Between Two Cities

God and Man in AMERICA

A COMMENTARY ON OUR TIMES

Cover design by Robert Borja

Library of Congress Catalog Card Number: 62-10907

Between Two Cities

Cities

God and Man in America

Edited by

Fathers of The Society of Jesus

Thurston N. Davis

Donald R. Campion

L. C. McHugh

LOYOLA UNIVERSITY PRESS

Chicago 13, Illinois

1962

IMPRIMI POTEST: John R. Connery, S.J., *Provincial of the Chicago Province,* December 11, 1961. NIHIL OBSTAT: John B. Amberg, S.J., *Censor deputatus,* December 11, 1961. IMPRIMATUR: ✠ Albert Cardinal Meyer, *Archbishop of Chicago,* December 12, 1961.

OPTIMUS MAGISTER BONUS LIBER

FIFTIETH ANNIVERSARY PRINTING · 1912-1962 ·

Preface

The title imprinted on the spine of this book suggests that between these two covers a reader might expect to find some sort of "tale of two cities." It is in fact such a tale, or a collection of such tales, but not of just any two cities.

An armchair traveler can readily locate many sets of paired cities around the globe: Paris and Rome, Berlin and Munich, Moscow and Leningrad, London and Birmingham. Here in the United States we could name San Francisco and Los Angeles on our west coast, St. Paul and Minneapolis in Minnesota, Baltimore and Washington on our east coast.

However, to those of us who have shared the experience of putting this book together, the twin cities suggested by the title of this volume might well be Chicago and New York. Chicago—because it is the home of the book's publisher, Loyola University Press; New York City—because on the western rim of New York's colorful midtown area stands Campion House, residence of the editors of AMERICA, the National Catholic Weekly Review. In a real though secondary sense the title of this volume acknowledges both these points of origin.

The fraternal bonds between AMERICA on one hand and Loyola University Press on the other have for years been tight and strong. Our two publishing establishments operate in distinct fields and according to different editorial tempos, but on each side we share the concern of brothers and

I

friends for the persons and the work of the other.

The late Father Austin G. Schmidt, S.J., former director of the Loyola University Press, was, all through his dedicated and scholarly life as a publisher, an object of admiration to the editors of AMERICA. Moreover, throughout the years we have come to know and esteem his able assistant, now Father Schmidt's successor, Father John B. Amberg, S.J. And it was Robert B. McCoy, a recent addition to the lively staff of Loyola University Press, who first suggested and has enthusiastically taken on the task of publishing this book. We are grateful to him.

But what are the two cities between which this volume is really poised? They are, of course, the City of God and the City of Man. AMERICA's editors, following the path marked out for all mortal *viatores*, are on pilgrimage from one to the other. In our professional lives as priests, we move back and forth, over and over again, from one of these cities to the other. Moreover, in our peculiar vocation as editors and journalists, we make this journey, back and forth every seven days, in obedience to the rigorous demands of an unending and inevitable series of press deadlines. From a study of the latest scarifying communique out of the Kremlin; from a discussion of the plight of the *braceros* in California and the Southwest; from a volume on demography and world agricultural statistics; from the halls of the United Nations or the Congress on Capitol Hill, we pack up and go each week—galleys and page proofs in hand—to a point beyond time and out of space, into a realm of unchanging truths, fixed principles, and stable values. Then back we come with another issue of AMERICA. In other words, we humbly attempt a weekly raid on the City of God in order to publish, in the City of Man, a journal that talks common Christian sense about the world of human events.

This may sound a bit pretentious. It is not so intended. We have no hidden or special revelations. We know no secret back door into the mind of God. But we do have certain advantages: an excellent library, a sound and long tradition as a journalistic team, and the circumstances of life that allow us the leisure (a very busy leisure, I can assure you) to explore and think and argue and write. Moreover, we are blessed in that we do all these things in the congenial company of able and hard-working colleagues.

In other words, AMERICA and its contributors are concerned with both God and man, and with the cities of both of them. Within the pages of this book a reader will find a hundred paths that crisscross the complicated world of contemporary affairs. But through it all, and written between every line, is the conviction that in all its diversity and change the world of man is God's world and that he who does not labor to return it to God redeemed in some small measure by his tears and worry and dedication has missed the meaning of man's job on earth.

This little preface gives me the occasion publicly to acknowledge my personal esteem for my colleagues, past and present, on the staff of AMERICA. To each and every one of this band of brothers who, for more than fifty years, have striven to publish a Review worthy of its name, I am deeply in debt for the inspiration and example of their lives and work. Finally, it should be noted that this book would not have seen the light of day without the collaboration of my two associates, Donald R. Campion, S.J. and L. C. McHugh, S.J., and of a valued colleague, William Holub, general manager of the AMERICA Press.

THURSTON N. DAVIS, s.j.
Editor in Chief
AMERICA

To
Austin G. Schmidt
and
Vincent A. McCormick
of the Society of Jesus

Table of Contents

God and Man

Arts and Letters

East and West

Christian Unity

Poems

IX

What would *you* talk about, if you were one of an army of pilgrims hiking to the cathedral of Chartres? Perhaps you would talk of shoes and ships and sealing wax, but it is more likely that you would talk of God and man; and your conversation might turn with regret to the scandal of Christian disunity. Why has the constructive dialogue on ecumenism, so far advanced in Europe, made so little progress in America, the land chosen to exercise leadership in freedom's darkest hour? Is there any way in which priest and layman can help make the Church overwhelmingly evident as the way to God? Or are we doomed to go on bickering over the proper highway to heaven, even as humanity begins to explore its destiny on the endless frontiers of space?

God and Man

The Story of a
Roman Catholic

John LaFarge, S.J.

I F YOU WRITE a book that people like, they are apt to
say nice things. In itself, this is not so bad, since
it may help you to discover what is really worth
your effort. Nice words also humble you, because the response you get, even if most kindly, is not quite what
you expected. Favorite passages remain unnoticed, while
people seem to delight in matters on which you set little
store.

They were reading my autobiography aloud at meals,
a couple of years ago, in a monastery refectory. After
four chapters had been completed, word came that they
were to cease and desist. Certain items in these first
four chapters, matters that did not seem to me particularly humorous, had caused chuckles among the brethren. The Very Reverend Prior Visitor, who was of another nationality and language, reminded the brethren
that reading at table should excite compunction, not
hilarity. Other monasteries and convents, so it is reported, have read the book through without remorse.
Even Père Jean Minéry's recent French translation
(which, incidentally, is a swell one) is being read in
refectories abroad. All this was a surprise to me, since

1

I had aimed at a merely factual narrative. Life itself, however, is full of anomalies.

More to be expected are honest corrections and disagreements. They are considerably helpful, even if they inflict minor wounds. I was much distressed when I received a strong protest from a very dear relative—now no longer with us—because on one occasion I had referred to the (temporary) color of her mother's hair. On consideration, I saw that it was possibly unfair to select a single item when so very much could be rightly said about her mother, a lovely, gifted and generous soul. So I made amends in the paper-back edition. Yet I stood by the accuracy of my original narrative. I cannot *prove* the occurrence, yet I distinctly recall it. So I invoked a principle, the guide of autobiographers. What you set down on paper is simply what you personally remember, as you remember it. You check the facts to the best of your ability, but certain of them rest in the realm of merely personal memories.

This is why I stood by my narrative when I expressed the disagreeable impression made upon me, as an undergraduate, by the late George Santayana, or the favorable one I received concerning the heroic Cardinal Stepinac, when I took supper with him in Zagreb just before the war. Stepinac was—and still is—a national hero of the Croatians, and Serbians and Croats have many bitter griefs against one another. But the best you can do, if you are not attempting to write history, is to record impressions. And on the other slope of that national divide, what finer impression could anyone receive than that afforded by AMERICA's valiant Serbian-Irish Balkan correspondent over the many years, the gifted Miss Annie Christich?

As I leaf through the apparently endless series of messages and comments that have continued from the publication of the book to this very day, or recall recent conversations along the same line, some do specially stand out. They give you heart, though they are of interest only to yourself. The confirmation of my own memory that perhaps I have most prized came last summer as I talked in Boston with Mrs. John Potter (Ellen Hooper) and her sister Mrs. Ward Thoron, nieces of Henry Adams, and friends of my college days. "You did a perfect picture of your father," they said. "Just as we knew him."

Why, after all, would such a story attract people? "What I notice in your story," writes one critic, "is that you were attracted by the personality of Jesus." Quite so. If that attraction has seized a person, especially one who speaks for Jesus, others may be attracted to him, and wish for his story. People after all are drawn to the priest, not by any tricks of his own personality, but by the very fact that he is the bearer and the messenger of the Church's imperishable hope. And people today are desperately in need of hope.

Words to that effect come from many sources. Dr. Karl Menninger, that famous oracle of psychic health, said recently that in his opinion people today are most of all concerned over the loss of hope. The crisis, as many think, is more of hope that it is even of faith. As Fr. Vincent McCorry puts it (AM. 1/16/60, p. 484):

> Some ages in Christian history have needed more religious faith; such, in general, was the 19th century. Other eras needed more religious love; such as the 18th century, insofar as it was the age of Jansenism. Our time almost certainly needs more religious hope.

The priest speaks for hope. He is not just a foreteller of some future glorious event. By his sacramental action as well as by his words and activities, he conveys to the world Him who *is* our hope. If the priest himself is accessible in the world of time, it is easier for us to communicate with the world of the Eternal, who has made His home—pitched His tent, as St. John says—in time.

I remember watching the dial of my fat old silver-cased watch the night of December 31, 1899, before turning out the gas light over my bed, and asking myself whether the new 20th century could ever equal the marvels of the one just expired. (Oh, I know, I was a year too soon, and all that.) The 19th-century tradition did everything possible to persuade people they could scrap their faith and yet—or thereby—be completely and comfortably cheerful. (Every Englishman might enjoy

3

his cup of hot cocoa on a fast electric train.) So life's rhythm could still proceed in secular comfort even though deprived of the logical foundation of any assurance. Today, the sabotaging of faith has developed its equally logical conclusion. Many of those who preserve the faith are not unaffected by the prevailing atmosphere.

STRESS ON CATHOLICITY

Yet, I must ask myself, has not the story something more personal to tell, something quite distinctive? If I review in my mind this chain of events and experiences, I note a lifelong refrain. This was a deep and abiding sense of the universal mission—to all classes and peoples —of the Church, that spiritual Kingdom of which I became a citizen on a cold day back in February some 80 years ago. (The pastor, incidentally, didn't enter my name in the parish register, since I was not expected to live. It was only years later, through the affidavit of the two witnesses to the baptism, that it was made historically certain that I did really enter the Kingdom. My mother habitually lived on hope. Indeed, I had only emerged into this world at all, because, as Ed Lahey remarked recently in the Boston *Globe*, Mrs. LaFarge was not over-concerned about the population explosion. But that is another story.)

Some may legitimately ask: what difference does your abiding view make to the rest of us? Perhaps none. Nevertheless, if the Church is to make its deserved impact upon the confused and divided contemporary world, its universal mission, and thereby its catholicity, must be made overwhelmingly evident. Unless that is done, and done with great imagination and comprehension, the Church's other famous "marks" of unity, holiness and apostolic origin are spoken to deaf ears and closed minds. I do not venture this remark just of myself. I find this same stress on catholicity running through the utterances of the Holy See in our times— as for instance in the great Christmas discourses of Pope Pius XII. Yet my own experience has forced it upon me.

Catholicity, to mean anything, must be in force here

4

and now: in my city, in my block or suburban section, in my own parish. In line with just such a viewpoint, for instance, the Holy See declared on February 22, 1951, in response to an inquiry from a Catholic diocese in the United States, that no more parishes could be set up on racial lines. By catholicity I mean not only that the mission of the Church is to all peoples and all mankind alike, but also—in a vertical sense—to all that is contained in man himself. It is certainly a vital part of the Church's present-day message that it loves the created world, as God's free gift, as it has evolved through countless ages; the natural world in its intricacy and multiplicity. This world remains, and will apparently remain until the end of time as a battleground between the Spirit of God and the Enemy of the human race. Yet this is the world to which God has said Amen, and waits for us to respond with our own Amen, having given us the awesome power of accepting or refusing His grace.

Or of ignoring the moral law, which has a catholicity of its own.

There is a catholicity of love, which is the forward-moving wave of the Church. But there is also a catholicity of justice, of the integral teaching and exemplifying of the moral law, without which love cannot freely operate. This I believe is the issue especially confronting us Catholics during the year 1960.

The moral issue is being put with sharpness and poignancy from various and contradictory angles, about matters of social or political conduct that most people are not used to consider as falling under the Ten Commandments. The use of nuclear weapons and the testing of hydrogen bombs have put a startling new face upon the Fifth (Protestant and Hebrew Sixth) Commandment: Thou shalt not kill. This commandment, as Herman Wouk notices in his remarkable book, *This Is My God*, isn't even expressed by that much rhetoric in its original form. The Hebrew simply says: Don't kill, *lô tirtzah;* don't steal; don't covet, etc. The searching test case of true catholicity at Deerfield Park, Illinois, and the defeat last summer of the Fair Housing Bill in my native Rhode Island put sharp moral queries to Catholic

5

consciences. Other queries face young married couples planning for future families, or candidates for high public office, not to speak of the moral questions that afflict the quiz-hero selling his presumed talents in the isolation booth, or the practitioners of economic power in management or labor.

As I see it, Christian moral teaching, if it is to be convincing to the contemporary mind, must also be truly catholic or universal. It can admit of no preferences or exceptions, for the simple reason that man is an integral whole, not a collection of propositions. Our teaching must speak the entire moral message in all its bearings: state the theory, but also apply it remorselessly to tangible and well-known situations. Prudence—that important but frequently distorted virtue—may suggest that we speak only a partial version and soft-pedal the rest. I suppose it would be highly imprudent today, at least in Governor-elect Jimmy Davis's Louisiana, to recall how, on the eve of World War II, a filibustering senator of that same sovereign State (where my paternal grandfather lived until he decided to sell his plantation, manumit his slaves, and leave *"pour les Etats-Unis"*), filled the halls of the U. S. Senate for days with pagan appeals to race prejudice and shreds of Hitler's "Aryan" lore, yet sent, over his own signature, along with Senators Connally and Pepper, a fervent message of congratulation to the Reds of anti-Franco Spain. But should we conceal these apparent inconsistencies?

CLIMATE FOR DIALOGUE

Indeed the same prudence, considering the present international scene, can be in fact the highest imprudence. So much so, that I would consider any evasive course today as suicidal for us Catholics, or indeed for believing people in general. The slight advantages we gain by avoiding one or the other painful issue are entirely out of proportion to the respect that is earned by

6

frankness upon all the great moral issues.

I believe there is no better or sounder climate for fruitful dialogue with all persons of sincere religious belief, especially here in the United States, than one created by a mutual confrontation of the entire gamut of moral problems, as they affect the individual, the family, society and community, or the nation. This would mean considering them, not—as is so frequently done—in splendid isolation, but as related to one another, and related to the great central idea of the full realization of man's destiny under God.

Such advice, however, must take into account that on many of these specific points our Catholic doctrine as yet is much subject to discussion. The obstacles we encounter frequently reveal connections and implications that otherwise would be passed over. The challenge of the birth-control issue, for instance, is making intelligent people on both sides of the dispute look more sharply into the allied moral questions of the nature of the family, of our country's international obligations, of the aims and purposes of American agriculture, as well as into the nature of moral law and its relation to revealed religion. Enthusiastic Planned Parenthood proponents are becoming somewhat more guarded in their utterances, while Catholics recognize they must present the issue not just as a one-two precept, but as framed in the wider context of all human experience.

Yet today how much general encouragement is given to long and patient conference and investigation, such—to take but a single instance—as the year-round program of the Catholic Association for International Peace? This is a work based upon the best knowledge obtainable from every source, and upon the scrupulously faithful study of the Church's official documents and the advice of competent scholars from every direction. There is a time, King Solomon says, to speak and a time to keep silent. So there are occasions that call for stern warning, the sensational exposé, even the harangue. But a continued diet of this emergency language is self-defeating. High school children write in to me and ask when the Pope will open "that letter." A widely read popular columnist in Catholic papers recently exhorted

7

our clergy to drop every other subject and concentrate all their preaching upon the sole issue of U. S. Communist infiltration. That way madness lies.

Certainly the preacher or writer who adroitly avoids any positive moral commitments enjoys many tactical advantages. He can always create the impression of saying something, without suffering any inconvenience by what is said. He can't be caught off base, because there is nothing definite to catch on to. Today's whirlwind means of publicity, too, favor the dedicated partisan, the professional liberal or anti-liberal. In both courses there are evident tactical advantages. Yet—and I offer this as the result of cumulative experience—the odds in the long run rest with the relatively small number who climb the long, uphill road and try to speak the many-sided moral message as an integrated whole. They will be reproached for mumbling where others speak with a clarion voice. But in the long run they succeed in being heard, and what they say sticks permanently.

A few weeks ago I spoke at St. Mary's City, Maryland, at a meeting to commemorate the 325th Anniversary of the founding, on that spot, of the original Maryland Colony. The event had for me a special significance, since I had spent many years as pastor of that territory, and had often tried to create anew in my own mind the happenings of those remote historical days.

LESSON OF MARYLAND

The gentlemen or burgesses of early Maryland—mostly, even if not all, Catholic—were not as free as they would have liked to make clear, public statements on certain delicate issues. Jealous royal eyes across the sea were watching them. Yet they stoutly held their position on civil liberties, as Englishmen and heirs to the tradition of Magna Carta. Respecting these same liberties, they proclaimed in guarded language the freedom of religious worship and personal freedom as well. For the first half-century of their existence under the tutelage of the Lords Baltimore—that is to say, until the proprietary or personal colony was forced to become a royal colony—these burgesses sedulously practiced the tolerance that they preached.

8

Today, we in the United States suffer no restraints upon our freedom of speech, and there is nothing but human respect to hinder our conveying to the public the total integrity of our faith, or of our moral message. Our spiritual strength lies not in the dialectical discomfiture of those who happen to disagree with us, and still remain unconvinced. Our strength lies rather in the partnership of all good men, of whatever origin or condition, in seeking agreement by the best means available on these capital issues, at least as far as is possible under the very different set of presuppositions by which we approach them.

"I find no difficulty," said a prominent Protestant clergyman to me of late, as we were discussing certain recent utterances of an ethical nature, "I find no difficulty about the term 'catholic.' Indeed, I like to consider myself a catholic in my own way. But the term 'Roman' causes me trouble. It seems to limit the term catholic, and associates the Church with a particular discipline. 'Catholic' would seem to imply the wide and comprehensive view, on the great issues of the day. 'Roman,' those of a sect."

It was not then the occasion to discuss the position of Rome, guardian of the tomb of St. Peter, and custodian of the sacred deposit of Christian faith. But I did call his attention to the "catholic" spirit in which Rome, through its official utterances, particularly the discourses and letters of the Holy See, approaches the intricate web of great moral problems. One cannot long read these documents, without being impressed by their agreeable lack of one-sidedness: not an owlish affectation of impartiality, such as little minds easily assume, but rather a concern so deep, a general perspective so broad, that each single question is seen in a broader setting. Questions are studied not only in a further context of kindred moral issues, but in the still wider perspective of the Church's entire view of man, the world, history and time. Attempts therefore to give a partisan twist to papal utterances are usually doomed to failure.

There is of course the other side to the picture. Papal discourses are necessarily so broadly pitched to a world audience, so traditional in style and so solicitous about how future generations may interpret them, that they usually are not as specific and concrete as we would like. The specifying is our job, and the job of the best minds in each country. In the meanwhile we continue to do everything in our power to clear up the strictly theological and historical misconceptions that hinder our progress on the rocky road to religious unity.

As I have said, the more truly catholic is our catholicity, the more easily all misunderstandings will be cleared away. Certainly, the more thoroughly Roman, that is, the more thoroughly integral and devoid of one-sidedness is our affirmation of every item in the whole entire gamut of moral rights and duties, the sooner will such a constructive dialogue be possible, and the better prepared we shall be for whatever the coming ecumenical council may bring forth. This is one reason that I am glad I wrote the life story of a Catholic, and of a Roman Catholic as well.

American Protestants

Erik von Kuehnelt-Leddihn

As a lecturer I frequently have occasion to tell American audiences about the increasingly fruitful relations which are developing in most of the free European countries between the Catholic Church and the denominations that stem from the Reformation. Almost invariably, when I speak on this subject, I am asked why this movement finds no counterpart in the United States. The answer is not simple. Responsibility for the situation in America rests not only on the shoulders of some Catholics and, in my opinion, in even larger measure on the "other side," but must also be attributed to certain theological, historical and social facts. Yet these, at least in part, could be overcome if only a real determination to bridge the abyss actually existed.

Catholics, needless to say, should be the very last to remain uncritical of themselves. Our Church continues to be "God's strength in the guise of human weakness"; our first Pope was *piscator et peccator*—fisherman and sinner; the smitten ear of Malchus and the mocking crow of the rooster haunt our memories down the centuries.

Though we never surrender the essentials, it is still true that our very catholicity, our innate tendency to annex, baptize and incorporate anything that is true, good or beautiful, as well as our inner urge to expand in every imaginable direction (what Karl Barth critically eyes as *das katholische Und*—"The Catholic AND") sometimes prompts us to get lost in what is purely marginal and unessential. Popular devotions have a way of ballooning to the point where they distract from the actual deposit of faith. The result is that we find ourselves exposed to perfectly legitimate criticism from the heirs of the Reformation.

Another subject calling for self-examination on our part is the not infrequent phenomenon of the "Catholicist" (as opposed to the Catholic) in the United States. He looks for all the world like a partisan of a sect rather than a member of the Church Universal. His "Catholicism"—a term coined in the Counter-Reformation and once criticized by Pius XII—is a genuine "ism." He knows practically nothing about the theological content and the spiritual yearnings of the Reformation and tends to read the attitudes of latter-day, relativistic Protestantism—now largely vanished from the European continent—into the history of the 16th century. This accounts, for instance, for the credence he lends to the fairy-tale version of Luther as an early liberal who believed in "private interpretation." Worst of all, the "Catholicist" (admittedly not a breed found exclusively in the American hemisphere) remains profoundly suspicious of the label "Christian."

ATTITUDE OF EUROPEAN PROTESTANTS

On the European continent, the Evangelical (Lutheran) and even the Reformed (Calvinist) Christians always had some sort of conscious `and subconscious realization that they had sprung from the Catholic Church. It is her renewed vigor which baffles them, over and over again. Thus, Harnack never concealed his surprise that the Catholic Church was still producing saints.

The members of the Reformation faiths in the United States, on the other hand, are frequently exposed to the illusion of having some sort of historical primacy. This stems, understandably, from the fact that, aside from Maryland and the Southwest, they actually had settled this country before Catholics came on the scene in any numbers.

A German Lutheran, however, worshipping in Nuremberg's St. Sebaldus or in Marburg's St. Elizabeth, where medieval art is so much better preserved than in many a Catholic church and where images of our Lady abound, cannot but be aware of the old unity. The *Simultankirchen*—churches owned in common since the Reformation—vividly bring home the fact of an even earlier common history through fifteen hundred years. But to the American Protestant, his colonial-style meeting house, tabernacle or church has no predecessor other than the wilderness which harbored the Indians. Little wonder that he resents the present Romanist challenge to his ancient birthright.

Even the continental Calvinist is aware of the common past. In Geneva's St. Peter's, the mother church of Presbyterianism, one still can see a papal tiara in the stained glass not far from where the altar once stood. Traces of a Catholic "prehistory" are also to be seen in the buildings of the Reformed Church in the Netherlands. These and other such Catholic memories and survivals lend a psychological assist to theological encounters in Holland, France and Switzerland.

Still, the fact should not be overlooked that the bulk of the followers of the Reformation on the continent of Europe are Lutherans and not Calvinists. One has only to compare the *Confessio Augustana* with either the spirit of Calvin's *Institutions* or the text of the Anglican *Thirty-Nine Articles* to discover that the split issuing from Geneva was of a far more radical nature than the schism begun by Luther. The dry, sober French lawyer did a far more thorough job than the German Augustinian—a "wrestler with Christ"—who, had his lot been other, might have become a great mystic. And whatever the contribution of Lutherans to the spirit of American Protestantism, the fact remains that the nation's cultural roots have been watered far more by the springs of Calvinism, Congregationalism, Anglicanism, Unitarianism, and even of the Quaker persuasion.

Thus, in spite of the many external affinities of Episcopalianism to the Catholic Church, the position of Catholics in the German Lutheran world was always more relaxed and better protected legally than in the British Isles or in colonial America. The Catholic monarch of Saxony was able to rule a 92-per-cent Lutheran population, while the Catholic subjects of the Hohenzollerns did not suffer the indignities of third-class citizenship imposed on their co-religionists in an otherwise more liberal country. All this is not so surprising, however, if we keep in mind that the German princes until 1806 were, at least in name, the vassals of the Holy Roman Emperor—whose very title could not have been more Catholic.

There is a German nationalistic spirit in Lutheranism, but it was always kept within limits. It could not have been otherwise, because the political center of the Germanies until the dawn of the 19th century was Catholic Vienna; Catholics inhabited the most ancient historical sectors of Germany (Westphalia, the Rhineland, Bavaria, Alsace and Austria); Catholic thought and concepts had influenced some of the most important non-Catholic German artists and thinkers—Goethe, Schiller, Novalis, Bach and Leibniz.

THE AMERICAN EXPERIENCE

In the United States, on the other hand, as in Britain, the various denominations which date their rise from the Reformation and its aftermath entered into the spirit of a nascent nationalism which, in America far more than in Britain, was linked with the rising tide of democracy. Indeed, as Prof. Ray A. Billington and others have pointed out, the religious tolerance practiced by the London Government in its overseas domains (in the Quebec Act, for instance) kindled the flames of American revolutionary fervor. Antimonarchical sentiment swelled in close harmony with hatred of the Church. This was the sense of the popular ditty dating from that day: "If Gallic papists have the right / To worship their own way / Then farewell to the liberties / Of poor Amerikay!"

It is evident that the prejudices imported from Britain played a significant role in the fermenting of this potent brew of religious and nationalistic drives. When liberal philosophers of 18th-century England denied full citizenship to Catholics, they acted entirely in harmony with prevailing sentiments. To the average Englishman, even today, "dark men begin at Calais." The shadow of the Armada, the fear of Jesuits in disguise, the threat of a foreign conquest by tyrannical potentates or of a new Inquisition by clerics lusting after power and hostile to sincere doubt or free research, the twin specter of ignorance and superstition emanating from the continent—all these partly real, but mostly imaginary, dangers have for centuries weighed on Britain's soul. And almost all these traumatic apprehensions have been transposed to the American scene.

The anti-Catholic biases of American Protestantism, however, are of a dual nature. In the United States, it must be remembered, two diametrically opposed attitudes of *protest* exist side by side. One of these is critical of the Catholic Church and faith after the manner of the Reformers. The other, representing a Protestantism influenced by the spirit of the Enlightenment and of relativism, passes a very different judgment on us. We have only to ask a preacher in the mountains of Kentucky what sort of people we Catholics really are. He will tell us that we appear to be half-pagans given to dancing, smoking, drinking, merrymaking and to sinful games of chance such as bingo. But a minister in some progressive, suburban church might insist that Catholics are medievalists ground under the heels of an infallible Pope and a greedy clergy, a melancholy and backward tribe deprived of birth control, divorces, salty books and breezy movies.

ROLE OF THE REFORMATION

The common bond between these two radically different views continues to be the emphatic rejection of the Catholic faith. But whereas the puritanical and, even yet, often fundamentalist outlook of an earlier

15

orthodoxy is on the wane in America, the symbolists, relativists and crypto-Unitarians still flourish. It is true that the clarion call of a return to the Reformation and its ideals and tenets has also been heard in the United States. But it sounds much louder on the European continent. There the Reformation remains part of the historical past. Its memory—with the help of monumental "visual aids"—can be more easily revived. And this in spite of the fact that certain theologians, like Rudolf Bultmann, are still fighting a rear-guard action.

We Catholics can only applaud this conscious return to the ideas and ideals of the Reformation because it implies a going back to the point where our separated brethren branched off from the common road. The discussion between Luther and Dr. Eck, which had been carried on in a murmur all through the centuries, has once again become articulate. In turn, our confrontation with the momentous problems and questions addressed to the Church four hundred years ago, and only superficially answered in many instances by our apologists, is being renewed.

Thus, we again stand face to face with the Reformation. Such an earnest book as Pastor Max Lackmann's *Katholische Einheit und Augsburger Konfession* (Graz, 1959), as well as the seriously questioning essays of Prebendary Hans Asmussen, merit well-pondered replies. Berlin's Bishop (now Cardinal) Julius Doepfner, last year during the Unity Octave, rightly said that we do not expect that our Evangelical brethren ought to come back into the Church on their knees and with empty hands. "Already [there are] so many institutions and insights deriving from Evangelical theology which we have incorporated into ours and which we would not like to miss."

It is true that such language is rarely heard among high Catholic ecclesiastics in America. Is this the case solely because America's theologians are more narrow, more "partisan" in their outlook? Or because America's Protestant theology has a less enriching effect on our theological thinking? Or is this due to other reasons which have an intrinsic link with the survival of Protestantism as opposed to an *evangelisches Christentum*?

16

Indeed, it is difficult to overlook the fact that the label "Protestant," originally attached to the Lutherans, today survives largely in the more or less non-Lutheran United States. There it continues to be proudly used by denominations which have nothing at all to do with the famous Protestation of the Lutheran estates in 1529.

On the other hand, we see how precisely a recent Lutheran meeting in the United States affirmed Luther's old dictum that papalism *is* anti-Christ. All of this shows that the old orthodoxy, in spite of the great watering down by the Enlightenment and relativism, can still be preserved in spots. The old orthodoxy, however, is by no means the new orthodoxy, which is the result of a return to initial positions after long and fruitless peregrinations in the desert of near-unbelief.

European neo-orthodoxy can look at the mysterious Church of Rome without fear or hatred. But it finds no *full-fledged* American counterpart. Hence the curious alliance of a "professional" U. S. Protestantism with nationalist sentiments and the consequent outcry that the Catholic faith is an alien religion. (It is this accusation which incites many U. S. Catholics to that 200-per-cent Americanism which, in turn, lies at the bottom of much of their anti-intellectualism.) Hence also the unpardonable ganging up with non-Christian forces—witness the POAU—in outbursts of singular pettiness and narrow patriotism so foreign to truly Christian groups.

The history of our Church is full of very dark pages, and intelligent Catholics are thoroughly aware of that grim fact. But I really cannot imagine a group calling itself "Catholics and Other Austrians United" trying to curtail Evangelical demands for Lutheran (or Presbyterian) instruction in our Austrian public schools. As a matter of fact, in Austria we have issued a series of stamps with a surcharge in order to raise money for the reconstruction of our oldest Evangelical school destroyed by bombs in World War II. Some of these stamps bear the portraits of outstanding Evangelical Austrians from Kepler to Hansen. Moreover, our Evangelical brethren have an established right to a holiday on October 31, the anniversary of a landmark in Reformation history. And all this takes place in a country which, together with Spain, was the driving force in the Counter-Reformation and in which Evangelicals today constitute only six per cent of the total population.

Much of the animosity of American Protestants towards the Catholic Church seems to be due to a spirit of uneasy competitiveness as well as to an absence of that broad historical outlook which recognizes—at least up to a point—the providential role the Catholic Church has played in the story of Christianity. It is precisely in this respect that they differ radically from Europe's Evangelical Christians. On the other hand, American Catholics should be more mindful of St. Paul's words *oportet et haereses esse* ("for there must be factions" I Cor. 11:19). They may rightly regret the dissent, but must rejoice in the survival of authentic Christianity wherever they find it. In their midst there is still too much naive denigration of the Reformation, too much of the neurotic-monk-wanting-to-marry-a-nun formula used in Catholic instruction about the Reformation.

Again, a great deal of the latent as well as open anti-Catholicism among Protestants in the United States may be traced to another aspect of their fundamentally parochial attitude. This is a tendency to insist childishly that without Calvin's *Institutions* there would be no dental care in the common schools, no modern plumbing, jet planes or voting machines. On top of it all there is the fear that without the Reformation America would have been just another glorified Quebec or Bolivia. According to this view, if the United States ever becomes Catholic, it will also be magically transformed into a Latin nation. To this must be added the nightmare of Rum, Romanism and Rebellion—plus bingo and Roman Catholic kids riding public school buses. Of course, the specter of wild demonstrations in Colombia or of a confiscated novel in Ireland helps to reinforce this curious pattern of thinking.

Yet, in the heart of the continent where once the Thirty Years War was fought in all its bitterness, the situation is radically different. It is true that Pastor Niemoeller still sticks to his formula, "Rather Moscow than Rome," but the learned institutes studying the opposite faiths are flourishing, Evangelical and Catholic Christians are writing for each other's periodicals, and mixed theological conferences are taking place. For now the 400-year-old division of the Church in the West clearly appears to both sides to be what it really was: a catastrophe of the first order for which the guilt, as Pope John has hinted, must be shared by both sides. And while it may be the role of Europe's torn and bleeding heartland to close the wound where it first was opened, it seems especially tragic that the healing process is slowest in the country which history has appointed to be the leader in freedom's most crucial struggle—a country where the mutual understanding of all Christians is therefore a command of the hour.

Royal Road to Chartres

Robert J. O'Connell

A BRIGHT, HOT sun shone down on the pilgrims around
me as we rounded the Gare Montparnasse. My
first glimpse was of a mob of students lining the
Rue Vaugirard. The last stragglers of the preceding
group, called Route Topaz, were trooping into the station. That meant the thousand still waiting belonged
to our group of the pilgrimage, Route Amethyst. Almost
all in hiking attire, they clustered round their chapter
emblems beguiling the time with talk. Each chapter
was theoretically broken down into ten teams of five,
and just looking down the long street at that buzzing
crowd, it was hard to imagine that six such "routes"
were going that day, and that the following weekend
would see a second wave start out in comparable numbers. Indeed, each year (depending on weather and
other factors) some 15,000 students make the pilgrimage
to Chartres.

No doubt it was a bit *à la mode*, and therefore all
complexions and mentalities were represented—the fervent, the Catholic Actioneers, the tepid, the doubters,
even some out-and-out unbelievers. Péguy himself, that
strange figure whose ambiguous history is at the root of

the Chartres pilgrimage, casts a shadow large enough to envelop them all. And, after all, a convivial hike of some 40 or 50 kilometers along those flat roads of the Beauce all aflower with early May—what more could a young student ask?

This was my first meeting with our chapter. Circumstances and malevolent chance had made it impossible for me to be present at their preliminary briefings, which were aimed at preparing the discussion of this year's theme, "The Priest and Us." Well, that topic should cause some minor explosions, given the position of the clergy on the French scene. Is the priest just a member of a caste, separated by privilege and taboo from ordinary humanity? And if Christ was admittedly the only priest in the fullest sense of the term, of what use is this cassocked creature of breviary and celibacy and all the other apparatus of clericalism? And if the faithful themselves are a priestly people, how does that fit in with this apparent relic of medieval and pre-medieval society? It was almost disconcerting to see how much the literature aimed at nourishing the discussion seemed calculated to sharpen every arm the critical intelligence of the French *universitaire* could lay hold of. Just two or three clever unbelievers in the group, I thought, and this would turn into quite a circus indeed!

At last came the departure signal, and off we wound into the trains waiting to take us out to the edge of the metropolis, where the columns could snake along side roads without tying up the main auto routes. The train ride allowed for some introductions, too, but, in spite of that, the atmosphere seemed somehow reserved, almost distant. Then we arrived at Epernon; there was a blessing of the group and their emblems; and the route to Chartres stretched out before us.

The first portion of each stage was devoted to discussion. The group chaplain flitted from team to team, inciting, encouraging, sharpening a point here and there, trying above all to assure that openness was the rule—the minimum of orthodoxy could be assured later. An hour or more of this and we arrived at our first brief halt. Out came the canteens, the oranges and lemons, and all at once it was apparent that the original reserve was beginning to evaporate. The first marks of that strange fellowship among the Chartres *routiers* started to show. Someone had brought too many oranges, too much water or tea, and wanted (naturally!) to lighten his pack—anybody have some? Chocolate, Père? These almonds you'll find good against thirst. Do have some! The budding intellectualism of the discussion gave way momentarily to banter and smiles and an easy camaraderie. The magic was beginning to operate.

The second stage was devoted to meditation. A few themes for reflection, and off we went. This time the chaplain hung back in case any of the lads wanted to confess en route. Some forty minutes of this, and the chapter leader led us in the Our Father. Then we sang the rosary—*Je vous salue Marie . . .*—to a marching air, and soon we had come to our halting place for dinner.

Once we had settled in the shade, the work of blazing sun, hot roads and heavy packs made itself felt. The' first blisters began to sting, the news that water was available was hailed with parched enthusiasm, and, in spite of fatigue, a friendly rivalry set in to see who would go and fetch it for the group. Dinner over, the time came for "chapter"; a report from each team on the issues raised in their discussion, the questions they proposed to the chaplain, then the latter's replies. (Where was this religious eggheadedness? These youngsters were talking about *life!* And the doubters, why something was bothering them, there was something they wanted to see!)

The sun was kinder now, the evening cool and melting into night as we trudged off for Esclimont and the spacious grounds of the chateau where the vigil service was to be held. Here, especially, the organization of the pilgrimage made itself felt; it was not over-organized, but remarkably adequate to an almost impossible situation. Places were marked for each chapter's packs and for the hearing of confessions for both girls and boys. In the flat center of a natural amphitheater, a huge canvas, floodlit and gracefully stretched on guyed poles, hovered like a great white bird over the altar. Hymns and chants and readings, a polyphonic choir excellently trained, light and dark, candle and torch and vestment all blended into a symphony for ear and eye and—the lines for confession and Communion seemed to say—for the heart as well. We were at one of the high moments of the pilgrimage, a moment when its religious core was laid suddenly bare. The last doubts began to wither; these youngsters were not just off on a weekend hike.

Hours later, as I tossed to find a comfortable position in a sleeping bag that was laid almost directly onto concrete, any residual doubts were gone. One didn't march some fifty or so kilometers only to spend an all but sleepless night, unless there was something deeper to this thing than mere fashion or fellowship. The next day, Sunday, confirmed that impression again and again.

The early morning sun soon turned from warm to hot. As the march wore on, with discussion leading into meditation, a certain gingerly quality in everyone's walk became more and more manifest; the blisters, so methodically punctured and taped the night before, had taken up their work again. The halt for lunch was welcomed. Then our road wound into the blazing eye of the afternoon sun. Again and again a boy would be seen carrying two packs instead of one, while a protesting girl hobbled alongside remonstrating for the right to carry her own burden. We had stopped at noon in one of the few bits of forest shade discoverable in that portion of the Beauce, but for the afternoon stop there was little such comfort.

Dinner, chapter and a few final thoughts for the last stretch all took place practically full under the cruel sun. Still there was no complaining; even the joking references to blisters lacked the slightest tinge of the dramatic. And suddenly it dawned that in a single day's time the group had insensibly become a unit, welded at a depth of unspoken understanding that few could understand and that no one alluded to. The doubters still doubted, yes. Their contribution was almost invariably an objection, a note of skepticism, a tired "Oh, Père, those are fine words, but. . . ." The others listened, patiently and without resentment, with no desire for cheap dialectical triumphs. This was a pilgrimage, a time for another kind of action, another kind of thought.

It was appropriate that the last lap came after discussion and chapter on the priesthood of the laity, for that last lap was the pure stuff of sacrifice. Now the moment for reflecting on that sacrifice was past. Dead ahead into the declining sun the column moved with sweat and fatigue and discomfort and sometimes naked pain. Minds had lost their edge; voices more sighed than sang the Aves; packs changed hands; arms wound round some slogging figure that refused to drop out so near to the goal. And yet, how often, when two glances accidentally met, there was that sudden, spontaneous smile!

Thank you, students of Paris, for that image, and for that résumé of the twilight journey we call the Christian life! From the sanctuary on which our hearts were set streamed a love that drew us all together at the same time it drew us on. When the spires of Chartres rose slowly over the purpling fields, and the greeting went up from a thousand throats—*Salve, Regina!*—which of us would have guessed there was that much spirit left in him?

Other Worlds – for Man

Joseph A. Breig and L. C. McHugh, S.J.

I: MAN STANDS ALONE

THE MORE one appreciates the marvel called man and the infinite wonder of the creation, Incarnation and Redemption, the less is one impressed by the thought that there may be, on some heavenly planet other than earth, creatures like us—that is, composed of material bodies and immortal spiritual souls, able to know and love and serve God consciously, and destined for an everlasting sharing in His divine life.

So, at any rate, it strongly seems to me.

Every consideration higher than the barest logic— every instinct and feeling for poetry and artistry, and every religious sense of the divine fitness of things, argues, I think, that mankind is utterly unique and will forever remain so; and that if the cosmos is to be populated by thinking beings, the populating will be done by us in breathtaking migrations through space, much like man's migrations across oceans and continents.

My case, I believe, can best be made not by negative debating against the idea that God may have created other beings like us, but by a positive presentation of the electrifying extraordinariness of what we know about ourselves, both by our own observation and by divine revelation.

THE NUB OF THE ARGUMENT

It strikes me that for those who share my religious beliefs, I can point up the whole matter by inquiring whether they can imagine more than one Virgin Mary— more than one Mother of God. This query, for me, goes to the heart of the question.

What confronts us is the following body of knowledge about the human race—that is, specifically, about you and me.

We are made in God's image and likeness. We have God's word on that—the word of God speaking to us concerning His will in creation and concerning creation's crowning splendor.

Such is the stunning unity—the oneness in diversity— of mankind that the fall from God's grace of the first, the representative man, was the fall of all.

Yet so loved—and so somehow valuable in God's eyes —were all of us that God Himself, in the Person of His Son became one of us for our redemption. He assumed a human nature in order to be born among us, flesh of our flesh and bone of our bone, of a woman who for that reason was preserved from the spiritual effect of our otherwise universal fall from the privilege of full companionship with God.

God, thus become incarnate, lived among us, shared our miseries and our joys, comforted and counseled and taught us, and by dying in unutterable anguish of soul and body and affections, reopened the way for us to enter into participation in His own eternal bliss through the door of our own deaths, incorporated into His.

What is it about human beings that makes them so priceless in the divine plan?

The answer that I see is this: God, in bringing man out of nothingness, created a being so marvelous that in him all the material creation, unto the farthest spiral nebula and the most distant boundaries of space, is gathered up and united with an immortal spirit destined for knowledge and love and service of the infinite Creator.

So it is that if I, by the grace of God—God grant it!—lift my mind and heart to adore and love and thank and petition my Maker and Saviour, in me the cosmos is lifted up in prayer. Not merely for myself do I pray, but for all my fellow men past and present and future, and for the stars known and unknown; for the planets and moons and meteors and meteorites; for the mineral and plant and animal kingdoms; for all that materially exists anywhere.

Adam was uniquely the Representative Man; but you and I too are representatives to God of God's material creation. In our bodies we are made of matter in its manifold forms: even the cosmic rays enter into us as messengers to us from outer space. And in our souls we are from God, breathed directly into existence. Principally in soul, but also mysteriously in body, we are His images and likenesses. Moreover, we are brothers of Christ through the Incarnation. We are caught up in Him and live by His life; we are members of Him; in us and through us He continues the work on earth which He began in His own body as one of us.

Here, it seems to me, we come to the crux of the matter. In the Incarnation, by taking flesh and blood and bone from us through the Virgin, God in a divinely wonderful way united to Himself not only mankind, but through mankind the whole of the visible creation. Thus we have the amazingly beautiful, and the divinely magnificent, ascent of creation from its lowest and most elementary forms into union with spirit, first in man, then in the God-man, and through Him with God, the infinite pure Spirit. We have the coming together of the finite and the infinite, of the lowest and the highest. The perfection and splendor of this divine work seem to me to leave no place for supposing that it is not unique.

To me, there is a divine rightness in the concept of this singular unity of mankind, of the cosmos and of the Creator, which cannot be present in any theory that there may be one or more other races of thinking beings composed of matter and spirit.

More than one Incarnation of God? I hold that the

27

answer is No.

More than one Mother of God? No.

More than one race into which God has poured His image and likeness? No.

But all this is not to say that the cosmos, save for our own planet, is to remain forever uninhabited by beings able to speak for the visible creation in adoration of its Maker. It seems to me rather likely that God's commandment to men and women to love each other, and in their love to multiply and fill the earth and subdue it, may include the conquest of space and the colonizing of frontiers more astounding than the frontiers already conquered by human migrations through the thousands of years—the hundreds of thousands of years—that lie behind us in history. Indeed, I think that our times call upon us, not to neglect history or to cast it away from us, but to look forward and upward and outward to staggeringly glorious visions of the future and of our amazing destiny in it.

Perhaps, in the technological achievements of the past few years, God is calling upon us to rise above the dreadful quarrels we have lately endured, and to lift our eyes to the countless worlds beckoning to us. Possibly He is reminding us of—and chiding us with—the fact that He made us more wonderful than we realize, with a dignity and splendor and power we have half-forgotten; and that there are immense works at hand to which we ought to be addressing ourselves.

In fact, it may be that by turning the minds of the people of Russia away from foolish Communist grubbing and toward the limitless reaches of space, God is preparing them for a return to Him, for a rejection of empty atheism and for a future of accomplishment beyond their wildest dreams. It is not to the conquest of other nations that the peoples of the Soviet Union ought to be addressing themselves, but to the crossing of the oceans of space—and to magnificent new insights into the majesty and goodness of God and the immeasurable riches with which He endowed mankind when He gave us worlds innumerable to explore and to represent in noble adoration.

JOSEPH A. BREIG

II: OTHERS OUT YONDER

I FEEL that intelligent life is common in those planetary oases which dot the "deserts of vast eternity" that stretch through space. The family of Adam, or *homo terrenus*, as I shall dub him, is not a lonely wayfarer in a wilderness of glowing cinders and icy cosmic dust.

At this moment, there is not one scrap of "hard" evidence to support my case. I have only suggestive analogies, a priori and statistical probabilities, and an individualized sense of the fitness of things. Frankly, therefore, I admit in advance that my position must be stated in arguments that show the forms of logic but have the probative strength of straws.

Already, serious astronomers are striving to find meaningful patterns amid all the random static that pours into the dish of a big radio telescope in West Virginia. That story was told by Ray Bradbury in the October 24th issue of *Life*. Project Ozma's outlay of tax money is not a boondoggle. It stems from the statistical implications and the intuitional thrust of modern cosmogony and biochemistry.

Increasingly, biochemistry favors the view that life will arise as a normal result of chemical evolution whenever conditions are right. If favorable circumstances prevail over sufficient eons of time, the evolutive quality of life verges naturally toward higher and eventually rational forms. As for astronomy, current theories of cosmic development generally suggest that planet formation is a common event in the evolution of the quintillions of stars which lie within our view. It is exceedingly probable that billions of planets occupy the "golden zones" of distant suns where temperature and other energy factors favor the emergence of life. Perhaps then the highest forms of organic existence are a widespread climax of cosmic history, rather than an isolated discontinuity that has appeared just once as a sort of "contamination" of the earth's mantle.

I have put this summary in materialistic terms that prescind from finality. But where science talks of the statistical probability that life may arise by chance and develop through random variations, the Catholic philosopher holds that there can be no real chance in a world created by God. There are only lines of causality, unintelligible to us but unified in the divine Mind and somehow expressive of His purposes. On the other hand, since we increasingly regard the origin of life as an event of the natural order rather than as a metaphysical problem demanding the miraculous intervention of creative power, there is no insurmountable difficulty in granting that life may arise whenever and wherever the apt conditions are present.

Moreover, in life as we know it, there are remarkable powers of adaptability, differentiation and movement toward rational organization. Organic life on earth evolved toward a specialized animal form that in God's design was apt material for the infusion of a spiritual soul, while at the same time the lower forms were ordained to serve as a substratum for rational existence and its needs. Why should these things not be generally true in a physical universe characterized by uniformity of law and process? Hence, where suitable conditions exist on a planetary mantle, we may expect life to emerge, perhaps as a normal aspect of development. Where the conditions persist for billions of years, may we not expect that God is preparing for a divine incursion of the biosphere which will manifest His glory in the phenomenon of man?

God made the universe for His glory, not as something to be gained but as a benefit to be bestowed; and above all it consists in sharing His happiness with rational creatures. Does it not seem strange to say that His power, immensity, beauty and eternity are displayed with lavish generosity through unimaginable reaches of space and time, but that the knowledge and love which alone give meaning to all this splendor are confined to this tiny globe where self-conscious life began to flourish a few millennia ago?

Let me put that differently. We teach that irrational creatures are God's "footprints," but that men are His images—radically through the possession of mind and will, accidentally through the doing of virtuous deeds.

Does it not seem odd to say that God has left His footprints everywhere, but has established His image only here? Faceless indeed seems the vast cosmos, if there is heard nowhere but on earth an echo of His knowledge, freedom and, above all, His holiness.

When God set Adam in Eden, He gave him a mandate to "subdue the earth." In the context of *Genesis,* it may be argued that man's image-quality is chiefly manifest in his lordship over created things, a lordship that does not consist merely in superiority of status but in proprietary dominion. But the note of genuine dominion is effective occupation. It would seem, then, that if the physical world is meant to serve genuinely utilitarian purposes and not be just an object of contemplation, it must lie open to exploitation by other rational beings than ourselves. For undoubtedly, most of the universe is forever closed to penetration by *homo terrenus.*

In his *Contra Gentes,* while discussing the providence of God, Thomas Aquinas notes that "the first thing aimed at in creatures is their multiplication . . . and to the gaining and securing of this end all things else seem to be subordinated." Aquinas held this position within the narrow framework of Aristotelian physics and astronomy. If he had considered the hierarchy of being within the framework of an expanding universe, how would he have expressed himself? Would he perchance have suggested that the irrational creation, where numbers proliferate, cannot meaningfully establish and conserve that to which it is ordained, unless rational life is also common in the physical universe?

31

Aquinas further argued that the good of the species transcends that of the individual, and that therefore the multiplication of species is a greater addition to the good of the universe than the multiplication of individuals of one species. He applied this principle with consistency even to the upper end of the spectrum of creation—the angelic realm; his stand was that every angel is of a different species and that the multitude of the angels exceeds every material number. If he had possessed our knowledge of the cosmos, would he perhaps have held that a few billions of our human stock, inhabiting an isolated corner of creation, inadequately manifest the goodness of God as it can be shown in rational animals? "Multiplication and variety was needful in the creation, to the end that the perfect likeness of God might be found in creatures according to their measure."

Perhaps then there are races that were never elevated to grace. We sons of Adam are a race elevated, fallen and redeemed—a testimony to His mercy. Who will say there are no races elevated but not fallen, as testimony to His holiness? Who can say that there are no races elevated, fallen but forever without redemption, to show forth the mystery of His justice?

I am not aware of any grave theological objections to the probabilities I have described. The purpose of revelation was to teach us what we needed for salvation, not to instruct us in science or philosophy.

I am not perturbed, for example, at the imagination of a second Mother of God, for I do not even find any difficulty in conceiving a thousand incarnations of each or all the Persons of the Trinity. Aquinas discussed several such possibilities centuries ago and found none of them repugnant to sound theology, though of course he did not suggest that they were actually realized.

Why do we normally resist the thought that man may not be alone in the universe? I think that our perennial jealousy of our status largely springs from the erroneous science which long ago placed us at the physical center of the visible creation. It was inevitable that we regarded ourselves as unique, when all the obvious signs indicated that the heavens revolved about us day and night.

During the course of the years, as we know, the supposed center of the cosmos moved from the earth to the sun, from the sun to the galaxy, until today man resides he knows not where in a metagalaxy of undisclosed structure and extent. Yet now that we have lost our physical centrality, we still cling to the prejudice that we are unique, solely on the grounds of our intellectual superiority.

Where does the evidence for that uniqueness lie? Man as such surely has no centrality in the total creation. The hub of that complex lies in the angelic world, not in any aspect of material creation. We on earth cannot argue uniqueness from the fact that we are images of God in a material mold: for the dignity of being such an image is endlessly shareable. And neither does our worth give any ground for complacency; the redemptive love which the Father showed us in sending His Only-Begotten Son was a proof of His generosity in the face of our desperate need, not an indication that God found some vein of gold in the corruption of our fallen nature.

Despite our lowliness, I feel that even our race has a splendid destiny in space. We may not be able to assign a farthest limit to our lordship over nature, but it will not be limited to the earth alone. Earthly man will go as far as his ambition and inventiveness can carry him. And since he will take the Mystical Body with him, wherever he goes, his colonization of space may be looked upon as a providential extension of the Incarnation in space and time. The Church, perhaps, has a physical dimension beyond our ken.

But, as I already observed, our destiny among the stars will be severely prescribed by the frontiers of impassable distances. C. S. Lewis, speculating on the formidable distances about us, conjectured that they might be God's quarantine precautions. "They prevent the spiritual infection of a fallen species from spreading." Perhaps God has restricted the ambit of our wayfaring, precisely lest we play the role of the primeval Serpent in Edens beyond our reach.

So I rest my slender case. My arguments were no

more than bumbling thrusts into the unknown. But while we wait for real evidence to be acquired, I like to think that the physical universe is a flourishing commonwealth, not a boundless waste where a lonely pilgrim sojourns in the silent dark. And when the evidence accumulates, I should not be surprised to find that Alice Meynell intuitively grasped the full truth in her poem "Christ in the Universe":

O, be prepared, my soul!
To read the inconceivable, to scan
The million forms of God those stars unroll
When, in our turn, we show to them a Man.

L. C. McHugh, s.j.

Moral Rearmament

Robert A. Graham, S.J.

WITH THE INSTINCT of true public-relations men, the leaders of Moral Rearmament found Premier Khrushchev's visit to the United States the ideal peg on which to hang their message. From the Swiss headquarters of MRA at Caux, an ex-Comintern official, Eudocio Ravines of Peru, found space in the U. S. newspapers of September 29 to declare that the Cold War was now entering a new and more perilous phase—and to add the operative part of the story: "Moral Rearmament is the total and categorical answer to the Communist danger." Thus the promoters of one of the most original moral movements of our times used the front-page news to draw attention to their work and to 'their claims.

Moral Rearmament, formerly known as Buchmanism and later as the Oxford Group, is four decades old. Its founder, Dr. Frank N. D. Buchman, now in his eighties, remains its guiding spirit, even though his activities have been necessarily reduced with his advancing years. Originating as a sort of revivalist movement in the YMCA tradition, it grew with the years and now operates on a wholesale scale in the international field. Today there appears no abatement of its progress. With abundant resources, a dedicated and experienced staff, and a lofty, appealing message pitched to the tastes of the top echelons of national and international society, the school of Dr. Buchman moves on with an obvious assurance. It has encountered ridicule, scoffing, suspicion; it has been condemned for its philosophy, its morals and its motivation. In 1940 it appeared totally discredited, but it survived this crisis as it had survived earlier setbacks. Though its full-time workers are still estimated at a bare two thousand at most, its program reaches many thousands of what MRA likes to term "key people."

If, as alleged, Moral Rearmament is *the* answer to communism, then it surely deserves attention. And, indeed, there are distinguished Americans who say it is just that. Thus Admiral William H. Standley, former U. S. envoy in Moscow, is quoted as saying only last March: "The choice for America is Moral Rearmament or communism." This is quite an alternative to put before the American public. The sweeping terms with which this claim is put forward suggest, on the part of its authors, more than an ordinary confidence in the validity of their mission and their message. It must be admitted that the recent record of MRA activities demonstrates that, for good or ill, the movement has made itself felt on the international scene and that the end is not yet in sight.

This past summer, at its two major world centers—one at Caux and the other at Cedar Point, Mackinac Island, Mich.—MRA was going full blast. Successive waves of invitees underwent the "courses" that MRA has designed to implant its message. The visitors consisted of men and women, young and old, from a wide variety of occupations, but all leaders in their own circles. They were flown in from all points of the world and maintained in that first-class-resort comfort —tobacco and liquor aside—to which most of them were accustomed. As the Mackinac Island delegates approached the scene of their coming indoctrination, their eyes met a sign at the gate of Cedar Point: "People of every nation, race and color come here from every

continent for training in an idea to unite men and remake the world." For the following week, or rather
weeks, carefully segregated from the ordinary vaca-
tioners on the island, they took part in what is entitled
the "Summit Strategy Conference." In a spacious hall
designed to resemble a wigwam—presumably to suggest the idea of a council of the sachems of all nations
—they met to hear ex-Communists, ex-agnostics, authors,
diplomats and other persons of note, or at least of interest, tell of the triumph in their lives of the four
Absolutes of Honesty, Purity, Unselfishness and Love.
In the evenings they attended morality plays and movies
created by MRA to bring out the central point of personal change. Here, in short, they were exposed to the
"only answer" to communism. One must admit that
only the Communists seem to carry on, at anywhere
near the same scale, such a systematic formation of
the elite of all nations and races. And there is more
to come. Next year, if rumors stirring island folk are
true, MRA will take over additional property. Mackinac
Island bids fair to become one big MRA citadel.

AN IDEOLOGY? OR A RELIGION?

Any way one looks at it, Moral Rearmament cannot
be ignored. It claims that it is not a religion; it claims
also not to be interested in political action. Yet it operates in a zone avowedly related to religion and politics. By its own description MRA is an ideological force.
An ideology, says the movement's literature, is "an idea
that dominates the whole of the person—his motives,
his thinking, his living—and fights with a strategy to
get everybody to live the same way." But this definition,
in its first part, necessarily involves a religious or quasi-
religious commitment, while the second part points to
inevitable involvement in the political or quasi-politi-
cal field. In this respect MRA compares itself to the
ideology of communism. It feels that only MRA has
the elements to cope successfully with the ideology
that emanates from Moscow.

The followers of Dr. Buchman first conceived themselves as the answer to communism in the aftermath

37

of the second World War. With the typically generous self-praise it habitually indulges in, MRA now claims to have had a major share in saving Western Europe from communism. According to a booklet issued this past July, three things saved Western Europe in 1947. One was the announcement of the Marshall Plan, the second the ascent of Robert Schuman to power in France—and the third "the ideological initiative of Moral Rearmament in creating, through changed men, totally committed to a superior ideology, the conditions under which the Marshall Plan and the Schuman Plan could work." The movement's literature also claims that through its work in the Ruhr, and in the British coal fields as well, it prevented a Communist takeover. The four Absolutes had dissolved the conflicts by changing men.

These claims are not taken seriously by those in a position to know the details of the developments in question. It remains, however, that MRA did succeed in attracting to itself a number of former Communists for whom MRA has obviously become an alternative to Marxism. One of these was Señor Ravines, already mentioned. Another, currently featured in MRA events, is Angelo Passetto of Italy, once a propagandist for Red chief Palmiro Togliatti. He is now engaged in creating songs and dramatizations of the "idea" behind Moral Rearmament. Other ex-Communists appear frequently on the movement's programs.

On the whole, the technical efficiency and professional polish of MRA's activities are in marked contrast to the naïveté of its efforts in the social and political field. For a while MRA directed its attention to the labor field. It succeeded only in earning for itself the indignation of labor organizations for its uninvited and unwelcome interference and its disregard for the legitimate procedures long established in the solution of labor disputes. In its well-intentioned fight against communism, MRA has given cause for great doubt as to its ability to carry through its program without serious mistakes.

The case history of *The Vanishing Island* is an instance in point and one that will not soon be forgotten by the United States Government. This is the title of an MRA "ideological musical play," one of the morality productions used (quite effectively) in transmitting the MRA message. Like most of the plays in the MRA repertory, this one was written by Peter Howard, former British newspaperman and for many years one of Dr. Buchman's closest aides. The play was presented in mid-1955 in Washington before a distinguished audience from all branches of the Government and from diplomatic society. It concerned the fortunes of the citizens of two countries, "I Love Me" and "We Hate You." In the former (the capitalist world, the United States in particular) there reign corruption, selfishness, materialism, licentiousness and hypocrisy. This nation is threatened by the other country, which carries on a vigorous anti-"I Love Me" propaganda. The leaders of the West are confused and weak, because they have no ideas. On the Eastern side, however, the rulers know precisely what they want and how to get it. As the play develops, war seems inevitable until an MRA team arrives on the scene and reconciles the postulates of capitalism and communism (somehow) through the four Absolutes. All admit their respective faults and peace is assured.

The play's over-all effect was anything but complimentary to the West. The Washington audience reacted with understandable coolness but seems to have taken it as they would take a sermon preached against well-known local abuses. What the invitees did not know was that plans were already in readiness to take this indictment of the West on a grand tour of the Far East, the Middle East and Africa, where at that precise moment neutralism was causing U. S. foreign policy the most acute concern. Still less did they know that the Secretary of the Air Force, urged by influential congressional friends of MRA, had agreed to put at MRA's disposal three Air Force planes to carry the troupe on what was described as a "Statesmen's Mission" for world peace. And so it came about that in June, 1955 this compromising spectacular, with its nearly two hundred people, left Washington on a mission that was bound to confirm the neutralism of the uncommitted peoples and make the United States, to boot, look like an idiot for appearing to sponsor this self-condemnatory exhibition.

Belatedly informed, the State Department issued instructions to U. S. representatives abroad that *The Vanishing Island* had no official backing whatsoever. When public opinion reacted to news of the junket at the expense of the U. S. Government, the tour's directors arranged to make compensation. But the damage was already done. In 16 countries the United States and all Western civilization had been given a black eye, and communism only the mildest of rebuffs. The tour ended at Geneva in September, but it soon took off again, this time labeled the MRA Ideological Mission, to present *The Vanishing Island* in West Germany and the capitals of Scandinavia. Altogether, according to an MRA statement, the musical play was seen by 243,000 people in 24 nations during a 40,000-mile journey. This was MRA's "answer" to communism. No one really can measure the ultimate harm done by this naive meddling in international politics.

The claim to be a bulwark against communism is being made by Moral Rearmament not only to Governments but also to the Catholic Church. MRA believes it is the natural vehicle which can bind together those world forces which are equally threatened by the onrushing tide of Marxist materialism. One of the relatively few Catholics active in the movement, a Filipino newspaperman, Vicente Villamin, reported early this year that he had presented to authorities at the Vatican a scheme according to which Moral Rearmament was to become a sort of common ground for all efforts to face and resist communism, particularly in Asia. If such a plan was ever seriously considered in Rome, there is no evidence of it.

THREE CATHOLIC DOCUMENTS

While the Holy See no doubt welcomes the stress on personal reform and spiritual idealism which is the essence of the MRA program, it cannot overlook the fact that in many respects this "ideology" is tantamount to a religion. Hence the extreme reserve manifested in

the past toward the Caux-Mackinac axis. It is not
necessary to review here the Catholic stand on Moral
Rearmament. Two Catholics studies in English are
particularly useful. One is by the Auxiliary Bishop of
Malines, Most Rev. Léon-Joseph Suenens, and is entitled *The Right View of Moral Rearmament* (Burns
and Oates, 1953). The other is a full-length article by
Edward Duff, S.J., "Verdict on MRA," which appeared
in the June, 1956 *Social Order*. In a class by itself, because of its official character, is the pastoral instruction
on faith which the Bishop of Marquette, Mich., Most
Rev. Thomas L. Noa, issued to his faithful under date
of August 15, 1958. (Mackinac Island is located in that
diocese.) The instruction terminated by stating that
Catholics living in the diocese "may not attend the
meetings of MRA, or participate in or promote its
activities." The same prohibition the bishop extended
to all other Catholics "whenever they may be within the
limits of the jurisdiction of the Diocese of Marquette."

The conclusions of these three sources, not to speak
of earlier condemnations and warnings emanating from
various bishops in Europe and elsewhere, are negative.
Nevertheless, no general ban on cooperation with MRA
has yet been issued by the Holy See, at least as applicable to lay persons. Consequently there are still a
certain number of Catholics who are full-time workers.
And there are many more who annually accept invitations to attend MRA assemblies or "Summit Conferences," at least at Caux. For these, obviously, the argument that MRA presents the "answer" to communism
still has some validity.

It would be unfair at this point to fail to acknowledge
that MRA has been, for many people, a sort of half-
way house to the Catholic Church. The number of indifferent or fallen-away Catholics who attribute their
return to the Church to their first contacts with Moral
Rearmament is too large to be just a coincidence. The
same is true for a fair number of converts. For this
reason and for perhaps others, many Catholics can be
cited as loyal defenders of the movement. These range,
to mention only names appearing in recent MRA literature, from the late Joseph Scott of Los Angeles to

41

Gabriel Marcel, the French existentialist. Even Richard Cardinal Cushing is cited as paying tribute to what MRA has done for souls, although just what the Archbishop of Boston really said is not a matter of record outside of MRA literature.

Don Luigi Sturzo, who died last August, is also quoted in Moral Rearmament literature. In this connection, however, it seems that MRA has overdone its zeal, at the expense of accuracy, if not of veracity. The founder of Italian Christian Democracy is quoted as follows: "In no other place do I feel the presence of God as at MRA Assemblies. Here one learns with the fullness of divine teaching how men can live together. These ideas must become the policy of nations." This is a startling encomium that, on the face of it, Don Sturzo could not possibly have uttered. The Don Luigi Sturzo Foundation in Rome, to which this writer referred the quote for verification, states that Don Sturzo never made any such statement and, in fact, that he never attended an MRA assembly in his life.

This loose and casual liberty taken with words is characteristic of the unguided course of MRA's relations with the Church. A few years ago, it appeared that some safeguards to eliminate potential dangers in theology and ascetical practice had been set up by an agreement between MRA and diocesan authorities in Switzerland. However, this "agreement" was later annulled by an MRA spokesman on the grounds that, after all, Moral Rearmament is not an "organization" but an organism, and that consequently there could be no question of an "agreement" with anyone. The effect of this repudiation was to restore the former ambiguities in MRA that have long troubled Catholic theologians. These indications are not calculated to bolster the Holy See's confidence in Moral Rearmament as an ideological alternative for communism, whether for Catholics or anyone else.

To the extent that Moral Rearmament with its message of spiritual rebirth awakens dormant souls and leads them to a serious reconsideration of the life they have been leading, the efforts of Dr. Buchman deserve the well-wishing of mankind. Who cannot but be sympathetic toward a cause whose object is "to unite men and remake the world"? But this is fundamentally a religious task, and Moral Rearmament has hovered perilously close to the religious field at all times. In view of the astounding progress of MRA since its beginnings and its undoubted influence on human lives, "Frank," as Dr. Buchman is known to the workers in the movement, should go down in history as one of the greatest Protestant missionaries in these modern times.

It is understandable, on the other hand, that the Catholic Church shies away when MRA presents itself as a guide in the spiritual redemption of souls, as it does in its "ideological" campaign. On the nonreligious plane, MRA can also be welcomed to the extent that it can unveil to confused minds the vision of a world where personal change can transform the atmosphere of society. The evidence thus far, however, is that MRA has neither the political sophistication nor the doctrinal cohesion that could enable it, at this moment, to cope with communism as one ideology against another. Men should be glad if MRA accomplishes good for individuals and for society; they will be vastly relieved, and even surprised, if it does not do harm to Governments or to souls.

This is an age of explosions: nuclear, technological, demographic—and cultural. Yes, art and literature are "busting out all over," at least if you rely on statistics. But what is the worth of the cultural explosion when people question whether art and letters are a true imitation of nature and life? Some critics look on modern painting and sculpture as a sort of private joke. Some think literature has so debased shock values that it runs the risk of becoming a mere commentary on sex and sadism. Where is the cultural explosion likely to end, when even an artist like Hemingway confesses that he does not know the meaning of Man?

Arts and Letters

The Culture Explosion

C. J. McNaspy

IT WAS REASSURING during the recent Presidential campaign to find both candidates stoutly in favor of "deeper and wider education, and the intellectual curiosity in which culture flourishes." These are Mr. Kennedy's words, but Mr. Nixon said much the same. A Secretary of Culture? No, replied our next President. Such a department "might even stultify the arts, if wrongly administered. We have more than enough conformity now." It was clear that America's new frontiers had room for the free, vigorous expansion of culture.

What seems significant here is not precisely what Mr. Kennedy stated, nor even his courage in quoting T. S. Eliot's poetry during a campaign speech, nor his eggheadish preference for Moussorgsky and Berlioz—a riskier choice than Mr. Nixon's choice of "Oklahoma!" and "Swan Lake." It is rather that both candidates should have had to submit to a cultural inquisition at all. Did General de Gaulle? Fearlessly, Mr. Kennedy's advisers did not stop there. A "Committee of Arts, Letters & Science for Kennedy for President" unabashedly brandished the most formidable list of intellectuals (from Aaron Copland to Thornton Wilder) in an open plea "to those who have not decided." Clearly, the eggheads now have it. After exhausting the "religious issue," political analysts should peer into the "cultural issue."

I have just read or reread some dozen recent books on culture in America. Most of them are unflattering, self-deflation being a national pastime. Now made acutely aware of our deficiencies as a society, we are, it seems, hideously and variously wasteful; alienated, over-organized, lonely, other-directed; victimized by power elites and all manner of pacifiers and hidden persuaders; in a word, a lot of ugly, status-seeking, vulgarian operators. This iconoclastic list could be endlessly prolonged, but with the title of one book at least we can hardly take exception: Eric Larrabee is surely safe when calling us *The Self-Conscious Society*.

This self-consciousness takes many shapes. In the campaign, however, it became increasingly alembicated into one simple essence—how was our *prestige* coming along? What was our *image* abroad? In a word, the question was *culture*—culture taken in the broad anthropological sense, but not excluding the popular meaning of education, fine arts, and what are generally called the "higher" things.

It would come as a shock to many of Mr. Casey Stengel's devotees to learn that in 1959 more than twice as many people viewed the art shown in New York's Metropolitan Museum as that performed in Yankee Stadium. The score, to be precise, was 3,947,365 to 1,552,030 in favor of the Metropolitan. In defense of our "national sport" one may point out that baseball has a shorter season than painting, that baseball isn't the only professional sport, that statistics can prove anything (almost). In rebuttal, the protagonists of indoor culture may add to their score the 568,744 who paid to enter the Museum of Modern Art, the 2,356,221 who visited the Museum of Natural History, the 435,943 viewers of the Brooklyn Art Museum (obviously after the Dodgers' departure), and some ten million visitors to other museums in New York. True, not all are "art" museums, but all are "cultural."

Dropping idle and odious comparisons (besides,

athletics and the fine arts are not incompatible), we note that the enormous number of museum visitors in New York is not a local phenomenon. Chicago's Art Institute reports 1,093,958 viewers in 1959, with 4,306,528 visitors to other municipal museums. The Smithsonian Institution in Washington had 6,662,126 visitors that year, and the National Gallery 961,883. In the West, Los Angeles reports 916,996 viewers in its County Museum, and the California Academy of Sciences, in San Francisco, 2,405,270.

Philadelphia's Franklin Institute numbered 410,443 visitors; Detroit's Art Museum 963,391; Boston's Museum of Fine Arts (not including the Isabella Stewart Gardner Museum or the Fogg Museum) 485,961 (with a paying, supporting membership of 9,153). The South now boasts several impressive museums. Among them, Houston's Museum of Fine Arts in the same year numbered 172,809 viewers. In these and other museums that I have visited in various parts of the country, the average is always roughly proportionate to population.

It is interesting to find that viewers in American museums are not outnumbered abroad, where American tourists do more than their part to swell attendance. The venerable Louvre reports 1,671,000 (Americans included) visitors in one year, less than half the number attending the Metropolitan in New York. The British Museum reports 752,826, less than Detroit. Amsterdam's celebrated Rijksmuseum had 490,426, far less than the Museum of Modern Art. In 1958 the world-famed museum of The Hague entertained 148,145 visitors, less than Houston.

Another noteworthy fact about our American museums is the steady, often spectacular increase in popular attendance. With few exceptions (such as during the temporary closing of the Museum of Modern Art, caused by fire in 1958), each of the museums studied shows continuous growth. In 1956, for example, the museums of New York registered 12,281,602, and the following year 13,190,033. The Metropolitan attendance grew from 1,326,955 in 1939 to 3,947,365 last year—an increase of almost 300 per cent. In 1924 the Houston museum had 33,959 viewers; last year, 172,809—a truly

Texan boom of more than 500 per cent. (I am grateful to all the curators who helped me assemble this information.)

The quality of our museums is almost as striking as their quantity. Eloise Spaeth's new book on *American Art Museums and Galleries* studies 84 important museums from Ogunquit, Maine, to Phoenix, Arizona, and 125 galleries (she had to choose, since there are over 300 in New York alone). To those who know their painting from books it may be surprising to discover that many world masterpieces are not in Europe but here. The Gainsborough *Blue Boy* is in California, the Brueghel *Wedding Dance* (the best-known version) in Detroit, El Greco's *Assumption* in Chicago. The richest collection of French impressionists is in Baltimore, not Paris; that of Vermeers in Washington and New York's Frick Gallery, not Amsterdam.

CONCERT music's growth in popularity has been so spectacular in the last generation that it is hard to give a fair sketch in a few words. While in 1920 there were not a hundred symphony orchestras in the United States, today there are 1,142, more than half the world's total, and 35 million concert-goers. Today just about everyone has a collection of "classical" records or has a friend who does. Such music is now available on radio almost all day and night in and near large cities. In fact, it has become almost as hard to escape being engulfed by Wagner or Brahms as by "rockabilly." The hi-fi industry is a multi billion-dollar one, and always growing.

The theatre, despite heralds of doom, shows signs of a vitality hardly matched in our history—and seldom perhaps in anyone's history. The American Theatre Society's subscription list alone has grown from 84,000 ten years ago to 116,332 this year. Alice Griffin shows that there are some five thousand theatres in the country today, with vigorous regional performing groups at a high professional level. "Gone," she says, "are the days of the militantly amateur group which performed to entertain its members rather than its audience."

"Nowadays nobody reads any more," is a common lament. Facts taken from the 1961 edition of the *American Library and Book Trade Annual* suggest the opposite. Not counting high school libraries, we find presently in the United States 12,852 libraries (7,257 public, with 3,566 branches, and 1,948 college libraries). The public library circulation for 1956 (the latest date available) was 489,520,000. Presumably, some of these books were read after being withdrawn. The number of new books printed in 1920 was 5,101; in 1958 it had doubled to 11,012. *Publishers' Weekly* for June, 1959, showed that the average per capita American expenditure for books was $7.00 for that year. *U. S. Income and Output* showed the following growth in annual expenditure for 1950 and 1957: books, $677 million to $1.026 billion; magazines and newspapers, $1.47 billion to $2.71 billion. If nobody reads today, a great deal of money is being spent on nothing.

These are a few of the facts regarding America's "culture consumption." While they need to be interpreted and appraised, they cannot be gainsaid or simply bypassed. Why then are our critics of culture so unhappy? Why does almost every week bring again the hue and cry of alarm? What is there to be said against the indisputable data of this cultural explosion?

The general objection is a real or imaginary application of Gresham's Law to culture. This law, it will be remembered, states that bad money will drive out good money. It is the law of debasement through dispersion. The renowned historian Rostovtzeff puts it well and has often been quoted: "Is it possible to extend a higher civilization to the lower classes without debasing its standard and diluting its quality to the vanishing point?" Stanley Edgar Hyman calls it the Law of Raspberry Jam: the wider you spread it the thinner it gets.

Doubtless there has been an increase in America of public contact with the higher culture, but has this brought a decrease of depth and meaningfulness? Is the whole cultural explosion real or just a superficial puff? Is "instant culture," if I may so call it, a genuine or a spurious brew? After Russell Lynes coined his triple cultural criterion—high-brow, low-brow, middle-brow—

the statusmongers began providing taste signals. Unsure of oneself, one was now shown just what were the proper reactions and even how to achieve them, not merely to pretend. Visual aids were provided, of course, by *Life* magazine: illustrated charts specifying the proper drinks, hobbies, likes and dislikes to fit the level of "brow" one aspired to.

The problem is not altogether new. In his *Phaedrus* Plato naturally wrestled with it, and so did Aristotle. More recently, De Tocqueville, with the hauteur befitting his class, feared the "tyranny of the majority," while Lord Bryce felt that democracy would lead us to a "self-distrust, a despondency, a disposition to fall into line, to acquiesce in the dominant opinion, to submit thought as well as action to the encompassing power of numbers." Americans, too, have always been concerned, and the booming H. L. Mencken leveled murderous attacks against the "booboisie."

A MONG THE LEADING critics of the "pessimistic school" are Dwight Macdonald, Hannah Arendt, Oscar Handlin and Ernest van den Haag. These and other respected scholars are deeply disquieted at the hollowness discerned in much enthusiasm for culture. Even more, the "mass media," they feel, are a serious danger, promoting standardization rather than standards, homogenization rather than humanism, passivity not creativity. The power, money and prestige of these media seduce and beguile; men of authentic gifts are lured away and lost to true culture. Mass culture has debased and prostituted class culture, lowering it to the level of entertainment. The mass media do not foster art; they replace it.

It is manifestly impossible to discuss fairly, in a brief summary, this serious position. Let me urge my readers to study the debate on mass culture in the special Spring issue of *Daedalus* (1960), in the symposium edited by Bernard Rosenberg and David Manning White, *Mass Culture* (Free Press, 1957), and issues 3, 4 and 5 of *Partisan Review* (1952).

The main source of malaise and the principal critical target today is, of course, television. Now that well over 90 per cent of our American homes possess (or are possessed by) these 50-some million sets, the average instrument is in operation for more than 38½ hours per week (see *Fortune*, December, 1958). It would be hard not to blame TV for our ills.

During the past thirty years, Mack Hanan points out in *The Pacifiers*, the average workweek has been shortened by the number of hours in a whole day. We are now a society of the leisure-stricken. Despite this, if Vance Packard's estimates are accurate, only one American adult in three hundred reads serious books with any regularity, and, again on his word, a recent poll showed that most Americans could not recall reading any kind of book in the past year. Moreover, despite our large investment in book publication, we were greatly surpassed in 1958 by the USSR, Japan, Great Britain and West Germany. It is suggested, if not stated, that TV is both cause and effect. Ennui is never-ending, and we now find people desperately escaping from leisure to new employment, causing the current problem of "moonlighting." Perhaps explicitizing T. S. Eliot's famed bang-and-whimper, Arthur Morgan has predicted: "America will not perish from a bomb. It will perish from boredom."

No one should underestimate the usual vacuity of TV. However, its positive danger, as well as the positive influence of most mass media, seems to have been considerably exaggerated. Joseph T. Klapper's new book, *The Effects of Mass Communication,* torpedoes many gruesome generalizations. Apathy, passivity and a playpen atmosphere seem, on the whole, the real threat. Having personally spent many hundreds of hours in television studios, as well as my normal quota in vigil before the "Happy Screen," I believe myself not insensitive to the problems and limitations of the medium.

The critics do seem oblivious to so much, especially the growing movement of Education Television throughout the nation. In New Orleans, for example, station WYES-TV provides regular programs of instruction, in cooperation with local universities and with a national exchange of select videotapes, in many areas of the liberal arts. In Boston and throughout New England, WGBH-TV and related stations have for several years carried out an elaborate series of courses in cultural subjects. In addition, they have provided a unique public service in cooperation with the Boston Museum of Fine Arts. The museum is completely wired for television and has produced some six hundred live programs, many of which are available on tape for other stations. More than fifty non-commercial educational stations now cover most of our country's highly populated centers.

This may be only one swallow and not yet a true spring, but it does urge us to return to even keel and reflect on some of our blessings. In one of the wisest books I have read on American culture, *God's Country and Mine,* Jacques Barzun reminds us that "what we have undertaken, no other society has tried: we do not suppress half of mankind to refine part of the other half." Without indulging in naive chauvinism of time or space, we can be humbly grateful for unprecedented opportunities. Had we been born at another time, how many of us who criticize mass culture would enjoy sufficient culture to be able to criticize it? In any but our own favored society, could we pass judgment from the Olympian heights?

Athens, it is true, created a high culture and gave us much that is best; but at the time it was for the few, and the few killed Socrates, the critic of culture. Florence could boast its proud moments and monuments; yet how many Medici enjoyed fully the golden fruits of a golden age? What percentage of the masses of Vienna or Salzburg had leisure and freedom to relish Mozart?

And how many contemporaries ever heard Beethoven's late quartets? "Class culture" is fine for the classes, but most of us are the masses.

Granted, the day of the finger-bowl has passed, save for chaplains in a few other-worldly convents. Lordly manners, too, that once characterized (did they really?) a few lords have yielded to unaffected considerateness. While delinquency, adult and juvenile, is always with us, life is notably safer (except for the possibility of complete annihilation) and the human dignity of more people more respected now than ever. Numberless millions of us share patterns of culture formerly enjoyed by a tiny enclave of the privileged. When millions of workers prolong their hours in adult education programs, it would be ungenerous to suggest that this is only conformism and a doltish quest for cultural status symbols. And how can a society that faithfully reads "Peanuts" by altogether philistine?

If we find the TV ratings of Welk and Westerns too high and their quality too low, it may be because we all have been given chances to know better things. Besides, TV sets are still equipped with a button that brings instant, blessed release. And the paperbacks (1,912 new ones last year alone) make the best—from Homer to Hemingway—comfortably available to everyone who still reads. For all its blemishes, the culture explosion can surely serve the good of man.

The Lid Life of
Herbert Matthews

Thurston N. Davis

C AN THERE POSSIBLY be a sort of Matthews' Law—a
rule-of-thumb by which to tell whether Herbert
L. Matthews did or didn't write a given editorial
in the New York *Times?* The question is worth asking
because, within a wide circle of *Times* readers, no name
in recent newspaperdom creates more controversial
reactions. Rightly or wrongly, many believe, and have
for years believed, that certain of the self-confessed
biases and strongly personal evaluations of Mr. Matthews' signed stories represent a point of view several
degrees at variance with the general editorial positions
of his newspaper. This viewpoint, they argue, must
inevitably be reflected in the unsigned editorials he con-
tributes. Hence, if such a thing as Matthews' Law exists,
thousands of readers will find it a useful daily tool.

Herbert Matthews, for almost forty years a news-
gatherer and news-analyst for the *Times,* has since 1949
been a member of the editorial staff of that esteemed
newspaper. For a generation, under the Matthews by-
line, the public has been accustomed to read his interpretations of Franco Spain. In fact, at the *Times,* all
Iberian and Latin American affairs come under Herbert

Matthews' eye in one way or another. Moreover, until recently, Mr. Matthews was the *Times*' "man in Havana"—the specialist assigned to watch the progress of the Cuban revolution of Fidel Castro. He no longer writes on this topic under his own by-line.

Editorials in the New York *Times* carry great weight in many quarters. Because they are unsigned, the full force and authority of the newspaper lie behind them. Since Mr. Matthews is a member of the *Times* editorial staff, it may reasonably be assumed that at least certain editorials on Spain, Portugal, Cuba and other Latin American countries come from his typewriter.

One's interest in trying to detect which are, and which are not, the editorials of Herbert Matthews is whetted by his own analysis of what it means to be a journalist. He expounds his theory in his recent enlarged edition of *The Yoke and the Arrows* (Braziller, 1961):

> I would never dream of hiding my own bias or denying it. I did not do so during the Spanish Civil War and I do not do so now. In my credo, as I said before, the journalist is not one who must be free of bias or opinions or feelings. Such a newspaperman would be a pitiful specimen, to be despised rather than admired. (p, 225)

Moreover, in a foreword to the same edition of that book, dated February, 1961, Mr. Matthews discusses his relation as editorialist to the newspaper he works for:

> The editorial policy of the New York *Times* toward the Franco regime is blamed on me. (As a matter of fact, editorials in the *Times* are expressions of the newspaper's opinions and when it comes to Franco Spain it does not matter who writes the editorials.)

One wonders whether the same two sentences could have been written with "Castro Cuba" substituted for the references to Spain and Franco. But this point need not be belabored here.

The modest purpose of this article is to suggest how certain of Mr. Matthews' editorials in the New York *Times* can be identified.

One discovers, without a taxing amount of research,

a sort of metaphorical thumb-print on the unsigned editorials contributed by Herbert Matthews.

Examine this recent specimen. It is from the July 18, 1961 editorial page of the *Times*—a piece of indubitably genuine Matthews copy on "The Spanish Civil War." Commemorating the 25th anniversary of the start of that war on July 18, 1936, the *Times* said:

> It was a bitter, bloody, heroic struggle whose greatest tragedy was that it left Spain unchanged. In fact, it turned Spain backward to its autocratic, hierarchical, feudal system of army, Church, land-owning, banking and industrial elite. The same Gen. Franco Bahamonde *sits on the lid,* waiting for the end which must come to him, but which will be a beginning for Spain. . . . (*Emphasis added here and below*)

Earlier this year, when Premier Salazar's Portugal began to make front-page headlines, a *Times* editorial ("Portugal's 'Wind of Change' ") said in part on May 4:

> The result is that a growing opposition is *pressing against the lid* with which he [Salazar] would keep it down.

Again, an excerpt from another unsigned editorial bears the tell-tale trace. Dated March 14, 1958, it discussed the state of affairs in the Cuba of General Batista:

> Now he [Batista] has *clamped the lid down again* and reimposed censorship of the press and radio, but he cannot turn the clock back.

The thumb-print on a Matthews editorial checks perfectly with that found in Mr. Matthews' signed articles. Here, from the Sunday *Times* of May 6, 1956, is a snippet of a lengthy discussion of Batista's regime in Cuba:

> The uprising last week was symptomatic of the ferment *under the lid* that General Batista sits upon. One of these days *the lid may blow off*—but not now.

Again, in the first installment of an extended signed report on Spain, in the *Times* for Sept. 17, 1956, we read:

> On top all is tranquil because there is nothing to be seen but *the Generalissimo sitting on a lid.*

Five "lids," however, do not make a law. Can we get this project securely out of the realm of hypothesis and assure ourselves that there really is such a thing as Matthews' Law? I believe we can.

Turn once again to *The Yoke and the Arrows*. The passages cited below can all be found, identically the same, in both the first (1957) and revised (1961) editions, although page references are supplied only for the revised version.

Early in this book, discussing the centuries of Spanish history that lie behind the regime of General Franco, Mr. Matthews writes:

> Each time the people rose or freedom asserted itself, one or other of them, or all together ["the kings, the aristocrats, the generals and the priests"] would *clamp the lid back again*. . . . That is what happened in 1939 when a *caudillo*—Generalissimo Francisco Franco—*slammed another lid down and sat on it*. (p. 25)

Then, within six pages:

> Franco *slammed a lid down and sat on it*. (p. 31)

Again:

> The irony of it! Here we all are in the year 1961 with Italian fascism a sordid memory and with Bolshevism triumphant, while *a Caudillo still sits uneasily on a lid* in Spain. (p. 54)

Some pages later:

> What Franco had to do was *to clamp a lid down—or a number of lids*—and *sit on them*. (pp. 64-65)

Perhaps the finest specimen of all is:

> In those years after the Civil War, Franco had far more to do than just to *sit on the lid of a Spain* which, in any event, was prostrate and licking its wounds. (p. 67)

Then, in rapid succession, we run across two more:

> If one had to seek a single reason why, twenty-two years after the Spanish Civil War, *the same Caudillo is sitting on the same lid* in Spain, this is it. (pp. 98-99)

and

> On top, all is tranquil because, as stated before,

there is nothing to be seen but *the Generalissimo sitting on a lid.* (p. 99)

Farther along:

There is *another lid on which Franco sits.* (p. 105)

Then, too:

A student of Spain can only be amazed and heartsick at seeing generation after generation of the Spanish clergy repeating the same mistakes and building up the same forces of hatred that take such a terrible toll when *the lid blows off.* As of today, it is *Franco who sits on that lid.* . . . (p. 169)

Finally, two more:

Meanwhile *Generalissimo Francisco Franco sits on the lid*—this one, too. (p. 190)

and

Is it any wonder that we who write about Spain refer again and again to *the "lid" on which the Caudillo sits?* (p. 200)

A student for the doctorate in journalism might some day—by wearisome research through thirty or more years of the *Times* on microfilm—push Matthews' Law on to its fully scientific conclusions. If he chooses this topic for his dissertation, he will doubtless find his best material in Mr. Matthews' pre-1961 period.

Christ or Credit Card?

Moira Walsh

H OLLYWOOD'S NEWEST multimillion-dollar, color-and-wide-screen, stereophonic-sound, three-hour-long biblical epic, *King of Kings*, which is being released by MGM, is the logical culmination of a gigantic fraud perpetrated by the film industry on the movie-going public. The fraud consists in persuading people that these films, as a group, have substantial religious or at least edifying qualities. It is closer to the truth to say that, with some notable exceptions such as *Ben Hur*, they are disedifying and even antireligious.

These are harsh words. They should be tempered by admitting that the public continues with unabated enthusiasm to support this fraud. And frequently enough it has had the well-intentioned backing of religious and community leaders. In defense of the religious and community leaders of today it should be said that their attitude is based on assumptions arrived at many years ago when the implications of the motion picture medium were very imperfectly understood by the public, by serious film observers and by the movie industry itself. If they now have doubts about the wisdom of this policy, as many of them do, they are caught up in an institutionalized tradition for which they feel a certain personal responsibility and from which it is extremely difficult to break away.

In defense of the film industry it might be said that their motives in making these pictures may be quite sincere. They have always had a stultifying tendency to believe in their own publicity and in box-office receipts as a sure test of cinematic excellence. When their own high estimate of their screen treatments of Holy Writ are confirmed, not only by the financial support of the mass audience but also by the unrestrained praise of the "opinion-making" segment of the community, which is generally freer with a denunciation than an endorsement, the movie makers can hardly be blamed for basking in a self-righteous glow.

In any case the sincerity of the members of this "society for the admiration of biblical movies" is not the point at issue. The question is: Are they, wittingly or not, caught up in an ultimately self-destructive vicious circle?

An increasing number of lucid and informed voices are saying so. The first group to express skepticism about the worth of these cinematic forays into Scripture were the serious secular critics. They were generally dismissed by the film industry as "out of touch with the tastes of the mass public," a remark which also served to indicate how far out of touch the industry was with the purpose of serious criticism. And film executives were not the only ones who were outraged by the critics' lack of enthusiasm for the Bible à la Hollywood. Their remarks were often, and usually wrongly, interpreted by religious spokesmen as contemptuous and even subversive of Christian values.

At the same time Catholics have always harbored reservations about some of these films, beginning with their objections to Cecil B. de Mille's *Sign of the Cross,* a "Christians-to-the-lions" epic enthusiastically spiked with pagan decadence, which was one of the contributing factors in the formation of the Legion of Decency. And the Legion itself has frequently taken note of one suspicious trend in these films—the tendency to give sex and/or sadism top billing over religion—by marking a number of them "objectionable in part"—for example, *Salome, David and Bathsheba, The Prodigal, Solomon and Sheba* and *Esther and the King.*

Another undoubted shortcoming of the gospel according to Hollywood is the habit of watering down the Bible in our pluralistic society so that it gives the least possible offense to the religious sensibilities of all shades of believers and unbelievers in the audience. Occasionally the Legion of Decency will make a notation to this effect, while at the same time classifying the picture in question as unobjectionable—as in the case of *The Robe*. More often they will let the omissions or distortions pass without comment.

Justice and charity sometimes dictate this course of action. In a fictional story which deals only tangentially with biblical incidents (and most of the films under discussion fall into this category), inaccuracies and elisions can in most cases be presumed to result from the clouded vision of the fictional characters rather than the shilly-shallying of the producer. At other times the Legion's "hands-off" policy may be pragmatic in a perfectly legitimate sense.

Contrary to popular belief both inside and outside the Church, the Legion's power to influence the content of films has always been extremely limited. And it has maintained what influence it possesses by the skillful practice of the art of the possible. In most cases dogmatic or scriptural accuracy has been too much to expect of Hollywood, so the Legion has reluctantly accepted what it could not change.

King of Kings, however, presents an entirely different kind of a problem. This is not a well-meaning bit of pious fiction in which Christ appears briefly as an off-screen voice or a faceless white-robed figure. Rather, it purports to portray the life of Christ with a popular actor, Jeffrey Hunter, playing the role front and center; besides, it bears a title which is one of the traditional titles under which Christ is invoked. Some regard for facts and some spiritual comprehension are required if the film is not to be literally blasphemous despite its impeccable air of surface reverence. The Legion found it so wanting in this regard that it placed the picture in its "Separate Classification" with the observation:

> While acknowledging the inspirational intent of this motion picture, the poetic license taken in the development of the life of Christ renders the film theologically, historically and scripturally inaccurate.

No doubt this verdict elicited cries of anguish, astonishment and outraged innocence from the movie's sponsors. If so, I must admit to having a certain sympathy for them. The reactions of religious spokesmen to biblical films over the years have certainly given the producers some grounds for concluding that there was absolutely nothing they could not get away with except possibly too much sex and violence. Yet if the Legion had not taken a stand on *King of Kings*, it would have found it almost impossible to take one in the future on any film that violated scriptural or religious truth. And with our expanding knowledge of the screen medium it is becoming increasingly clear that violations of other Commandments than the Sixth and Ninth must be reckoned with, and that films sinning against the intellect and the human personality are, in the long run, the greater threat to faith and morals.

My sympathy for the film's sponsors, faced with the bad news that their sure-fire, time-tested formula for appeasing everyone has failed in this case to appease one important segment of the public, was short-lived, however. It has been replaced by a certain grudging awe for the virtuosity with which the company is using the "gamesmanship" approach in promoting the film among religious groups. The purpose of this maneuver is to divide and conquer, to confuse, to throw off balance, to blunt potential criticism by tricking some segments of the various groups into giving a seeming endorsement. Its chief weapon is apparent altruism—for example, the gratis distribution in schools of handsomely gotten-up film strips equipped with impeccably Catholic or impeccably Protestant captions.

An even grander gesture consists of the donation of preview theatre performances of the picture in key cities all over the world to religious leaders with no strings attached, except the concealed one that the company is hardly going to hide its candle under a bushel. Its publicity releases about these newsworthy events are designed to make it sound as much as possible as though the religious leaders were endorsing the film.

The company's sleight-of-hand technique with a press release was further illustrated a few days before the film's New York opening when they announced that "*King of Kings* has received the highest rating from the Catholic Cinematographic Center, the Vatican's film rating and reviewing organization." All this means is that the Italian equivalent of the Legion of Decency classified the film as their equivalent of "unobjectionable for general patronage." To grasp this, however, one must know that in context the words "highest rating" have no positive connotation, that the C.C.C. is an Italian Catholic national group and not "the Vatican's film rating and reviewing organization," and that Catholic film-classifying groups in various countries often come to different conclusions on the same film.

What the uninitiated can be counted on to infer from the release is 1) that Pope John himself has personally pinned a medal on the picture and 2) that, in expressing reservations about it, the American Legion of Decency is just not showing proper respect for the central authority of the Church. As long as film companies persist in these tactics, the chance of a fruitful dialogue between the churches and the film industry in this country seems fairly remote.

The task of tracking down all the liberties the picture takes with Scripture rightly belongs to a biblical scholar, which I am not. I mention one crucial falsification with reluctance. This is the trait common to most modern biblical films of rearranging facts to absolve the Jews of all blame for Christ's death. I mention it with reluctance because I acknowledge that the Jews have suffered for nineteen centuries from a terrible misunderstanding of this event by Christians. Or perhaps they have suffered rather because individual Christians were unwilling to accept the awful and essential truth about the Incarnation—that Christ was crucified for *my* sins—and have sought a scapegoat instead. But however legitimate is the grievance of the Jews on this point and however understandable their desire to rid themselves of an unjustly applied stigma, no good can be accomplished by letting Hollywood rewrite history according to wishful thinking. From a purely practical point of view it produces an effect diametrically opposed to the one sought after.

The application of this revisionist principle to *King of Kings* makes for an impossible situation dramatically as well as historically. The picture cuts from Christ being examined privately by Pilate (Hurd Hatfield) to Lucius (Ron Randell) releasing the imprisoned Barabbas (Harry Guardino) and saying in effect: "You are free. Christ will be crucified. Your followers yelled louder than the others." (Lucius is the good pagan centurion who figures, without aging, throughout the film's 33-year span, and Barabbas is pictured as the prototype of an Israeli freedom fighter.)

Thus, with one line of dialogue, the crucial matter of Christ's condemnation, how it came about and who was present at it, is casually glossed over and misrepresented. In the film the unspecified "others" are not present at the Crucifixion either. Nobody is there, in fact, except Christ's faithful few and some Roman soldiers.

How Christ came to be crucified in the first place is still more inexplicable. In the gospel according to scenarist Philip Yordan, His betrayal resulted from a not-ignoble miscalculation. Judas (Rip Torn) was a friend of Barabbas and, like him, an advocate of armed rebellion. When a premature rising of Barabbas' followers on Palm Sunday was mowed down by the Roman phalanx (in one of the film's few dramatically and pictorially exciting sequences), Judas, close to despair, had only one last hope. If the Master were delivered into the hands of His enemies, He would be forced to use His supernatural powers to strike down the oppressors and establish His kingdom on earth. To whom Judas betrayed Him is not clear, since the film introduces us to no one who had anything against Him. The thirty pieces of silver are nowhere in evidence.

Other stratagems employed by the film to keep it from having what might euphemistically be described as "sectarian orientation" might be cited. For example, any miracles that Christ is seen to perform are ones that could have a psychological explanation. The primacy of Peter among the apostles is not mentioned, but for that matter neither is the sending of the Twelve on their apostolic mission. And when the centurion (Lucius again) utters his great act of faith, it is not the ringing biblical phrase, "Truly this was the Son of God," but comes out instead: "Truly this was the Christ."

But criticism of the film on the grounds of scriptural inaccuracy only operates to discredit individual parts. It has to my mind a more fundamental failing which vitiates the whole. It is bad art, and bad art of a particular and precise sort designed to convey a surface impression to the unwary that is totally at odds with its real content and impact.

To understand the significance of this indictment it is necessary to understand the essential dynamics of films, how they actually work and how they affect audiences. The above-mentioned secular critics, by and large, were the first to perceive this all-important point. All too often the policies of film-betterment groups were formulated without sufficient comprehension of the screen medium, which has led them, at one time or another, to endorse some very strange films indeed.

A few months ago in AMERICA I attempted haltingly to explain how the film form operates:

The essential impact of a work of art flows, not from what is said, but from the intangible synthesis or climate that is created by the collision of the artist's vision of life and his chosen material. Furthermore, this climate, this implicit outlook on life, is the basic quality that a film communicates to the public and the communication is subliminal, on the level of emotion rather than intelligence.

These remarks were made as a preliminary explanation for taking the position that a superficially disedifying film, such as *La Dolce Vita*, can be in reality both moral and worth-while. They serve equally well to demonstrate how a superficially inspirational film such as *King of Kings* can prove in actuality to be nothing of the sort.

If a film about our Lord is going to communicate to the audience "an intangible synthesis or climate created by the collision of the artist's vision of life and his chosen material," then producer Samuel Bronston, director Nicholas Ray and scenarist Yordan have to start off by answering the biblical question: "What think ye of Christ?" But from the movie it is obvious that these gentlemen have no opinion on the subject except that at the moment He is a "hot" box-office property if properly exploited. This attitude, or lack of it, poisons the wellsprings of the movie.

Christ is there as a physical presence, but His spirit is absent. No serious attempt is made to establish who He is, what His motives and purpose are or what His relationship is to the various social forces around Him. Consequently there is no "dramatic engagement" between Him and the audience, and not the slightest possibility that anyone will derive from the film any meaningful insight into what Christ's life and sufferings signify for us. On the contrary, the picture bends all its efforts in the other direction—to keep Christ as neutral and undynamic as possible while at the same time lulling the audience into a pleasurable state of pietistic euphoria by parading the familiar words and images of the New Testament in pageant style before them.

The Sermon on the Mount sequence, staged with mobs of people and an effective eye to cinematic movement, is a case in point. Having spoken the Beatitudes with great earnestness and some skill, Hunter falls to answering some of the famous questions proposed to Christ in the Gospels. The words sound fine but they have no integral connection with any of the film's dramatic action. Therefore in the context of the picture they have no more impact than audience participation on a Jack Paar show.

This avoidance of the fundamental issues is not due to ineptitude or even to the muddleheaded but understandable wish to avoid offending anyone's religious sensibilities. Rather it is based on the same shrewd commercial instinct that poisons so much of the entertainment shown in the mass media today. An important function of art after all is to make us see ourselves more clearly. This can be a very painful experience, so painful in fact that vast numbers of the mass audience have demonstrated that they will not support it with their ticket or grocery purchases. They prefer the kind of entertainment with the opposite but ultimately de-Christianizing message: "You are fine as you are."

"One of the weaknesses of some popular religion today is that it aims to make people feel good rather than be good," said Methodist minister Ralph W. Sockman recently. That is certainly the weakness of *King of Kings.* A life of Christ should be an irresistible challenge to man's conscience. Instead, this one is a tranquilizing drug.

Bishop Paul J. Hallinan of Charleston, S.C., has pinpointed this dichotomy even more pungently:

The greatest challenge to Christianity today is a popular, bland, respectable faith termed secular humanism. It is often called "the American Way of Life." It is not godless but it keeps God in His place—the pulpit. It equates the Christian moral code with such terms as decency, brotherhood, the Golden Rule. It is the orthodoxy of non-believers, but it is a ready refuge for the half-believer too. . . . It simply says: "Take up your credit card and follow me."

King of Kings is perfectly at home in a credit-card society. It is at opposite poles from Christ's exhortation: "Take up your cross and follow Me."

What Do the Scrolls Tell Us?

Raymond E. Brown, S.S.

T IS NOW close to fifteen years since the first scrolls
were discovered in a cave near Qumran. Today
unbroken silence cloaks the ruins of the quasi-
monastic settlement that has been excavated at Qumran
in the intervening years. Eleven caves that yielded up
documentary treasures once more open their gaping
mouths only to bats and flies, and some passing Bed-
ouin. If the dust seems finally to be settling at Qumran,
so too in the scientific world of biblical studies a certain
peace seems at last to hold sway in the matter of the
scrolls.

As Joseph A. Fitzmyer, S.J., pointed out in AMERICA
earlier this year (3/18), the mavericks with their cries
of hoax are heard in ever fewer numbers. Also, calm
weighing of the evidence has silenced or, at least, exposed in an embarrassing light the professional agnos-
tics and the opportunistic scholars who saw a chance to
make headlines by claiming that the new scrolls challenged the uniqueness of Jesus Christ. The years of investigation have resulted in a generally accepted view
on the dating, nature and significance of the scrolls.

It is commonly agreed today that the scrolls come
from the library of a group of Essenes who inhabited

the Qumran area from shortly after 150 B.C. until 68 A.D. The Essenes, according to the Jewish historian Josephus, were one of the three major Jewish sects in the first century of the Christian era. But the Essenes were more truly a sect than their rivals, the Pharisees and Sadducees of Gospel fame, who were actually parties of political and theological opinion. As reconstructed from the scrolls and from sources like Josephus, Pliny and Philo, Essene history began with a breaking away from the main body of Judaism shortly after the Maccabean revolt of 166 B.C.

Most pious Jews cheered the attempts of the Maccabee brothers, Judas, Jonathan and Simon, to free Judea from the political and religious tyranny of the Syrians. Not all were equally enthusiastic about the usurpation of the high priesthood by Jonathan (152 B.C.), a usurpation that was more or less legalized for Simon and his descendants in 140 B.C. (I Mac. 14:41). The Essenes seem to have sprung from a revolt of the real high-priestly family (descended from Sadoc) and of their followers against that usurpation. Withdrawing into the wilderness of Judea, these priests and laymen formed a community whose purpose, as they wrote, was "to clear the way of the Lord in the wilderness." They were to be a penitent nucleus which, by strict observance of the ancient law and adherence to the sacred solar calendar, and by absolute purity in matters sexual and ritual, would be prepared for the imminent coming of God.

The Qumranians were persecuted by the Maccabean high priests and by their successors, the Hasmoneans, who earn in the Qumran writings such epithets as "Wicked Priest," "Man of Lies" and "Vessels of Violence."

Shortly after the Essene movement began, there arose at Qumran a man who bore the title of "the Righteous Teacher." This nameless priest was a man of great spiritual attainments, for, according to the scrolls, God revealed to him secrets which He had held back even from the prophets of old. Although the personality of the Righteous Teacher left its mark on the community's ideals, we know little of his career, save that he was persecuted. Of his claim to be a messiah, of his crucifixion and resurrection, the writings of the community say nothing. For these items one must consult the vivid and creative imagination of certain modern writers on the scrolls.

During the century before Christ, the community at Qumran grew in numbers. The buildings were enlarged about 110 B.C. They soon included an elaborate system for conducting and preserving water, a bakery, a pottery shop, storehouses and a community dining room. Most of the sectarians must have lived in tents and caves near this settlement. The swelling numbers may have included fugitives from the increasingly irreligious activities of the Hasmonean high priests like John Hyrcanus (d. 104) and Alexander Jannaeus (103-76). Jannaeus' wife, Salome Alexandra, who ruled from 76-67, is mentioned by name in the Qumran writings, as is the first Roman governor of Syria, Aemilius Scaurus (62).

Even the troubled times that saw the rise to power of Herod the Great (c. 40 B.C.) seem to have left their mark at Qumran, for fire and earthquake desolated the building. For about forty years, roughly contemporary with Herod's reign, the settlement was virtually deserted. Shortly after Herod's death in 4 B.C., however, the sect returned to settle at Qumran and remained there until the Jewish revolt against Rome. In 68 A.D. the Tenth Roman Legion reduced the buildings to ruins and ended the history of the Qumran community.

The library of this community must have been quite extensive. One of the caves near the community settlement, Cave IV, contained over four hundred manuscripts in Hebrew, Aramaic and Greek. Unfortunately, only a small part of the total library has come down to us. Among eleven caves discovered so far, the first and last have yielded complete scrolls. The rest have produced only fragments—some torn deliberately in antiquity (perhaps by Roman soldiers), many of them encrusted with dirt and bat dung, eaten by animals and insects, and worn by two thousand years of exposure to the elements. Nevertheless, these few scrolls and many fragments have proved to be one of the most important legacies left in Palestine by the people of the

Book. William F. Albright has characterized it as "the greatest manuscript discovery of modern times."

ABOUT one-quarter of the discovered manuscripts are biblical. Every book of the Hebrew Old Testament except Esther is represented. Of the deutero-canonical books (those found in the Greek Old Testament, but not in the Hebrew—accepted by Catholics, but not by Protestants and Jews), some of the original Hebrew of Sirach and the Aramaic of Tobias have appeared. Consequently, it is in the field of the Old Testament that Qumran has made some of its greatest contributions.

Before the discovery of the scrolls, the oldest Hebrew manuscripts of the biblical books dated to the ninth century A.D. Now we have, in whole or in part, over a hundred manuscripts going back to the period before Christ. In fact, some of the manuscripts are older than the Essene community itself, for instance, fragments of Exodus and Samuel from Cave IV, dating to the third century B.C. These must have been heirlooms brought by the founding fathers. One of the fragments of Daniel dates from about a half-century after Daniel was written (probably about 165 B.C.).

We must not jump to the conclusion that because the Qumran texts are older than previously known Hebrew manuscripts, they are necessarily better. At the beginning of the second century A.D. there was an organized attempt in Judaism to compare biblical manuscripts, to choose those that were carefully done, and to reject those that were textually poor. The standard Hebrew text of the Middle Ages is the heir to this tradition of critical scholarship. With the Qumran scrolls we find ourselves back in the precritical period with all sorts of textual traditions, some good and some bad. For example, two scrolls of Isaiah were found in Cave I. One was virtually identical with the Hebrew text we know; the other had a myriad of slightly variant spellings (only a few of which actually gave significantly different readings).

It should be added that even when different readings

of the biblical texts are supplied by the Qumran manuscripts, many of them are not new to scholars. After all, the medieval Hebrew texts have not been the scholars' only keys to the Old Testament. The old translations of the Bible into other languages play an important role. For instance, the Greek translation (Septuagint) of the Old Testament, made centuries before Christ, often departs considerably from the Hebrew text familiar to us. Until the Qumran discoveries, scholars could only make educated guesses at what sort of Hebrew underlay this Greek translation. Some even thought that the Septuagint was simply a free translation. The discoveries at Qumran gave us, for the first time, fragments of the variant Hebrew texts that underlay the Septuagint, and we have found that in books like Samuel and Jeremiah the Greek translators were being faithful, but to a Hebrew text quite different from the one we knew.

The scrolls, then, provide a good deal of interesting material for study of the Old Testament text as well as for auxiliary sciences such as Hebrew paleography and Hebrew pronunciation. But perhaps we should close this section by adding an assurance for the timorous of heart. The variant readings of which we speak largely concern phraseology. There will be no substantial changes in the Old Testament narrative. In fact, many modern critical translations, like our Catholic Confraternity translation of the Old Testament, have already incorporated the best of the variant readings, which were known from the Septuagint and from the Vulgate, St. Jerome's Latin translation of the Bible.

T HE QUMRAN SCROLLS have also made a great contribution to the history of Judaism between the two Testaments. The Old Testament literature breaks off in the second century B.C.; the rabbinical literature has its roots in the second century A.D. Very little of the in-between literature had survived until the discovery of the scrolls. Now, from the nonbiblical Qumran writings, we can get a more realistic picture of the political, intellectual and theological ferment of the period from 150 B.C. to 70 A.D. It is true that we have to look at this period through the eyes of the Essenes. If we had some of the Pharisee and Sadducee literature, we might get a more rounded idea of the times. Yet the scrolls have given us many insights that otherwise might have been lost.

We find, for instance, that a dualistic theology had come into Judaism. Perhaps, ultimately, it came from Persia. In Essene thought, the world was divided in two, under the leadership of the angel of light and the angel of darkness. Both angels were created by God, but they were allowed to struggle in this world on an equal footing until God's final intervention on the side of light. Yearning for God's intervention produced a strong eschatological and apocalyptic interest at Qumran, and messianic expectations were especially vivid. The Essenes expected the coming of a prophet (perhaps the prophet who would be like Moses—cf. Deut. 18:15) and of *two* messiahs, one a priest, the other a king of the house of David.

The moral theology of Qumran was highly developed. There was some sharing of personal goods; amassing of wealth was severely condemned. There seems to have been an ideal of celibacy; most of the community rules concern only men. Josephus, however, speaks of celibate and marrying Essenes, and female skeletons have been found in some of the smaller Qumran cemeteries. It is not entirely clear whether the married Essenes represented a different congregation alongside the celibate community or a later relaxation in community discipline to foster membership. Fraternal charity was another virtue greatly emphasized at Qumran, far more, indeed, than in the Old Testament.

The discipline of the Qumran community is most striking as one reads the scrolls. Newcomers were submitted to a year of postulancy and a year (or two) of novitiate before being admitted to the community. In these years of trial the candidates were carefully scrutinized on behavior and adherence to the strict Qumran interpretation of the Law. Only gradually were they allowed to participate in the ritual cleansings of the sect, and only full-fledged members were admitted to the sacred community meal of bread and wine. Nothing so close to a monastic community has hitherto been found in pre-Christian Judaism.

THE INCREASED knowledge of Judaism gained from the scrolls has also given us a better insight into the background of Christianity. For instance, John the Baptist now seems less lonely in his wilderness ministry. Living and working in the same area as the Qumran Essenes, he quite conceivably had some contact with them. Like them, he insisted on repentance and a cleansing baptism; like them, he regarded his mission as preparing the way for the imminent coming of the Lord (both John and Qumran use the "voice in the desert" passage of Isaiah 40:3 to characterize their missions); like them, he tried to form a penitent nucleus in Israel. Obviously, his ministry was of wider appeal and was less legalistic, but John still stands closer to the Qumran Essenes than to any other Jewish background.

Our knowledge of Qumran thought also throws light on many of our Lord's sayings. After all, Jesus had to speak to all the Jews of his time and in their own terms, and some of the Essene doctrines may have been fairly widely known. Josephus tells us that there were Essenes scattered in various towns. Consider particularly the way Jesus speaks in St. John's Gospel. Sections like John 3:19-21 and 8:12, which emphasize the division between light and darkness, are quite intelligible against the framework of Qumran dualism. The presence of abstract dualistic terminology had led critics to deny authentic Palestinian origin to St. John's Gospel. Now, in some ways, it turns out to be the most Palestinian of all Gospels.

The scrolls have also shed light on the Epistles. A section like II Cor. 6:14-15, for example, sounds almost as if it had been copied out of a Qumran document.

The whole argument of the Epistle to the Hebrews seems clearer, thanks to Qumran. The author is probably writing to a group of converted Jewish priests who are beginning to fall away from Christianity. Yet, in the arguments he uses with them, he does not seem to have the priesthood of the Jerusalem Temple in mind, but the priestly practice of a more ancient period. Now the hypothesis has been advanced that the epistle was written to convert Essene priests. Then the comparisons drawn from the older priesthood would make more sense, for the Essenes regarded the current Jerusalem priests as usurpers. Also, the argument of the epistle that Christ is superior to every angel would be clearer against a Qumran background, in which all the sons of light were subject to a supreme angel. Finally, this hypothesis would explain the great emphasis in the epistle that Christ is a priest, even though not a Levitical priest. To satisfy Qumran expectations, Jesus would have to be the Davidic messiah and the priestly messiah all in one. We might remember the early Christian designation of Jesus Christ as prophet, priest and king. In Him, then, were to be found the three messianic expectations of Qumran.

The Qumran finds may help, also, to clarify some details of early Christian practice and organization. The ideal of a community of goods was shared by both Essenes and Christians (Acts 2:44-45). One of the Qumran officials bore a title (*mebaqqer* or *paqid*) which is the exact Hebrew equivalent of the Greek word for bishop (*episkopos*). Like the Christian *episkopos* (Acts 20:28), this Qumran official was regarded as a shepherd. His functions of teaching and guiding the small Qumran groups resembled closely the functions of the early bishops (Titus 1:7-9). Also, the large assemblies of the Qumran community were called the "sessions of *the Many*," a term very close to that used of the Christian community sessions in the Acts of the Apostles (6:2; 15:30). The Qumran practice of a daily sacred meal in which the priest blesses bread and wine has interesting parallels in the daily "breaking of the bread" in the Christian communities (Acts 2:46), although, of course, there is nothing at Qumran to suggest the body and blood of the Lord.

A final verdict as to the full significance of the Qumran discoveries is still to be achieved: the fruit of further patient investigation. Enough, however, has already been acquired to dissipate the flock of fantastic speculations occasioned by the first discoveries. Far from upsetting the credibility of the Christian narrative, the scrolls, in many cases, have offered valuable interpretations of Old and New Testament documents. We may look forward with much interest to the eventual completion of this fruitful enterprise.

New Images of Man

W. Norris Clarke

"NEW IMAGES OF MAN" is the theme of an unusually interesting and thought-provoking exhibition of contemporary sculpture and painting on view until Nov. 29 at the Museum of Modern Art in New York City. The 23 American and European artists here represented by some hundred of their works are not content with the absorption in pure abstract form which up to now has dominated about 80 per cent of contemporary exhibited art. They all feel in some way the urgent call to body forth in canvas and paint, in wood, metal and stone, their inner vision of what modern man is really like, of what has happened or is in the process of happening to him, under the veneer of his well-tailored, superficially healthy surface.

Though these artists are for the most part quite independent of each other and belong to widely different schools, there is enough unity of idea, imagery and feeling among them to make their silent judgment on our age unusually significant. The artist has always held up the mirror to his own time for those who have the eyes to see and the courage to want to see. His own eyes may not always be perfectly clear, and he may not see all that is there. But it is dangerous for the rest of us not to stop periodically in the headlong rush of our daily living and take a long attentive look at the products of his vision. This is what I would like to do in what follows, speaking not as an art critic, but as a Christian philosopher, focusing on what these men are trying to express rather than on the artistic adequacy of how they express it.

I am aware that to many the attempt to disengage any definite meaning or idea-content from a piece of modern art will seem a hopelessly arbitrary and subjective enterprise. This may well be true for most of the dominant abstract art. But one of the significant things about the present exhibition is that it marks a notable departure from pure abstractionism. The latter movement had worked out its own inner genius to such a pure degree that it was bound sooner or later, like all particular movements in art, to call forth its own counterpoint. Though the present group could not express themselves in the way they do unless they had learned the lessons of abstractionism, still I think it is undeniable that most of them are seriously concerned with giving expression to a vision or image of man that is in some recognizable sense a criticism of life. I am supported in this by the commentary of the director, the excerpts from the artists' own writings on the aims of their work, and the perceptive preface of Paul Tillich, distinguished Protestant theologian and critic of culture —all contained in the excellent book of text and photographs which serves as catalog for the exhibit. The comments of four sculptors—Leonard Baskin, Reg Butler, Balcomb Green and Theodore Roszak—on the opposite page illustrate what these artists are trying to do.

A CREATURE OF TENSIONS

What sort of images do we see in this hall of mirrors for contemporary man, so skillfully mounted for our benefit by Peter Selz, curator of painting and sculpture exhibitions at the Museum of Modern Art? The most powerful over-all impression that struck me was that nowhere here could one find man at peace, man in harmony with himself, with his fellows or with the world that is supposed to be at least temporarily his home. Almost every artist lays him bare, in his own arresting way, as a creature of taut, often agonizing tension, confused as to who and what he is, painfully lonely and isolated from his brothers, the depersonalized victim of his own triumphant technology or of dark primitive forces unleashed from his own subhuman depths.

It is as though these painters and sculptors felt it was no longer safe to allow themselves or us to focus on the external beauty and grace of the human form, as earlier artists had done, mercifully concealing the machinery and obscure forces at work within. This would only flatter us, dull our sense of danger and lull us into a fatal slumber, while the poisonous gases of self-complacency and illusion continued to do their deadly work. We must rather be taken brusquely by the shoulder and vigorously shaken up, made to see what is happening to us within. Hence in most of these works all protecting surfaces are stripped away. Man is laid bare to the engine room, so to speak, with all his inner wheels, wires and power lines exposed. Even where an outer surface is apparently kept, the taut lines of bone, nerve and muscle pierce so transparently through that the veil of skin and flesh serves rather to reveal than to conceal what is underneath. This insistent urge to analysis in depth, leaving no recess of privacy unprobed, no refuge of illusion unexposed, reflects unmistakably those two typical techniques of our day for exploring the hidden dimensions of man: the X-ray camera and psychoanalysis—or rather, to be really up to date and actually more accurate— "existential" psychoanalysis. It would be hard to portray more aptly the pervasive spirit of inner tension and anxious self-analysis so characteristic of modern man in an urban technological society.

Let us now explore in detail the characteristic feelings about himself and his world that emerge from these new images of man. What are the sources of his anxiety and tension? He appears, first of all, as the depersonalized victim of his triumphant but soulless technology. Who can forget the pitiful dejected shell of the once noble hero Jason, created by the British sculptor Paolozzi out of old bits of discarded metal, wheels and tubes, pierced by jagged holes revealing the emptiness within? Or the heavy, earth-bound Icarus in the same style, stretching out helplessly his stunted (or fractured?) wings? With a little meditation one begins to share the artist's vision of man as fallen from his human dignity and his once heroic grandeur to the level of a run-down robot, a discarded reject of his own technology.

A similar theme recurs in the works of the French sculptor César, especially in his arresting figure of a female torso roughly welded of old bits of metal, whose iron blisters and amputated legs and arms, ending in jagged splinters of corroded steel, speak of human precariousness and the decay of the flesh more eloquently than any materials formed by nature herself could do. It breaks out again in a violent cry in the tremendously dynamic "Iron Throat" of the American Roszak, a great eroded skull in steel plate and tubing, its mouth open in an enormous shout—an image, one cannot help but think, of the power of communications: all voice, but dead within.

THE LONELY MAN

A second common theme is that of lonely man, isolated both from his fellows and the world of nature with which he was once in harmony. This is marvelously evoked by the "thin people" of the Swiss Giacometti, undoubtedly one of the most gifted sculptors of the group. His figures in bronze rise tall and indescribably thin, sometimes only a few inches in width for a height of six feet or more, each one infinitely withdrawn into itself and remote from every other, even when they form a group on a public square. As one critic has said, his figures may stand or walk, but they never rest; they are too tensely introspective and self-enclosed for repose. Aside from "ideology," however, for sheer artistic magic with the utmost economy of materials, his evocation of space and its mystery in the soaring figure of a "Man Pointing" has few equals that I can recall.

Something of the same impression of loneliness and isolation in the midst of the world is reflected also in the stiffly awkward couple in two of Diebenkorn's canvases. They seem to be strangely lost and out of place in the coolly indifferent and impersonal space of the room that is presumably their home. Francis Bacon's painting of the huddled figure of a man in the center of a landscape, completely alien to the nature around him and absorbed in himself, is another striking example. This lack of a sense of organic harmony and at-home-ness with his environment is one of the most frequently recurring themes of the exhibition. The same inner loneliness breaks out again in quite a different way, it seems to me, in the hectic gaiety of De Kooning's pathetically erotic women, with their desperately extrovert eyes and fixed toothy smiles. The restless, agitated flow of lines, masses and colors in these paintings achieves an admirable interpenetration of idea with artistic form.

Germaine Richier's sculptures make us pass from the isolation of man from his fellows and the world around him to his own uncertainty about himself within. Her strange, half-human figures, hovering ambiguously between man and animal or plant, like "The Grasshopper" and "Don Quixote of the Forest," seem to suggest that modern man is no longer so sure whether he is really human or only a mask for something more primitive.

A milder form of the same inner uncertainty and loss of self-identity is reflected in the blurred or faceless figures characteristic of several of the painters. Their image of man suggests someone who has lost all awareness of who and what he is, as he moves through a mysteriously opaque and alien space. Such are Bacon's two "Studies for a Portrait of Van Gogh" and Nathan Oliveira's "Man Walking" and "Standing Man with Stick," although the latter warns us: "My concern for the figure is primarily a formal one, growing out of the problems of painting itself. The implications are unconscious."

The last major theme of the exhibition, if one can call it a separate theme, I can best describe as a kind of pent-up outburst or explosion of indignation at all man's inhumanity to himself and his fellow man. The unbearable anguish of man's self-imprisonment and self-mutilation bursts out at us with brutal explicitness from

Bacon's painting of the "Man in a Blue Box," in which a powerful figure is shown rising from his chair, his whole face exploding in a vast cry of agony, his pose suggesting with sinister ambiguity that he is both judge and accused at once. Compassionate indignation flames out at man's regression to the beast in Rico Lebrun's paintings, "Buchenwald Pit" and "Study for Dachau Chamber." In a similar but more muted and resigned vein are Leon Golub's paintings of "Damaged Man," a pathetic yet heroic figure systematically dislocated in every member, and his more normal and at the same time more deeply moving "Orestes" with its strangely haunting face, the essence of bewildered pain beyond words borne with Stoic resignation and the determination to endure despite it all.

An affirmation of human dignity, however, shines through Lebrun's work in the strange light of glory that seems to radiate from his tangled heaps of limbs, some of them marking as on a clock of human history that

the time is well past high noon (the fancy struck me that it was also the time of the Passion of the Son of Man). As he himself tells us, "I wanted to express the belief that the human image, even when disfigured by the executioner, is grand in meaning. No brutality will ever cancel that meaning. Painting may increase it by changing what is disfigured into what is transfigured." Golub, too, with his "Colossal Head," points to man's heroic will to endure despite his tragic vulnerability and the enveloping threat of mutilation or annihilation. "The ambiguities of these huge forms," he writes, "indicate the stress of their vulnerability versus their capacities for endurance."

Let us call a halt reluctantly to our very incomplete inventory and reflect a moment on what we have seen. (I have had to omit many minor themes and outstanding individual works, often of stirring power and beauty, such as Roszak's "Skylark," a poem in shining steel of a figure alive with motion, half-bird, half-human, pivoting on tiptoe in the act of taking flight, with a burst of stars for a face; or the seated thinker in squared stone of the Austrian Fritz Wotruba. [*See our cover.—*Ed.])

What is the significance of it all, if any? The image of man which emerges here is certainly not one which would be greeted with enthusiasm at a Rotary Club convention. Despite the compassion behind it and the occasional flashes of hope, grandeur and beauty which break through the storm clouds, it is on the whole a somber and threatening picture: an image of inner tension, anxiety, uncertainty, depersonalization, vulnerability to powerful subhuman forces seething just beneath the thin veneer of civilization—an image, in a word, of the extreme precariousness of man's human dignity and the dangerous erosion it is undergoing on all sides.

THE ARTIST CONFUSES US

The spontaneous reaction of the non-professional, "man-in-the-street" observer tends at first to be a sense of disorientation and bafflement at being suddenly confronted with this strange and disconcerting picture of the man he thought he knew so well. This can quickly turn into a feeling of resentment—even indignation—as though he were being presented with a deliberately distorted and unflattering portrait of himself. "What have you done to our humanity?" one feels like complaining to the artist. "Why have you so mercilessly laid bare the dark corners of our soul, why have you so dislocated and dissected our natural beauty in order to reconstruct the parts in such artificial and disturbing patterns?"

But the artist can with justice throw the challenge right back at his accuser: "My images reflect what I see. What I have been watching is yourself. The real question is: What have *you* done to our common humanity, to yourself, to your brothers and to me? You accuse me of taking man and nature apart like a machine and refabricating them in unnatural new forms.

84

But isn't that exactly what you have done to the world around you with your technology, sometimes creating new beauty but often, with careless ruthlessness, leaving only ugliness and distortion behind as the price of utility or comfort? And isn't the taking apart and artificial reconstruction of man exactly what 'social engineering' has already done in Russia and China and threatens to do in any technological civilization?

"I am not trying to paint you as you look, or would like to look, from the outside, but as you really are, or fear that you are, within. I am not judging you, but only trying with compassion and sympathy to give expression to your own secret, inarticulate image of yourself. Do not people always experience a moment of resistance and resentment when brought face to face with their hidden selves for the first time? Yet is this not the only path to self-renewal? I am doing nothing else than what you pay your psychiatrists for doing. You should thank me, rather than blame me, for having revealed to you the hidden face of your own soul."

And I think the artist would be right. Admittedly he does not see all that is to be seen among us. Perhaps his hope and faith are not as strong and obvious as his spirit of protest. This may be his defect. But what he does see and image forth for us is certainly there. It would be wise for us not to turn away our eyes because the face in the artist's mirror is not the beautiful and inspiring one we had hoped to see, but one furrowed with agony and fear.

The people who had to live through Buchenwald and Dachau have good reason to want to bury their trauma in oblivion. But the facts behind these names, and their all too numerous counterparts in other sections of the world, remain an ineradicable scar on the face of 20th-century man which neither the historian nor the artist has the right to forget. As Tillich puts it in his perceptive preface, these makers of art

are fighting desperately over the image of man, and by producing shock and fascination in the observer, they communicate their own concern for threatened and struggling humanity. . . . If they depict the human face, they show that it is not

simply given to us, but that its human form itself
is a matter of continuous struggle.

Who of us would be willing to deny that our century
will stand out in history as the one in which the ultimate
precariousness and vulnerability of man were unveiled
for the first time? Perhaps our artists have read the
record better than we like to think.

PESSIMISM DESPITE SUCCESS

A problem remains in my own mind, however, that
has long puzzled me and that the present exhibition
has only brought to a head more acutely. I would like
to propose it to the readers of AMERICA for their reflection and for what further light they can throw upon it.
Why is it that, despite our constantly increasing pros-
perity, comfort and technological mastery over nature,
the majority of our outstanding contemporary artists,
both literary and otherwise, remain quite unimpressed
by this aspect of our culture and the widespread optimism it generates, and persist in presenting a predominantly somber image of the decline and dehumanization
of man? Are they merely expressing their own private
resentment at their loss of prestige compared to the
businessman and the scientist; at their isolation within
the highly organized, team-work society around them;
at their inability to feel at home and come to terms
with the machine age; or possibly at their alienation
from the ancient religious roots of art?
It is true that the artist, who must necessarily remain
a lonely individualist in the disappearing tradition of
personalized craftsmanship, and who for long has had
to live as a kind of vagrant on the margins of society,
has felt the pressure of the technological age more
keenly than most people. He has had to face the difficulty not only of finding a place for himself within it
that will not suffocate his art, but also of keeping himself from being so spiritually, imaginatively and emo-
tionally overwhelmed by its complexity that his art itself
cannot get it into focus with adequate unity, totality
and depth. Could it be, then, that the artist's darkly

colored portrait of lost and anxious contemporary man is really only a disguised projection of his own ambiguous and frustrated predicament?

On the other hand, his very distance from the world which nourishes him gives him a better vantage point, like that of the philosopher and the saint, for discerning what is truly significant within it. Is it he, then, who has seen more clearly than the rest of us? I do not know the answer. But while we wait for more light on the matter, it would be wise for us to give our artists the benefit of the doubt and meditate humbly on how we might provide them with the model for the happier and more harmonious image of man that we hope to find in the art exhibits of the next generation.

The Recognition of Shock

Harold C. Gardiner

THE VIRGINIA KIRKUS SERVICE is an organization that
reviews books far in advance of publication as a
means of alerting booksellers. Its biweekly bulletin is, as a rule, admirably outspoken in calling spades
exactly spades when it is necessary to warn booksellers
that such and such a book ought to be "handled with
care." It is one of my chores to read the bulletin, and I
have been much impressed of late by the number of
books that have called forth cautions like these:

> It is, in fact, the author's concentration on bed-
> room/bathroom obscenities that the publishers
> commend as a "selling point" (*Drum and Bugle*,
> by Terence Fugate, Simon & Schuster).

> The lives of Amber Falls' citizens are exposed and
> the picture presented is one of unbridled sexuality,
> desperate squalor, intellectual and moral whore-
> dom, despair nursed in alcoholism (*The Mill*, by
> Bradley Robinson, Random House).

> The antagonist is the occupation army . . . where
> boozing, wenching and brawling are the antidote

for army apathy and boredom (*A Fever for Living*, by R. A. Roripaugh, Morrow).

There she seduces him, disgusts and degrades him and finally completes his destruction. . . . It is a study in dissolution, in the fascination of the flesh which almost approaches an exaltation of evil (*The Gouffé Case*, by Joachim Maass, Harper).

The situation bursts as stickily as a lanced boil and one sniffs sensationalism at the core (*Lord Love a Duck*, by Al Hine, Atheneum).

More than the weather is steamy—there's lots of sex, cheap rather than seductive (*The Long Goodnight*, by Carl D. Burton, Morrow).

Strictures like these are common—increasingly common, I believe—in the bulletin, and though this source is hardly infallible in its estimates, its judgments do serve to spotlight a trend that is well summarized in a review of Grace Metalious' (of *Peyton Place* "fame") *The Tight White Collar* in the London *Times Literary Supplement* (January 6):

> Vulgarity informs almost every page [of this book], an account of the sex lives of the inhabitants of a small New England town hung on a plot about a witch hunt involving a teacher in the local school. The defilement of the most intimate of human experiences by language worthy of an advertisement for underwear; the prepackaging of sex in clichés so that an anxiety-ridden orthodoxy may masquerade as the ultimate in frankness and daring—these things are not uncommon in many contemporary novels, but *The Tight White Collar* is the epitome of the genre.

If these damning criticisms are accurate straws in the wind (and dozens of similar examples could be adduced), a question inescapably rises: what has happened to our contemporary recognition of shock? To pose the question in this term is to engage in an obvious play on the title of a famous book edited by Edmund Wilson in 1943, *The Shock of Recognition*. That book consisted of a series of studies by famous American writers of other equally famous literary compatriots— Melville assayed Hawthorne, for example, and Twain judged Cooper. The theme of the book was indicated in the words of Melville: "For genius, all over the world, stands hand in hand, and one shock of recognition runs the whole circle round." This tingling sense of awareness of kinship still runs like an electric current among the truly eminent of our creative writers; we find Mauriac writing probingly about Graham Greene, or, to take a very recent instance, Phyllis McGinley saluting the achievements of fellow poet Daniel Berrigan, S.J. (see AM. 10/26/57, pp. 110-111).

But the point I have in mind is concerned with the problem in reverse, so to speak. Why is it that many concerned with current literature—who, if they are not geniuses, at least ought to have basic good taste—do not recognize that much of the "shock" in that literature is a cheap and tawdry and debasing fake? Perhaps it is because, as Wilson says in his introduction to *The Shock of Recognition*, "it requires gifts just as rare—since they are just the same gifts—to be fully aware of the bad as to be fully aware of the good" (Doubleday, Doran, 1943, p. xiii).

But no—that certainly cannot be the basic reason, for it does not take "rare gifts" for readers, critics and, above all, the publishers to realize that, as critic Hannah Arendt once said: "The fact that pornography is infinitely boring is unrecognized only by the truly vulgar."

If Miss Arendt's touchstone in this matter still works, I am afraid that we are forced to the conclusion that not only a wide reading public but even more portentously **a large circle of critics and a segment of publishers are persistently and perhaps all unconsciously revealing their own fundamental vulgarity.** In an endeavor to attract a reading public, some publishers seem to be progressively pressing into service the tactics of the advertising agencies that whoop up the motion pictures. This particular book, like the film at your neighborhood Bijou, is sold to you (see the Kirkus statement about *Drum and Bugle* above) as "daring, frank, uninhibited, revealing, shocking," when, in sober critical fact, the excess of suggestive detail adds up to nothing more than utter boredom for the reader—unless, of course, he happens to be itching with curiosity.

WHY HAS the failure to recognize the vulgar nature of this kind of shock taken on such an unhealthy emphasis in American publishing? I believe that one clue is provided by the reference above to the influence of motion-picture promotion. It is not a large leap from the film to that other spawner of moving images that engages so much of the U. S. citizen's entertainment hours —the TV screen. Everyone has heard by now that there is much concern in all sorts of circles about the amount of violence in our TV shows. If we need anything to convince us that there is indeed a surfeit of violence, perhaps the remarks in a hardheaded business paper will do the trick. The *Wall Street Journal* (October 20, 1960), reporting a boom in the sale of U. S. television programs abroad, remarked:

> Excessive violence in some U. S. video programs has already raised difficulties abroad. Australia's censorship board last year barred 42 U. S. TV films and demanded cuts in 1,595 additional films. Sweden and Japan and other countries have also voiced objections to brawlings and shootings in American programs.

In the same issue John G. McCarthy, president of the Television Program Export Association, conceded: "There's no doubt about it; we're going to have to tone down our violence if we want to get the most out of the foreign market."

This lofty commercial motive has not yet made itself so markedly felt in the field of American publishing. Though U. S. publishers obviously do hope to pile up sales abroad, the vulgarity pays off here with American readers, where the big money is. But as the U. S. public gets more and more inured to violence through the gentle ministrations of TV (and of the "mature" films), it seems some publishers and authors feel that the only way they can attract attention is to pile violence upon violence, shock upon shock.

A most convincing case can be argued, I believe, that television violence is not merely coloring the moral attitudes of millions of younger and older viewers, but is subtly shaping the thinking of other media of entertainment as well, and not least the publishers of fiction. Al-fred A. Knopf, president of the publishing firm that bears his name, has gone so far as to state recently that it's out-of-date to complain about sex in fiction today, for the simple reason that it has been replaced by sadism. Is it a mere coincidence that the replacement in fiction has followed the course of violent incidents on the television screen? Mr. Knopf may have indulged in a bit of oversimplification, but his point underlines the one I am making: we have become so used to violence in one form or another that it no longer shocks, or will shock only if dealt out in consistently larger and stronger doses.

I F THIS TYPE of shock is less and less recognized for the vulgarity it is, there is another type of shock that is—what shall I call it?—proper and human. This is the kind of impact a book makes, not through the external and sensational images of sex and sadism, but through its quality to shake the reader into a realization of what an awful (in the proper sense of the word) creation of God any human soul is. Jean Mouroux put this succinctly and superbly in his *The Meaning of Man* (Sheed & Ward, 1948, p. 268): "On the day when, by some flash of intellectual enlightenment, or some effort at spiritual progress, we come to realize what we really are, we are seized with a kind of shiver."

And, strange to say (or apparently so), this shiver is precisely what true literature can and does provide. Arnold Bennett pointed this out many years ago in his *Literary Taste:* "The pleasure derived from a classic is never a violent pleasure—it is subtle, it will wax in intensity; it does not at all knock you down; it steals over you." In the same context Mr. Bennett observes, apropos my remarks about the vulgarity of the other kind of shock: "The artistic pleasures of an uncultivated mind are generally violent."

There is a ton more of legitimate shock—legitimate in this sense of a realization of the mystery of man—in the pages of Alan Paton's *Cry, the Beloved Country* than there is in a dozen books like James Jones' *From Here to Eternity*. Paton's great book had this quality while it was being read; the quality is there when one relives it in memory (it "waxes in intensity") and detects in one's inner self the silent canker of a pride that *could* burst out into open racial injustice. There is more genuine shock in the recently published (and churlishly received in some Catholic circles) *No Little Thing*, by Elizabeth Ann Cooper, than there is in a carload of *Peyton Places*, as one sees dramatically the Hopkinsesque "cliffs of fall" that can yawn before a priest—the fall all the more abysmal as the heights were lofty.

But susceptibility to *this* kind of shiver or shock is deadened by too frequent reception of the vulgar shock. The "daring" of a James Jones or a Grace Metalious creates such a din that the mental ear is deafened to the vibrations of the shiver set up in the soul by a Paton or a Greene, who make us face the realization that within oneself couch those awful capacities of glory and degradation—and *that* is the mystery of man.

I am inclined to think that one essential way of keeping alert to the shiver and insensitive to the shock is to preserve in one's self a deep sense of the reality of sin. I also am inclined to suspect that one basic reason why some Catholics think that the themes of a Greene or a Cooper ought not be treated rests exactly on a lack of such realization.

We would be smug indeed if we labored under the impression that we are assured of possessing this sense of sin by the mere fact that we *are* Catholics. We live in a world and are surrounded by an atmosphere in which a sense of sin has been lost. Henri Rondet, S.J., puts this well in his rich little book, *The Theology of Sin* (Fides, 1961, p. 84):

> In Kantian philosophy and its derivatives, God unfortunately remains exterior to moral obligation. Since then, morality has been secularized. In the best situations they only talk about duty, truth, justice, brotherhood and human solidarity. Moral fault is kept, responsibility remains, but whom is man responsible to? Sin as such implies a personal attitude to a personal God. In order to recover the consciousness of sin, we have also to recover the consciousness of God, His grandeur, His rights, the demands of His love.

In our efforts to deepen this realization of God and thereby to make more interior our "vivid consciousness of the world's sin by knowing ourselves to be sinners or capable of sin" (this is Fr. Rondet's phrase, which he applies even—perhaps I should say especially—to the saints), the shiver set pulsing by good and great books can be an immense help. But this implies that we are open to, sensitive to the shock of recognition, that we can appreciate the fact that a Greene, a Mauriac, a Cooper are not talking about "such things" for the sake of the vulgar shock that appeals to uncultivated minds, but rather for the sake of making us realize interiorly that not only genius, but our common fallen human nature stands, in Melville's phrase, "hand in hand all over the world." And if one still questions why Catholic authors have so often provided the shiver by concentrating on the theme of adultery, Fr. Rondet's words offer an explanation:

> In the Old Testament sin is disobedience, ingratitude, adultery. This last analogy, though difficult to manage, is the best. A modern man understands what an offense against love, against friendship, is. There are relations between God and man which are comparable to those between a man and his wife, between friends. Sin is an offense against a father, a friend, a spouse (p. 84).

As one grows in such a realization of the inner, personal relationship between God and one's true self, which knows the world's sin by knowing its own (either actual or potential), one grows progressively deafer to the specious attractiveness of the shock that has no basis in a sense of sin, but can do no more than flaunt violations of the conventions. Then one becomes attuned to the recognition, in the work of genuinely creative writers, of the true shock of "what we really are."

Novelists who send this shiver coursing through our fibers always make a demand on our humility and reward it. We must go to them with no thoughts that we are "not as the rest of men"; we come away from them saying to our inner selves: "Lord, be merciful to me a sinner." And if all this brings us to conclude that a spirit of prayer has something to do with really creative reading, that, at least, is a salutary shock of recognition.

Portrait of Hemingway

Charles A. Brady

"By my troth, I care not; a man can die but once; we owe God a death . . . and let it go which way it will, he that dies this year is quit for the next."—Henry IV (Ernest Hemingway's favorite quotation)

IT SEEMS a rule of human nature that one writer— and not necessarily his generation's greatest— should seize upon the imagination of his time. It was so with R. L. Stevenson yesterday, and with Byron before that. It has been the case with Ernest Hemingway in our day. In the end he, who had in life been so obsessed by death, did not have the luck to die their kind of hero death after which he had quested all his days. He died, instead, the less seemly sort of death that overtook those two other European romanticists whom he also so strangely resembled, Pushkin and Lermontov.

Because Hemingway was a man greatly loved, on the whole the newspapers have shown themselves strangely forbearing toward the not so very short and not so very happy life of a writer who, ideally speaking, should have kept his last appointment with death in Uganda or Kenya, not in Ketchum. Death came for him, not on some hot Spanish afternoon, but in a cold American dawn. His art had been dying slowly over the six or seven years before. While no other traveler between life and death has any right to speculate on a fellow pilgrim's passing, one cannot help but wonder if flagging creative vigor did not play its part in this final sinister installment of the Hemingway legend.

That same self-fostered legend, which occupied so disproportionate a share of our attention in Hemingway's regard, was, when all is said and done, not really so very important. Much of it was downright silly: the boxing poses for the rotogravure sections; the slangy baby talk—the "Bwana," "Papa," "Maître" business; the Byronic remarks, like the one to Fitzgerald, that his idea of heaven was a bull ring in which he owned two *barrera* seats, with a trout stream outside that no one else was allowed to fish. This was the side Lillian Ross made such savage fun of in the celebrated *New Yorker* profile. It was the side that took over far too many of Hemingway's own pages. Wolcott Gibbs used to parody it magnificently, until the inadvertent self-parody of *Across the River and Into the Trees* rendered all other lampoons forever anticlimactic —at least so far as Hemingway's art was concerned.

In everyday life the self-protective buffoonery went on right up to the time of and after 1954's near-fatal airplane crash in Africa, with the highly publicized diet of bananas and gin which Ogden Nash affectionately mocked in his calypso:

I land in the jungle by the teeth of my skeen.
Big gorilla walk up to me and talk very mean.
He put up his mits and I sock him in the cheen.
Then gorilla and me, we begin the beguine
With a bunch of bananas and a bottle of jeen.

Yet underneath all the embarrassed and embarrassing exhibitionism, beneath all the popping of corks and cocking of rifles, there was a good side to the shield. Hemingway *did* go to war, after all. Until the bitter end, Hemingway *did* escape from death like some latter-day Herakles. The admittedly too-often-

97

photographed hair on his chest was not ersatz at all. The old Mohican, who, in his art, was as fastidiously paleface as Henry James himself, was as tenderhearted underneath as he was tough-minded on the surface. It is always dangerous to underrate Hemingway's intelligence. Though, like Eliot in his poetry, Hemingway deliberately filtered out all evidence of overt cerebration, he gave the game away when, in *Green Hills of Africa*, he quoted an Australian hunter saying impatiently to him: "No. Go on. Do not try to be stupid." Reversing the little girl with the curl who, when she was bad, she was horrid, it might be said of Ernest Hemingway that, when he was good, he was incomparable.

For Ernest Hemingway stands as our greatest master of fiction between the wars—and for a decade after. I am not forgetting William Faulkner, either, who objected so strongly to Hemingway's self-imposed classic limits (and rated Hemingway fifth, among his contemporaries, after Thomas Wolfe, himself, John Dos Passos and Erskine Caldwell) on the grounds of Hemingway's esthetic cowardice: ". . . he stayed within what he knew. He did it fine, but he didn't try for the impossible." The difference between Hemingway and Faulkner is the difference between a cat and a dog. For the sake of objectivity, let me go on record as stating that I am a cat man myself.

Nor am I overlooking those limitations of Hemingway which by any computation must be accounted bad: his sentimentality and his adolescent bravura, especially in the matter of sex—his heroines, for example, are really no more than the dream-boats of an adolescent's fundamentalist reverie. But these strictures concern his attitudes, not his stylistics. Hemingway's one-finger prose music is writing like the painting of Matisse. He was far from being a naturalist. His fiction reveals him to be a symbolist-moralist poet "exhaling" allegory like cigarette smoke. Limitations are one thing, limits another. He transcends and cunningly makes the best of his limits to the point where, next to James, one is inclined to rank him as our *strictest* artist. This probably means that he is, at bottom, one of the greater lesser writers, rather than one of the lesser greater writers. But there is real greatness here from many points of view.

What qualities make for this greatness? These: integrity; grace under pressure; a style whose purity produces the paradoxical impacts of obscure clarity and complex simplicity; compassion for the human condition; above all, utter honesty of intention and effect. "He could not be bought," said John Peale Bishop. "A writer's job," said Hemingway, "is to tell the truth." Needless to say, no one writer ever latches on to more than a portion of the truth. But Hemingway got hold of an astounding amount of it. He remains, moreover, the only major writer in our tradition who succeeds in sympathetically mediating the great Hispanic ethos. One must add these qualities also: a strong historical imagination; a keen sense of place and period; a power of precise observation; a subtly cadenced, stylized conversation that brings the movement of his stories curiously closer to ballet and archaic ritual than to drama; a romantic view of love which, for all its inadequacies, has the great merit, for our day, of being sexually normal.

Hemingway was a part-time expatriate with deep-seated indigenous roots. His art grew alongside one of the two main streams of the American literary tradition. He is not an Emersonian idealist, and he has no particular regard for this particular tributary of the American genius, which he once stigmatized as "the small, dried and excellent wisdom of Unitarians." No, he visits the dark side of the moon along with Twain and Crane and Poe, with Sherwood Anderson and two greater writers whom, however, he did not much admire, Hawthorne and Melville. Malcolm Cowley was right when he said of the stories: "Here are nightmares at noonday . . . a haunted and nocturnal writer."

BUT IF THE THEMES are dark, the much-praised much-maligned style is bright with the brightness of fine crystal. Once Hemingway had moved away from the first primitivist excesses of the echolalia Gertrude Stein taught her young Paris disciples, his effect justified Ford Madox Ford's famous encomium that his words like "pebbles fetched fresh from a brook . . . live and shine, each in its place." All this clean, mosaic splendor is at the service of what Hemingway himself called "the good and the bad, the remorse and sorrow, the people and the places and how the weather was," which is just about as good a definition of essential fiction as anyone has ever hit off.

Now stylistics as obtrusively tesselated as these are likely to fit the short story better than the novel. For all the poignancy of *Farewell to Arms* and the sheer brilliance of that glittering, comic *Waste Land, The Sun Also Rises*, it seems to me that the best of Hemingway's roughly sixty stories will last longer. These best must include: "Fifty Grand," "A Clean, Well-Lighted Place," "The Killers," "The Gambler, the Nun, and the Radio," "The Undefeated," "The Short Happy Life of Francis Macomber."

Hemingway has been accurately termed one of the obsessed artists. But it should never be forgotten that he was as much obsessed by God as by death, and that he was a critic rather than an apostle of nihilism, a moralist who did not approve of the rich bums and rootless expatriates who infest certain of his novels and with whom his great friend, Scott Fitzgerald, to some degree at least, was in collusion.

It has become a critical truism to describe Hemingway's muse as Catholic and Faulkner's as Protestant. (The tangled question of Hemingway's exact religious status, after his early conversion to Catholicism, might be resolved by saying that he stayed *croyant* even while his marital coil prevented his being *pratiquant*.) For once, a truism turns out to be true. Hemingway's habit of imagery is ritually Catholic. So is his sense of limits. So is his admiration for the Spanish thing, even for the Jesuit *mystique*, as we note in a reference to "the same town where Loyola got his wound that made him think." Look, moreover, at the sympathy with which nuns and priests are drawn in his fiction. If his controversial defense of the Spanish Republic comes in question here, it might be noted that this is precisely Belloc's stance where the men of 1789 are concerned.

Look also at Hemingway's fundamental admirations: courage, first and foremost, and fidelity; after these, love, generosity, chivalry, humility, a sense of the ridiculous. One remembers his credo after the announce-

ment of his Nobel award: "I do not know what Man (with a capital M) means. . . . I do know what man (with a small m) means and I hope I have learned something about men (small m) and something about women and something about animals."

Hemingway felt about animals much as the cave artists of the Dordogne felt, or a Siberian shaman. He loved them, hunted them, knew how to make them the vehicles of his deepest spiritual intuitions. Consider this, the most famous of his symbols, from the beginning of *The Snows of Kilimanjaro:*

> Kilimanjaro is a snow-covered mountain, 19,710 feet high, and it is said to be the highest mountain in Africa. Its western summit is called by the Masai "Ngaje Ngai," the House of God. Close to the western summit there is the dried and frozen carcass of a leopard. No one has explained what the leopard was seeking at that altitude.

No one has to explain. It is God, of course. As Brett said to Jake Barnes in *The Sun Also Rises:* "It's sort of what we have instead of God." And Jake replied:

101

"Some people have God. Quite a lot." In his own articulately inarticulate way, Hemingway's writing, too, had quite a lot of God about it.

A less famous but equally good self-symbol in animal terms occurs in the little-known "Fable of the Good Lion." The old man in *The Old Man and the Sea* used to dream of the lions on the beaches. This Good Lion, on the other hand, while he was in Africa, used to dream of the griffons, the winged lions, of St. Mark's. Only, when he got back to civilization, he went into Harry's Bar and asked for a Hindu-trader sandwich and a dry Martini made with Gordon's gin, an action which shocked all the habitués—for habitués, read Hemingway's bourgeois readers—most deliciously.

Like the Snow Leopard, the Good Lion tells us a good deal about the heraldic side of Hemingway, and about something else as well. If journalistic legends are so often false, it is partly because they mythologize too little, not too much. The Hemingway legend is already dead. The Hemingway myth is just beginning. On this higher mythic plane, he is many things: what Wyndham Lewis once called him, a "dumb ox," though "dumb" is surely the wrong adjective here; a sentient woodchuck capable of describing what he tastes and feels; even better, a medieval armorer-chronicler; a gladiator; a helmed legionary; Huckleberry Finn grown up and gone kudu-hunting; a sea-god even, a Triton or a Neptune. Above all he is a saga-hero defending a cave-mouth; a Viking gnawing his oar and well able to tell us the flavor of the bitten wood. Now that Ernest Hemingway has been released from the oar he manned in life, we can begin to view his saga-art in perspective and to discover its ultimate secret, which is precisely this: it was saga-art essentially, and that saga-art was better than any other body of writing in this grim century of ours; it was able to isolate the saga-essence, which remains one of the permanently recurring essences of man's tragic experience.

Death of a Dog

Joel Wells

ITEM: *A dog was struck and killed by a car at 9:30 last night on the highway north of town, an unidentified boy reported to the police this morning.*

The Old Dog and the Cars

after Ernest Hemingway

HE WAS AN OLD DOG and he had not chased a car for four years. But he would chase a car tonight and the boy would see him and know that he was not afraid.

He had not been afraid when he was a pup. There were not enough cars on the highway then, or big enough, or fast enough. He took them as they came, every afternoon with the sun in their eyes so they could not see him, which tripled the risk. Or at night, when there was no moon, he had run with risk so big he could feel it crowding against his flank.

There was a Sunday in his third year when he ran four Buicks within ten minutes, making three of them cross the centerline and putting the last one in the ditch. The boy had given him a tire for that.

But the Ford got him the very next day, driven by a woman. She hooked to the right, catching him on the rusty bumper so that he had lost his footing and fallen before the feet of the boy. And the fear had moved up from the tip of his tail and strangled his courage as he lay there.

He did not run again and the boy got another pup. For four years he sat in the afternoon dust under the porch and listened to the applause of brakes on the highway. Tonight they would squeal for him.

Put Out More Dogs

after Evelyn Waugh

"**M**YLES! I DO WISH you could remember to steer to the right."

Lady Distraught dug bone-white fingers even deeper into the leopard-skin upholstery of the Rolls and glared at her husband.

"Damned nuisance!" His Lordship muttered, veering the wheel sharply to avoid a large moving-van already half off the road and heading for the safety of a concrete embankment.

Trust the Americans to muck up a perfectly simple thing like motoring. During the war, he remembered, some Lend-Lease-happy idiot had come before Parliament with a proposal to make England "keep to the right to make the Yanks feel at home." The fool had gone on to read a forty-minute tract about "not having to change the roads, you know, not even the center-stripes."

Well, he'd dodged more than his share of Americans at home, let them dodge him over here. And, having retrieved the hand with which he had been adjusting his tails to a better lie (they had a terrible propensity to bunch against leopard-skin), he steadied the Rolls for a fresh charge.

A promising petrol tanker was just settling into his sights when Lady Distraught gave one of her well-known screams and something struck the car's right fender with a thud.

"Clement Attlee!" swore His Lordship, sure that he had run up against one of those rural American types whose clothing is covered over with copper rivets and buttons, "that's bound to have marred the finish."

The Matter of a Hound

after Graham Greene

THE OVERHEAD FAN moved no faster than the minute hand of his watch. A fly clung to the underside of the blade with contemptuous ease. Through the open door the heat bulged in at him like a penny balloon filled with water. At any moment it would burst and inundate him in his own sweat. Under the porch lizards stirred and rubbed against each other with the sound of dry sticks.

Inspector Hoad opened the bottom drawer of his desk and took out a bottle. Frowning, he held it before his mouth but did not drink.

"Drunk again!" buzzed the fly, "drunk before eight in the morning."

He opened his lips and let the gin slide over his tongue and down the desolate road of his throat. Very quickly, Hoad hoped, it would reach his soul.

The balloon burst. Sweat oozed over his lashes into his eyes and the station-yard began to shimmer through the doorway like the high-noon prospect of an English country pond. Something white was moving across its surface. Slender and white: a swan? The swan stopped in the doorway surrounded by a salty nimbus.

"You killed him," the boy said. "You were drunk and you ran over him but you didn't have to stop because you are the police."

Hoad blotted his eyes on the encrusted khaki sleeve of authority. So it had come to that at last: one night you finally succeed in capturing that elusive nymph, oblivion, and in the morning a boy in a white shirt comes and stands in your door to tell you that you've killed someone.

"You have the only car," the boy said, passing sentence.

Reverently, Hoad recapped the gin and placed it back in the drawer. The moment was too sacred to spoil with sordid curiosity. This boy, Manuel, would tell it well in his careful mission-school English: "He looked at me but did not ask whom it was that he had killed."

To Hoad's lips the barrel of the pistol felt even cooler than had the bottle.

The Weakling and the Dog

after François Mauriac

IT WAS during the summer of his fourteenth year that the dog had been destroyed. His parents, in the manner of those who have only sons who are frail, ran continually to bearded physicians who assured them that all that was required was a month under the sun at X, on the coast. Heeding this divine word as faithfully as had the Israelites in going out of Egypt, they fled the city, driving their firstborn and animals before them, until they came to a halt beside the sea.

But the waters had neither divided nor performed to prescription and the boy had grown thinner while a certain cough, muted in the din of Paris, became more audible in nights as silent as a tabernacle. They baked and watered him by day and rubbed and wrapped him at night until his body became as pliable and porous as a pudding. The days ached on interminably to the drone of his mother's reading and the snuffling sounds which rose from behind his father's newspaper.

The dog had been his great consolation. On the beach it leaped and circled his chair, attacking the waves impetuously with a bravado both comic and inspiring. At night, after the droning and the snuffling in the adjoining room had merged themselves in a rich counterpoint of snoring, the dog would leap over the sill of the boy's room and settle himself in the blankets over his feet.

But doctors, as everyone knows, are able to see far more than ordinary men, and it was not long before one of them discovered dog hairs among the boy's bed-clothes.

"And you ask why he coughs and grows thinner," pronounced Zeus from the hallway outside his room.

"But he is so attached to the beast that he will never consent to being separated," his mother responded in the voice of one who knows that what they are saying is of no consequence.

"Here is what you must do. . . ." The doctor outlined his murderous plot without the least diminution of his superbly professional voice.

In the midst of a death struggle with communism, the United States carries on within itself a debate about our national purpose. In large part this debate is prompted by the moral ambiguity of our foreign policy and by worry over the image of America abroad. But even smaller nations in the West seem to float in a vacuum of national purpose. Why? Is it because the West has lost contact with the tradition of reason, the public philosophy that must underlie any fruitful dialogue on ends and means? Perhaps we cannot define our national goals until we know the real meaning of morality. Perhaps we cannot project an image that wins acceptance until we know more about ourselves. And one asks himself: can the new Peace Corps contribute modestly to America's excruciating search for self-definition in this troubled and exasperated world of ours?

East and West

Morality
and Foreign Policy

John Courtney Murray, S.J.

URING THE DECADE of the Tentative 'Fifties the course of events has thrust a number of basic issues into the forum of public argument. One of them goes under the rubric, "morality and public policy." Chiefly in question is foreign policy.

My introduction to the state of the problem took place at the outset of the decade in a conversation with a distinguished journalist who is now dead. In public affairs he was immensely knowledgeable; he was also greatly puzzled over the new issue that was being raised. His first question revealed the source of his puzzlement. What, he asked, has the Sermon on the Mount got to do with foreign policy? I was not a little taken aback by this statement of the issue. What, I asked, makes you think that morality is identical with the Sermon on the Mount? Innocently and earnestly he replied: "Isn't it?" And that in effect was the end of the conversation. We floundered a while in the shallows and miseries of mutual misunderstanding, and then changed the subject to the tactics of the war going on in Korea.

THE OLD MORALITY PASSES

I have only a fragmentary acquaintance with the growing body of literature on morality and foreign policy; the subject is outside my field. But listening, as it were, on the edges of the public argument, I have come to the conclusion that my journalist friend properly introduced me to the fundamental problem. It does not lie in the concept of policy, or even in the concreteness of actual policies, though these matters are complex enough. It lies in the concept of morality itself. Rarely does the argument get to concrete issues of policy. And even when it does, the talk quickly turns back to the root of confusion—the question: what is morality?

The reasons for this fact lie in the history of moral theory in America. But that story is long, not to be told here (I don't think it ever has been fully told). An important event, of relatively recent occurrence, has been the recognition of the shortcomings and falsities of an older American morality that dominated the 19th century and still held sway into the 20th.

Its style was voluntarist; it sought the constitution of the moral order in the will of God. The good is good because God commands it; the evil is evil because God forbids it. The notion that certain acts are intrinsically evil or good, and therefore forbidden or commanded by God, was rejected. Rejected too was the older intellectualist tradition of ethics and its equation of morality with right reason. Reason is the dupe of interest and passion. And how is one to know, or dare to say, whose reason is right? In the search for moral principles and solutions reason can have no place.

In its sources the older morality was scriptural in a fundamentalist sense. In order to find the will of God for man it went directly to the Bible. There alone the divine precepts and prohibitions are stated. They are stated in so many words, and the words are to be taken at their immediate face value without further exegetical ado. When, for instance, the Gospel tells the Christian not to resist evil but to turn the other cheek, the precept is clear and absolute. The true Christian abdicates the use of force even in the face of injury.

In its mood the old morality was subjectivist. Technically it would be called a "morality of intention." It set primary and controlling value on a sincerity of interior motive; what matters is not what you do but why you do it. And it was strong on the point that an act is moral only when its motive is altruistic—concretely, when the motive is love. If any element of self-interest creeps in, the act is corrupt and sinful.

Finally, in its whole spirit the old morality was individualistic. Not only did it reject the idea of a moral authority external to the individual conscience. It also set its single focus on the individual existence and on the moral problems that arise in interpersonal relationships. As for society, it believed in a direct transference of personal values into social life; in principle it would tolerate nothing less than Christian perfection as a social standard. Its highest assertion was there would be no moral problems in society, if only all men loved the neighbor.

Within the last generation this older morality has come under severe criticism, in itself and its later historical alliance with certain trends in secular liberal thought. The attack has centered on its simplism. The discovery was made that this morality of facile absolutes was ill-suited to cope with the growing complexity of an industrial society, domestically and in its foreign relations.

It did not go beyond the false notion that society is simply the sum of the individuals living in it, and that public morality is no more than the sum of private moralities. It did not understand the special moral problems raised by the institutionalization of human action. It did not grasp the nature of politics, the due autonomy of the political, the limiting factors of political action, or the standing of success as a political value. It had no sense of the differential character of morality and legality, no theory of jurisprudence, no idea of the distinction between private sin and public crime (witness the laws

that it has left on the statute books—notably the Connecticut birth control statute).

In consequence of all these shortcomings, the older
morality possessed no resources for discriminating moral
judgment. It tended to thrust its simple yeas and nays
upon political, social and economic reality without any
careful prior analysis of the realities in question. It
disregarded the duly autonomous character of their
lines and life. It distorted the meaning of Plato's famous
dictum and understood it to say that society is the
individual (not "man") writ large. In a word, what
the older morality failed to understand was the nature
of man himself.

ETHIC FOR A NEW WORLD

The critique of the older American morality seems
to have been not only just but also successful. The
older morality, though still around, is no longer dominant. This is good. It is perhaps particularly good that
the older morality is still around. Doubtless it is useless
against the demons that inhabit the organized structures
of society and exert their sway over history from these
seats of institutionalized power. On the other hand, it
had a certain virtue of exorcism against the demons
that dwell in the life of the individual. And it is always
good that at least some demons are cast out from among
us even though their departure still leaves us in combat
with the "rulers of this world of darkness," whose
dominion will endure until the Day of the Lord.

The avowed purpose of the newer American morality
is to reckon with the full complexity of man's nature
and of human affairs. Hence against the absolutism
of the old morality, in which the contingent facts got
lost under insistence on the absolute precept, the new
morality moves towards a situationalism, in which the
absoluteness of principle tends to get lost amid the
contingencies of fact. Against the abstract fundamentalist literalism of the old morality the new system is
consciously pragmatist; not the wording of the precept
but a calculus of the consequences of the act is the
decisive moral norm. Whereas the old morality saw
things as so simple that moral judgment was always

easy, the new morality sees things as so complicated that moral judgment becomes practically impossible. The final category of moral judgment is not "right" or "wrong"—but "ambiguous."

Finally, against the self-righteous tendency of the old morality, the new theory teaches that to act is to sin, to accept responsibilty is to incur guilt, to live at all is to stand under the judgment of God, which is uniformly adverse, since every act of moral judgment is vitiated by some hidden fallacy, and every use of human freedom is inevitably an exercise in pride.

The current argument about morality and foreign policy goes on within the climate of moral opinion created at once by the older American morality, and by the newer morality, and by the conflict between them—a conflict which does not rule out certain similarities, notably their common rejection of the whole style and structure of natural-law morality. Three basic problems, each related to the others, furnish the focus of concern.

THREE RELATED PROBLEMS

The first is the gulf between individual and collective morality. Since the day of Roger Williams and his separation of the "garden" (the Christian community) and the "wilderness" (society or "the world"), prevalent American moral theory has never found a way to bridge the chasm between the order of private life and the order of law, public policy and institutional action, especially when the question concerns the nation-state. The private life is governed by the will of God as stated in the Scriptures; it is to bear the stamp of the Christian values canonized by the Scriptures—patience, gentleness, sacrifice, forbearance, trust, compassion, humility, forgiveness of injuries and, supremely and inclusively, love.

On the other hand, it is the plainest of historical facts that the public life of the nation-state is not governed by these values. Hardly less plain is the fact that it cannot be. What, asked my journalist friend quite sensibly, has the Sermon on the Mount got to do with foreign policy? Pacifism, for instance, may be a dictate of the individual conscience, but it cannot be a public policy. What then is the will of God for the nation-state? How and where is it to be discovered? There is no charter of political morality in the Scriptures. Must one, therefore, admit that all politics is simply *Realpolitik*—the selfish pursuit of national interest in a nicely calculated play of power to which ethical norms are irrelevant?

The other two questions are consequent. First, is it not the historical fact that the nation-state acknowledges only one imperative, the dictate of national interest? And is not the fact itself also normative? Is it not right that the nation should so act? Would it not be *wrong* for the nation to act apart from the national interest, short of it, or beyond it? But if you hold this, do you not come into open conflict with the basic tenet of both the older and the new American morality, which is that self-concern is the primal sin? that the pursuit of self-interest is the pursuit of evil? that the whole function of Christian morality is to call self-interest into question, deny it all theoretical justification, and condemn it in practice? This is the moral theory. Strictly applied, it must assert that the nation is sinful and guilty in all its actions, since they are never free of the taint of interest.

Faithfully held, this theory requires that the nation should be called upon to transcend self-interest, resist its dictates, and act beyond them in a spirit of disinterested altruism. Or, since this moral call would have the ring of nonsense in the field of politics, and since morality is not supposed to sound like nonsense, one could choose not to hold and apply the theory strictly. One could fall back on the position that self-interest is a legitimate motive for the nation, even though it is an illegitimate motive for the individual. Then the question is, in the name of what theory do you make this distinction? Is this to bridge the gulf between private and collective morality, or simply to fall headlong into it?

The final issue is perhaps the most basic. It certainly is the most inclusive, since it spans all the prominent issues of the day—armaments, the politics of the Cold

War, the economics and politics of the revolution of rising expectations. It is the issue of power. As far as the sheer fact goes, most Americans seem to have finally awakened to the central relationship between foreign policy and force. But the awakening was to a state of moral bafflement and anxiety, insofar as it took place in the climate of moral opinion described above.

In the climate of this moral opinion a cold breath of evil more than faintly emanates from the very words "power" and "force." It seems to have been part of the American dream that this nation could go through history with clean hands by the simple Kantian expedient described in Péguy's genial phrase: "Kantianism has clean hands, because it has no hands." Concretely, a nation's "hands", wherewith it shapes the stuff of

history, are its instruments of power—military, economic and diplomatic power, together with the power of sheer presence and prestige. We have never wanted to have such hands, much less to get them dirty by handling any history save our own. Our historic declaration was that power-struggles were for the "barbarous" nations of Europe, not for us. Now we have become suddenly conscious of our hands—that they are sinewy beyond comparison; that they are sunk in the affairs of the world; that they are getting dirty beyond the wrists.

At least we feel them to be dirty, and the feeling is one of guilt. The United States today is an imperialism, like it or not. And we like it so little that we are even unwilling to admit the fact. The cause of our anxiety is not that there has been little in our past political experience to teach us wisely to wield the instrument of empire, which is power. It is rather that there is nothing in current American moral theories to teach us the moral quality of power itself. The prevalent teaching is simply that power is evil. The teaching, in fact, is that the evil in human nature is precisely a will to power. The will is activated as the hand closes on the thing; at that moment innocence is lost, never to be regained. To be human is bad enough; but to be powerful is to be corrupt, with a corruption that increases with each increment of power.

In what moral terms, therefore, is America to justify itself in its possession of power? And in what terms is America to justify itself to the world for its uses of its power? Can these hands be cleansed? Or must the scriptural phrase be inverted to read: Let him who is unjustified become still more unjust? The national straits are even more narrowed when· one considers that the teaching says one further devastating thing. It says that to refuse to use power is to be "irresponsible," and therefore to be more guilty yet.

ONE THING COMES CLEAR

These seem to be the basic issues involved in the current controversy about morality and foreign policy. I have found myself in a fog as I have listened intermittently, while cynics dispute with moralists, and political realists dispute with ethical idealists, and fundamentalists dispute with "ambiguists" (I apologize for the barbarism, but I must have a descriptive term for this school of thought, whose favorite word is "ambiguity").

Only one thing is clear. The real issue does not concern the moral quality of this or that element of American foreign policy. The real issue concerns the nature of morality itself, the determinants of moral action

116

(whether individual or collective), the structure of the moral act, and the general style of moral argument. One cannot argue moral issues until they are stated; but what are the terms of statement of the moral issues involved in foreign policy? One cannot come to practical solutions until one has first formulated the relevant principles and also analyzed the factual situation in which the principled solution is to be practiced; but by what methods do you arrive at your principles and establish their relevance, and what is your analysis of the factual situation? As these issues are touched, or as they are avoided, the whole argument flies off in all directions.

The proper bafflers are the ambiguists. Their flashes of insight are frequent enough; but in the end the fog closes down. They are great ones for the facts, against the fundamentalists, and great ones for "conscience," against the cynics. They insist on the values of pragmatism against the absolutists; but they resent the suggestion that they push pragmatism to the point of a relativism of moral values. My main difficulty, however, is that I never know what, in their argument, is fact and what is moral category (surely there is a difference), or where the process of history ends and the moral order begins (surely there must be such a point).

When they undertake to describe the historical-political situation for which policy is to be framed, one has the same feeling that comes on seeing a play by Sartre. No human characters are on the stage, only Sartre's philosophical categories. So, in the ambiguist descriptions, the factual situation always appears as a "predicament," full of "ironies," sown with "dilemmas," to be stated only in "paradox," and to be dealt with only at one's "hazard," because in the situation "creative and destructive possibilities" are inextricably mixed, and therefore policy and action of whatever kind can only be "morally ambiguous."

MORALITY BASED ON A PARTI PRIS

But this is to filter the facts through categories. So far as one can see by an independent look "out there," the dilemmas and ironies and paradoxes are, like the beauty of the beloved, in the eye of the ambiguist beholder. They represent a doctrinaire construction of the facts in terms of an antecedent moral theory. And every set of facts is constructed in such a way as to make the moral verdict "ambiguous" a foregone conclusion.

The ambiguist rightly puts emphasis on the complexity of the situations with which foreign policy has to deal; no one could exaggerate the complexity hidden under the phrase, "the Cold War." But does the fact of complexity justify the vocabulary of description or the monotonous moral verdict? It is as if a surgeon in the midst of a gastroenterostomy were to say that the highly complex situation in front of him is so full of paradox ("The patient is at once receiving blood and

losing it"), and irony ("Half a stomach will be better than a whole one") and dilemmas ("Not too much, nor too little, anesthesia") that all surgical solutions are necessarily ambiguous. Complicated situations, surgical or moral, are merely complicated. It is for the statesman, as for the surgeon, to master the complications and minister as best he can to the health of the body, politic or physical. The work may be done deftly or clumsily, intelligently or stupidly, with variant degrees of success or failure; but why call it in either case "ambiguous"? The philosophers of moral ambiguity will, of course, say that the ambiguity, properly speaking, is not in the political situation but in political man, who carries into politics the paradox, irony and ambiguous amalgam of virtue and corruption that reside in his own nature (or in the human "self," as the ambiguists prefer to say, since they have a peculiar meaning all their own for the word "nature"). There you have it.

In point of sheer method there is no reason why the ambiguist should not make use of a conceptual scheme to guide his analysis of political fact, and to furnish the terms for his statement of moral issues, and to determine the style of his argument in favor of his solutions. Every moralist does this. Every moralist has his concept of the moral order. All practical moral inquiry has theoretical presuppositions. Each moral theory has its own categories of statement and its own style of argument. And in the end every structure of moral doctrine and decision rests on a concept of the nature of man.

NO PROGRESS HERE

To this concept of man's nature the critical argument comes back. The ambiguist indicts the fundamentalist and the secular liberal for their one-dimensional views of man. But he does not recognize that the same indictment recoils on his own head. He easily disposes of all the utopianisms, both "hard" and "soft," that result from the one-dimensional fundamentalist and secular liberal views. He then spins an enormously complex analysis of the "real" nature of man in personal and political life. And at the end of it (this is the real paradox) he has again compressed the moral life of man into one dimension. Inescapably, beyond all help of divine grace—and even further beyond all help from human reason and freedom—the life of man, personally and politically, is lived in the single moral dimension of ambiguity. He who relishes irony should relish this— that the whole complicated argument against simplistic

119

theories should result in the creation of a theory that is itself simplistic; that the smashing attack on the bright and brittle illusion of utopianism should win its victory under the banner of an opposite illusion that is marshy and murky but no less an illusion.

I have outlined the argument about morality and foreign policy in a way to suggest that it is an intramural argument within the Protestant community. So it is.

The question I have asked myself is, whether and on what terms it might be possible to me to enter the argument, as a representative of the tradition of reason in moral affairs. (It is also called the tradition of natural law; but the term "natural law" is so widely misunderstood today that it gives rise not only to semantic difficulties but also to emotional antagonism.) It might be worth while to essay an answer to this question in a later issue of AMERICA.

REMARKS ON AN ARGUMENT: PART II

RECENTLY, within a segment of the American people, an argument has been set afoot concerning morality and foreign policy. The parties to it have been Protestants; hence they have defined the issues in terms of Protestant moral theory. Protestant moral theory, however, is in a sort of fluid transitional state, considerably in conflict with itself; hence the problem of defining moral issues in public policy has been further complicated by a more fundamental argument about the norms and methods of moral judgment itself.

Against an older fundamentalism that found in simple scriptural maxims the solutions to even the most complicated social and political problems—with disastrous results to the structure of the problems—a newer school has arisen. I have called it "ambiguism," because of its fondness for the word "ambiguous" as a term of moral judgment. It emphasizes the complexity of moral issues as they arise in society and state; it asserts that in all the concrete situations with which public policy has to deal the elements of right and wrong are so inextricably mixed as to be indistinguishable; hence it claims that every public action or policy is "ambiguous," that is, both right and wrong. Nonetheless, the ambiguists, like the simplists, protest their opposition to the political realists or cynics, to whom all public issues are simply issues of power in which moral judgments have no place at all.

PSEUDO-PROBLEMS

My own terms of moral definition, argument and judgment are, of course, those of the tradition of reason in moral affairs—the ancient tradition that has been sustained and developed in the Catholic Church. Consequently, listening to the public argument on morality and foreign policy, I have found it difficult to discover just what all the shooting is about. Three major issues have come to the fore. The trouble is that all three seem to me factitious. From where I sit, so to speak, in the moral universe, they are all pseudo-problems. Were I to enter the argument, this is the first point I should have to make.

The Protestant moralist is disturbed by the gulf between the morality of individual and collective man. He is forever trying somehow to close the gap. Forever he fails, not only in doing this but even in seeing how it could possibly be done. Thus he is driven back upon the simplist category of "ambiguity." Or he sadly admits an unresolvable dichotomy between moral man and immoral society.

I am obliged to say that the whole practical problem is falsely conceived in consequence of a defective theory. No such pseudo-problem arises within the tradition of reason—or, if you will, in the ethic of natural law. Society and the state are understood to be natural institutions with their own relatively autonomous ends or purposes, which are predesigned in broad outline in the social and political nature of man, as understood in its concrete completeness through reflection and historical experience. These purposes are public, not

121

private. They are therefore strictly limited. They do not transcend the temporal and terrestrial order, within which the political and social life of man is confined; and even within this order they are not coextensive with the ends of the human person as such. The obligatory public purposes of society and the state impose on these institutions a special set of obligations which, again by nature, are not coextensive with the wider and higher range of obligations that rest upon the human person (not to speak of the Christian). In a word, the imperatives of political and social morality derive from the inherent order of political and social reality itself, as the architectonic moral reason conceives this necessary order in the light of the fivefold structure of obligatory political ends—justice, freedom, security, the general welfare, and civil unity or peace (so the Preamble to the American Constitution states these ends).

It follows, then, that the morality proper to the life and action of society and the state is not univocally the morality of personal life, or even of familial life. Therefore the effort to bring the organized action of politics and the practical art of statecraft directly under the control of the Christian values that govern personal and familial life is inherently fallacious. It makes wreckage not only of public policy but also of morality itself.

Again, the Protestant moralist is deeply troubled by the fact that nations and states have the incorrigible habit of acting in their own self-interest, and thus violating the fundamental canon of morality which sees in self-concern the basic sin. Here again is a pseudo-problem. I am, of course, much troubled by the question of the national interest, but chiefly lest it be falsely identified in the concrete, thus giving rise to politically stupid policies. But since I do not subscribe to a Kantian "morality of intention," I am not at all troubled by the centrality of self-interest as the motive of national action. From the point of view of political morality, as determined by the purposes inherent in the state, this motive is both legitimate and necessary.

There is, however, one reservation. I do not want self-interest interpreted in the sense of the classic theory of *raison d'état*, which was linked to the modern concept of the absolute sovereignty of the nation-state. This latter concept imparted to the notion of national self-interest an absoluteness that was always as illegitimate as it is presently outworn. The tradition of reason requires, with particular stringency today, that national interest, remaining always valid and omnipresent as a *motive,* be given only a relative and proximate status as an *end* of national action. Political action stands always under the imperative to realize, at least in some minimal human measure, the fivefold structure of obligatory political ends. Political action by the nation-state projected in the form of foreign policy today stands with historical clarity (as it always stood with theoretical clarity in the tradition of reason) under the imperative to realize this structure of political ends in the international community, within the limits—narrow but real—of the possible. Today, in fact as in theory, the national interest must be related to this international realization, which stands higher and more ultimate in political value than itself.

No false theoretical dichotomy may be thrust in here. The national interest, rightly understood, is successfully achieved only at the interior, as it were, of the growing international order to which the pursuit of national interest can and must contribute. There is, of course, the practical problem of defining the concrete policies that will be successful at once in the national interest and in the higher interest of international order. The casuistry is endlessly difficult. In any case, one ought to spare oneself unnecessary theoretical agonies, whose roots are often in sentimentalism; as, for instance, the effort to justify foreign aid in terms of pure disinterested Christian charity. To erect some sort of inevitable opposition between the pursuit of national interest and the true imperatives of political morality is to create a pseudo-problem.

POWER AND POLITICS

The third source of Protestant moral anxiety is the problem of power. The practical problem, as put to policy, is enormously complicated in the nuclear age, in the midst of a profound historical crisis of civilization, and over against an ideology of force that is also a spreading political imperialism. This, however, is surely no reason for distorting the problem by thrusting into it a set of theoretically false dilemmas—by saying, for instance, that to use power is prideful and therefore bad, and not to use it is irresponsible and therefore worse. The tradition of reason declines all such reckless simplism. It rejects the cynical dictum of Lenin that "the state is a club." On the other hand, it does not attempt to fashion the state in the image of an Eastern-seaboard "liberal" who at once abhors power and adores it (since by him, emergent from the matrix of American Protestant culture, power is unconsciously regarded as satanic). The traditional ethic starts with the assumption that, as there is no law without force to vindicate it, so there is no politics without power to promote it. All politics is power politics—up to a point.

The point is set by multiple criteria. To be drastically brief, the essential criterion is the distinction between force and violence. Force is the measure of power necessary and sufficient to uphold the valid purposes both of law and of politics. What exceeds this measure is violence, which destroys the order both of law and of politics. The distinction is teleological, in the customary style of the tradition of reason. As an instrument, force is morally neutral in itself. The standard of its use is aptitude or ineptitude for the achievement of the obligatory public purposes. Here again the casuistry is endlessly difficult, especially when the moralist's refusal to sanction too much force clashes with the soldier's

classic reluctance to use too little force. In any case, the theory is clear enough. The same criterion which governs the state in its use of coercive law for the public purposes also governs the state in its use of force, again for the public purposes. The function of law, said the Jurist, is to be useful to the community; this too is the function of force.

The community, as the Jurist knew, is neither a choir of angels nor a pack of wolves. It is simply the human community which, in proportion as it is civilized, strives to maintain itself in some small margin of safe distance from the chaos of barbarism. For this effort the only resources directly available to the community are those which first rescued it from barbarism, namely, the resources of reason, made operative chiefly through the processes of reasonable law, prudent public policies, and a discriminatingly apt use of force.

(Note here that Christianity profoundly altered the structure of politics by introducing the revolutionary idea of the two communities, two orders of law and two authorities; but it did not change the nature of politics, law and government, which still remain rational processes; to the quality of these processes Christian faith and grace contribute only indirectly, by their inner effect upon man himself, which is in part the correction and clarification of the processes of reason.)

The necessary defense against barbarism is, therefore, an apparatus of state that embodies both reason and force in a measure that is at least decently conformable with what man has learned, by rational reflection and historical experience, to be necessary and useful to sustain his striving towards the life of civility. The historical success of the civilized community in this continuing effort of the forces of reason to hold at bay the counterforces of barbarism is no more than marginal. The traditional ethic, which asserts the doctrine of the rule of reason in public affairs, does not expect that man's historical success in installing reason in its rightful rule will be much more than marginal. But the margin makes the difference.

All this is the sort of thing that the theorist of natural law would have first to say were he to enter on the ground floor, so to speak, of the controversy about morality and public policy. He could not possibly argue con-

crete problems of policy in the moral terms of the ambiguist. Insofar as these terms are intelligible to him at
all, they seem to him questionable in themselves and
creative of pseudo-problems in the field of policy. In
turn, the Protestant moralist, whatever his school, cannot
possibly argue questions of policy in the moral terms of
the tradition of reason. The tradition is alien to him
at every point—in its intellectualism, its theological
emphasis, its insistence on the analogical character of
the structures of life (personal, familial, political, social), its assignment of primacy to the objective end
of the act over the subjective intention of the agent,
and its casuistical niceties. At best, the whole theory is
unintelligible; at worst it is an idolatry of reason and
an evacuation of the Gospel.

It has also become customary to point out that,
whatever the merits of the tradition, it is dead, in the
sense of Nietzsche's dictum, "God is dead." So I was
told recently. It happened that I wrote a little piece
on the traditional moral doctrine on the limitations of
warfare, as fashioned by the tradition of reason. A
friendly critic, Prof. Julian Hartt of the Yale Divinity
School, had this to say: "Father Murray has not, I believe, clearly enough come to terms with the question
behind every serious consideration of limited war as a
moral option, i.e., where are the ethical principles to
fix the appropriate limits? *Where,* not *what*: can we
make out the lineaments of the community which is
the living repository (as it were) of the ethical principles relevant and efficacious to the moral determina-
tions of the limits of warfare?" This is a fair question.

After a look around the national lot, Professor Hartt
comes to the conclusion that the American community
does not qualify; it is not the living repository of what
the tradition of reason has said on warfare. I am compelled regretfully to agree that he is right. Such is the
fact. I would further say that the American community,
especially in its "clerks," who are the custodians of
the public philosophy, is not the repository of the
tradition of reason on any moral issue you would like
to name. This ancient tradition—like the Eternal Reason
of God, to which it makes its initial and final appeal—

is dead. (It lives, if you will, within the Catholic community; but this community fails to bring it into vital relation with the problems of foreign policy; there seems, in fact, to be some reason for saying that the Catholic community is not much interested in foreign affairs, beyond its contribution in sustaining the domestic mood of anti-communism.)

But if it be the fact that the tradition of natural law, once vigorous in America, is now dead, a serious question arises. What then is the moral doctrine on which America bases its national action, especially its foreign policy?

"DON'T SHOOT FIRST"

One could put the question in the first instance to the Government. It is clear that the Department of Defense and its allied agencies find sufficient moral warrant for their policies in their loyalty to the good old Western-story maxim: "Don't shoot first." With the moral issue thus summarily disposed of, they set policy under the primatial control of that powerful dyarchy, technology and the budget, which conspire to accumulate weapons that, from the moral point of view, are unshootable, no matter who shoots first. Those who are disquieted by this situation—which is not ambiguous but simply wrong—are invited to find comfort in the emanations of crypto-pacifism from the White House, which seems to hold that we shall never shoot at all. The moral argument for this unambiguous position, whose simplism rivals that of the ambiguists, is never made clear. The inquiry into the moral bases of policy would likely produce other weird and wonderful answers, if elsewhere pursued—within the Department of State, for instance, with regard to disarmament, foreign aid and diplomatic démarches among the uncommitted or emergent nations.

In any case, the question is perhaps more appropriately put to the American community at large. The theory of American government seems to be that public policies borrow, as it were, their morality from the conscience of the people. Right policies, as well as due powers, derive from the consent of the governed. There-fore, on what structured concept of the moral order does the American people undertake to fulfill its tradi-tional public moral right and duty, which is to judge, direct, correct, and then consent to, the courses of foreign policy?

There is a sentimental subjectivist scriptural funda-mentalism. But this theory by definition has nothing to say about foreign policy; it is at best a theory of inter-personal relationships and therefore irrelevant to inter-national relations, which are not interpersonal. There is also moral ambiguism. But this, in the final analysis, is not properly a moral theory. It is perhaps a technique of historical analysis, highly doctrinaire in style; but it is not an ethical philosophy. It is an interesting paradox-ical structure of rhetorical categories; but it is not a normative doctrine that could base discriminating moral judgments. All norms vanish amid the multiplying para-doxes; and all discrimination is swallowed up in the cavernous interior of the constantly recurrent verdict: "This action is morally ambiguous."

The school of ambiguist thought has done some use-ful negative service by its corrosive critique of older types of moral simplism and political utopianism. But it has no positive constructive power to fashion purpose-ful public policies in an age of crisis. It can throw rocks after the event, but it can lay no cornerstones. It points out all the moral hazards, and takes none. The self-contradiction inherent in sin is indeed a massive fact of the human condition; but not for this reason, or any other, does ambiguity become a virtue in moral judg-ment. Ambiguism can judge no policies save those that history has already judged. It can direct no policies be-cause it can specify no ends toward which policy should be directed. And it can correct no policies since all pol-icies deserve by definition the same qualification, "am-biguous," and what use is it to correct one ambiguous course by substituting another? We can discard am-biguism as the moral premise of public policy.

WHAT IS LEFT?

What is there left? There is, of course, the pseudo-morality of secular liberalism, especially of the academic variety. Its basic premise is a curious version of the Socratic paradox, that knowledge is virtue; it asserts that, if only we really could get to understand everybody, our foreign policy would inevitably be good. The trouble is that the past failures of the political intelligence of secular liberalism, and its demonstrated capacities for misunderstanding, have already pretty much discredited it.

Finally, there is the ubiquitous pragmatist, whose concern is only with what will work. But he too wins no confidence, since most of us have already learned from the pragmatist source of truth, which is history, that whatever is not true will fail to work. We want to know the political truth that will base workable policies.

It would seem, therefore, that the moral footing has been eroded from beneath the political principle of consent, which has now come to designate nothing more than the technique of majority opinion as the guide of public action—a technique as apt to produce fatuity in policy and tyranny of rule as to produce wisdom and justice. It was not always so. In the constitutional theory of the West the principle of consent found its moral basis in the belief, which was presumed sufficiently to be the fact, that the people are the living repository of a moral tradition, possessed at least as a heritage of wisdom, that enables them to know what is reasonable in the action of the state—its laws, its public policies, its uses of force. The people consent because it is reasonable to consent to what, with some evidence, appears as reasonable. Today no such moral tradition lives among the American people—certainly not, as Professor Hartt suggests, the tradition of reason, which is known as the ethic of natural law. Those who seek the ironies of history should find one here, in the fact that the ethic which launched Western constitutionalism and endured long enough as a popular heritage to give essential form to the American system of government has now ceased to sustain the structure and direct the action of this constitutional commonwealth.

The situation is not such as to gladden the heart. But

at least one knows the right question in the present matter. It is not how foreign policy is to be guided by the norms of morality. It is, rather, what is the morality by whose norms foreign policy is to be guided?

◆

Cassation for Good Friday

Space drains from the air between the woman and son;
They seem closer together; dark overleaps the land
As hope and memory pour into the shape of time
And time, at its full, at crux, crashes.
Silent, the woman of fifty and her sudden son
Keep their eyes empty of refusal, continue to stand,
Continue to watch the high man leap to his iron limit
In shortening thrusts.
                    Feathered by the lash
Like a love-wild bird he leaps for breath.
At the end of the dance he invents death.

At the end of the love-dance, the used-up man
Bows mystery-high in the quiet, exploded air.
The dancer hangs. The lover goes. The sky bends
Up, back and away from woman and boy, who stare
As if at each other; home, she goes to the window;
A lion lounges down the street.
The boy is waiting for friends.
Every unsuitable thing takes place.
The day never ends.   MARIE PONSOT

130

How We

Look to Others

George H. Dunne and C. J. McNaspy

I

THE AVERAGE AMERICAN is puzzled. He sees himself as reasonably decent, good-natured, peace-loving, generous. He has no colonies and no designs upon alien territories. He sees Fidel Castro as an unbalanced revolutionist who has betrayed the democratic hopes of many of his own followers and is busily mortgaging his revolution to the Communist powers. Why, then, should there be so much anti-Americanism about? And why, on the other hand, is Fidel Castro so popular a hero that almost every Latin American government is fearful of angering its own people should it anger him?

It would help the average American to understand if he had the gift to see both himself and Castro as others do. Two quotations from the same issue of *Time* (8/8/60) may give him just the perspective he needs. One concerns "Che" Guevara, the *éminence grise* of Castro's movement. A friend who knew him in 1953, when he held a minor job in Guatemala's agrarian program, says:

Once we came across a group of undernourished, belly-bloated kids. We were in United Fruit land. Che went into one of his rages. He cursed everybody from God to North American "exploiters" and wound up with a frightening asthmatic attack that lasted two hours.

The other concerns an American bean grower who is fighting efforts to provide a minimum of schooling for the children of migrant farm workers who, full-fledged field hands at nine years of age, are doomed by illiteracy to dreary servitude for life. Says the bean grower: "When a migrant goes to school beyond the seventh grade, you've ruined a good bean picker."

Examine these two images side by side! The dedicated revolutionary who admits to being a Marxist, and the typical representative of American democratic society—Guevara cursing himself into asthmatic rage at the sight of underprivileged children, the American coldly assaying the value of the stunted human as bean picker.

It may be objected that the American is not typical. The objection does not stand up. He is typical of Americans who make their money growing beans or tomatoes or lettuce or fruit. The proof lies in the fact that the farm lobby bitterly opposed this same effort, as it and the ranchers' associations generally have coldly and successfully resisted for years every effort to improve the wretched lot of the migrant field hand. He is also typical of other average Americans who are unmoved by, and indifferent to, the miserable exploitation of the migrant worker.

There is more than a sermon in this confrontation of images. There is a key to an understanding of a large part of contemporary history.

There are perhaps no people more generous with their wealth than Americans, but the image which impinges itself upon world consciousness is not one of American largesse. It is rather the image of the calculating and unfeeling bean grower, and in sharp contrast to it the dramatic image of the deeply feeling, raging Guevara.

It is not the exceptional Tom Dooley, but the hard-nosed bean grower who appears to be the normal product and expression of the social and economic system which has reached its highest development in America. This, as much as anything else, is what "colonialism" and "imperialism" mean to downtrodden people everywhere. This is why there is so much anti-Americanism about.

In a recent article in the *Commonweal* (12/30/60), Fr. Albert Nevins, M.M., quotes Karl Marx:

It is quite easy for Mister Hegel in his well-heated office in Berlin to resolve the problem of man's captivity solely in speculative fashion and to explain all human contradictions on the plan of a dialectic philosophy. But while there are women and children working 18 hours a day in the mines of Manchester I cannot feel myself free.

Here is the idealism which explains the tremendous appeal Marx has had and—despite the demonstrable errors of doctrine, despite the blood which has flowed, the tyrannies which have been spawned—continues to have for millions of men everywhere.

It is basically the same idealism, the same concern, which triggered Guevara's rage. It is the same idealism, the inability himself to feel free so long as the peasant masses were poor, hungry and illiterate, that sparked Fidel Castro. Guevara sacrificed a medical career, Castro a legal career, to set the peasants free. (Recently in Rome a Benedictine priest, who only a few years ago was in British government service in Malaya, where his job was to interrogate Communist prisoners, told me what a sobering experience it was to discover how many of them were professional men who, driven by the same idealism, had sacrificed their own careers to advance the revolution. I had the feeling the experience had something to do with his decision to sacrifice his own career in government and to join the Benedictines.)

What matters is not whether Castro is destroying more than he is building, or whether the sum total of human suffering in Cuba has been halved or doubled, or whether he falls from power tomorrow. What matters is that three years ago he was a man with a handful of poorly armed followers holed up in the mountain fastnesses. Today he is master of Cuba and still a hero to the mobs which wildly cheer his interminable harangues. What matters is to understand that his strength lies in the kind of image he projects to those mobs. It matters to understand what that image is: the image of an angry man bent upon destroying a social structure which says that the poor must be kept poor and ignorant so that we will have good bean pickers.

Take the case of China. The Republican thesis which would explain Communist success in terms of an alleged American betrayal engineered by a Democratic Administration is sheer nonsense. My right to this opinion rests upon the fact that 28 years ago I was urging—there are documents to prove it—the necessity of what today would be called a "crash program" to develop an imaginative Chinese leadership to destroy the frightfully disordered social structure which produced luxury for a few and illiteracy, beggary, misery or poverty for the teeming multitudes. If this were not done, and soon, the Communists, so I argued, would inevitably come to power.

At that time the Communists were an isolated body, holed up and surrounded in the mountainous regions of south-central China. But they were the only ones who projected a sharp image of protest against an intolerable social structure. Crushed by taxes, bled white by rapacious war lords, gouged by landlords, exploited in factory and field, millions of Chinese lived in a gray misery.

One day I climbed a path to a Buddhist temple outside the city of Suchow. For half a mile I walked a solid gantlet of beggars squatting elbow to elbow, empty rice bowls held out in the age-old suppliant gesture. In Shanghai 12-year-old children worked 16 hours a day in foreign and Chinese-owned cotton mills and slept at night on their hard workbenches. What voices were raised in angry protest? Who cursed themselves into fits of asthmatic rage? Who swore not to rest until these slaves had been set free?

Missionaries, with compassion and often heroically, went about their work of corporal and spiritual mercy, but they accepted the misery as part of the structure of

Chinese life. Foreigners went to and from their factories, in and out of their offices, back and forth from
their clubs, without a second thought about the misery.
The great "New Life" reform movement of Chiang Kai-
shek consisted largely in propaganda campaigns against
the indubitably noisome habit of ubiquitous spitting.

The only ones who denied the inevitability of misery,
damned the system which perpetuated it, and promised
an end to it were the Communists. They were a symbol
of protest and of hope. That was the source of their
strength. That is why, abandoned as early as 1927 by
Stalin, who neither then nor later was interested in the
Chinese revolution, without outside support, surrounded
by Nationalist forces, they could not be destroyed. That
is why 28 years ago their ultimate triumph was inevitable—unless someone else could project an even more
powerful image of protest and of hope. But no one else
did, and in 18 short years, with an assist from Japanese
aggression, which only advanced the date of their ultimate triumph, and in the last stages with considerable
help from American military equipment delivered to
them by defecting Nationalist troops or sold to them by
corrupt Kuomintang politicians, they were masters of
China.

This is not to say that the Communists were swept
into power on a great tide of popular support. This

would be a gross distortion
of the facts. No doubt the
larger mass of the people
were uncommitted, but their
very passivity was an asset
to the Communists. Outside
of its own bureaucracy, the
Kuomintang had no real
roots in the people. What did
it offer but a perpetuation of the old ways, which is to
say the old misery?

This is not a tract in support of communism. I am well
aware of the mess of pottage the Chinese have bought.
Many today in the communes eat their bread, if they
have any, in sorrow. Probably many of the young idealists, the students of fifteen years ago, who rallied in

overwhelming numbers to the Communist cause now wonder what happened to their great dream. It would be wishful thinking, however, to believe that the dream has died for all. The hundreds of thousands of young people who turn out for parades and demonstrations do not have the look of sullen prisoners of the regime. For them the Communists still manage to project the image of promise. They are still carried along by the specter of an evil world to be destroyed and a better world to be built. It is quite likely that they still sing with gusto the song of Communist Youth:

> We are the builders.
> We build the future.
> The future world lies in our hands.

There was a time when America projected an image that enflamed imaginations, set feet jiggling and hearts dancing. That image does not come through today. What comes through is the hard-faced image of the bean growers, the hate-contorted faces of New Orleans housewives screaming epithets into the ears of a bewildered Negro child.

Far more important than guns for Laotians is the projection of a new image of America. President Kennedy in his Inaugural Address projected such an image, and it is significant and symptomatic that it stirred excitement around the globe. But it will take more than words, or even the deeds, of one man, even a President. What is needed is the image of an angry people, people who react, not blasphemously like Guevara, but like Christ in the temple, against a social structure which creates, perpetuates, or tolerates human misery anywhere.

Where will this fury arise? Is our society capable of producing this kind of rage, this kind of central concern for human beings, for other human beings? Is any society whose central concern is money and profit? These are questions which I should not presume to answer, but, on the record, I reserve the right to a certain amount of pessimism.

There have been profound changes in our social structure during the past thirty years. There will be profound changes in the next fifty years. Amidst those changes we had better find a way to do away with the bean-grower mentality and become a people who, like Karl Marx, can never feel free so long as Guatemala children or West Virginia children or Indian children have bloated bellies, or Mexican-American children slave in the fields, or Negro children are treated like medieval lepers. If we don't find a way, there will be other Castros and more surprises, and our grandchildren may learn that Khrushchev was right about them.　　GEORGE H. DUNNE

II

THERE IS a Canadian proverb that says: When the wild ducks fly over, the tame ducks flutter their wings furiously—and stay on the ground. A distinguished missionary quoted this to me the other day during a discussion on the forthcoming Peace Corps. Like almost everyone else I had interviewed, he thought the Corps a splendid idea. But he wondered, and many others wonder, how many of the thousands of enthusiasts will only flutter their wings when the time comes to take off.

A random, unscientific sampling of student opinion at a recent NSA (National Student Association) meeting showed remarkable unanimity about the Peace Corps. All those questioned showed real zest for the idea. But when confronted with the question: "Are *you* going to go?" 94 per cent cleared throats and answered: "Well, no, but . . . ." Doubtless the sampling was inadequate, and possibly not even representative, but it did give one pause.

Another set of attitudes came to light during interviews with United Nations personnel (AM. 4/8, pp. 49-50). I was fortunately able to meet a number of officials from the "developing countries" (the word "underdeveloped" is no longer used), but received only standard, innocuous replies. It seemed more useful, accordingly, to talk to younger, unofficial members of these nations, with the promise that they and their nationalities would be kept anonymous. They seemed to speak freely, though how freely is hard to judge.

Rather like the NSA members, all of them assured me that they were favorably impressed by the Peace Corps ideal. They had lived in America long enough to realize personally that not all Americans are callous, dollar-mad imperialists. The real problem would lie back at home. There, innate skepticism would be hard to put down. In stately phraseology one young African warmly insisted that "America must somehow eradicate apprehensions felt by my people."

These "apprehensions" are obviously centered in the lingering dread of imperialism. Having just won political autonomy, many nations are intensely anxious to avoid anything that "savors of even the mildest form of colonialism," as one man put it. "After all," he said smiling, "we cannot forget that Americans are traditional allies of the British, Belgians and French." If the Corps is not skillfully conducted, said another, international relations will "jump from the water into the fire, as our people say."

The problems of adaptation will be even more mammoth than Americans anticipate, a young Asian assured me. "My own family back at home is rather well-to-do. An American could quite easily live with us, I believe. But it wouldn't serve the purpose of the Corps." The phrase "cultural shock" is being used to describe the probable reaction of most young Americans coming from a push-button world into many of the countries envisioned by the Corps. Even the "toughening-up" program to be given in Puerto Rico left some of my UN friends unimpressed. "They must have as stiff a training as the astronauts are getting," was the way one of them put it.

Even the very idea of the Peace Corps provokes misgivings and some skepticism. "Our countries need to be strongly reassured that the Corps is not to be given in place of money—the money we already receive or that we hope to receive," I was told more than once. For the problem in most countries, as the "locals" see it, is largely financial.

It was interesting to interview some Americans working in the UN. After our editorial "No Children's Crusade" appeared (4/8, pp. 49-50), a UN technician wrote in approval: "You are expressing an opinion strongly held 'in the house' here." It would indeed, I believe, be very wasteful if the Corps did not make extensive use of the findings of a number of the experienced UN agencies.

In this connection, several of these American experts were of the opinion that it would be more helpful in the long run to train *local* people than simply other Americans for short-term service. In any case, whatever is done, they felt, we must always avoid replacing the "locals." These developing countries vary widely: in some areas, experts are needed at high levels; but in most, the need is for intermediate workers, neither at the top nor the bottom. Above all, such practical skills need to be taught as how to sharpen tools, how to repair simple machinery, how to drain a swamp, when to plant, how to rotate crops, how to fertilize, how to improve the technique of thatching huts, how to install and use sanitary facilities, and how to maintain them. This unpretentious type of work, the UN people said, is not likely to cause unemployment nor to be interpreted as masked "neo-colonialism."

It was reassuring to learn that the Peace Corps has now released a guide insisting that the Corps is to "help, not replace," private and religious agencies already working in the field, and learn from their experience. The appointment, too, of the respected missiologist, Fr. John J. Considine, M.M., was a heartening step. I was able to meet with Fr. Joseph B. Gremillion, director of Socio-Economic Development, and F. Robert Melina, coordinator for Peace Corps, both of Catholic Relief Services—NCWC, and found that their suggestions largely corroborated the opinions of my contacts at the UN.

The executive secretary of the Mission Secretariat, Fr. Frederick A. McGuire, C.M., kindly allowed me to use answers to an important questionnaire. Inquiries had been sent out to CRS workers, to missioners and to local educators and religious leaders in the developing countries. Their answers should be of real service to Corps leaders.

THE GENERAL REACTION to the Peace Corps from this source was again favorable, but again there was the strong proviso that "the project must be properly conducted." Thomas Cardinal Tien, S.V.D., writing from Taiwan, stated: "May I suggest that this seems necessary: to train not too many young people, but very thoroughly, especially in the ethical respect." In India, Valerian Cardinal Gracias contacted heads of four important Catholic universities. Their replies echoed those of Cardinal Tien, with strong emphasis on the "need for suitable personnel, careful selection, and a cautious and slow beginning." One educator urged "something akin to military discipline, under the control of a mature officer who by previous experience knows the character and temperament of the people."

Community development is seen as a pressing need, and "social workers, medical, agricultural and veterinary graduates would be extremely useful," a missionary comments. "Let not MEDICO's experience be lost. Consult them. Use the experience of the International Voluntary Service. Discipline must be very, very rigid."

A rather blunt caution comes from another missionary: "Men with only State Department background should never be leaders, even if they have been overseas. Their attitude centers around housing, PX, motor pools and the like." More explicitly, for some areas "a person with a country background is an absolute necessity. A city-raised boy cannot adjust enough to a country living 100 years in the past."

Corpsmen must beware of chauvinistic attitudes and "must be screened for tact, understanding and psychological stability," says a native priest. "Material aid, however eagerly accepted, is suspect as to its motives." Moreover, in Americans especially there is often, he notes, an "almost inevitable sense of superiority which is resented."

A missionary in South America urges the Corps to be wary of close association with local governments. Oth-

140

erwise, "the personnel will too soon become disillusioned by corruption, graft, feet-dragging, inefficiency and general lack of co-operation." Moreover, as another puts it, "the government here would take all the credit. Some 99 per cent of the people don't know anything of the millions already given by the United States."

"The hardest job," in the mind of another priest, "is to find out what the people in the host countries want. Some Corpsmen should go with the attitude and announced purpose of learning. It would be a good idea," he adds, "to invite people from other countries to participate in the Corps, and probably some young local people would like to be invited to take part."

An acute problem in the minds of several observers is how to reach the needy. "The big, already-rich land owner doesn't care about the poor. All projects should be directed at personal contact with the masses." He goes on to specify: "What I feel is needed are not the high-priced technicians living in expensive houses in the cities, but dedicated, skilled technicians living among the poor as friends and companions."

"Teaching is our prime need," notes one CRS worker. "But teaching what? Skilled trade teachers are most needed. Not highly technical teachers, but down-to-earth practical teachers." A missionary notes: "The country I am in has enough doctors and lawyers. What it needs is a skilled middle class of workers." With some acerbity he adds that "so far the United States has helped the rich man become richer. This is a point that the Communists use to the hilt."

Another missioner concentrates on the personal traits of a prospective Corpsman. "He must be sincere, sym-

pathetic, hardworking, indifferent as to where he sleeps or what he eats, not emotional, not easily discouraged, determined, rugged, the out-of-door type, self-reliant and even-tempered." This sounds very much like the qualities needed in a missioner.

After long interviews with persons differing in religion, race and background, and after reading reports from many lands, I am impressed by their overarching theme: while the ideal of a Peace Corps is unexceptionable, the hazards and problems are colossal. Knowledgeable missionaries, who have personally made the huge sacrifice of adaptation and who work with the highest motives of dedication, know this better than anyone else. Better than anyone else they know that there will be no glamour involved, that this will not be a "lark," that an inept Peace Corps would be not only futile but worse than none at all.   C. J. McNaspy

♦

Dies Sanctificatus Illuxit Nobis

This poor god shepherds once stumbled
off their hills finding and kings
groped their starred night to worship
comes to sit at the gates of the world
and judge it. And there is not one,
not one man will dare to watch
his whipped face then saying my god
it was not I that scarred your face.

Rejoice in your flocks shepherds, kings
your palaces: today the hands
of love have soothed him in a crèche,
the unimaginable word,
where men may cry for joy for him
who came to weep for every man.

JOHN KNOEPFLE

Red Bear and
Pink Toenails

George H. Dunne

PINK TOENAILS, the painted kind, have never found favor with me. They seemed a move in the wrong direction, taking us back toward a "bells on my fingers and rings on my toes" kind of primitive society. Neither have I been known as a champion of Madison Avenue. I have looked with jaundiced eye upon the world of advertising which exalts the dubious merits of products most of us could well do without and persuades people that they need a variety of things they really don't need at all. And although by nature not disposed to look kindly upon any sort of censorship, the blatant vulgarity of cheap cheesecake cover illustrations exploited by so large a part of the magazine trade has seemed to me from every point of view indefensible.

Perspective is an interesting phenomenon. There is a church in Rome, St. Ignatius, where you must stand on one spot, marked by a small mosaic, in order to see in proper perspective the rather remarkable fresco which covers the ceiling of the nave. Move even a few feet away to right or to left from that point of view and the perspective changes. Things look radically different.

When I passed through the Brandenburg Gate from West Berlin into East Berlin things immediately looked radically different. And the farther I moved into East Berlin the more different they looked. Like everyone else, I had read about the striking contrast between West and East Berlin. I had not doubted what I had read, but I had not really grasped the profound nature of that contrast. There is no use trying to describe this passage from light to shadow, from life to death. Only those who have actually themselves crossed the river Styx can understand what the passage is like. There is no reason to suppose that I could make it more understandable to others than others were able to make it to me. To grasp it, one must oneself experience the almost shattering impact of crossing from West to East Berlin.

West Berlin is a city bursting with life. East Berlin is a city which looks upon you out of the lustreless eyes of death. It is not simply a question of West Berlin's streets crowded with autos, sidewalks brimming wth people, shops crowded with customers, stores bursting with food, with furs, with clothes, with appliances. Nor is the contrast merely between the stark ruins which are still the predominant landscape of East Berlin and West Berlin's new and modern buildings, which have sprung up at an extraordinary rate where at war's end there was only rubble. For even when, as along their Stalinallee, the Communists have made a determined and deliberate attempt to match West Berlin's building display, the effort has come to naught. The buildings are there—apartments above, showcase state-owned stores below. They are massive and grandiose, each one exactly like its neighbor, all done in a heavy, stolid Soviet style, and all totally incapable of distilling a breath of life into the broad street upon which they stand. Stalinallee remains as dead as Alexanderplatz or Wilhelmstrasse, where Hitler's death bunker is now just a grass-covered mound, or Unter den Linden, where the once-famed Adlon Hotel is a rubbish heap probably inhabited by rats.

When I came back through the Brandenburg Gate into West Berlin, leaving behind the hostile faces, the uncertain faces, the fearful faces, the pathetic faces, it was like a resurrection. Never had I seen anything as lovely as the painted pink toenails. Eagerly I drank in the colorful advertisements on every side: *Konditorei Mohring, Zum guten Bier, Wunderbarer Jacobs Kaffee, Imperial Weinbrand, St. John Rum!* Even the magazine kiosks with their too generous display of flesh and sex (though not as generous as those in Rome) were a welcome sight. Like the pink toenails and the flaunted ads they cried out: FREEDOM! FREEDOM! FREEDOM! and their cry seemed to make a song which echoed through the streets and, like sunlight, touched the buildings into life, dispelled darkness from alleyways, made eyes sparkle and laughter ring and hearts rejoice.

It came to me that this is what makes the contrast so shocking. It came to me that this is what our world is all about. This is what the world-wide struggle is all about. It is about freedom, and therefore about life; for the two are one. Girls free to paint their toenails every color or no color. Men free to flaunt their commercial boasts. Other men free to be foolish or not to be fooled. Free to believe or to disbelieve. Men free to follow Christ or to serve the devil.

I saw a sign ride by on the side of a beautiful double-decker bus. *"Mach mal Pause, Trink Coca-Cola, das erfrischt richtig,"* it commanded. A moment later another sign rode by with just the contrary advice: *"Dir zum Lohne trink Darbohne!"* Again it came to me that this is what it is all about. I don't have to drink Coca-Cola or Darbohne. I can take them or leave them, drink either or both or neither. This is what makes our kind of world a world worth living in. This is what makes West Berlin a city that teems with life and East Berlin a city of death.

It came to me that this is not only our kind of a world. It is God's kind of a world. God's kind of a world is a world in which men are free to make their choices, to choose heaven or to choose hell. People who say: "How could God permit sin?" don't know what they are saying. A world in which men could not sin is a world in which men are not free. If you want a microscopic view of that kind of world visit East Berlin. The tragedy of communism is that it thinks man can be brought

145

to salvation by being deprived of his freedom to choose.

I saw no pink toenails in East Berlin. Apart from dreary party propaganda slogans hanging on red banners across dismal factory fronts, I saw no advertising. I saw no vulgar magazine displays. The party has done away with the occasions of sin, the temptations to be frivolous or foolish or wicked. God's world, on the contrary, is filled with temptations and occasions of sin. That is the way He made it from the beginning when He began by planting the tree of forbidden fruit in the Garden of Eden: something to be remembered, not only by Marxists, but also by others who easily succumb to the temptation to appeal to the Inquisition or the Holy Office or the police power of the state to save us from the occasions of sin.

It is not just a matter of painted toenails. These may one day come to East Berlin. They may even be there now, unnoticed by me. But painted toenails will look entirely different in East Berlin than they do in West Berlin. No more than the imposing Georgian architecture of Stalinallee will they be able to lift the pall of death that hangs over this city from which people were fleeing at the rate of 300 a day when I was there, a figure greatly swollen since. Because, no more than the buildings on Stalinallee will they symbolize freedom. Like those buildings, they will be only another manifestation of death. For when painted toenails appear it will not be because girls have *chosen* to paint their toenails pink or green or some other outlandish color, but because a Communist bureaucrat or a faceless Communist bureau has decided that painted toenails serve the ends of the regime and are therefore to be cultivated. Freedom—and therefore life—spring not from decisions imposed, but from choices made.

I spent the evening of my return from East Berlin leaning out my open window, like a true Roman, gazing upon the human pageant in the street below: the boys and girls holding hands, the crowded sidewalk cafés, the throngs pouring out of theatres, even the silly people craning necks like Hollywood simpletons to catch a glimpse of some featherbrained movie star (it was International Film Festival Week in Berlin), the neon signs, the noisy cars, the murmur of human voices, the ready laughter, the beautiful sight of faces that were neither sullen, nor hateful, nor filled with fear.

I realized exactly what Khrushchev means when he says that West Berlin is a chicken bone stuck in his throat. How can he permit this confrontation in a Communist heartland between this small island in which men are free to make their choices and which throbs with the pulse of life worth living, and the city where death walks through the streets because freedom has died?

Fresh Look at Cuba
and Castro

John Meslay

E VEN WHEN ONE IS allowed to travel freely to Havana today, it is not easy to form a judgment on the impact of communism on the life of the Cuban citizens, or to say which phase (according to Leninist theory) the Cuban revolution has presently reached.

My first impression of the scene about me, as I drove in from the airport, was its strong similarity to what I had experienced in the streets of Warsaw in Poland, several years ago: heroic-sized pictures of national or Communist heroes like Yuri Gagarin, who visited Cuba on July 26 for the anniversary of the Castro revolution; posters and slogans inviting the passer-by to work, to study and to take up his rifle.

In Havana, militiamen and militiawomen with rifles mount guard at nearly every corner, in all the public buildings and even in some private shops. The mere sight of them is enough to create a climate of fear and to give the ordinary citizen a vague feeling of guilt. Everyone is afraid of being denounced to the Committees of Defense of the Revolution (there is one on every block), or to the famous G2 (the secret police).

In such a political climate, one can hardly expect to find objectivity of judgment. Apart from some in diplomatic circles who are not directly involved, the people you meet in Havana today are either strongly favorable or strongly opposed to the regime. The dominant feelings are nervousness, anxiety and fear. The foreigner, walking through the streets of the city, cannot but notice the lack of joy and the tension plain on so many faces. The shortage of food, without yet reaching any dangerous proportions, obliges the women to queue for many hours to get meat, fruit or fish. (According to what high officials of the new regime told me, the shortage of food is not due to less production, but to the necessity of exporting agricultural produce in order to buy machines, spare parts—and weapons.) Besides, even though a great majority of Cubans were rather lax Catholics, they now resent the constant interference of the government in religious affairs. Probably Castro has not measured the strength of the religious resistance to his plans.

My visit coincided with the Literacy Congress (*Congreso de Alfabetización*) in Havana. Schoolteachers came from all over the island to comment on the literacy campaign which has been under way since April and is slated to last until January. All the boys and girls between 12 and 18 years of age who volunteered for the campaign have been sent to the villages in the country and in the mountains to help the teachers in a full-scale adult education program.

The very ambitious objective of doing away with illiteracy in Cuba by next January will most probably not be reached, but the campaign is already yielding very important psychological and ideological results. For one thing, public opinion has been mobilized on one common aim, the achievement of which is objectively good and can hardly be criticized. Moreover, the textbooks used, as well as the indoctrination campaign which goes along with the educational effort, provide the regime with a powerful instrument for the propagation of its socialist ideology.

The paradigms chosen to teach reading and writing all convey some "socialist" meaning. For instance, the very first lesson on the vowels is used for a pungent commentary on the "imperialist" character of the Organization of American States (the abbreviation in Spanish is O.E.A.).

Finally, the young people taking part in the campaign get special treatment. They appear on TV programs and on the whole seem to enjoy their work. These young persons get a sense of *participation* in the life of the country. For the first time, they enter into *communication* with the people of the remotest districts. These teen-agers appear proud of the Cuban revolution and this experience will certainly have a profound and lasting influence on their lives. On the other hand, the sending of boys and girls together without guidance for a long period of time to faraway districts is highly objectionable from the point of view of morality, and I heard many complaints about this.

There are 285 collective farms already in operation in Cuba. These are called *granjas del pueblo* and belong to the strict type of Russian *sovchoz*. I visited one of them just outside of Havana, where the administration is building nice, clean little houses for the villagers.

I also visited a co-operative plant for sugar-cane growers. Here the government is capitalizing on the agricultural progress which had been made in the preceding years by the now-expropriated big landowners. Of course, it is not quite certain that collective farming will yield better crops.

The government has not divided the land into small plots or parcels, nor handed them over to the individual peasants. Instead, it has made these people believe they are now the collective owners of the farm and has thus transformed them into employees of the government. They receive fixed wages just as they did under the preceding system. But propaganda indoctrination, which goes along with various substantial advantages, gives them, too, a higher sense of "participation." I use that word again deliberately. This class of very poor land laborers who now have their own houses will probably become the defenders of the regime. Even if the urban workers fall away from the revolution and lose their enthusiasm, these very poor peasants—together with the very many militiamen and militiawomen to whom a fixed

150

salary and a job have been given, all over the country —will, in many cases, though by no means all, prove the best allies of the regime in case of crisis.

The weakness of Fidel Castro is that he probably no longer controls his own revolution. It is true that his figure or image is still largely popular (perhaps more so in other Latin American countries than in Cuba, where the anti-religious measures have made him lose ground). The propaganda machine leads everyone to believe that the Castro revolution has set a pattern for all future upheavals in South America. But the striking resemblance between the Cuban situation and what we have seen in other countries on the eve of a Communist take-over leaves little doubt that the uniqueness of "Fidelismo," if it was unique, has been lost, and that the point of no return on the road to "classical" communism has been reached.

Around Fidel Castro, men schooled in Soviet political doctrine are slowly preparing conditions for the final takeover, and I do not see how the trend can be reversed. It is even probable that the coming-to-power of the Communist party, as such, will coincide with some bettering of the Cuban economic situation. Cuba will receive foreign aid because, for propaganda purposes, the USSR cannot let Cuba starve.

Therefore, the chief lesson to be drawn at this moment does not concern Cuba, but the other Latin American countries. Just as the Marshall Plan in 1947 came too late to save Eastern Europe but did save Western Europe, so the Alliance for Progress program drawn up at Punta del Este last August will not pull Cuba back into the Western fold (at least not directly and immediately), but it may help some of the other Latin American nations to resist the terrible stress and temptation they are now facing.

In these nations, many influential young men are ready to overthrow their own government and to imitate Castro's shortcut to economic independence. If they are to overcome this temptation, which is so strong in the young generation of economists and left-oriented intellectuals, more will be needed than very generous and large-scale help from the United States. Required also is an effective and self-sacrificing resolution, on the part of the economic ruling class in Latin America, to take the lead in a redistribution of the national income. Unfortunately, however, this ruling class seems to think mainly in terms of military defense against the Communist threat they see embodied in the Cuban regime.

It is not difficult to find out where the secret of Fidel Castro's success lies. It is to be located in the two ideas which I have already cited: "participation" and "communication." For the first time, millions of Cubans are invited to "participate" personally in the building of their own country. And for the first time there is an effort to make all men equal and to create "communication" between the different elements of Cuban society. Lenin, with his usual shrewdness, assigned this task of making "one people" out of many elements—in sociological jargon, the function of participation and communication —to the nationalist period, which, according to his theory of the evolution of societies, was a necessary preliminary step to the Communist takeover, particularly in underdeveloped, that is to say, pre-industrial and colonial countries.

Of course, there is a great deal of bluff and lying in this pretension of building up the unity of a nation. Many people in Cuba today are neither "participating" nor "communicating." On the contrary, they live in fear of their neighbor and take no part in any public activities. The policy of the new regime has alienated a large part of the population, but these are precisely those who, in the Communist terminology, are called "the enemies of the people." In Cuban Communist slang they are termed *gusanos* (worms), that is, those who formerly lived on the work of others and who felt safe and secure through money, status and property.

As background to the panic which today seizes so many Cubans and prompts them to seek refuge abroad, a sense of insecurity is very strong. The regime will take steps to increase this insecurity for a while among this class of people who previously had status. It is an essential part of the strategy of the Communist system. In a regime like that of Castro, it is part of the usual build-up to destroy the framework of security that obtained in the old society and to build a new framework where only those who adhere to the regime feel safe and comfortable. For the others (the *parasitos*, the "worms"), life must be made impossible. They have to convert or go away.

A FTER THE ABORTIVE April invasion, religious were jailed and were there subjected to threats, but they were finally released. They were not expelled; they themselves asked to leave the country. This is what the regime wanted: to get rid of them without risking bloodshed or martyrdom.

It was only in mid-September that the government finally organized a large-scale deportation of priests. This operation included an element that is really something new in international law: the deportation of Cuban citizens without a trial, and their forcible exile to another country prior to any agreement with that country.

What set off Castro's conflict with the Church? Well, what started the present acute conflict with the United States? Is Castro's feud with the U.S.A. fully explained, as certain propagandists in Latin America and in Europe would have us believe, by long-standing U.S. abuses? The thing to remember is that when the Communists step in, *any* conflict is bound to become acute. Much the same can be said of Castro's contest with the Church. It would have been the same no matter what the Church might have done, and even if her members had always been inspired by the purest Christian spirit. A totalitarian system like communism refuses to accept any sharing of the loyalty of human beings.

Therefore, it is painfully true that the lack of justice and of love of the poor on the part of some Cuban Catholics has provided a stepping stone for Castro and for the Communist revolution. But our duty is not to judge the past. The Catholics in Cuba are now passing through the fire of persecution. If the fire consumes, it also purifies. Many formerly lax Catholics are returning to the fervent practice of their faith. Many deeds of generosity and even of heroism are performed every day. It is too early to report them because such a report would endanger young men and women who have chosen to be faithful to God. The outside world cannot do much to help them except by prayer and brotherly comprehension for the difficulties and trials of this new "Church of Silence."

The most immediate duty incumbent on us is to change the social and economic conditions in those countries where communism has not yet seized political power. We must strive to do this so radically and thoroughly that the Communist system appears in a clear light for what it really is—a quick, very primitive, half-barbarian solution to social evils through brutal despotism and destructive totalitarianism: a purge which cures the illness by killing the patient.

However, let us be perfectly clear about one thing: if no other solution is proposed now—and rapidly—then the temptation to try communism will grow stronger in all the underdeveloped countries. That is exactly what makes Khrushchev so confident about the peaceful triumph of communism all over the world.

My own conclusion is that probably the situation created by the Castro regime and the Cuban power-grab by the Communist party is something that is here to stay, at least for a long time. But the drama of Castro and Cuba may yet help us to draw some badly needed lessons for other countries and other continents.

The Past Is Prologue
Leo A. Foley

FREEDOM and tyranny are common words today. They form the slogans of new nations arising out of violence, while the most tyrannical enemy of the United States calls itself a champion of freedom. In the midst of this confusion and danger, we Americans might well ask ourselves not only what we mean by freedom and tyranny, but also what our entire national purpose is. Actually, we have a model of our national purpose. We have the outstanding definition of our own aims and purposes in the American Revolution.

The American Revolution was many things. In England, it was an extension of parliamentary politics, marked by the opposition between the Tories and the Whigs. Thus it was that many such British leaders in America as Lord Howe, Lord Cornwallis and Thomas Gage were often in sympathy with the Americans simply because they themselves were influenced by Whigs in politics. In America, the revolution was not only a blow for independence. It was also a civil war, an Indian war, a vast unifying process, but always a movement proceeding from the people. In the eyes of the world, it was a startling social phenomenon soon to become the model for every progressive movement. It excited the admiration of political figures on a world-wide scale. *Democracy in America,* by Alexis de Tocqueville, is but one example.

Let there be no doubt about it, the American Revolution was one of the greatest political events since men began to congregate into tribes, cities, states and nations. Its success was, among many things, the reason for William Lyons Mackenzie's inchoate revolution in Canada, the reason why Englishmen and members of the British Commonwealth are today among the world's freest people. During these several years when we are commemorating the hundredth anniversary of the American Civil War, we might well remember that Southerners and Southern leaders would be written off as traitors and insurgents were it not for the Declaration of Independence. Yet, whereas most Americans know the Civil War almost by heart, there are many phases of the Revolution that are almost completely unknown and which by their very nature demand examination and re-examination by every American, rather, by every human being.

First, the American Revolution did not start with the killing of innocent people. It started with a document containing a theory, a statement of rights in the *Declaration of Rights and Grievances* drawn up in Philadelphia in 1765. Furthermore, the rights expressed were not those of a few. They were the rights of man given a startlingly new expression, namely, that man's rights are an extension of God's authority simply because God is God, man is man, and freedom is the manner of man's existence. The philosopher will recognize therein the position of St. Thomas, St. Robert Bellarmine, Francis Suarez and John Locke.

Nevertheless, this had been developed in a typically American manner, that of the New England town meeting. This institution was typically Protestant insofar as it was an extension of the Congregationalist Sunday meeting. The Congregationalists were Calvinists who maintained a priesthood of the people, making the layman equal in God's sight to a bishop. In civil affairs, they looked to the citizen as equal to anyone and just as capable of a correct civil decision as an appointed governor.

We Catholics should be aware of this Protestant contribution to American democracy. We have a tendency to envision St. Thomas Aquinas as the author of the Declaration of Independence. We overlook the fact that although he and Bellarmine and Suarez admired the Roman republic, they still lived in a monarchical society and wrote against the evils of tyranny by bespeaking the rights of man with a view to a benign monarchy.

The town meeting, still a potent force in many New England areas, was the model for the Continental Congress. It was also the model for co-operation of States under the Articles of Confederation and the interco-operation of citizens and States in the House of Representatives and the Senate under our present Constitution.

Europeans looked with open astonishment to see if these upstart colonists could make this sort of thing stick in a world given over to monarchy and colonialism. We Americans should be as proud as we can be of the fact that our predecessors did establish the American Republic, establish it on a sound metaphysics of man, and created a model of government that has been the ideal of every struggling state that aspired to freedom.

Second, the Revolution, as a war, was won by the people. From this emerged a new social entity, a new perfect society, a new state. Although James Otis and Samuel Adams may have breathed fire, it was the American volunteer, the minuteman, the militia man who had to learn tactics under fire, who kept that fire burning with his sacrifices. Although John Adams proposed the plan for independence and Thomas Jefferson wrote it up in the spring and summer of 1776, it was the slum dweller in New York, the waterfront scrounger in Charleston, the Philadelphia and Boston workman who fought for it. Although James Madison was to be the constitutional lawyer in the Constitutional Convention, he wrote with a background of a new nation that had begun from the ground up, from the people themselves.

157

Even the carrying on of the war was by amateurs. The only professional soldiers in the American army were Horatio Gates and Charles Lee. Gates was no military genius, even though later research seems to show that Gates rather than Benedict Arnold was the victor at Saratoga. Charles Lee was better at spreading dissension than at organizing troops and winning battles. Washington's outstanding generals and officers, Nathaniel Greene, Anthony Wayne, Henry Knox, Daniel Morgan, Henry Lee, Francis Marion, Israel Putnam, and the rest, were ironmasters, farmers, booksellers and amateur gentlemen—almost anything but soldiers. Yet, they rose to the challenge and defeated the finest professional army in the world by unorthodox strategy and improvised tactics. Even Washington himself had been only a colonel in the colonial forces when John Adams proposed him for command of the Continental armies.

These amateurs did a far better job than, with few exceptions, the professionals were to do during the Civil War. Military historians marvel at the audacity of a few poorly trained militiamen standing up against a professional group on Lexington Common. Yet, this was the pattern of the whole: the people against tyranny, the citizen who will not fight until he has to, and who then improvises brilliantly in order to win promptly.

There were all kinds of legalistic snarls at the beginning of hostilities. New Yorkers were fighting citizens of New Hampshire over possession of the Hampshire Grants, now the State of Vermont. When Henry Knox was dispatched by Washington to bring the cannon captured at Ticonderoga to Dorchester Heights in order to drive the British from Boston, Knox had all he could do to get any drivers to cross from one State to another. In fact, he had to depend upon local committees in township after township to supply him with relays of drivers. Yet, at the end of the war there was common unity under a Virginia Commander-in-Chief when a Rhode Islander, Nathaniel Greene, led a mixed army, and with the help of Southern officers enticed Cornwallis out of South Carolina, sniped at him, did battle with him, and nudged him into Yorktown where Greene promptly bottled him up to await the French fleet.

One cannot overestimate the unifying force of George Washington during and after the Revolution. Although he had the reputation of being a rather cold type from Virginia, he soon won the love of his men to such an extent that when Congress was unable to hold the army together, Washington fulfilled that task. When he had finally starved Sir Henry Clinton out of New York two years after Yorktown, tears flowed freely at Washington's farewell dinner for his generals.

This was the end of a process that had begun when all of the colonies leaped to the relief of beleaguered Boston. We might well remember in these days of remnants of acrimony between Northern and Southern States that Boston was indebted not only to the fiery eloquence of a Virginian, Patrick Henry, but also to two generous donations of hard, cold cash from South Carolina. In a period of 24 years, from the *Declaration of Rights and Grievances* to the adoption of the United

States Constitution in 1789, again largely because of the prestige of George Washington, a nation was born, a nation that has become the champion of the rights of man.

Today leadership of the free world is thrust upon the United States. Great nations and small nations look to the United States not only for its military strength but also because of its prestige in defense of the rights of man. We Americans can scarcely begin to appreciate the flame of hope that was lit by the American Revolution. Despite our complaints about legislation, taxes and big government, we do not know what it means not to be free.

The establishment of the United States as one nation was a process that involved the co-operation of many individuals of different opinions and viewpoints. Our forebears realized that there are limits to individual freedom. They also learned that co-operation for a common cause does not require coercion of opinion into a single, tolerated conviction. Monolithic political tenets are the property of tyrannies.

Members of the Continental Congress, colony by colony, individual by individual, disagreed, wrangled and argued before they achieved the unity of the closing of the Declaration of Independence: "And for support of this declaration, we mutually pledge to each other our lives, our fortunes, and our sacred honour."

The realization of that pledge is found in the opening words of the Constitution: "We, the people of the United States. . . ." This new unity was also preceded by discussion, argumentation and—always—serious purpose. If Herodotus is right, and if what is past is prologue, there are several truths that cannot be avoided. We cannot allow one opinion to oppress free discussion. Nor can we allow discussion to dissipate all conviction. Above all, no one can afford to identify the "American way of life" with The Great, Big, Good Time. Our existence and our future are a challenging responsibility based on a sound appreciation of our principles, our heroes and their sacrifices in their achievements.

Ireland: Vacuum of National Purpose

Gary MacEoin

THE VILLAGE in the West of Ireland seemed fuller of young people in August, 1959 than I had seen it in half a century. They were gay, well-spoken, well-dressed and free-spending. They took advantage of once-in-a-lifetime summer weather to throng to football games on Sundays, picnic at the beaches, explore the countryside in rented automobiles and see Grade-B westerns in the village movie house.

The people are living better than ever before. The selection of material comforts is sometimes odd. An electric washing machine confers prestige rather than comfort when one must carry the water half a mile in a bucket from the river. Forty years ago the village road was worn into three deep ruts, a center one by the plodding horses and donkeys, two side ones by the narrow iron rims of the cart wheels. They were so deep a cyclist could not move from one to another without dismounting. This year I drove at eighty miles an hour (Ireland has no speed limits) over its excellent macadam surface.

But the surface does not, unfortunately, tell the entire story. The prosperous young people having a gay time are home on vacation from England and the United

States. There were never so few young workers on the farms. No sooner do they finish school than they emigrate, attracted by high wages and steady work. The money they spend on vacation and the substantial remittances they send their families account in large part for the improved living conditions of those who stay.

Ireland's economy is overwhelmingly agricultural, with over 40 per cent of the population engaged in farming. The typical farm is undercapitalized and not very efficiently operated. But the currents which have affected international trade in this century have not bypassed Ireland. Agriculture, providing the bulk of its exports, must try to maintain competitive production costs, and accordingly machinery and agricultural chemicals have cut the labor input. For every four men employed on the land 20 years ago, there is room today for only three. And the trend is not yet exhausted. Output per farm worker, though up nearly 65 per cent in 20 years, is still far below that of competitors. The alternative to dwindling returns is more farm efficiency, which usually means less labor per unit of production.

Fewer farm workers, each producing substantially more, give a total agricultural output some 25 per cent higher in volume than 20 years ago. The increase is praiseworthy, though far behind the typical Western European achievement of the same period. Indeed, it is doubtful if it even pays for the higher living standards today enjoyed by the smaller farm population, for these improvements represent in substantial part the remittances from overseas of a new generation of emigrants, perhaps also some depletion of capital resources.

WHY DO THEY EMIGRATE?

What to do, however, with the people displaced from the land? This problem has been vexing the country for a century. Emigration seems the only answer.

Now the average Irish boy or girl has no wish to emigrate. The persistence of the little villages and towns, where the owners of the old-time general purpose stores and saloons lean against their doorways and wait patiently for the approach of the rare customer, shows the strength of the ties. So does the energy with which those who must go accumulate their earnings in London and New York, both to subsidize those who stay and to take frequent trips back, trips that today often pledge the future under pay-later plans.

Those who stay agree with those who go in deploring emigration. At one time, there was a lot of talk of settling more people on the land. More recently, they talk about expanding industry, and there has in fact been a small but steady annual increase in industrial employment. Yet the paradox remains. The greater the industrialization, the lower the total employment.

Today, Ireland exports automobiles to the United States and television receivers to Britain. This year its first oil refinery with an annual capacity of 2 million tons has gone on stream. A West German firm completed construction of a plant at Killarney to manufacture cranes for export. Another West German firm is building a cheese factory. Two American companies announced formation of Irish companies to produce cosmetics and chewing gum.

All of this is impressive, but it does not begin to change the basic situation. No technique has been devised to overcome the economy's persistent tendency to increase imports at a more rapid rate than exports, which is another way of saying that the Irish insist on consuming more than they produce. They settle their account by exporting their children.

I'd like to think a little about the attitude of trying to get something for nothing. Reasons exist, both technical and historical, for low labor productivity. Likewise, exposure to and facility of movement to England and the United States foster a desire for living standards which the economy does not justify. Yet, I think that the real problem is more basic. As I see it, the Irish lack a philosophy of work or, at least, a Christian philosophy of work. There is no pride of achievement, no concept of vocation, no aspiration after perfection.

This is, and is deliberately intended to be, a judgment on the moral condition of the country, for such an attitude runs counter to the whole Catholic concept of life. The existence of the attitude is, nevertheless, unquestionable. Indeed, I found no disposition to deny it. On

163

the contrary, for many this general mediocrity is a virtue, and for others a fact of life.

"Slipshod performance is universal," a priest commented, "and still you can't say that it is inherent in our character. The Irish make excellent workers abroad. My own belief is that the climate is mainly to blame."

"On the contrary," interjected a journalist friend, "this is the way God meant people to live. We in this country have found a human tempo of living. We're doing fine."

This argument—or sophistry—is frequent. It shows up, for example, in the tourist publicity, which presents the happy-go-lucky attitudes of the native as one of the country's picturesque features.

Be that as it may, optimum production is impossible with such an attitude. There is no use, for example, having modern telephone equipment, if a switchboard operator tells you there is no reply rather than make the effort to complete a call, or if the long-distance service in a major city takes ten minutes to look up a number in the London directory. I had both these experiences, and all to whom I recounted them agreed they were normal.

Similarly, there is no hope for the new industries, no matter how excellent their equipment, if the moral atmosphere considers it neither shameful nor sinful to deliver such inferior work as it is possible to get away with. And unfortunately, the monopolistic system devised—unavoidably, often—to encourage nascent industry makes it possible to get away for a time with very inferior work and haphazard schedules. However, even the worm turns. Such practices have contributed to the high mortality among new industries.

Thinking people are unhappy and frustrated with the situation. They blame the leaders for failing to devise ways of rewarding performance. Now, as I have suggested, I don't think this criticism goes deep enough, for the problem is more moral than technical. Nevertheless, it has validity. Society functions best when individual advantage and moral obligation run together. In Ireland, performance is seldom adequately rewarded.

The property structure, not only on the land, but also in commerce and industry, erects a barrier between employer and employe. The best guarantee of advancement is membership in the boss's family. The likelihood of raising oneself by honest merit out of the rank and file is so remote that the intelligent employe—and intelligence is plentiful—knows that only a fool would try.

"Longevity," as a cynic remarked, "is the country's greatest curse." Nobody is willing to relinquish authority while a breath remains in his body. Even the son slated to succeed to his father's enterprise is an old man before he can make an independent decision. By then, any enthusiasm or ideas he might once have possessed are atrophied. His concern is to enjoy his tardy power, not to risk it.

Politics suffers a like fate. Here, the men who fought in 1916 and in the War of Independence remain unchallenged in 1959. In the interval, they have concentrated all power in the central Government in Dublin and given to permanent civil servants a dictatorship over the lives and decisions of the people without parallel in the free world outside France. The county councils, which played so big a part in the struggle for independence, demonstrating at that time the possibilities for self-government existing in the country, have been made rubber stamps. The police, education, the law courts, public assistance, hospitals, transport, all are under central control. The citizen is a child who could not be depended upon to make any decisions in matters affecting the community in which he lives.

It would be strange if these trends and attitudes were not also reflected in the Church, the transcendental importance of which in Irish life is universally recognized. And when I say the Church, I am not thinking exclusively of the institutional framework of Catholicism, though obviously this is the major influence, especially in the Republic, where Catholics are 93 or more per cent of the total population. The statement may shock some, yet I am convinced that the moral values and social attitudes of the Irish Catholic and the Irish Protestant are all but indistinguishable. If only they could both see this plain fact, they would be two-thirds way toward ending Partition, and a long way, too, toward mending the rift in Christ's seamless garment.

165

The Church, taken in this broad sense as a social institution, offers, in the opinion of many, the most acute expression of the tendency to treat the general public as too immature to make its own decisions.

TOO MUCH BANNING

Censorship provides a good example. Here Church and State work closely together in censoring both books and films. The wording of the book-censorship legislation ("in general tendency indecent") parallels and was no doubt inspired by the Canon Law ("*ex professo obscena tractantes*"), but the application runs wildly beyond the rules laid down by the most rigid canonist. Such absurdities have resulted as the banning of a book carrying the Nihil Obstat of a Catholic archbishop and the condemnation of books as being "in general tendency indecent" because of a single objectionable incident, perhaps only a single phrase.

Censorship is also performed administratively by the Customs outside the framework of the Censorship of Publications Act. Such discretionary authority might be justified against pornography, but it is in fact used to seize shipments from reputable publishers to their dealers, and they have in practice no redress. A recent victim was Joyce Cary's novel *The Captive and the Free.* (Another Cary novel, *The Horse's Mouth,* is banned.)

Unofficial but real censorship exists at a third level, that of the public library. Twenty years ago, when I lived in Ireland, a librarian friend (now with God) used to select for me books she considered good and important. These were books withdrawn from circulation on the basis of instructions with which she disagreed but had to follow. Yet she was an exemplary and indeed militant Catholic, thoroughly qualified to make her own decisions. And the situation she endured has not improved.

The stress on book censorship would be less extraordinary if there was any substantial book-reading public. A recent survey of London publishers, the main suppliers of the Irish market, found them in agreement that 750 copies of a new hard-cover novel was the absolute top "best-seller" limit. In nonfiction, only the life of a saint or other Church personality, or a book of recent Irish political history, might exceed this figure, going as high as 4,000. The exception for recent Irish political history is not surprising, for politics remains an obsession, while social and economic thought is neglected. The other exception is curious. It suggests that the clergy attend to their spiritual reading, and no other.

Film censorship produces equal absurdities. For example, you can't have a bum tell a priest on the screen to go to hell. The phrase is cut out, even though it means that now the priest, without any provocation, knocks the bum into the gutter with a left to the jaw. One is left under the impression that it's quite proper for a priest to toss bums in the gutter, where presumably they should have been in the first instance. And, of course, you can't show a priest dressed in lay attire watching the floor show at a night club. So this scene is cut, turning what was a priest's pastoral concern for a parishioner's slightly errant daughter into a middle-aged cleric's infatuation for a starlet.

I apologize for devoting so much space to censorship, because I don't think it really makes too much difference to the average Irishman if the censors ban Kate O'Brien or cut a slice of tripe out of *Say One For Me*. But I do think that the attitude behind the censorship is important. It is the work of people who equate sanctity with the absence of sin, of a society which lacks any great purpose. It bespeaks a defensive mood, an anxiety to hold on and to conserve, not to push forward and to create. Here we are face to face with people who regard themselves as guardians of a completed society, one which has achieved its purposes and has no further great business to transact.

PATERNALISM

The civil servant, as I said, thinks of himself as guardian of a public incapable of pursuing its own welfare. But he in turn has his problems. On the plane from New York to Shannon, I spent half the night chatting with an Irish pastor returning from his first trip to the United States. Incidentally, his observations on his visit had confirmed his previous belief that the Catholic

Church in the United States has nothing to give the Catholic Church in Ireland but money. I mention him not for this, however, but for his exemplification of a trait frequently encountered in the clergy, a naive belief in his own omnisapience and in his absolute right and duty to override all contrary opinions. He had built several churches, he told me, without ever employing an architect (something to remember, when one is looking at Irish churches), and he always rejected Education Department school-building plans and substituted his own. The civil servants, knowing what's good for them, go along. After all, it's only public money.

The Irish, however, are not fools. They have traditionally a tremendous respect and affection for their priests, who were their only leaders and protectors during centuries of defeat. And from that historic experience they have learned great patience. But their patience is being exhausted. I was horrified by the bitter criticism of the clergy I heard everywhere I went. This is something quite different from old-time European anticlericalism, which throve mainly among nominal Catholics. Here the feeling is strongest among devout people, who remain intensely faithful to practice. And their criticism is less of the action than of the inaction of their spiritual leaders.

Ironically enough, one of the things that seems to have served to focus the dissatisfaction is a social action movement conceived and promoted by a remarkable Irish priest, the late Canon Hayes. *Muintir na Tire* (People of the Land) was designed to rejuvenate the dying countryside. The Canon effected a social and economic transformation in his own parish through the application of principles of extension education, self-help and cooperation. Others followed his urging and example, and the movement grew to national dimensions and achieved similar results wherever priests with his zeal and intelligence were willing to encourage without dominating.

And there's the rub. One wanted nothing to do with this new-fangled nonsense. Another made all the decisions. Yet another sought to channel the enthusiasm into an additional fund-raising organization for his own parish purposes. It is a pattern frequent in Ireland, where the tendency is always strong to subject the social and civic to the ecclesiastical—in effect a denial that the State no less than the Church is a perfect society seeking its own ends by its own independent means.

I should like to end on a note of optimism, but the truth is that I feel far from optimistic. The mood of the country is static and protective when the challenge calls for change and action. The danger, as always in such circumstances, is that youthful enthusiasm—lacking constructive leadership—will follow false prophets. The persistent attraction of the banned Irish Republican Army, pursuing an outmoded policy of force in keeping with the over-all arrested emotional development of the country, demonstrates alike the altruism of youth and the absence of legitimate objectives. It should serve as a warning to those who think of the present vacuum of national purpose as normality.

That American Way

Walter J. Ong

WITH THE CRISES on the international front today and the obvious fact that we Americans
are not the most beloved people in the world,
the importance of our attitude toward other nations
should be brought home to us more forcefully than ever
before. Is the lack of total success of our foreign policy
connected with some deep-set attitude in the American
psyche? What is wrong with the "American attitude"
toward those of other lands?

One possible answer is, nothing at all. Other countries are inhabited by goldbrickers, who are very happy
to take our money and, for compensation, to dislike us
as having more than they. We are the most generous
people in the world, doling out cash, credit and supplies to every other country out of the sheer goodness
of our hearts without hope of any profit or reward. And
what reward do we get? None. Absolutely none. It is
not just. Who ever heard of anyone's being so good and
unselfish as we are, looking for no reward, and then, to
cap everything, getting no reward after all, not even
that of being the most highly esteemed of all people
on earth—a reward which would be little enough, to

tell the truth, since we so richly deserve it? No wonder our blood curdles with indignation.

We have all encountered this type of reaction in others, and probably also in our own hearts. Its presence among us more than hints that there may be something wrong with our attitude toward peoples of other countries. And what is wrong with our attitude seems to be in great part a consequence of our country's history. Our own great American achievement has somehow become a positive psychological handicap. The United States has been a vast and successfully working machine for converting into ourselves persons from every nation of the world. We have met the entire human race (provided they came to the United States) and have found ourselves able to deal with them successfully. We can make anyone over into ourselves. Unfortunately, the conversion process has so far proved a one-way operation. We cannot make ourselves over, even imaginatively, into other people. As a nation and, for the most part, as individuals we have never been trained to deal with persons of other nations and cultures on their own terms.

The situation would not be so bad if we had assimilated only one or two nationalities. But our assimilation of everybody gives us illusions of grandeur. Knowing that we and all the rest of the human race can be "adjusted" to one another, we forget that the adjustment is successful, as far as we are concerned, only if all the other persons are subject to adjustment. We assume that we ourselves are born automatically "adjusted" to everybody everywhere.

THEY TALK OUR LANGUAGE

I recall a conversation a few years ago with an American businessman who stated with glowing self-satisfaction: "Whenever I do business with foreigners, I insist that they write me in English. It makes for better understanding all the way around." "Half-way around," I wanted to emend. I thought of German businessmen I had heard of who would hire Swahili-speaking clerks just to write the Bantus in their own language. But for

171

my American friend, understanding was a one-way street; if the other fellow understood *your* language, that meant that *you* were adjusted to *him* and understood him thoroughly. There is a dangerous and insulting innocence in this state of mind. Curiously enough —or disastrously enough—my American businessman friend was a genuinely devoted Catholic layman, particularly interested in international relations within the Church.

To dislike foreigners as foreigners is of course a common human failing. All nations suffer from it. Other English-speaking peoples do not particularly like foreigners. The British do not. Their insular aversion to those not like themselves, perhaps matched or surpassed only by that of the Irish, was celebrated a few years ago with infectious humor by George Mikes, who, in the role of a displaced person in Great Britain, produced the well-known book *How to Be an Alien*. Nevertheless, though foreigners feel foreign in Great Britain as elsewhere, it is no great surprise to an Englishman that a foreigner does not speak English. To an American in the United States it is a little more of a shock.

Our attitude toward the language is quite different from that of the English. The Englishman feels that the language is his and is inclined to want to keep it for himself. The American feels that it is his but should not be kept to himself. On the contrary, it ought to be enforced on everybody whether everybody likes it or not. Typically, he does not even state this feeling of his. He takes it for granted. Imposed for generations on masses of non-English-speaking immigrants, American English is a reassuring badge of conformity which —unless he watches himself—the American simply assumes the rest of the world should be made to wear.

The conviction underlying this linguistic attitude is simple: it is that everyone else in the world wants to be an American. I have some European friends who can wax amusedly eloquent at this bumptious assumption, and others who are fiercely indignant when it obtrudes on them, as it all too frequently does, from

American tourists and visitors. Again our own history has confused us. In our personal lives, or in our schoolbooks and other reading, we are familiar with non-Americans of all sorts who have come to America and want to be Americans. Our schoolbooks and folklore are full of the America-refuge-of-all-the-downtrodden-and-woebegone theme. We have inscribed this theme on the Statue of Liberty—"Give me your tired, your poor . . . wretched refuse . . ." Some present American descendants of the same "refuse" are now agitating to have the inscription changed, but most of us still relish its thought. Intoxicated with a heady appreciation of our own charity, we forget that the non-Americans—refuse or not—who did not come to America, very often did not come because, all things considered, they did not think America was worth it. When you are visiting a foreign country, you may as well face the fact that you are visiting the descendants of those who did not want to be Americans.

LOYAL NON-AMERICANS

This is truly a shattering thought for unthinking Americans. It is very difficult for an American to believe that anyone could not particularly care to be an American, and all but impossible for him to believe that anyone could coldbloodedly want not to be one. The inscription on the Statue of Liberty, and its many equivalents in all that we learn, consciously and subconsciously, at home and in school, keep our collective ego bright and shining by sheltering us from the thought of such repulsive possibilities. They condition us to the persuasion—which is something less than self-evident—that all men regard the United States as the most desirable country on earth. We are conditioned to this with such thoroughness and profundity that I am sure that by this point many readers are bristling with indignation and that some have already broken off diplomatic relations with me and are now writing to the editor.

Still, some roots stand more or less clearly exposed where even commonplace analysis can reach them. This

173

conviction that all the world wants to be American is obviously a strong defense reaction to the guilt feelings of our ancestors, which our culture subtly, but inevitably, conveys to us. We are all descended from ancestors who, if they were not violently torn from their homes as slaves or as prisoners, political or otherwise, came here, most of them if not all, by leaving behind persons to whom they were bound by affection and obligations of all sorts. Our highly commercialized folklore likes to dwell on more consoling things, making heroes of those who left but not of those who stayed. But the facts of our history which lie behind us tell a more complex story. Tearing away from family and other ties may well have been the most sensible move, but it is not accomplished without psychological hardship. The emigrant is haunted by the fact that he has abandoned others to their fate. For he has, after all, run away from home.

In such an event, to save face it was imperative that America eventually be thought of as the land of opportunity, whether it was originally so thought of or not. For the negative element in turning away from home had to be countered by building up all possible positive reasons for the abandonment. What was behind one had to be forgotten. It occasioned too much pain. One had to talk of opportunity in a new future. Much has been written about the consequent tendency of Americans to build their families around the children, who look into the future and do not know the past, even to the extent that after one generation they no longer speak the language of their fathers. Second-generation Americans become ashamed of the foreign ways of their parents—which is to say that, just as these parents felt guilty about leaving their own parents, so their own children feel guilty about them, in a different but related way. Now that the third generation is learning from sociological studies that their own parents, born in this country, felt ashamed of their parents for not having been born in this country, the third generation becomes ashamed of its parents for having felt ashamed of theirs. The American family itself, oriented through the children into the future, thus becomes an instrument for smothering the past in vague and confused, but terribly real, feelings of shame. Henry James' novels show that such feelings are not restricted to the descendants of recent immigrant groups but go back to the colonial beginnings of America.

Just how real this situation is was borne in on me a few months ago when a recent immigrant to the United States from Central Europe, who had just become an American citizen, wrote an article for a national magazine explaining his reasons for coming to the United States and his reactions to his new home. In the article he mentioned that people in the United States like to think of our country as the land of opportunity, but that, try as he might, he could find no such thinking in his own decision to come here. His impulse was not at all framed in the idea of seeking "new opportunity." It was far more elemental. He simply wanted desperately to "get away."

Shortly after he had published this article, having the good fortune to meet him, I mentioned my fascination with this particular point in his account of himself. "Yes," he said pensively, "and I had much more in the article on the same point, but the editors suppressed it." Did they suppress it because they did not want to believe it? or because they did not think their readers wanted to hear it? or perhaps for both reasons and others, too? The Statue of Liberty approach is much more comforting—until you get to thinking about it too much. Strangely, then it makes you, of all things, ashamed of your ancestors again.

Are we so ashamed of immigrant ancestors, however remote, that we are repelled at the idea of further immigration into the United States? Since the recent Hungarian revolt against communism, the United States has had the lowest record of all major Western powers in the receiving of refugees. Both in terms of our total national income and in terms of our total population, we have taken in a far smaller proportion of these refugees than the war-torn countries of Germany, France and England.

Connected with our difficulties in adjusting to other persons is our extreme sensitivity to criticism of the United States by others. Again, such sensitivity to criticism of one's homeland is natural to all men. Citizens of other countries are hurt and angry when their country is the butt of criticism. But they are ordinarily not greatly surprised. The American is surprised, and his hurt and anger the greater for this. He cannot believe that there are people who would not like the United States. Otherwise, how could it be that everyone in the world wants to be an American?

AS OTHERS SEE US

I recall the Dutch priest who was a very good friend of mine and was visiting in this country. He had shared with an American priest who had lived in England the fun of *How to Be an Alien*. The American priest wanted to read anything else which George Mikes had written. With some misgivings, his Dutch friend was persuaded to lend him another book by the same man, *How to Scrape Skies: The United States Explored, Rediscovered and Explained*. The humor of this second book was lost in startled and hurt resentment on the part of the American. He could not understand how an author who poked fun at England so cleverly could so crudely and stupidly misrepresent American ways.

The American's understanding of other countries is complicated by the position of America in the technological civilization which is rapidly becoming the

176

civilization of the entire human race. As man everywhere moves toward greater and greater technological developments, the United States is, for certain historical reasons, in the vanguard. (This judgment is made from the over-all viewpoint; in some details, of course, the United States lags behind.) Seeing others moving toward the same goal as himself, but somewhat behind him, the American is likely to believe that they have their eyes on him and his achievements rather than on the goal. This is a human misinterpretation, comforting to the ego, but hardly one which endears the American to a European, who is, also quite humanly, annoyed by the fact that the American has, by quitting home, in some matters gotten ahead of the civilization which bore him and without which he would be an impossibility.

A related complication is the superior wealth of the United States, not all of which is the product of America herself, much coming from other countries in which Americans have played the complicated role of both benefactors and exploiters—and, being human, chiefly the latter. Americans console themselves commonly here by representing other peoples as venal, panting after American wealth. They will do anything for American money, the tourist and the taxpayer thinking of foreign loans both tell themselves. This argument is a two-edged sword. Turned over, it says that the only way Americans have of getting along with other persons is money

The truth is often that Americans do attract the venal elements in other civilizations because we are venal ourselves, making up for our linguistic and other deficiencies by throwing our economic weight around. It is certain at least that we have become symbols of venality all over the face of the earth. Here are some excerpts from a recent language examination for advanced elementary education in the schools of the Netherlands: "Mr. Coppergold, a rich American, had visited several countries in western Europe. . . . And everywhere they spoke English to him, especially when he threw his dollars around." Dutch elementary school

177

children can be expected to find translation of this passage in a foreign language not too hard. They know the elements which make up the rich American.

Monetary considerations are often operative in what has been styled the American's European neurosis. I recall the incident when a group of Americans on a tour in Italy were treated to a spectacle of a compatriot of theirs, a middle-aged woman, who without warning dramatically rose from her seat in the tourist bus and, for the benefit of all the passengers, asked the guide in a loud voice why he did not point out what was the truth, that all the rebuilding they saw in the war-torn countryside was due entirely to the kindness of Americans and to the money which "we" were sending, without any recompense, to Europe. Unfortunately, all the bus passengers were not Americans. There were a great many Italians—perhaps some whose sons' bodies were still lying under the rubble to which the American tourist so gallantly waved.

The problems of Americans in adjusting, or even in wanting to adjust, to ways of life other than their own not merely unnerve tourists but also affect our foreign policy in a myriad of ways. There are the American technical teams in foreign countries who, observers report, are, not all of them, but most of them, definitely less loved by the people around them and less in contact with these people than the corresponding Soviet teams. There is our utterly miserable record in providing diplomatic staffs able to handle the language of the country to which they are sent.

When this serious state of linguistic affairs was reported recently to President Eisenhower, his answer was that money should be raised to train suitable men. The answer certainly caused many a smile in foreign lands. There are your Americans again: more money will cure all human ills. Of course, what is needed in human relations is not just money but a certain quality of understanding and love. Money will not create in Americans the desire to learn foreign languages, which is what we so desperately need. Generally speaking, the American abroad who wants to learn the language of the people among whom he lives is the American capable of understanding and adjustment. The attitude toward the language is likely to be the attitude toward the civilization. Perhaps for this reason, in my own experience, it is Americans from academic circles, teachers and students, who do best in adjusting themselves to foreign living.

The American's difficulty in accommodating himself to others is becoming a great matter for concern in the Church as American Catholics are called on more and more to bear their share of the burdens in manning the Church's supranational offices and to share her supranational concerns. The American clergy and religious suffer of course from the same psychological disabilities as other Americans, and the results are there for everyone to see. An old-time missionary complains that newly arrived Americans take for granted that the local people will do everything the way it is done in America —or at least they *must* want to do it that way. A religious superior in Europe writes to an American religious superior with obvious concern over the fact that in the international house of which he has charge, clergy from all over the world live happily under the local regime—except the Americans, who need all sorts of preferential treatment. What can he do? He begs that some adaptable Americans be sent to the house.

It is notorious that in the Church's curia at Rome, Americans are woefully underrepresented. It is hard to get them to Rome or, once there, to keep them. We shall send money instead, and pray to be excused in our persons. The reasons for begging to be excused are by no means all invalid. Even when they wish desperately to serve, Americans are often incapacitated to do so by the fact that they are Americans. Their psychological difficulties are real and give rise even to physical disabilities.

In the present crisis of adjusting ourselves to other men, what we need to do, first of all, is to think. For it is the unthinking "innocence" of Americans vis-à-vis the rest of the world, so profoundly caught in the novels of Henry James, which dogs us, to the detriment of ourselves and others, still. Our thoughtlessness is caught in phrases such as "un-American activity" (imagine "un-British activity," "un-Irish activity," "un-Venezuelan activity," and how campaigns dealing in such slogans would impress us). It is caught in our assumptions that what we do is never chauvinistic or nationalistic, though what others do may well be. Thus, for British missionaries to teach cricket or Canadian missionaries to teach lacrosse would be chauvinistic, but for American missionaries to teach baseball is not spreading American culture but merely enabling the benighted natives to be human beings.

Our thoughtlessness is perhaps most profound in our attitude toward citizenship. For a citizen of any other country to become a citizen of the United States is admirable and a compliment to the country of his origin, which should be proud to have given birth to a potential American. For an American citizen to become a citizen of another country is quite a different thing. It is treasonable, an affront to the United States, and shows a dastardly streak which will bring no good to the adopted land. I have talked to persons who were led to suppose all through their schooling that T. S. Eliot was a treacherous and suspect character simply for having taken up residence and citizenship in England.

Such unthinking attitudes sound fantastic when they are actually formulated, but I think most of us Americans will recognize them as real, as being rooted in our hearts and not easy to eradicate, even when they have been brought to the light by explicit formulation and statement. All the picture is not black, of course. There are the bright spots of which we do not ordinarily need to be reminded and which I have consequently not shown here. There are hundreds of Americans in foreign parts who adjust thoroughly and gracefully and with love to those around them. These are the cultural ambassadors of whom we can well be proud, and the response to their behavior on the part of those of other countries is gratifying beyond expectation. For most persons do wish to like Americans. We are, after all, not more repulsive than other people in the world, provided we try not to be.

But we have to try, not only in ways we like, but in ways others like. We must work hard for acceptance by others if we want to be loved. We cannot assume that we are accepted, and scream when we are not, as the immature do. We must understand that while our psychological heritage breeds in us an
overpowering desire
for acceptance, to se-
cure acceptance in
foreign lands we need
more than wishful
w a r m - heartedness
and candy bars for
the children. We need
imagination and hu-
man sympathy f o r
those unlike us. And
a b o v e all—a hard
thing for us Ameri-
cans—we have great
need to understand
ourselves.

Back in 1948 President Truman felt that it was high time for the churches to man the parapets of civilization against the menace of godlessness. But he failed in his efforts to have the Christian forces in the West make common cause for the Kingdom of Christ against the Kingdom of Satan. Such is the scandal of Christian disunity in the face of the monolithic solidarity of communism. Ecumenism is still in its unstable infancy and has a rugged road ahead. Catholics like to lay the blame for division upon our separated brethren. Too often, however, the fault lies in our own stars. Too many Catholics still lurk in the ghetto, fearing to be "engaged," not daring to become "involved." God grant that the Second Vatican Council may show us how to open the path to Christian unity before it is too late.

Christian Unity

In a Catholic Ghetto?

Robert I. Gannon

"GHETTO" has been a fighting word for centuries—
like "Inquisition." It refers to the formerly restricted parts of certain European cities where,
by law, all Jews were compelled to live. Some insisted
that as an institution it was well meant, but, no matter
what could be said of it as assuring the safety of the
Jews and promoting their solidarity, it was recognized
as a symbol of Gentile aversion and fear.

In the last few years, the word has become almost as
popular in some Catholic circles as "dialogue" and "pluralistic." Every time a good long convention is held where
lots and lots of papers are read, someone is sure to condemn "the ghetto mentality," which is said to have
resulted among us from the fact that we were so long
an ostracized minority. They point out that in Colonial
days we were like the *gens lucifuga* of Penal England—
the "people who shunned the light"—and although there
was a breather after the American Revolution, the
Nativist movement, following the heavy immigration of
underprivileged Catholics, kept us on the defense for
generations, and forced us to live in a more or less
restricted circle. Now we are taken to task for continuing a situation which we did not create—a situation
which has become a symbol of Protestant fear to some

183

and of Catholic solidarity to others. "Ghetto," therefore, is today not only a fighting word among us, but a very confusing one as well.

There is, first, a false sense in which the word is used by apologetic Catholics. These are the brethren, with us almost from Apostolic times, who shrink from identification with a Church that prides itself on being the Church of the poor and the humble. They would like to remove their identification tags, the last differences that set them apart from the non-Catholic world around them. To these people the parish is a social ghetto. They resent getting permission for anything from a pastor, pride themselves on the fact that they have never met any of the priests, and, of course, would not be caught dead at a meeting of the Bona Mors. The reading of Catholic books and periodicals creates, they say, a mental ghetto. But it takes the Catholic schools to combine the social ghetto with the mental. When children are confined in that sort of atmosphere too long, they will believe for the rest of their lives that there is only one true faith and that the Pope is the Vicar of Christ. They may even want to go on to a Catholic college, and eventually to marry their own.

This sort of thinking is encouraged by a wave of exaggerated self-criticism that is spreading from our uninhibited juniors to the ranks of our neglected intellectuals. It is considered the healthy thing to belittle accomplishment, to ignore the handicaps which have been so nobly overcome and to shout our defects from a sound truck in Times Square. The whole world must hear that there is not one single St. John Chrysostom to be heard in St. Patrick's Cathedral, not a single Oppenheimer among Notre Dame's alumni, not even a Rodgers or a Hammerstein, and the reason is that American Catholics are living in a ghetto.

It may be embarrassing to be caught agreeing with this type of coreligionist, but wrongheaded as they are, there is something in what they say. We are in a sort of ghetto, but not the sort that they like to talk about. Our parishes are not ghettos. They are the extension of our homes, and being identified with them is like fostering the family spirit. Our Catholic press is not a

184

mental ghetto designed for isolation. It is a constant reminder that ours is an eternal faith that is eternally adapting itself to a changing world, and this makes us all the more eager to study contemporary society. But no one with a day's work to do can keep up with the modern problems of the Church unless he learns what the best-informed Catholics are thinking about them. As for our schools, far from being ghettos, they are lighthouses in these tempestuous times, and the Protestants and the Jews who attend them appreciate what they mean for the future of America. Like the parishes and the press, they are symbols, not of fear, but of Catholic solidarity.

WHAT OUR GHETTO IS

What, then, is the ghetto that too many of us *do* cultivate? It is the ghetto of social aloofness. Too many of us are living in the past, nursing slights of another generation, aloof from our fellow Americans, where no aloofness is called for.

It is true that not too many years ago Catholics were excluded from ordinary neighborhood activities and snubbed by an intolerant majority. Unless these new arrivals would give up the Mass, they were not welcome on any committees that worked for the community as a whole. Today, however, in the urbanized United States this attitude is exceptional. A new generation of Protestants has matured, and the aspect of their maturity that interests us is the fact that they no longer believe what their fathers believed about the Roman Catholic Church.

A professor of the University of Virginia once told, at the end of a faculty forum, how his father had warned him as late as 1910 that Catholics were dangerous only when they started to be friendly, because every Catholic was pledged to make friends with one Protestant and kill him. Tales like that have retreated to the hills, and ordinary Protestants can joke about them now. They still find many of our practices and assumptions irritating, and they are not completely reassured about the future; but it is worth noting that the uneasiness of some admirable ministers of the gospel in the present campaign reflects their reading not of *The Awful Disclosures of Maria Monk* but of commentaries on what Leo XIII wrote in his *Immortale Dei* (1885) about the Christian constitution of states. That indicates considerable progress. The professors of philosophy and religion at Colgate University last spring were troubled about this same encyclical, the only one they were studying in their classes, but they were eager to get to the bottom of the misunderstandings.

The deep South looks different from up here in New York and some of the blasts that are coming from the Texas Baptists sound like the roaring 1840's, but even in Dallas itself a Jesuit was asked only last year to open the drive for the Community Chest. He spoke at a traditional luncheon that had formerly been restricted to Protestant ministers and their congregations, and afterwards he was congratulated in the good old Protestant way. The line formed to the right, and one after another each said to him: "Thank you, Reverend, for your message!" Later he spoke to 14 old-fashioned preachers who sat in the front row of a series of meetings in Tuscaloosa, Alabama, and had the leader, a venerable Methodist, say at a little reception afterwards: "Reverend, I had no idea that a Roman Catholic priest could preach such a good Methodist sermon." Needless to say, it was not a Methodist sermon. It was a Christian sermon on the matter found in the first two pages of the catechism, and it worked. It stressed the fact that there was much common ground to be shared by all of us, and its selection was in line with the conciliation that has characterized the reign of "Good Pope John."

This conciliation involves no compromise in any essential, still less any risk of indifferentism. The dictionary says that conciliation is "the gaining of good will by pleasing acts." Madison Avenue might call it public relations, but the Pope would call it in the present circumstances spreading the charity of Christ by imitating the amiability of Christ. See how the Holy Father has gone out of his way to change the wording in several passages of the liturgy, not because they were untrue, but because they were unnecessarily harsh and offensive to people who would like to be friendly.

Our minimum program, then, in removing the bitterness that wells to the surface of our national life when the spirit of politics gets out of hand, is to make sure that intelligent Americans of good will, Protestant, Jewish and whatever, know us for what we are. If we are real Catholics we are worth knowing; and our character answers more objections than any sermon would. And yet, out of habit we keep on being clannish; we cling to our ghetto. We still hesitate to join non-Catholics in social, charitable and recreational movements that are city-wide and even national. What leadership do we give the Red Cross, for example, or the Boy Scouts, or the public library, the art galleries, symphony orchestras and movements for better parks? And yet, what is more conducive to seeing God in my neighbor and having my neighbor see God in me, than to work with my neighbor when we are both at our best working for others?

What public-spirited people do for the community is good, but the fact that they do it together is even better. By working shoulder to shoulder for the public weal, men of every religion and no religion can build up what we need more than ever in the gathering chaos—American unity.

Perspectives for the Council

Yves M.-J. Congar, O.P.

PERE CONGAR, distinguished European theologian, is a consultor to the Theological Commission of the coming Ecumenical Council. Among his many significant books, *Lay People in the Church* is perhaps best known to the English-speaking world as an outstanding contribution to the theology of the laity. For a quarter of a century Fr. Congar has been in the forefront of the ecumenical movement in European circles. His pioneer work of the mid-Thirties, *Chrétiens désunis*, is still cited as a great leap forward in Catholic thinking about the separated brethren.

Recently this gracious and very busy man invited the interviewer to the Dominican House in Strasbourg, France, to discuss some of the salient problems facing the Church at this turning point in its history. The astoundingly rapid change in all fields today compels us to reconsider the role of "the little Church in a vast world." The quest for the most effective ways of witnessing to the truth that is in us forms the supreme challenge for all Catholics who are living in this new age a-borning.

✽ ✽

Q. You have mentioned in your writings that the coming Ecumenical Council should rethink the role of bishops in the Church. Would you like to develop this idea?

A. I think many bishops desire that the Roman Curia be more international, with better representation in Rome for the various national churches. One could imagine a number of ways of achieving this, for example, enlargement of the College of Cardinals, or perhaps the setting up of a new permanent commission.

Even more important is the question of the theology of the episcopal college. You are aware that, from a theological point of view, the bishops are successors of the apostles, not in the sense that each bishop succeeds a determined apostle, but in the sense that the college of bishops as such succeeds the college of apostles as such. This is important, because the apostles had a universal jurisdiction; thus, the college of bishops has in itself a universal jurisdiction in the Church.

Each individual bishop is limited *de facto* in his authority to a determined territory, but as a member of the episcopal college he possesses a certain power and obligation in regard to the whole Church. This power and duty to the whole Church is exercised mainly in an Ecumenical Council. The Council is the perfect realization of the episcopal college. When the bishops are dispersed in their own dioceses, each bishop individually is not infallible. But when the bishops universally preach a doctrine, it becomes a matter of faith, a matter of infallible teaching. This was the chief argument of Pius XII for declaring the dogma of the Assumption.

Furthermore, each bishop in his individual diocese should show an interest in the universal Church. He shows this interest, first, in the administration of his own diocese.

A diocese is only part of the whole Church, but it carries within itself the nature of the whole Church. Thus, for a diocese to be truly catholic, its bishop must govern it not as an independent unit, but rather as a portion of the universal Church. This implies that the bishop actualize in his diocese all the great causes of the universal Church.

Moreover, a bishop should interest himself in questions that are distant from his proper domain. Pius XII strongly underlined this in his encyclical *Fidei Donum*, in 1957, when he said that bishops are missionaries for the whole world. You have a striking example of that in Louvain, where you live. Cardinal Van Roey and the Belgian bishops constructed there a seminary for Latin America. The Belgian bishops felt that they had a certain charge of South America, where, as you know, the pastoral needs are very great. Of course, the Belgian bishops will not intervene in the diocesan affairs of Brazil or Chile, but they are pastorally interested in these dioceses, as the creation of this seminary signifies.

Q. *What attitudes do you think the Council will take regarding the mission countries?*

A. I feel that the Church of the 20th century has already begun to have a completely new outlook on the missions. This is to be understood in two ways.

First, the Church today understands better that it is missionary by nature, missionary in all the aspects of its life. There is no role or position in the Catholic Church that is not missionary. This should be strongly marked in the Council. And when I say that the Church is missionary in all its members, I am thinking especially of the laity.

Recent pontifical documents and the recent conventions of laymen in Rome have all expressed this thought.

Second, the Church has had to revise its attitude toward the missions because of the gradual collapse of colonialism. The 19th century was the most glorious missionary epoch of history, but it was also a century of colonialism. It was the century of the geographical discovery of the world, of Africa and Oceania in particular. Missionaries were sent on the heels of the explorers, and under the protection of Western governments. This protection seemed necessary at the time. But it linked the missions to the West, to colonial interests and to a certain form of imperialism. Today this is absolutely impossible. Wherever the missions are tied to Western powers, they are meeting serious obstacles. The missions remain alive and vigorous only in places where for at least a decade they have separated themselves from too much dependence on Western powers.

Today there are native hierarchies and native clergies. Of course, these indigenous churches have not been very active in theology, but I think they will bring to the Council their authentic problems. Instead of being represented at the Council by Western powers, as was the case in 1869, the mission countries will be represented by men who have firsthand knowledge and intense interest in the evangelization of their own lands. This should bring to the Council an extraordinary broadening of perspective in matters of canon law, Catholic Action, liturgy, and maybe even in the formulation of certain doctrines.

Q. *What position do you think the Council can take on the thorny question of non-Catholic groups evangelizing in previously Catholic areas?*

A. I do not believe that the Church can directly declare the right of non-Catholic Christians to evangelize in already Catholic areas. After all, the

Church must be honest with its own conscience; it must be loyal to its most profound beliefs. What it can do, and should do, I feel, is to make a firm declaration of tolerance, of respect for the religious liberties of other consciences.

In place of bitter rivalry, a disagreeable and very negative thing, the Church should seek an amicable understanding with the separated Christians, especially in missionary areas. Such understanding, I am happy to say, is coming more and more into evidence.

This question of tolerance is very important. The World Council of Churches in Geneva expressly requests that we take up the subject. In May we brought together 12 Catholic and 12 non-Catholic theologians (appointed by the WCC). This semiofficial meeting was to discuss religious tolerance and freedom of conscience.

Today this problem of tolerance must be seen as forming an indivisible unit in the world. I mean that it is impossible to demand tolerance in one country and not practice it in another. The question cannot be divided like that. A few years ago the Catholic Church in a certain country desired that Protestant citizens support the Catholic stand for religious liberty in Hungary. The Protestants did not want to co-operate; they said that they suffered from injustices in Catholic countries—Spain and areas of Latin America. This was not overly generous on their part; it would have been better had they not raised that matter. But one can certainly see their point of view. The example shows that this question of religious liberty must be viewed on an undivided, world-wide basis.

Q. *You have said that a whole new chapter on the laity could be written today, that the Church must go beyond the canonical notion of the laity and see the place of laymen in the sacral order of the Church. Would you like to comment on this?*

A. Yes. When the word "layman" is used, it makes

some theologians think of a canonical distinction which says that a layman is neither a cleric nor a monk. Actually there is much more to it than that.

The laity would be very disappointed if the Council just says that laymen are neither clerics nor monks. They already know that. They want to know just what they are, and this in a positive way, not only as regards their rights, but also concerning their duties. The laymen are anxious to take on the responsibilities of the Church, but they ask to know just how intimately they belong to the Church and form the Church.

On these points we have reached a sort of consensus since 1950, thanks to two world congresses of the lay apostolate, to the discourses of the Pope, and to a number of books. I think it is quite possible today to determine the ecclesiological role of lay people in a positive and constructive way.

Of course, there are some delicate points, such as the obligations of married people and the role of spouses in the Mystical Body (which is not made up of individuals but of families). Marriage must be seen as a Christian state in and of the Church. Pius XII, you know, speaks of such a state in his encyclical *Mystici Corporis*.

The role of lay people in the liturgy constitutes a considerable problem. First, there is the question of a more active lay participation in the liturgy as it is today. Much good work has been done. We have just recently celebrated the Holy Week and paschal ceremonies. I found them very impressive when the lay people had been properly prepared. But, in my opinion, there is a much more fundamental problem facing our liturgy. I doubt whether the Council will be able to take it up, since it will demand much time, work and gradual experimentation. I refer to the problem of a less clerical or monastic liturgy than our present one.

Let me give an example. Take the "Exsultet" preface of the paschal vigil. As a cleric who knows

Latin, who has an ecclesiastical, patristic and monastic background, I find myself relatively at home in this prayer. I recognize a quantity of poetical and biblical and traditional allusions in the song. It says something to me; it profoundly touches my religious spirit. But I imagine that for laymen, who have none of this Latin, traditional, clerical formation, it must have much less meaning. Many of the images say nothing at all to them; their formation has in many cases been just the opposite of a Greco-Latin traditional schooling.

I really think that this is *the* liturgical problem for some time to come. The difficulties will first present themselves in the far-off mission lands, like India and Africa, which totally lack the Western tradition. It is evident that in France our whole culture has a Latin foundation; the problem is, therefore, somewhat less urgent here than on the missions. But this liturgical "gap" will become more and more pronounced even in Western Europe. It will be necessary to envisage forms of expression that are more accessible to the laity, if we do not want to see the liturgy restricted to a specially trained elite. Such a restricted liturgy would have no contact with the masses.

I am very much impressed, having followed closely the French liturgical movement, by the fact that the liturgy did not really become popular until the singing of psalms in the vernacular was introduced, thanks to the translation of the Bible of Jerusalem and to the melodies of Père Gelineau. The movement is encouraging, but it is not an ideal solution. It is rather a paraliturgical, or peripheral, solution. I regret that in our student Masses we do not sing the Mass itself but, instead, various psalms distributed throughout.

Q. In your major work on the laity you explain how lay people participate in the priestly, prophetic and royal roles of the Church. Which of these functions do you think is the most important for the layman?

A. I would hesitate to say that one of these roles is more important than another. I think that the priestly function of the layman is the most comprehensive, that is, if one understands it, as I did, in conformity with the text of the Epistle to the Romans: ". . . offer up your bodies as a living sacrifice, consecrated to God and worthy of his acceptance; this is the worship due from you as rational creatures" (12:1). All the life of a layman is included in this complete offering to God.

The prophetic role is also very important. This is what the apostle Peter underlines in his first letter: ". . . that you may declare the virtues of him who has called you out of darkness into his wonderful light" (2:9). It is the prophetic people of God, the Church, like Israel of old, giving witness before the world of the existence of God, of His greatness and the need for serving Him.

And concerning the interior life, the royal role is very important. It is the domination of one's self, the conquest of one's liberty. I think that we could formulate all of Christian morality in terms of the conquest of liberty. It would then appear as a baptismal and paschal morality, that is, the escaping from the slavery to sin to live in the spiritual liberty of the sons of God.

Q. *Would you like to say something about the relation between the priest's and the layman's roles in the Church's mission of evangelization?*

A. If we understand "evangelization" in the sense of preaching the gospel, it is clear that this role is exercised mainly by priests. Under certain circumstances the priesthood could perhaps suffice for this mission. One would have to find out, though, whether the priests could establish contact with all the parts of a given population, and whether these clerics could express themselves in a language understandable to certain groups. Here I would insist on the need for lay people to evangelize among the workers and especially in the proletarian milieu.

But there is a special mission of the Church which the priest simply cannot fulfill adequately, and which becomes the special domain of the layman. This task is the influencing of the temporal directly.

By the nature of his calling, the priest cannot place himself completely in the political and professional order. This area is one of competition and of rivalry; the priest must remain the man of God, the man of charity. The priest in the Latin Church has no family; usually he doesn't have a secular occupation, except in an accidental way as teacher or researcher, etc. Thus, it is the layman who actually carries the cause of the Church, the cause of the "consecration of the world" of which Pius XII spoke.

This consecration does not mean a ceremonial consecration of the world to the Sacred Heart, which can be a very external affair. This consecration consists in an orientation of the world toward God. It cannot be achieved unless the world is reformed according to God, unless we reform the sordid structures of money, of sex, of egoism toward structures of service, fraternity, justice, truth and love. That is what it means to remake the world according to God. It is the laymen's role to carry forward this task of the Church. The priest must second their efforts by forming them spiritually, by advising (and being advised by) them.

Q. *I noticed in one of your articles that you hoped the Council would refrain, in the interests of Church unity, from making any Marian declarations. Why do you feel this way?*

A. I think that if the Council made some of the Marian declarations that are talked about in various theological publications and congresses, it would constitute an almost definitive obstacle to the unity of Christians.

It is a fact that the definition of the Assumption has created a new obstacle that is very difficult to overcome not only for Protestants—that's too clear —but even for the Orthodox, who nevertheless admit the Assumption. From the very day that it was dogmatized unilaterally by Rome, the Orthodox said: Ah no, we can't go along with that; it's not the same thing.

If we were to make dogmas of subjects not yet mature in the conscience of the Church, such as the co-redemption or the universal mediation of Mary, I think it would create an almost insurmountable obstacle to unity. Fr. R. Leiber, as you know, was a close adviser of Pius XII. In his memoirs of Pius XII, he stated that the Pope considered these questions not yet mature in the conscience of the Church, not sufficiently clear to be the subjects of a dogmatic declaration. I would ask those who want to make a dogma out of the co-redemption of Mary to give me first a good theology of the redemption. I'm sure they would have to admit that it is not an easy thing to do.

Q. *There seems to be a desire among many Christians to see a greater simplicity and modernity in the Church's modes of expression and in the ways of her ecclesiastics. What is your thought on this?*

A. I think the Council must express itself in language that will be understood by the men of today, that is, in clear, pastoral, and nonacademic words which have a truly evangelical and religious tone. As far as I can see from my personal contacts, this is the formal desire of the bishops. They absolutely do not want to propose to the world a theological dissertation. They want to address a pastoral message. The Church must become more and more aware that it is speaking not only to a believing but also to an unbelieving world.

On the question of external forms of clerical life in the Church, yes, it would be well if we simplified our ways. But what is of much more importance, and I say this from personal experience, is that men be able to express themselves freely. Men are not happy unless they can express themselves. In fact they do express themselves. But where? In their family lives, their diversions, their work—not in church.

Now it seems to me that because of the pomp that surrounds and imprisons them, bishops and Cardinals are practically never in occasions and places where men freely express themselves. They are with men, yes, but in formal ceremonies where men do not express themselves, where they enter into a ready-made rite that is perhaps too solemn. These high dignitaries have a certain contact with men, but this contact is fenced around with protocol and the marks of respect. In these circumstances men are careful not to say too much.

Thus, members of the upper hierarchy generally encounter artificial rather than real situations. One would wish that they had contact with men in those domains in which the latter express themselves freely. How to achieve such contact practically, you ask. One suggestion would be that members of the upper hierarchy four times a year take a worker's train for half an hour during the rush period. Of course, they would have to present themselves in a way that would not obstruct the liberty of expression of the men around them.

Q. *You have been engaged in the ecumenical movement for many years, Father. What do you think are some of the best means for furthering Christian unity?*

A. One must first understand that the ecumenical movement is a process of long duration. Success cannot be achieved by a resourceful five-year plan, as in the economic order.

On both sides we need a profound change of attitude, a revision of many ideas—not only prejudices, but also certain formulations of doctrine that could be improved. This will take a lot of time.

198

This gradual movement toward unity is advanced by numerous means. The first step is to see that there is correct and adequate information about one another in our schools and press. Second, we must all convert our hearts and abandon egoistic ideas of self-righteousness, of possessiveness, of a sort of religious imperialism. In short, it means becoming truly Christian. One of the principal means for this is prayer.

As you know, prayer does not always obtain what we pray for, but it always makes our heart more true, more fraternal, more humble. A prayer in common with our separated brethren is particularly significant. The directive of 1949, *Ecclesia Catholica,* approves the reciting together of the Our Father or any other prayer approved by the Church. Thus, for example, Compline (Evening Prayer) could be recited together. What is forbidden, of course, is liturgical worship together: Mass, Holy Communion, etc. Also, Catholics cannot ordinarily participate in non-Catholic services. This should not be looked upon as a spirit of opposition, but rather as a fundamental honesty and respect for one's own conscience.

Common prayer within the limits that I have mentioned is a very important and profound means of furthering unity. If something has already been accomplished in the Western countries, it is in large measure due to prayer, especially during the unity octave in January. I have had the privilege of preaching this octave for the last 25 years, and I must say that it is during this time that I find the audiences in the most attentive mood.

There are many other ways of preparing the ground for unity: historical studies, informal as well as theological discussions, and, yes, even the practical suggestion of M. Oscar Cullman about mutual collections, which are a good means of disinterestedness. All this has a role to play; nothing must be neglected. It is a world-wide process that is gradually leading us to something that only God foreknows. What this will be, we must not try

199

to learn too early.

What we must try to develop more fully as an essential condition for dialogue is confidence in our separated brothers. This implies that we treat "the others" as persons, as subjects and not as objects—objects of study, objects of sanctions, objects of repulsion, objects even of interest and of solicitude. This demands more than an exterior attitude, a certain form of politeness; it must come from within, from a conversion of heart. Yes, there is an intimate kinship between the dialogue and a confidence in others that treats them as persons.

Q. *Has the study of the ecumenical movement made much headway in European schools?*

A. It is a fact that ecumenism is becoming a subject of study in universities, seminaries and other institutes. I have drawn up a list of 17 universities which have one or more chairs dedicated to ecumenical problems. Last year I gave a course on the subject at the University of Strasbourg. As you know, the Holy See asks that a certain period of time be devoted to Orthodox theology in our seminaries; the same should certainly be done for the various forms of Protestantism. The important thing in this is that a few key ideas be developed well; it is not a question of covering much ground, but of delivering what is authentic.

In other words, one learns more in one hour of authentic conversation with a separated Christian than in years of artificial controversy. What counts is not to have at hand many facts and figures, but to have grasped the genius of the Orient and the inspiration of the Reformation. For this we must seek the authentic, whether that means inviting a minister into our seminaries from time to time or some other means. Surely we must cast about for new avenues of rapport if we are to be faithful to an inspiration for reunion that comes from the Holy Spirit.

Pope John XXIII:
Teacher

Philip S. Land, S.J.

A RECENT issue of AMERICA (9/30, p. 820) found it necessary to return once more to the defense of Pope John's encyclical on "Christianity and Social Progress." The most recent occasion for this defense had arisen in the form of a letter to AMERICA from one of *National Review*'s editors, Frank S. Meyer (AM. 9/30, p. 813).

Much more moderate in tone than *National Review*'s now notorious editorial on the encyclical, Mr. Meyer's letter no less firmly rejects the authority of the Pope as a teacher on social, economic or political matters. Commenting on the Meyer letter, AMERICA deplores the fact that, whereas we ought to be getting on with the work of interpreting and applying *Mater et Magistra,* it is discouragingly necessary to continue to defend the very right of the Pope to be heard on questions which involve both the temporal and the spiritual orders.

Why does AMERICA continue to stress this right of the Pope to act as teacher? Are its editors excessively preoccupied with this problem?

It assuredly does not seem so to me. I say this after three months of lecturing on and discussing the new encyclical in U.S. cities from coast to coast. Repeatedly I met the challenge: "What right has the Pope to talk about social questions?" and "Why doesn't the Pope just stick to preaching what's in the Gospels?"

Such questions, needless to say, come from people who are disgruntled because the Pope has said things in *Mater et Magistra* that they don't like. Such questioners were—it will be no surprise to learn—all members of the so-called conservative Right. Many of them declared themselves to be avid readers of *National Review*, from which they said they draw their personal social creed.

This challenge to papal authority in social matters was not exactly new to me. I had already been familiar with it in Europe while engaged for seven years in teaching and writing on Catholic social thought, principally in Rome. Moreover, I have had frequent contact with social developments elsewhere on the Continent. Thus, I have come to know Europe's strong element of *laïcisme,* which repudiates papal authority in all social matters. Says the laicist: Let the Church confine her exhortations to the Gospels and to the law of love. These are things of the spirit, and it is only things of the spirit that are or should be properly the concern of the Church. The task of civilization is purely temporal, wholly secular, and the Church has nothing at all to say about it.

In Europe, this laicist mentality finds its principal expression on the left wing of society. For there it is the left-wing Catholic who wants freedom—in his case, freedom to turn to what he believes to be the only vital source of social thought today, that is, to Hegel—and to Hegel as expounded by the Marxists.

During a long summer of travel in the United States this year, I continually met up with a strange variant of this European mentality. The only difference is that here in the United States I everywhere encountered it among extreme right-wing Catholics, notably those identifying themselves with the *National Review*. Aiding and abetting this mentality, if only unconsciously, were a small number of priests who—themselves also followers of *National Review*—are totally out of sympathy with Pope John's new encyclical, and in consequence are inclined to give it the silent treatment.

While these priests do not *ex professo* reject the Pope's right to teach in these fields, their silent treatment amounts in practice to just that; and it is so interpreted by some members of the laity who, in their encounters with these priests, find encouragement for their own rejection of papal authority in social questions.

AMERICA's editorial of September 30 devoted itself to the task of bringing about a better understanding of papal authority. The editorial is a clear statement, backed up by the weight of a century of the Church's own express teaching. It should be quite enough to convince loyal Catholics of what their attitude ought to be.

However, there is another approach that could be taken to bring us to the same conclusion—an approach that I made frequent use of this past summer. This is to point out a simple fact always missed by the dissenters: *there is in fact an already existing body of Catholic social thought.* The implication of this idea will escape no well-instructed Catholic. What the Church *in fact* has done and does today with regard to matters of faith and morals—namely, teach—she *rightly* (*de jure*) may do. And this is obviously no less true in matters of social morality than in those of personal morality.

I have made use of this approach because the current debate often goes on as though Pope John were the first Pope to try his hand at writing a social encyclical. The fact is that to an already existing and considerable body of Catholic social thought, one Pope after another throughout the past century has continually been adding more and more material. Most notable, of course, are the writings of Pope John's predecessors, Leo XIII, Pius XI and Pius XII. But others, too, made contributions of considerable importance.

Furthermore, all of these Popes recognized that they were contributing to an already existing body of Catholic doctrine, which, if it needed organization, growth and adaptation, nevertheless constituted a true *corpus doctrinae ecclesiae.* Each Pope in turn relies upon his predecessors; directs attention to what they have already written; insists that it is truly and properly the Church that is teaching; asserts that he himself is merely applying the existing body of Church doctrine in a new situation and covering a field hitherto left untouched (*Mater et Magistra*'s extended treatment of agriculture, for example), or that he is resolving a disputed question.

There is no more striking evidence of the truth of what I have just been saying than the encyclical *Mater et Magistra* itself. There Pope John devotes practically one-fourth of a lengthy document to the point of recalling the teachings of his predecessors and to reaffirming their authority.

In brief, centuries of papal practice refute the supposition of those who dissent from *Mater et Magistra*, claiming that the Popes do not have a right to speak to the Christian conscience in questions of social policy. If one cannot understand the limpid reasoning with which AMERICA explained to Mr. Meyer the theological basis of the Church's right—and duty—so to speak, surely this formidable fact of the Church presuming over centuries to do precisely what Mr. Meyer rejects, that is, to inform the Christian conscience in social as well as personal morality, should make the Catholic's dissent seem awesomely brash.

I repeat: *in social as well as personal matters.* What a singular prejudice it is which reduces morality to not cheating, not telling lies, not fornicating, not eating meat on Fridays, while dismissing from the realm of morality all questions that touch justice in economic life. And just such a rejection of Catholic tradition is involved in denying to the Pope an authoritative voice in social policy. Evidently, it cannot be repeated too often that wherever moral values are at stake, there the Church rightfully speaks in the name of Him who entrusted to her the task of guiding men to their eternal destiny.

In asserting thus vigorously the Catholic's obligation to heed any message propounded in a social encyclical, I do so in full awareness of the fact that it is not the competence of any individual, but that of the Church, to lay down norms for the proper fulfillment of that obedience. The Church, it should be remembered, is a loving mother who will not bruise the bent reed. Much less will she impose anything that is against reason.

It would take many more paragraphs than I have space for in this brief article to set forth the Church's norms for the reading and interpreting and applying of an encyclical. But those acquainted with them will recognize how eminently satisfactory they are.

It has been reported that Pope John has manifested a desire that Catholics engage in serious but loyal discussion of what he has written. He wants commentaries to be written and questions to be proposed. There is nothing at all surprising in this, because each of the social encyclicals has inevitably been followed by such discussion. The Pope recognizes that one may legitimately question the prudence of his decision not to enter into a detailed condemnation of the economic systems of socialism and communism. If this question is raised, the Pope would like the opportunity to answer it. He recognizes, too, that in some countries his use of the word "socialization" has given trouble. He welcomes clarifying comment on the topic.

The Holy Father realizes that the half-dozen general lines of "socialization" that particularly interest him will need both comment and careful application. He is keenly aware that the application of these policies calls for great discrimination, in view of the differing situations in which many nations find themselves—some well advanced along lines of sociative activity, others scarcely embarked upon any sort of organized group enterprises for the common good.

The Vicar of Christ acknowledges that "socialization" can and does have negative aspects. He will not consider it a disloyalty if some, commenting on "socialization" in local situations which they know well, wish to insist upon these aspects more than he did.

However, in the preparation of all such commentary and in any application that may be made to his principles, the Pope hopes that we will attend most carefully to his nuances of language, to his emphases, to what he states as certain and to what he sets down as reputable and authoritative opinion. Finally, he would certainly want a manifest distinction made between statements of what is truth, generally and everywhere applicable, and what is rather exhortation to a line of action which, according to circumstances, is mandatory or advisable or less advisable in one part of the world or another.

Among the dissenters I met this summer some few justified their slowness in accepting the new encyclical on the ground of a certain familiarity with the normal procedures by which encyclicals are prepared. They begin with the fact that a Pope must rely upon collaborators who have the technical competence he may lack in certain purely economic aspects of some questions, questions on whose social and moral implications he believes it timely to give guidance. These dissenters also recognize—and argue from the fact—that the Pope freely seeks help in setting forth accurately and fully those elements of Catholic social thought which he intends to bring to bear upon the questions at issue in his encyclical.

If Pope John had relied on more conservative collaborators—so these hesitant ones argue—a different (and to them more acceptable?) encyclical might have emerged. If, therefore, such a different teaching might have existed, how, they argue, can they be forced to accept the presently oriented document?

It is not altogether easy to answer this question, put in this way. And certainly, something must be conceded to the questioner of good will. It is perfectly true that the Pope's collaborators can be more liberal or more conservative in orientation. Indeed, the same could be said of Popes themselves. Hence, certain inevitable emphases will be reflected in what they write or in the manner in which they express themselves.

At this point, however, ends the comfort which the so-called "Catholic Right" can draw from the above consideration. For the collaborators of a Pope, whether liberal or conservative, would certainly know that a corpus of Catholic social doctrine exists. And this body of doctrine necessarily channels and confines whatever line their individual conservative or liberal tendencies might seek to take.

Moreover, as one whose life work has been the assimilation and the teaching of Catholic social doctrine, I can say with absolute certainty that *no* collaborators Pope John might have turned to—European or American or other—could have or would have prepared an encyclical that would be acceptable to the editors of the *National Review.*

An Appeal for
Christian Unity

Robert Pell

THAT distinguished lawyer and businessman, Myron C. Taylor, who dedicated his latter years to
diplomacy in the highest sense of the term, has
quietly "set sail," as he was wont to say, "for that other
shore." He has left behind with those who knew him
and worked with him memories of unflagging loyalty
to principles and men, of tireless devotion to what he
conceived to be his duty and his unquenchable Christian faith. I had the privilege of working with Ambassador Taylor from 1938, when I was assigned by
President Roosevelt as his Assistant at the Evian Conference on Political Refugees, until he left public life
in 1950 upon resigning as the Personal Representative
of the President of the United States to His Holiness the
Pope. I can think of many episodes which would illustrate his high qualities, but none more poignant than
his conversations in 1948 with leading churchmen to
promote unity—among Christians and others who believe in God—in the face of the mounting threat of international atheism and materialism, and in the interest
of peace.

Early in 1948 President Harry S. Truman decided

that the time had come to appeal for the cooperation of the religious forces of the world to resist communism and turn the influence of all those who believed in God toward the positive preservation of peace. The President had held informal preparatory exchanges to this end with Pope Pius XII through the mediation of Mr. Taylor. He had discussed this "thought," as it was regularly described, with Protestant leaders, notably Bishop G. Bromley Oxnam and Dr. Samuel McCrea Cavert. He had consulted outstanding Jewish personalities and was in communication with Muslim leaders.

By March of 1948, the President decided that the time had come to translate his "thought" into action. Accordingly, he called Ambassador Taylor to the White House in the week of March 20 for talks about his plan. This review of the possibilities led to the President's decision to send Mr. Taylor on a "voyage of exploration," in which the Ambassador would discuss the President's "thought" with the outstanding churchmen of the Christian world. Then, if agreement could be reached among Christians on a simple, positive formula, others who believed in God would be brought into the conversations. Accordingly, on March 23, President Truman gave Mr. Taylor a commission appointing him as his Personal Representative, with the rank of Ambassador, for these exploratory conversations. At Mr. Taylor's request, the President designated me to accompany Mr. Taylor, with the rank of Minister.

At once, Mr. Taylor set off for his post at Rome, as his point of departure, by way of Lisbon and Madrid.

In Lisbon, Mr. Taylor conferred at length with the Catholic Patriarch of Lisbon, Cardinal Emanuel Gonçalves Cerejeira, to whom were confided the revelations of the three children who had the vision at Fatima. On the basis of these revelations, the Cardinal was confident that the tide of godless communism would recede when faith was restored in the Christian world. Mr. Taylor, fortified by the Cardinal's confidence, then flew to Madrid where, at the suggestion of highly situated persons in the Vatican, he had an appointment to meet Cardinal Pedro Segura y Saenz, Archbishop of Seville, who was reported to be unbending with regard to any contact between the Catholic Church and the Protestants.

Ambassador Taylor met Cardinal Segura in the Episcopal Palace in Madrid, with Cardinal Pla y Deniel, Archbishop of Toledo and Primate of Spain, acting as host. The ensuing conversations between Ambassador Taylor and the Cardinal were on a high plane of objectivity, although it was clear that Cardinal Segura had serious doubts about the feasibility of joint action by Catholics and Protestants. Nevertheless, he seemed to be won to sympathize with Mr. Taylor's moving message in behalf of President Truman. Those of us who were present concluded that, at the very least, the Cardinal would not raise his voice in opposition to the President's appeal to the conscience of the world.

Thereupon, Mr. Taylor continued his flight to Rome, which he reached on April 4. The next day he visited the Vatican for a protracted review of the President's "thought" with Pope Pius. Mr. Taylor carried a brief, courteous letter from the President, but the main body of the message was oral, developed at some length by Mr. Taylor in a series of meetings with His Holiness, which took place on the balcony outside Pope Pius' private apartments.

Pope Pius XII was not only favorable to President Truman's "thought," but was prepared to support it in a letter to the President. This letter His Holiness handed to Mr. Taylor some days later, and it was considered by experts with a broad knowledge of Vatican practice and history as unusually liberal. Moreover, His Holiness gave Mr. Taylor permission to show a copy of the letter to other Christian leaders in the course of his exploratory tour.

President Truman thereupon directed the Commander-in-Chief in Germany to place his "Potsdam plane" at the disposal of Mr. Taylor. The Ambassador took off from Rome in the second week in April—I was with him and so was Miss Bushwaller, his confidential secretary—with Geneva as the first stop.

PROTESTANT REACTIONS

The object of Ambassador Taylor's visit to Geneva was to confer with the Provisional Executive Committee of the World Council of [Protestant] Churches, notably with Mr. Visser 't Hooft, its secretary. Immediately upon our arrival in Geneva Mr. Taylor sent me to notify Mr. 't Hooft that he wished to confer with the members of the executive committee on a matter of grave importance affecting the Christian world, and an appointment was arranged for the same afternoon. The American Consul General had advised the committee previously that Mr. Taylor would come to Geneva on a special mission, so that the Ambassador's arrival was not altogether unexpected. At all events, Mr. 't Hooft stressed to me that the committee was committed irrevocably to the principle of the separation of Church and State. For that reason it could not receive Mr. Taylor as the representative of a temporal sovereign. The members of the committee, as a courtesy, would talk with him, however, as a prominent Episcopalian layman who had important things to say.

At the appointed hour, Mr. Taylor and I presented ourselves at the headquarters of the executive committee. At the gate we were met by a spokesman for that austere body who repeated once more that the committee would not receive Mr. Taylor as the representative of a temporal sovereign. However, the members would be pleased to talk with Mr. Taylor in his capacity as a prominent Anglican, or Episcopal, layman. Mr. Taylor agreed to these terms and was ushered into the Council Chamber, where he was received coldly but with dignity and seated in a stiff-backed chair— I beside him.

Ambassador Taylor then outlined his mission, stressing the vital importance of union among Christians in the cause of world peace, threatened as they were by international atheism and materialism, and urging agreement on a positive statement of their intention of standing together under the banner of Christ. The members of the committee who were present heard Mr. Taylor through politely but without comment. However, they declined to read his Commission from the President or the copy of the letter which he carried from Pope Pius. Indeed, Secretary 't Hooft suggested that a wiser approach would be for the Protestant Churches to come together in the first instance with the President's "thought" in mind. Then, when they had agreed on a formula, approaches might be made to the Orthodox and Roman Catholic Churches. The secretary of the executive committee observed, moreover, that the Protestant Churches were planning to meet in the near future in Ecumenical Conference at Amsterdam. This would be the appropriate place and time to give further consideration to the possibilities of cooperation of the religious and moral forces of the world. He stressed, however, that this meeting would be held completely free from all governmental pressures. There would be no place at Amsterdam for Ambassadors or Personal Representatives of Heads of State. Mr. 't Hooft added that the World Council embraced over 150 Protestant communions in five continents. The Council, and as a consequence its proposed reunion at Amsterdam, was as inclusive as it had been possible to make it by several years of constant endeavor. There did not seem to be any possibility of widening its membership and scope at that late hour, despite Mr. Taylor's appeal to make the meeting inclusive of all Christianity.

I should like to take this opportunity to underscore that Mr. Taylor did not propose on this occasion, as some publications suggested later, that he should go to Amsterdam. Nor did he try to complicate "with the apparatus of diplomacy" what had already been accomplished. He confined his presentation to a solemn and very fervent appeal for contact between *all* Christian leaders, and those who believed in God, in the interest of peace and in defense against the inroads of international godlessness. He urged that this action be taken before it was too late.

From Geneva Mr. Taylor flew to London for a conversation with the Archbishop of Canterbury, Dr. Geoffrey Fisher, in his capacity as head, under the sovereign, of the English State Church. The Archbishop, accompanied by a Coadjutor and an Under Secretary of State at the Foreign Office, joined Mr. Taylor at luncheon in a private dining room at Claridge's Hotel. Dr. Fisher was most cordial but at the same time most cautious. He read President Truman's Commission without comment and expressed pleasure with Pope Pius' letter, which he read over twice. He indicated that the President's initiative was worthy of careful consideration, but indicated that there might be obstacles. However, they could be overcome, and he gave Mr. Taylor his full blessing and expressed the hope that his mission would lead to a concrete result. He would give much earnest consideration and prayer to President Truman's "thought" and would remain in contact with Mr. Taylor through diplomatic channels.

Paris was Mr. Taylor's next destination, where the ground had been prepared for conversations with Pastor Boegner, speaking for the French Protestant, or Huguenot, Church. Mr. Taylor sent me to sound out the Pastor preparatory to a meeting, and I found him far from conciliatory. Indeed, at first he was not sure that it would be possible for him to meet Mr. Taylor at all. Finally, with marked reluctance, he agreed to lunch with Mr. Taylor in a private dining room at the Ritz Hotel. However, he said over and over again that he could not see his way to coming to agreement with the Vatican and that the only form of cooperation which was conceivable, or desirable, was that based on a reaffirmation of their faith by the Protestant Churches, with which the Orthodox Churches might be associated, including the Patriarch of Moscow.

In any event, Pastor Boegner kept his luncheon date with Mr. Taylor, but merely reiterated his previous position. He was uncompromising with regard to co-operation with the Catholic Church, and those who were present could not help recalling the stand taken some weeks previously in Madrid by the Archbishop of Seville. They hoped, moreover, that the Pastor would unbend as far as the Archbishop had.

Finally, Mr. Taylor asked the Pastor point blank if he was to regard the statement of his views as closing the door to any form of further conversation with regard to President Truman's "thought." The Pastor replied that Mr. Taylor might consider his statement in that light. Mr. Taylor, a final time, asked Pastor Boegner to hold the door open at least a cranny while he continued further explorations, but the Pastor replied that he could not in all conscience do this. At least he would interpose no obstacle during the early stages of the talks and would be interested to hear how they progressed. The following day Mr. Taylor wrote Pastor Boegner, renewing his appeal. The Pastor replied with a letter firmly closing the door to further exchanges.

Thereafter, Mr. Taylor met in Paris with representatives of the German and Scandinavian Lutheran Churches. They were less obdurate than Pastor Boegner, but cannot be said to have been encouraging. The Ambassador also talked with the new Patriarch of Constantinople, Athenagoras I, an American citizen who had been obliged to assume Turkish nationality in order to take possession of his see. He was on his way to Constantinople and was most gracious in his meeting with Mr. Taylor. He expressed profound interest in the conversations initiated by President Truman, al-

214

though he stressed most honestly that he foresaw that many obstacles would have to be overcome. For instance, he must not break irrevocably with the Patriarch of Moscow.

REPORTING TO WASHINGTON

It was now June, and Mr. Taylor believed that he should make a full report to President Truman before entering upon a further phase of the conversations. Above all, Mr. Taylor wished to avoid anything which might appear to be a break. Accordingly, he suggested to the President that it might be wise to have a breathing spell, while emotions cooled. The groundwork had been laid. The Amsterdam Conference of the Protestant Church would be opening shortly. It might be well to wait and see what transpired there. Later, when the atmosphere was more propitious and there was a greater possibility of reaching a concrete accord, the conversations might be resumed and further considerations given to President Truman's "thought."

Mr. Taylor thereupon prepared a lengthy report for the President, to which he joined the memoranda of all his conversations and such documents as might be useful as background. Mr. Taylor instructed me to fly to Washington with this report and place it directly in the hands of the President. He would return to Rome, the seat of his Embassy, from where he could piece together the various skeins and threads of his preliminary talks. Moreover, Mr. Taylor directed me to go to Washington via London, where I was to send word to the Archbishop of Canterbury through the Foreign Office of what had transpired.

I reached Washington, after completing my mission in London, on June 13. On the 15th I went through what was then called "the State Department passage" to the White House and placed Mr. Taylor's report in President Truman's hands. Three days of deliberation followed, and on June 18 the President handed me a letter which he instructed me to deliver personally to Mr. Taylor in Rome. In his letter, Mr. Truman, after congratulating Mr. Taylor on the manner in which he

215

had conducted his delicate mission, agreed that the conversations should be suspended for a time. He said it was deplorable that the Amsterdam Conference would embrace only a section of Christendom and re-affirmed that both State and Church had a solemn obligation to man the parapets of Christian civilization.

In the meantime, plans for the Conference of the Protestant Churches at Amsterdam had been completed. It had been announced, moreover, that invitations had been extended to leaders of the Orthodox Churches. Indeed, it has been especially stressed that these invitations had included one to the Patriarch of Moscow, who had accepted. Finally, the Congregation of the Holy Office on June 5 had warned Catholics that they would not be permitted to attend the meeting. Every day the prospects of agreement among the leaders of Christendom seemed to be more remote. Nevertheless, in the thinking of Mr. Taylor, with which I understand President Truman agreed, the conversations were merely suspended. At some time in the future they would be carried forward from the point where Mr. Taylor, to his profound disappointment and undying regret, left off.

In conclusion, it is my duty to stress that Ambassador Myron C. Taylor's negotiation in the spring of 1948, seeking unity among Christians in the interest of the preservation of peace, was conceived in the highest idealism and carried out step by step with profound sincerity. Mr. Taylor spoke as one modest, faithful Christian to other Christians, in moving, simple language straight from his heart. He tried earnestly to lift the conversations from the slough of politics. He offered modestly to serve as a simple workman in building even one bridge to cross the ravines which separated the churches. He strove mightily to help them find together a few positive words to express their unity in the interest of peace and in their rejection of international godlessness. He may have seemed to falter at one split second in the eternal course of history. But surely Mr. Truman's message, and Mr. Taylor's, still and small though it may seem amid the thunder of jets and missiles, lives on. It is not yet too late to heed it. But it may be, very soon.

A Catholic-Protestant Conversation

Thomas F. Stransky, C.S.P.,

and Claud D. Nelson

 STRANSKY: Dr. Nelson, would you please tell me something about the response of non-Catholic Christians to the fact that the Catholic Church is going to hold an ecumenical council?

NELSON: Well, Father, there was the in-evitable first reaction of surprise, a second reaction of gratification, and perhaps, in the first few weeks, a certain amount of over-optimism, particularly since the question of unity and even of union was on the lips of so many who spoke about the council. My own re-actions were—"well, it's about time!" And then: "What will come of it?" In a word, profound encouragement and limited expectations. These reactions have not changed substantially. The fact of the council—the fact that Pope John feels the need of a council and sees the possibility of something constructive from its work—remains an event of fundamental importance.

STRANSKY: What do you mean by "It's about time"?

NELSON: The discouragement of non-Catholics by what was done in the unfinished council of nearly 100 years ago has been profound and, of course, prolonged. My impression of the First Vatican Council is one of fellow-Christians outside being completely ignored. If anything can be done to lighten that darkness, it is important that it be done, particularly since we are in a period when Christian unity, not only in a spiritual and emotional sense, but in a practical and co-operative sense, is certainly more important than it has ever been.

STRANSKY: Pope John hopes to lighten that darkness you speak about. So often he stresses the necessity of bringing the Church up-to-date—of an *aggiornamento.* If the council can clarify some of the doctrines misunderstood by non-Catholics, if it can inspire a more intensified Christian life among Catholics, and modernize many of the Church's external disciplines, I am sure the Catholic Church's image will become clearer to our separated brethren.

That, after all, is the best task the Church can perform at this stage of the ecumenical movement. Neither the Protestants, the Orthodox—nor, I'm afraid, Roman Catholics—are prepared for a "reunion" council, with the hope of reaching some general agreement.

Our council is a domestic affair. Yet, in its preparations, the Secretariat for Promoting Christian Unity is trying to help guide the council's theological and pastoral decisions in such a way as to aid our separated brethren to see the Church as the Church believes herself to be.

Furthermore, the very fact that there will be a council shows that the Church is conscious of its many imperfections on the human side and is, therefore, conscious of the need for much self-purification.

NELSON: I would like to underline one of your comments and to express deep gratification over another. Even those Protestants (and I believe also Eastern Orthodox) who are engaged actively in ecumenical or unity movements, apart from Rome, are certainly not ready to discuss union with Rome. They are not yet aware of what they must do to unify themseves, Protestants with Protestants, Protestants with Orthodox.

But it seems to me that the Roman Catholic confession of humility in the face of our human imperfections and of the situation of our divided churches is one of the surest and most necessary signs of an ecumenical spirit. Its very expression, both by the Pope's calling of the council, as you said, and by statements of other persons in positions of responsibility, draws us together in a way that an older attitude—one that sometimes has seemed to be self-satisfaction, almost arrogance—assuredly did not do.

 It seems to me that the calling of the council is not only a factor in the development toward Christian unity, but it also gives evidence that the time is ripe for some actual advance in that direction.

I think of all the signs within the Roman Church: the fact that two former Popes have either thought of calling a council or have been urged to do so; I think of the creation of the World Council of Churches and similar councils of smaller scope over the last fifty years; then there is the new surge toward unity within Orthodoxy. All this together indicates that the Holy Spirit is working among many, many Christians.

I wonder to what extent you would connect this movement of the Holy Spirit and the widespread movement toward Christian unity with renewed interest in the Bible?

STRANSKY: It is always difficult, often presumptuous, to trace God's handwriting in specific historical events. Yet, as I read the Holy Office's Letter on the Ecumenical Movement (1949), I don't think it presumptuous of the Catholic Church to see the workings of the Holy Spirit both in the mood of non-Catholic Christians and in Catholic desires and efforts to promote Christian unity.

Christ works through the Holy Spirit, and one can hear Christ's voice and feel the breath of His Spirit in the growing and ever firmer conviction that a divided Christianity is against Christ's will and a scandal, and that His prayer "that all may be one" is also a command for our own prayers and actions.

NELSON: Consider the biblical revival. The Bible, after all, is the Book of all us Christians, and by searching into God's mind and will as revealed in the Bible, Catholics better understand not only themselves but their separated brethren.

Catholic and non-Catholic biblical scholars are following more closely and more objectively each other's exegetical work (which, in large part, is itself becoming more objective). For example, recent studies on the Epistle to the Romans prove to be a fruitful ground for discussions with Protestants, for around that epistle, as we know, centered much of the Reformation theology of Luther, Calvin and Melancthon. And a developing biblical theology—expressing doctrine in biblical categories—finds closer rapprochement with Eastern theology.

STRANSKY: Interestingly enough, Cardinal Bea, president of our Secretariat, had his first serious theological discussions with non-Catholics in the 1920's at congresses of biblical studies, meetings at which scholars of various confessions discussed their common Book on objective, scientific grounds.

NELSON: Indeed, we do well to bear in mind, with reference to Christ's prayer for unity, that our unity is not simply important in itself, as evidence of our faith—for our own reassurance, guidance and salvation. It is more than that. Jesus seems to have held it as indispensable evidence to the non-believer. Only if we are united will the world believe that He was sent by the Father.

STRANSKY: The division of Christianity certainly makes it very difficult for the rest of the world to believe. It is a tragedy that we have had to pass through this bitter experience of history in order to prove Christ's words.

NELSON: The experience of Protestants bears you out. It is the missionaries who have been most eloquent and most impressive in saying that a divided Christianity cannot bear effective witness among those who have never heard of Christ. In fact, most Protestants date the concrete beginnings of the modern ecumenical movement from the International Missionary Congress in 1910 at Edinburgh. At first there was concern only for correcting the scandal caused by diverse mission methods, but soon Protestant missionaries had to face honestly the blunt judgment of Bishop Brent of Edinburgh: the division of the churches is itself the fundamental cause of the scandal.

STRANSKY: From another angle, I would like to paraphrase a remark of Bishop Newbigin, General Secretary of the International Missionary Council. It is not surprising to the non-Christian, he said, that Christians are concerned with promoting Christian unity; what is surprising is that they are *content* to be divided.

NELSON: One of the things I am sure many Protestants would hope will be encouraged by the council is more sustained and intelligent activity on the part of laymen. My own experience has been largely through the Y.M.C.A. Surely, the work of laymen in the Y.M.C.A., which is not necessarily nor exclusively Protestant, indicates how laymen may be effective in the Christian cause, without interfering in any way with ecclesiastical prerogatives and responsibilities.

 STRANSKY: When Pope Pius XII said that "the Church *is* the laity," I suspected many Catholics, including priests, were shocked that a Pope could sound so "Protestant." The statement implies that the very authority Christ gives to Pope,

bishop and priest is given that they may act under the
same title the Pope has assumed for centuries—"servant
of the servants of God." And the laymen—the servants
of God—have a specific role to play in the Church's
mission to the world—something far more than supply-
ing for the lack of priests.

Just what the layman's role is, and its consequences
in modern pastoral practices—well, the council will
handle that, through the Theological Commission, the
Commission for the Lay Apostolate and our own Secretariat.

But no matter what the council decides, I hope that
non-Catholics, as well as Catholics, will be patient. It's
hard enough to teach a small child to walk without
stumbling, and it is much more difficult to teach that
full-grown giant of a child—the laity—to take his first
mature steps. Furthermore, many of the laity's au-
thorized teachers—bishops and priests—are not yet
mature enough in this field to guide them. We are still
in the era of *talking about* the laity, surely not yet in
the era of the laity. And it will take a long time, I fear,
before the whole Church will work out, in practice,
the layman's apostolate.

The council would issue only guiding principles on
the layman's role. It will not decree their minute applications, for that depends on the varied circumstances
of nation, diocese, parish, etc. Even then, conciliar
decrees require a long time before their implications
filter into the conscious spiritual life and activity of
the Church's members. (Look how long it took for the
Council of Trent's decrees on seminary training to
shape a somewhat uniform practice throughout the
world!)

Yet, this "filtering process" can be hurried along if
every Catholic—not just the Pope and the bishops who
will gather in Rome—considers the calling of the council as a summons to the whole Church to commence a
vast spiritual retreat. As we prepare for it, our prayers
should be for the enlightened guidance of those who
will formulate and approve the council's conclusions,
and for all the laity, priests, religious and bishops, that
they may accept these conclusions in faith and love, and

live them and practice them, in that same faith and love.

NELSON: Is it foreseeable that after the council more Catholic laymen will feel competent and confident enough to engage in dialogue about religious matters with their Protestant neighbors who are willing and interested?

STRANSKY: The Council will try to make the layman more conscious of his duty and privilege of witnessing the Catholic faith by word and action. Of course, no matter what his competency, the U.S. layman must challenge that prevalent and enigmatic commandment of the American way of life, namely, that religion is not a topic for conversation. Besides, a layman is often afraid to talk about his faith because he doesn't trust his own information. Many non-Catholics have been referred to me by Catholic laymen; the issues raised in those conversations have been so simple that I failed to see why the average Catholic could not have answered them on his own, in his own language, and in the circumstances which provoked the questions originally.

As for serious dialogue, we have some very competent laymen. Often the layman can do much better than a priest in discussing Christian issues in the educational, political, social and economic fields. There he earns his daily bread and butter, and, if observant, he is quite conscious of their religious implications.

NELSON: My reference to "dialogue" probably put too much emphasis on its formal aspects. Of course, I think that's where we are at the present moment. "Dialogue," however, is also the proper word for that natural spontaneous conversation which ought to take place whenever Christian brethren—laymen or priests—have occasion to discuss common problems, or simply to meet and talk with each other. At present, however, in many, many cases, the occasion has to be created and even made formal before real conversation—any real dialogue, any truly attentive listening and honest speaking —can take place between Catholics and Protestants, at least in this country.

There must be a lot of casual, spontaneous conversation going on which is not recorded or formalized. I'm sure there is. However, I'm also sure that there are a good many Protestants who feel it really isn't worth while to talk with a Catholic layman, or perhaps even with a local priest, because they don't feel he is free. We feel that he is somehow restricted.

Sometimes that impression is due to what we read in the press, or in an encyclical meant for a certain specific situation, but we don't know which situation, and, therefore, read it as a general thing. I think of the common understanding of prohibitions for membership in the Y.M.C.A. or the Rotary Club, and also of the fact that there are areas where Catholics participate in the National Conference of Christians and Jews, and other areas where they do not.

 STRANSKY: Divine Truth is binding, and every Catholic, be he pope or layman, believes that Christ reveals His Word through His Church. In this sense, we are all "restricted" in what we believe. A Protestant who will talk to a Catholic layman or the local priest only if they are allowed to speak apart from the authority of the Church—well, he doesn't want to talk to a Catholic, but to a fellow-Protestant.

The authority of the Church is understandably a crucial, divisive issue between Roman Catholics and others. (Here I may mention that much of this problem of "Catholic authority," at least in America, is not theological but philosophical—what is authority and its relation to human liberty?)

Your mention of Catholic universal prohibitions is ticklish. Christian organizations, such as the Y.M.C.A. and the World Student Christian Federation are beginning to catch an ecumenical spirit to which Catholics could subscribe. I say "beginning to catch." How widespread this spirit is, how reflected it is in policy and action, requires much more honest and common study

225

by Catholic and non-Catholic authorities. The question for us will be whether or not universal prohibitions or approbations for Catholic memberships in such organizations are the most prudent and practical, or whether these decisions should be left up to local hierarchies.

Even a prohibition does not exclude all cooperation or dialogue. Last May at Louvain, I took part in a most fruitful discussion between thirty leaders of Pax Romana and the World Student Christian Federation on the provocative theme: "Technology and Christian Faith."

NELSON: You refer to certain practical fields—fields in which practical understanding and cooperation are necessary. Certainly we are agreed that conversation in such fields is necessary. Would you mention two or three of those fields and what specifically one ought to hope for from this coming council or within a short range of time?

STRANSKY: There are abundant opportunities for fruitful discussion and action, and they are already within reach, if we but open our eyes and catch an authentic ecumenical spirit. I think, first of all, of our mission lands. Faced with the increasing influence of communism and materialism, with the new problems of the scientific, economic and national revolutions, Christians as such in many African and Asian countries should realize their obligation to defend and promote their common deposit of truth and goods in the Christian patrimony. With all the shared social and political problems of a Christian minority, Christians can meet to discuss advisable ways and means of defending the fundamental principles of the natural law and the Christian religion and of re-establishing a sound social order.

What providential occasions for common discussion and much concrete cooperation are the relations we have as Christians with national governments and international organizations (e.g., Unesco, FAO); questions of mission schools and the religious orientation of public schools; questions of racism, just wages, the dignity of marriage and womanhood; problems of over-population, urbanization, immigration, alcoholism, etc.

Then there are the more properly theological issues that must be discussed together: Church-State rela-tions, religious tolerance, false proselytism, catechetics and liturgical worship, mixed marriages, the question of a common Bible translation, problems confronting the personal and social life of Christian ministers and priests, etc. Of course, you can see that most of these problems are not confined to the mission lands.

What can the council do? The 1949 Holy Office Let-ter on Ecumenism recommended the lines of action I've already mentioned. Such cooperation is implied, too, in Pope John's latest encyclical, *Mater et Magistra.* I doubt whether the council should do anything more than reinforce and clarify these general principles. Then it will be up to the local churches or international organizations to work out the details.

 NELSON: We've been speaking of dia-logue, and certainly one of the things we both hope will be encouraged by the council is the mutual respect, confidence, trust and tolerance between Catholics and non-Catholics, which is in one sense a condition of Christian conversation.

It seems to me that a very important foundation in the field of tolerance was laid by Pope Pius XII when —without recognizing the religious pluralism which exists, not only within countries but internationally (I mean what we call Christian pluralism)—without rec-ognizing it ecclesiastically—the Pope indicated to Cath-olic statesmen, in Catholic countries, that they must respect it as a political fact.

That statement seems to me to have represented, at least in the attitude toward Protestants, a change in policy, not in doctrine, which may be very significant. I have been encouraged to hear Cardinal Bea say, and others not usually thought of as being quite so ecumenical-minded as the Cardinal, that the council will not go back on that change of direction, will not reverse it.

Would you have further comments in this whole field of religious liberty, particularly as to how the activities of the Secretariat for Promoting Christian Unity are affecting and may affect mutual respect and tolerance and, in a civic sense, the protection of religious liberty?

STRANSKY: Yes. The Secretariat itself, as well as its members throughout the world, have been receiving so many similar questions, that I am convinced that Catholic relations with other Christian communities cannot be securely founded until a Catholic doctrine of tolerance is fully developed.

A growing school of Catholic theologians is pleading for more than a "policy change," that is, for a deepening and development of our doctrine. Such a doctrine of tolerance cannot be based on mere social or political expedience, or on the intellectual abstraction that "error has no right," but rather on the nature of human liberty itself and of divine faith. Of course, we cannot foresee how much time the council will spend on the question, or what it will decide.

NELSON: It seems to me that we have to realize—and we are beginning to realize quite generally—that tolerance, religious liberty, is something not conceded, either by the person who has power, or the person who has truth, to one who, in his opinion, does not have truth and who obviously does not have power. There is a mutuality about Christian tolerance which is essential to it.

In the various fields of which we have been speaking it seems to me that the creation of the Secretariat for Promoting Christian Unity and what it has done so far are of tremendous significance. For one thing, it has made possible two-way conversation. Indeed, without too much hesitation as to who speaks first, such conversations are going on between groups assembled jointly. For example, these conversations are being held between the World Council of Churches and the Secretariat. The mutuality we've been speaking of certainly exists in these encounters. This is very desirable.

I can think of nothing more significant likely to come out of the Council than the encouragement and development of the Secretariat and the process which it typifies. It seems to me to represent a willingness to talk on the part of Roman Catholics, which heretofore has not been evident, or so officially evident, one might say. This is so necessary if we are ever to arrive at a practical Christian unity.

STRANSKY: All I can say to that is that the Council itself will determine if and how the Secretariat should continue as a permanent official organ in the Church. But even as it stands now, the Secretariat gives witness that the Church is taking an official position on the dialogue. We treat our separated brethren more as *brethren* than as "separated"—not as adversaries to be conquered, but as brothers who ask questions that deserve an answer.

The short experience of the Secretariat has already shown how the Holy Spirit speaks to us Catholics through our separated brethren in many of their criticisms of the Church of 1961. As a Catholic, I believe that the Roman Catholic Church is the Church of Christ. Her structure cannot change. But, as Pope John has said, we should try to eliminate as much as possible the human obstacles that obstruct the work of showing the Church to be what she is. Many non-Catholic Christian criticisms, positive and negative, that have been received by the Secretariat, have given us a clearer insight into what these obstacles are.

Pope John has asked us Catholics not to rest until we have overcome old habits of thought, our old prejudices, the use of expressions that are anything but courteous. Thus, we are to try to create a climate favorable to the reconciliation to which we look forward. Thus, too, we must strive to cooperate with the work of grace.

The union of all Christians in the Church of Christ

will be a work of God's grace. If and when He will work His wonder, I do not know. But this I do know: we must begin now, in a very humble and patient way, to prepare for His gift. I hope you and all the rest of our separated brethren may look on our council as just a step in this preparation. So pray for us. I know you will.

NELSON: As you must for us. *Fiat Voluntas Dei!*

In the view of Teilhard de Chardin, evolution became self-conscious in man and the vital process ultimately converges toward a sort of divine togetherness which he called the Omega Point. We will let Mother Church judge the validity of this challenging synthesis of the phenomenon of man. But there is no doubt about our human heritage under God's providence and revelation. He is our Father. We are His children, born spiritually from the loins of Abraham. We must love not only Him, but all those who bear His image. One can wonder at the quality of that neighborly love, when he weighs our attitudes toward the poor, or even when he thinks about our treatment of criminals. Yes, man has come a long way from his origins, but he is still a far distance from any conceivable Omega Point.

All God's Children

Ethics at the
Shelter Doorway

L. C. McHugh
S.J.

T HE AMERICAN people are burrowing underground
in a grassroots movement for survival; the shelter business is booming. Civil defense officials
have already noted that many citizens are very furtive
about building a modest haven in the cellar or yard.
The more secret the nuclear hideaway, the less likely
they are to be troubled by panicky neighbors at the
shelter door when the bombs start falling.

Some rugged householders are not banking on mere
secrecy to insure their families a fair chance of survival.
Time, on August 18, cited a Chicago suburbanite who
intended to mount a machine gun at his shelter in order
to keep unwelcome strangers out, and it also quoted a
Texas businessman who was ready to evict unbidden
guests with tear gas if any such occupied his shelter
before his family did. Inevitably, *Time* raised the question: what do the guardians of the Christian ethic have
to say about the pros and cons of gunning one's neighbor at the shelter door? *Time* got some strange answers

in its brief clerical poll, and one was rather remarkable:

> If someone wanted to use the shelter, then you
> yourself should get out and let him use it. That's
> not what would happen, but that's the strict Chris-
> tian application.

I cannot accept that statement as it stands. It argues
that we must love our neighbor, not as ourselves, but
more than ourselves. It implies that the Christian law
runs counter to the instinct of self-preservation that is
written in the human frame. If I am right, then the
American people need more than blueprints for shelter
construction. They also need a little instruction in the
grim guidelines of essential morality at the shelter
hatchway. Are there any moral constants that apply
when unprepared or merely luckless neighbors and
strangers start milling around the sanctuary where you
and your family have built a refuge against atomic fire,
blast and fallout?

This aspect of nuclear warfare has received no attention, but its relevant principles were the common
property of Catholic moralists long before Hiroshima.
They are generally treated under the discussion of what
kind of activity is permissible when one's life is under
attack. These principles are worth reviewing, if only to
show that sound Christian morality does not solve
moral problems by appeal to sentiment, but by the cold
light of reason.

Each of us has a natural right to life and the essential goods, such as liberty and food, without which life
is brutish—or impossible.

The right to life and its equivalent goods is a curtain
of inviolability drawn around the human personality.
But if that curtain is torn aside by unreasonable interference with one's freedom, nature still provides a
second line of defense against injustice. This is the right
to use violence as a last resort or emergency measure
for securing the just needs of the human person. This
right to employ violence, which the moralists call "coactivity," is a *limited* grant of power, just like the rights
for whose protection it is given. Nobody enjoys unlimited rights, simply because no human being can have

unlimited needs.

Working from this basis, Catholic moralists teach that the use of violence to defend life and its equivalent goods is justifiable, when certain conditions are met, even if the violent defense entails the death of the aggressor. It will be very enlightening to reflect on what these conditions are.

1. The situation is such that violence is the last available recourse of the aggrieved party. Either you take desperate action now or, in your best judgment, you are going to be done in.

2. The violence used is employed at the time of assault. It is not vengeance for a deed already done, neither is it a preventive against a merely projected assault. The violence is leveled against an attack which, in the prudent estimation of the victim, has been actually initiated. How is one to determine that an attack upon one's life has truly begun? Sometimes the intent to work deadly harm is obvious, as when a known killer runs at me with a drawn gun or an unsheathed knife. But this is not always the case. In the actual circumstances of life, a man under assault has no time for academic niceties. He is not a logical machine but an excited and harried individual. He cannot be blamed if his use of violent defense is based on nothing more than a quick and honest judgment that he will suffer most grievous harm unless he resists promptly.

3. The third condition is that the violence is employed against an attack that is unjust. In other words, the violence is used to ward off an unwarranted invasion of one's undoubted rights. In the technical vocabulary of moralists, the assailant is called an unjust aggressor, but the term refers to an objective situation, not to a state of soul. The delirious madman who thrusts at me with a rapier may be incapable of moral guilt at the moment, but his invasion of my basic immunities is as objectively unjust as if he were a paid emissary of Murder, Inc.

4. Finally, when one uses violence to defend his essential rights, he may employ no more violence than is needed to protect himself. Coactivity is thus a marginal grant, strictly tailored to the end it serves. Moral-

ists have argued for centuries whether this grant ever allows one to intend the death of his adversary. We do not need to resolve this scholastic dispute here. What moralists agree on is that a man under grave attack may take those emergency measures which will effectively terminate the assault, even if they include the death of the assailant. Moreover, common sense tells us that men under attack seldom have a nice discrimination of weapons to employ in self-defense. They must use the means at hand, rough and ready as they are. Unless they use them in the surest way, they are likely to come out on the worse end of an unequal contest.

So much for the general conditions that cover the use of violence in defense of life. Two more observations are very much in order before the picture is complete.

To say that one has the right to employ violence in defense of life is not to say that one has the duty to do so. Indeed, in the Christian view, there is great merit in turning the other cheek and bearing evils patiently out of the love of God. But it should be noted that people who consistently manifest this exalted brand of supernatural motivation are deservedly called heroic Christians. Their conduct reveals a dedication to the full Christian ethic that is far above what God requires under pain of eternal loss in the way of the Ten Commandments. Nowhere in traditional Catholic morality does one read that Christ, in counseling nonresistance to evil, rescinded the right of self-defense which is granted by nature and recognized in the legal system of all nations.

Again, we must observe that because of special responsibilities the individual bears to other members of society, circumstances may easily arise in which it is positively immoral to turn the other cheek: one may have a positive duty to employ violence in his own behalf and/or for the sake of others. Secret Service agents are bound in justice not to bear ills patiently when the President is set upon by assassins. So, too, a well-armed hunter who surprises three hoodlums attacking a lonely woman in the forest cannot absolve his grave and obvious duty in charity with a shocked "tsk-tsk" and a resolution to inform the State police when he gets to the nearest telephone. . . . More relevant to our immediate interest, we ought to note that the father of a family is tied to his wife and children by bonds of both love and justice. His every normal instinct prompts him to nourish and protect his dependents. He cannot carelessly squander their essential welfare for the needy stranger and call this irresponsibility an act of charity. He may not idly stand by while his brood is robbed of what is necessary for life and then explain that his cowardice is actually a wholehearted obedience to the Biblical injunction to overcome evil by good.

I think that this review of some constants in the general morality of human survival has an obvious relevance to the questions that are raised in the mind of the cautious householder when he thinks about building a family shelter, and wonders how he can insure its availability, in the moment of greatest need, for those in whose behalf it was intended. But I would prefer that every man apply the principles to his own set of circumstances, although I am not averse to setting out a few practical norms that I think would be broadly acceptable to Catholic teachers of morality.

What is your family shelter? It is more than a piece of property that should be secure against trespass. It is a property of a most vital kind. When the bombs start falling, it is likely to be the one material good in your family's environment which is equivalent to life itself. The shelter is your ultimate line of defense against fire, blast, radiation and residual fallout. Moreover, because of its strictly limited resources (space, food, medical supplies, etc.), its use must be carefully regulated if it is to guarantee even marginal opportunity for survival over a protracted period. If you go underground with just one occupant above the maximum number for which the shelter was designed, the survival value of the shelter diminishes for all that take refuge in it.

If a man builds a shelter for his family, then it is the family that has the first right to use it. The right becomes empty if a misguided charity prompts a pitying householder to crowd his haven to the hatch in the hour of peril; for this conduct makes sure that no one will survive. And I consider it the height of nonsense to say that the Christian ethic demands or even permits a man to thrust his family into the rain of fallout when unsheltered neighbors plead for entrance. On the other hand, I doubt that any Catholic moralist would condemn the man who used available violence to repel panicky aggressors plying crowbars at the shelter door, or who took strong measures to evict trespassers who locked themselves in the family shelter before his own family had a chance to find sanctuary therein.

I shall even go so far as to offer a partial code of essential shelter morality. This will offend those who dread to think that the points could conceivably have serious bearing on human survival within the next few months. I am more interested, however, in finding what response such a code might have among readers and "guardians of the Christian ethic."

1. If you are an unattached individual and wish to yield your shelter space to others, God bless you. You can show no greater love for your neighbors.

2. Think twice before you rashly give your family shelter space to friends and neighbors or to the passing stranger. Do your dependents go along with this heroic self-sacrifice? If they do, and you have not yet built a shelter, don't bother to do so. Go next door and build one for your neighbor. In an emergency, he can take refuge there more quickly if it is on his own property instead of yours.

3. When you have sheltered your family, you may make a prudent judgment as to whether you may admit any others to your sanctuary without undue risk to the essential welfare of those who are most closely bound to you in justice and charity. It would be hard to

prove that you have any grave obligation to do so.

4. If you are already secured in your shelter and others try to break in, they may be treated as unjust aggressors and repelled with whatever means will effectively deter their assault. If others steal your family shelter space before you get there, you may also use whatever means will recover your sanctuary intact.

5. The careful husbandman who has no heroic aspirations will take precautions *now* so that his shelter will be available for those for whose safety it was built. If it is marginally equipped, it would be a normal exercise of prudence to conceal the entrance, if feasible, or make it inaccessible except to the members of the family. Does prudence also dictate that you have some "protective devices" in your survival kit, e.g. a revolver for breaking up traffic jams at your shelter door? That's for you to decide, in the light of your personal circumstances. But as Civil Defense Coordinator Keith Dwyer said in the *Time* story: "There's nothing in the Christian ethic which denies one's right to protect oneself and one's family."

—More on the Shelter Question—

MY ARTICLE on "Ethics at the Shelter Doorway" (9/30, p. 824) produced quite a bit of critical comment. This week's State of the Question (p. 288) reflects only a minute sampling of the varied reactions which greeted the article at home and abroad.

I grant that the article took a somewhat technical approach to a crisis of conscience that could arise for thousands of householders under thermonuclear attack, if our families had to rely, for survival, on the minimal protection offered by a do-it-yourself fallout shelter program.

Viewed in this light, my treatment of the principles of self-defense generated much emotional revulsion, especially among rabbis, Protestant clergymen and the gentle souls who make too simple appeals to the "unequivocal ethic" of the Sermon on the Mount.

Theologian Reinhold Niebuhr, for instance, said that I had given a "new and horrendous" twist to the shelter debate by "justifying the murder [sic] of anyone who dared to usurp" one's family refuge. Few indeed conceded, with Dr. Paul Ramsey of Princeton University, that my code of emergency morality might be the one to which we are impelled, "not by the cold light of reason, but by the warm light of Christian charity."

I do not apologize for the article, even though it posed some very unpleasant choices for a national community in panic and threatened with that shocking relaxation of normal social bonds which must be anticipated in any realistic forecast of thermonuclear war. Indeed, I am happy that my controversial discussion, by evoking the unwelcome thought that some of us may be driven to liquidating our neighbor even before Mr. Khrushchev's bombs can incinerate him, helped to highlight the essentially moral aspects of the Great Shelter Debate that is now engaging our attention.

For as *Look* will say in its December 5 issue (p. 21), "A moral debate with few parallels in American history is sweeping across the land. . . . Should every American prepare to claw his own hole in the ground in a lone effort to escape the lethal radiation of a possible nuclear war?"

The chief elements of this debate are well worth noting, and after following its development for more than a month, I believe they can be expressed in a series of rather excruciating questions:

■ Are all forms of fallout shelter a cruel governmental hoax foisted upon our people? Are they a fraudulent type of insurance against what must be an unbounded catastrophe? Does reliance on shelters encourage acceptance of nuclear war, even though such a war involves the death of civil society and the survival of no more than a barbarous tribe of mutants for whom life is short, brutish and raw? It is amazing how many people, paralyzed by despair and the fear that any nuclear war must end in the total ruin of all that they value, greet every proposed shelter program with the cry: "Noah's Ark? Include me out!"

■ Are all shelter precautions "immoral" because they either siphon off the energies that should be devoted wholeheartedly to the search for peace, or because they upset some delicate "balance of terror" and thereby bring on the inevitable holocaust that must terminate the open-ended arms race? Many are expressing the perilous view that a vote for shelters is a vote for nuclear war.

■ Is the family shelter in particular an immoral device, because it puts survival on a competitive basis that favors the affluent and leaves the poor with nothing more than the hope of seeing God sooner? Again and again, in the shelter debate, the note is sounded that private indulgence of the instinct of self-preservation is not just un-Christian but subhuman, and that the people who build private shel-

240

ters are an inferior breed who cannot possess the pioneer virtues that would be needed on the radioactive frontiers of a post-Armageddon Era.

■ If shelters do give some assurance that we can maximize human survival in a moderate nuclear assault, or at least insure the continuance of a germinal community after a saturation attack, then where does the primary duty of building shelters lie? Is a vast investment in community shelters, planned and controlled by government, the only program that can be reconciled with the demands of distributive justice? Many are talking as though shelter construction is an unjust and discriminative prescription for survival, unless it shows a common effort to meet the common defense—something that sounds suspiciously like saying that until Uncle Sam controls the weather, one cannot buy an umbrella without doing an injury to his neighbors.

THESE ISSUES are of pressing importance. Their universality far transcends the narrow problem to which my recent article was addressed, and the confusion that exists about them calls loudly for informed discussion, especially if, in the uncertain years ahead, shelters, like indoor plumbing, must become part of our way of life.

So far, we have had little more than emotional reactions to the rationale of what may come to be called the Subterranean Society. For that matter, the Administration has not yet developed a meaningful shelter policy, although it is four months since the President took note of the urgency of the present crisis. L. C. McHugh

241

God Bless America!

George H. Dunne

Rome, May 23—This is one of those days which make one proud to be an American. "The Stars and Stripes Forever. . . DA da-da-DA da-da-DA." "God bless America, land that I love." "Columbia, the gem of the ocean." Land of the free and home of the brave! You can see the Statue of Liberty standing there welcoming to her shore—urging them to come—the poor, the outcast, of every color, land and creed. The melting pot of the world! Irish and English, French and Germans, Dutch and Indonesians, Algerians, Liberians, Laotians, Cambodians, Burmese and Vietnamese. "Send me your poor from every land!" What a proud boast. You can hear the bands playing, the crowds cheering; see the flags flying, the orators orating. "God bless America, my home sweet home!" This is a day to make an American hold his head high and step out lively, conscious of the eyes of the world upon him.

The eyes of the world are upon him. You know it from the moment you step out the front door here in Rome. There is the story in every paper; the great black headlines screaming from every *chiosco*; the photographs on every front page, arresting the eye, making the heart beat faster, thrusting the proud American chin up higher. Oh, it's a great day to be an American! Not just in *L'Unità*, the Communist paper; but in *Il Messaggero*, the middle-of-the-road paper, and in *Tempo*, the right-of-center paper, and in *Il Popolo*, the Christian Democratic paper, and in *Il Quotidiano*, the Catholic Action paper, and in *Osservatore Romano*, the Vatican City paper. Not just in the papers in Rome and in Italy, but in the papers in France and in Germany and in Spain and in Portugal, the papers all over Europe, the papers all over the world—rejoicing our enemies, dismaying our friends, alienating the undecided.

Let the Russians boast of their sputniks and their shots around the moon and their astronauts circling the globe. Cheap publicity stunts! Propaganda flares! When it comes to capturing headlines, Americans can give them hearts and spades and beat them every time. Look at those headlines: RACE RIOTS IN ALABAMA! . . . WHITE MOB ASSAULTS BUSLOAD OF NEGRO AND WHITE YOUTHS. . . . . TWO GIRLS AMONG INJURED TAKEN TO HOSPITAL. Thank God, that vaunted Southern chivalry lives on, come hell, high water or the day of doom!

Look at those great photographs! A young white man, blood streaming down his face, dyeing his white shirt red. Red, white and blue! Oh, it's a grand thing to be an American! He'd been riding around the country in the Freedom Bus with this crowd of young colored people, being a friend. Well, that'll show him. That'll show the world how red-, white- and blue-blooded Americans handle that kind of thing. Look at this other picture! A young Negro man knocked to the sidewalk and three big, tough Alabama cops closing in to grab him and give him the works. That should teach those Baluba tribesmen down in the Congo a thing or two. They think they're primitives. It'll take them a few hundred years to catch up with us. They don't even know what being primitive means. Look at this picture here. Brave, frightened Negroes watching the long wakeful night hours through, besieged in a church by a howling mob of whites outside. A young woman, face

243

contorted by sobs, broken up, broken to pieces by the pounding waves of hatred beating in through the windows, through the doors, through the walls.

I know what she feels, the tearing sickness of feeling yourself hated for nothing that you have done or could undo, but only for what you are. I stood on a debating platform once in Boston and felt waves of hatred coming up at me out of the audience. They came from only part of the audience, a small part, from two or three hundred people who hated me because of what I was—a Catholic and a priest defending the Catholicism they hated. Nothing I could say or do could reach them or touch their hearts or stop those waves of hatred which were tangible, which I could feel and almost taste. When it was over, I went back to New York and into a hotel and was sick. I was sick for three days. So I know what makes this girl sob her heart out. Mine, however, was an isolated, single experience. She has had to live with hatred all her life, surrounded by it, engulfed by it, and tonight it howls about this church where she is at bay.

Yes, sir, those Communists think they are real good haters. "Imperialists," they call us. "Capitalists." Sticks and stones. We can give anybody lessons in hate. Remember those magnificent pictures a few months back that made the newspapers all over the world? Those New Orleans housewives, good solid American housewives, their faces grotesquely contorted with hate, screaming epithets at a bewildered little Negro child and her quietly courageous father? There was an orgasm of hate that even Hitler might have envied.

We have erected and maintained for a hundred years a segregated social system based upon hatred; hatred and pride, a (literally) God-damned pride in the whiteness of our own skin. A kind of skinolatry. That's what it means to be an American. Always out there in front. Firstest with the bestest. Maybe not in sputniks, shots to the moons, men in orbit, but first in the things that count, the things that *really* make the world sit up and take notice.

"There's a great day a-comin'." Yes sir, today is one of those great days, a come-and-get-it day. A day when it feels great to be an American.

Feels great to be a Catholic, too. Associated with those Catholic racists in New Orleans—frequenters of the sacraments, the papers said—who keep the fires of hatred burning bright. "Keep the home fires burning." Great to be a priest, along with those priests who encouraged their racist friends to defy their Archbishop and who quietly sabotaged his efforts to destroy the white-skinned calf in his own diocese.

A day indeed for a Catholic to be proud. A day for all Christians to be proud. For Alabama, like Mississippi, like Georgia, like all of the Deep South, is God-fearing, go-to-meeting country. You may be sure most of that howling mob besieging the church and trying to set it on fire to make a holocaust to the Lord of those who huddled within will be in their own Baptist and Methodist and Evangelical churches next Sunday, piously and proudly shouting their Christian hymns.

Some years ago a Jesuit missionary, after twenty-five years in India, said to me: "Stay in America and fight racial segregation. You can do more for the missions and for the cause of freedom that way than by returning to China, because the example of racial segregation in America is the biggest obstacle we have to overcome in trying to sell people on the merits of both Christianity and democracy."

We were looking out the window upon a Marian procession of young college men and women, of surpliced priests, and a resplendently robed bishop. "As long as they can gather a few hundred well-scrubbed boys and pretty girls to walk in a procession carrying banners on a sunny day, they think God's in His heaven and all's right with the world," he said. "And all the time the earth is crumbling beneath their feet."

Since that day China has gone, Eastern Europe has gone, Southeast Asia is tottering, Africa is threatening, Latin America is in doubt. And we still talk about "prudence" and "gradualism" and reduce to silence the voice that is raised in warning or in protest and say we must tread quietly here and walk softly there.

But this is such a complicated question! As complicated as charity. No doubt Christianity has become quite complicated. But the essence of the Christian way of life remains as simple as Christ said it was: love of God and love of neighbor, summing up all of the law and all of the prophets. And unless we have this, we do nothing more than tinkle the brass and sound the cymbals. Love is a hard saying and, because in two thousand years we have not learned to practice it, the thunder gathers on the left while we sing our pious hymns and walk in pleasant processions.

But enough of these melancholy thoughts. This is a day to exult in. Unfurl the flags! Strike up the bands! Thrust our your chests! Lift up your chins! "I pledge allegiance to the flag and to the Republic for which it stands, one nation, indivisible, with (come on now, shout it out) liberty and justice FOR ALL!" That's it! Now all together: "God bless America, land that I love . . . From the mountains, to the ocean. . . ." Hold it! Hold it! Wait a minute! How did that nigger back there get in? Ushers! grab that jigaboo and throw him out on his ear. . . . That's the way to do it. Wait'll *those* pictures hit the papers. That'll make them sit up and take notice. Now—let's hear *EVERYBODY* join in. "Onward, Christian soldiers, DA, DA, DA, DA, DA. . . ."

Freedom Now

I ASKED a young Freedom Rider in New Orleans last week: "How long have you felt the way you do now?" She smiled politely at the simplicity of my question. "Why, ever since I realized I was a Negro and was treated as something different."

Some thirty faculty members—priest, religious and lay—in New Orleans's two Catholic universities gave a variety of answers to my questions. Almost unanimously, they felt that the Freedom Rides were a good and probably a necessary thing. "Thank God," said one, "these youngsters aren't throwing bombs!" There was some division on the matter of timing: was this the best step here and now, or would it set interracial progress back? However, such division as existed followed lines of age, not race.

When I spoke to Negro university students, no difference of opinion could be found. It was always: "How much longer do we have to wait to be treated as human beings?" I asked about gradualism. "Our grandparents could wait a hundred years. We can't. We *have* to act." What had brought the change about? "It's simple. We read the same books as other Catholic Americans —St. Thomas, the Constitution, Lincoln. We want the same things. No more, no less." Had the explosion in Africa affected them? "Of course. At last we could feel that we didn't have to have white blood to want freedom and even to die for it."

With no pose or trace of braggadocio, one of them said quietly: "I don't want to get killed, but I will go on protesting even if it does mean I get killed." He had spent time in jail for taking part in a sit-in and had been beaten by an Alabama mob. His buddy nodded and explained: "We don't want freedom in 1963. We want it in 1961."   C. J. McNaspy

The Old Neighborhood
Katharine Byrne

E RIC LARRABEE has observed that one of the unan-
swerable arguments in the American conversation-
al repertory is "for the children's sake." These are
the words which may yet kill the City. This is the inscription on the banner which leads the "leavers,"
though there is, among them, occasional evidence of a
faint regret.

Whenever I see my friend Marcia, she asks: "How
are things in the old neighborhood?" In a way I think
she misses it despite the blatant charm of life in far-out
Homogeny. Somewhere in our conversation she is likely
to ask: "Does Miss Claussen still unpack her trunkful
of dolls each Christmas and ask the children in to drink
chocolate out of those cups her mother brought from
Sweden?" Or: "Does Mrs. Calvin still follow the garbage
truck down the alley with a broom and a dustpan?"
Or: "Does old Mr. Stein still wear his Prince Albert to
temple on Saturday morning?" Life on a square block
where there is no child over ten and no parent over
forty, has made my friend lonely for some of our aging
eccentrics.

I assure her that things are pretty much as they were

when she lived here, except that Mrs. Calvin is now too old to tidy up the alley, and must content herself with hollering out the window at the garbage men.

"I really should bring the children back sometime," she often says. Perhaps she has read the recommendation of the social scientist who notes that many children are growing up in great metropolitan concentrations without ever seeing the City. He recommends that thoughtful parents plan an occasional excursion back into town, presumably so that the children of this generation may enjoy the exotic sights and smells, the varied colors and customs of those who live here. (I have also heard, but do not believe, the story about the earnest PTA member who petitioned her Human Relations Chairman to find a way to import a busload of "less fortunate" children from the City to share the toys and treasures of the local kindergarteners. "How can our children learn to share," she wondered, "when all of them have the same things?")

We live in Marcia's old neighborhood, but it is really not old, even as areas are dated and outdated in a profligate City which uses up and abandons in such a hurry. It's only middle-aged, and bears up fairly well, especially in summer, which covers soot-colored stucco with bright Boston ivy, and makes green archways of the elms and maples. The streets are quiet. The alleys are where the noise is. There are collapsible pools in some of the yards, but out in the alley it's more fun to jump off an old kitchen chair into a garbage can of icy water, or play a peer-directed brand of baseball which can accommodate any child between the ages of six and twelve. Forty-year-old lilac and mock orange bushes push through the fences and over the gateways. The peonies and roses were planted by Nordic Protestant burghers who moved in when Taft was President.

When summer is gone, the sagging fences show their years and weather cracks the seams of stucco slipcovers. Only the handful of really handsome houses can stand the stark glare of winter. The Old Settlers will not be seen again until spring, unless one of them dies. Otherwise they are locked in until an April primary brings them out to vote the straight Republican ticket.

249

All but Mr. Ramsey, who hasn't voted for anyone since Norman Thomas stopped running. To their homes come the grocery boys, balancing on their handlebars the orders called in by the arthritic and weatherbound. The butcher's wife listens patiently. ("I'm sorry about your back, Mrs. Wesley. Will there be anything else today? Yes, I'm sure George has a nice knucklebone for Queenie. I'll send Jerry right over with it.")

Very early yesterday morning, I saw two of my neighbors leaving home. I am *not* peeking at people from behind drawn drapes at six o'clock. It's this early-rising baby beagle that has me prowling the streets and alleys at dawn. With a houseful of loving friends at all other times, at this hour he is mine alone. First we met Dr. Newland, whose wife was about to drive him to the airport. He was off to address a world congress of neuro-ophthalmologists meeting in Barcelona to discuss the control of glaucoma. A few houses later it was Mrs. Lipman who greeted us. She was off to the early shift at the girdle factory. A Polish DP, she has a five-figure tattoo on her left forearm, and other concentration camp mementos. Once in a while my eight-year-old travels around the block with hers, offering girdle "seconds" at half-price to any lady who will answer her back doorbell. And he wants to know why *his* mother doesn't produce anything a boy could sell from door to door.

This is a neighborhood of contrast and diversity. On a warm day with the windows open the incense which is wafted heavenward during the high Mass may mingle with the insistent smells of the bagel-and-onionroll bakery nearby. We have the lady who bakes cookies and loves children, and we have Mrs. Marshall. She's the one who turns the hose on the man-next-door if he dares to place a ladder a few inches over her property line when he wants to clean the leaves out of his garage gutter. We have the little girl whose clothes come from Best's and the children whose mother has discovered the joy of browsing in the Thrift Shop's perpetual rummage sale. Bobby Richardson's grandmother still walks him to school and calls for him, but there is another six-year-old who is on his own all day and may appear at your kitchen door with a breakfast quarter which he wants to trade for some orange juice and a bowl of cereal. If you are looking for a Finnish bath, a German-language movie, or a slice of almond-filled, honey-dripping Greek *baklava,* all are close by and available.

In American urban society clever and ambitious elements of the population are often able to move from

a poor ghetto to a plush ghetto in three generations. Here we seem to have bogged-down permanently in heterogeneous Phase Two. The voting roll reads: Bantsolas, Batka, Becker, Binkowski, Blumfield, Bongiovanni, Borge, Brooke, Brye, Byrne. At the other end of the line are the Yoshimuras, who always win the garden contest. There are other evidences that we are obsolete. We have a paperboy whose father is dead and whose mother *needs* the money he earns. Our backyards have fences between them, and neighbors who have known one another for years call each other by their last names. Dogs wear leashes. The other day I saw a Davy Crockett sweatshirt.

Harry Golden, in one of his syndicated slices of nostalgia, speaks in admiring reminiscence of the lower-East-Side mother of other years who used to keep the delicatessen open 16 hours a day and literally put her boy through law school with the contents of her pickle barrel. She isn't dead. Now she lives a few blocks from us. At a busy intersection, early and late, she's selling newspapers. Depending on the season, she wears a flowered housedress, a patrol boy's slicker or army boots and a combat jacket. Her boy will enter medical school this fall.

Sociologists will tell you that a good community spirit implies standards to which each member of a group feels forced to conform. Here some of us score low. While the general level for the care and feeding of front lawns is fairly high, no one gets excited because Mr. Richter, who teaches violin lessons in his basement studio, attacks his grass with a sickle once or twice a summer, and no oftener.

The evening paper features a daily column on the women's page called "Split-Level Living" or something. It's a serial chronicle about life in a certain bucolia on the edge of our metropolitan area. The author recounted an interesting episode recently. It seems that on a warm spring afternoon all the well-slacked and loose-shirt-tailed girls on her block were surprised to find one of their number out of uniform. Unaccountably, she appeared on her driveway dressed in the manner of a young woman about to be taken out to dinner. They asked her for an explanation. She told them that it was her birthday, that her husband had apparently forgotten the fact, and that she hoped that this subtle hint, when she picked him up at the station, would inspire him, et cetera, et cetera.

Now her motive and method are routine and incontestable. The fascinating point, to an outsider, is that all her neighbors knew what she was wearing, that they cared, and that they demanded and received an explanation for her wearing it. Fierce old Mrs. McCorkle, in a wide-skirted flannel nightgown and with an iron gray braid hanging to her waist, has been seen weeding her moss roses in the early hours. On our block the item is not considered newsworthy. And if it were, I wouldn't want to be the one to ask why she doesn't wear a more suitable gardening garment.

Not far away lie the newly-hardened arteries, the expressways built to move the hot-and-cursing or the cold-and-cursing multitudes who daily fight their way to the City's edge and far beyond. What has kept us from joining them? Is it social inertia, an unwillingness or an inability even to approach the starting line for the great push which engages the best energies of so many able people? Or is it because the woman of this house cannot face the prospect of cleaning out an attic crowded with tropical fish apparatus, the operating room of an abandoned doll "hosbidel," all those little pens from the time the guinea pigs had guinea pigs, fifty pounds of moldering raw data from one doctoral dissertation, who-knows-how-many Halloween costumes, and the boots which keep accumulating because no one ever seems to be the right size at the right time of the year?

THE TRUTH IS, of course, we like it here. And this in spite of the fact the City never had a good press. As far back as the days of Dick Whittington, it has been beaten down in print as a source and a magnet for the forces of evil. In our day, advertising, the great status-conferral instrument of our culture, has done nothing to improve the image. Who ever saw a boy in a Crest commercial come bounding up the steps of the ancestral two-flat to tell his mother he had no cavities? Who ever saw a beautiful young wife toss the laundry in with the sponsor's product and walk carefree from the basement of a 35-year-old octagon-front bungalow?

The City, "like a patient etherized upon a table," lies naked to the probings of the attending social theorists. What is the prognosis for one of its well-preserved but aging parts? The mature community, as they call it, cannot long prosper on the limited commitment of the elderly, watching life with waning interest from the sidelines of their screened front porches. It needs bright and scrappy young parents, interested, involved. People who will fight with the alderman or petition the pastor, if necessary, and whose move in this direction is not an interim expedient, but a positive choice made —and why not?—"for the children's sake."

If they come back to the Old Neighborhood (and I do not see them in great numbers), it will be because they find something of value here in spite of embarrassing deficiencies. (Eighth grade graduation parties are backyard barbecues with little brothers and sisters hanging around; 16-year-olds walk to school or take a bus; there is no local of the John Birch Society.) They will come, if they do, as independents bucking a dominant mobility pattern. Not as self-consciously different, perhaps, as the society column's "young marrieds," buying up the central city's "divine old houses with the magnificent leaded panes in the bay windows," but different, nevertheless. Candidates for the last place in the list of those whom the predictors suspect may ultimately inherit the City: "the very rich, the very poor, and the slightly odd."

On Being Slightly Odd

A NYONE who has lived through a generation which gave rise to successive epidemics of Davy Crockett hats, Jack Paar viewing and collegiate conservatism must be aware of the deep-rooted American compulsion to conform at all costs. Then, too, what contemporary parent hasn't wilted before the lament: "Aw, gee, all the kids are doing it"? From the cradle on, the pressure bears down on one—conform or (the horror of it!) be considered "slightly odd."

Now conformism in the matter of coonskin caps presents no serious problem for most people. The same goes for many of the other manias that capture the people's fancy and defy common sense. But for American Catholics the urge to be part of the faceless throng can be a real threat at times. Take, for instance, some prevailing family-life patterns in the typical American suburb.

The rub here, as Fr. John L. Thomas, S.J., leading Catholic student of family-life sociology, put it in an address at the recent 23rd annual convention of the American Catholic Sociological Society, is that "the Catholic family is clearly defined from the point of view of norms—its philosophy and theology."

History shows only too clearly that these norms have faced challenges from the general culture in the past. But for American Catholics, particularly for young parents, the difficulty lies in the fact that the move to suburbia puts them for the first time in a position of finding their "way of life in sharp conflict with what is considered normal by other Americans." It's a question that deserves close attention.

In this issue of AMERICA (p. 41), Katharine Byrne points the finger, in slightly less direct fashion, at the same sore spot. Speaking of self-exiled former residents of a big city's "Old Neighborhood," she suggests that a visit back there will help them to "find something of value" in the community life they abandoned when they fled over the expressway to cook-out land.

What could be more quaint, indeed, from a split-level viewpoint, than celebrating eighth-grade graduations by "backyard barbecues with little brothers and sisters hanging around"? Or more primitive, in the eyes of some Crestview Manor, with its fierce parking problem at the local high school, than the sight of 16-year-olds who "walk to school or take the bus"?

Neither Mrs. Byrne nor Father Thomas, we feel sure, is plugging a back-to-the-farm or even a back-to-the-metropolis movement for their fellow Catholics. What both hint at, however, is that there may be some virtue, not to mention necessity, about being "slightly odd" in a pluralistic society such as ours. Their observations make it clear, too, that the time has come to pose a few questions about the impact of so powerful a social force as advertising, "the great status-conferral instrument of our culture."

Whether it be a question of eating fish on Friday when everyone else is biting into prime beef, or the more serious issues of early dating and other matters subject to family decision, the Catholic has to recognize that living up to his faith inevitably demands on occasion that he be *different*. What makes the demand more painful for many of today's Catholics is the fact that they are more than ever cast as members of a minority "trying to preserve its values when the rest of society is not."

Angular Catholicism for the sake of angularity has nothing in particular to recommend it. But the risk of being labeled "slightly odd" by the conformist herd is a price worth paying for the sake of basic Catholic ideals.

On Loving the Poor

William A. Schumacher

S T. VINCENT DE PAUL once said: "The poor are our most demanding masters; we must love them so they will forgive us the bread that we give them." We rarely think of him as a master of paradox, yet in that epigram St. Vincent struck, three centuries ago, a profound truth about Christian charity. It seems strange at first glance to think of the poor as our masters; we tend, rather, to regard them as our inferiors, the recipients of our liberality.

But St. Vincent was looking to the real fruit of Christian charity, the spiritual benefit of the giver. It is axiomatic in theology that pure, disinterested love of God is impossible; the virtue of charity—that is, the love of God for His own sake—will always have overtones of our own spiritual profit from the very act of loving God. This is also true when the same virtue of charity is directed towards its other proper object—namely, the children of God, who are to be loved for His sake. When we truly love the poor, we stand to profit thereby. The poor, then, are really our benefactors, our masters, who have the right to demand love in God's name, and who confer on those who love them an eternal benefit.

A VISIT TO THE POOR

However, we cannot love what we do not know. True love is intensely personal; it cannot be accomplished by remote control. We cannot love the poor merely through a check or a gift; we must first come to know them. Come with me into the homes of the poor, here in the affluent United States, 1960. Whatever their race or color; whatever their religion or lack of it; whether they speak broken English, sloppy Spanish, or in the heavily accented tones of the Southern hills and fields—all the poor are very much alike. Climb the steps to the third-floor rear of a tenement, making your way past abandoned baby buggies, old tire casings and discarded clothing. Be careful to step over gaps where boards are missing from the stairs. (When there are no locks on the doors, removing a few planks from the back steps makes an effective barrier against surreptitious entry into a third-floor flat.) Don't forget to look for the poor living in so-called cottages, shacks located on the backs of lots which seem to be occupied completely by small factories and filling stations. You will find the poor there, too, down that littered path and behind that broken fence—living where you would never expect to find anyone at all.

Wherever they live, you will find the poor enveloped in an all-embracing odor, with mingled scents of unwashed bodies, moldy clothes, strong cooking smells, escaping gas and, in winter, the piercing reek of fuel oil from their stoves. The buildings in which the poor live were erected some fifty to eighty years ago; time and neglect have taken their toll in broken door jambs, sagging floors, peeling walls, leaky pipes and balky plumbing. Be sure to bring a flashlight if you make this trip at night; it will spare you many a bad fall and embarrassing situation.

Beyond learning where the poor live, we must meet them face to face. From a natural viewpoint they are not very attractive people. Defeated by life, old before their time, they seem suspicious at first acquaintance.

257

When you come to know them better, you will learn that this is a deep-seated shrewdness born of years of experience in detecting phonies and frauds. Surrounded by crudity, living in the midst of every sort of degradation, accustomed to disease and corruption, grown used to all varieties of sin from childhood, these people cannot be fooled or tricked. All the effects of original sin are well known to the poor; the weaknesses and shortcomings of human nature are drilled into them every day of their lives. Hammer blows of human cruelty and selfishness have fallen on their hearts, uncushioned by the conventions that protect the rest of us. What wonder, then, that something twisted and misshapen has occasionally resulted.

These, then, are the poor who are our most demanding masters; these are the people whom we must love if we are to love God. But what is lovable about them? Only the image of God in their souls is an adequate object of true charity. The whole problem lies in seeing this image in such a place. Philosophy tells us that God is Goodness, Truth and Beauty. His image is hard to find in those whose lives are choked with evil, lies and ugliness. Only the virtue of faith, the acceptance of God's word that these are, indeed, His beloved children and the brothers of His Son—only such faith makes this kind of love possible. In the world's eyes they are worthless, yet the price which God paid for each one of them was the death of His own Son on the cross. Only the crucifix is the correct price tag for each of the souls of the poor.

But once we have come to know the poor, then we must learn to love them. More than this, we must learn how to love them in such a way that the expression of our love will not corrupt its spiritual fruits and make a hollow mockery of the love itself.

We cannot truly love the poor with "charity" in the do-gooder, Lady Bountiful sense, because this sort of charity is often only a disguised selfishness. Those "charitable Catholics" whose acts of love consist of graciously bestowing a gift on some waif with a photographer in attendance remind me always of Christ's story of the Pharisee, who gave his alms to the accompaniment of blaring trumpets. In His words, "they have had their reward." If they have had their reward in public praise, whether by a fanfare of trumpets in the streets of Jerusalem or by a picture on the society page, there is no spiritual reward to be gained. What could have been profitable for eternal life has been wasted in attempting to buy the fickle praise of men.

This love of God in His own poor will never be carried out in practice merely by writing a check, even for those whom we have come to know. What young lady would take a lover seriously who made his proposal by mail, money order enclosed? If we claim to love the poor, it must be with the qualities of a lover—a burning personal interest in their happiness both here and hereafter, a concern for their welfare in every sense, a compassion for their weaknesses, an understanding of their all too human frailties.

It would be easy to love the poor if they would respond in kind; it is very difficult to offer love to those who take it for granted and spit in your eye. Yet only this kind of love is worthy to be called by the noble

name of Christian charity, since Christ our Lord loved us in this way. As St. Paul reminds us: "It is hard enough to find anyone who will die on behalf of a just man, although perhaps there may be those who will face death for one so deserving. But here, as if God meant to prove how well He loves us, it was while we were still sinners that Christ, in His own appointed time, died for us" (Romans 5: 8-9).

The poor are shrewd, and all our protestations of

interest and concern, all our well-meaning compassion and understanding will be rejected as a sham and a fraud unless it is backed up by self-sacrifice. This is the ultimate test of love, the willingness to put oneself out— in time, in convenience, in cold cash until it hurts. The poor are realists; they know from bitter experience that pious words do not put food in children's mouths, nor do beautiful sentiments put shoes on their feet.

But if merely writing a check is not enough to love the poor, how then are we to do it? Did you ever think of learning about a poor family and then visiting them, literally feeding and clothing them? An experience of this sort can teach us more about poverty and its effects than all the sociology texts ever written. It can also be quite humbling and thought-provoking.

WHEN LOVE IS PRACTICAL

Could you pick up a poor expectant mother and drive her to the prenatal clinic, saving her a long walk in the cold? Could you visit some of the most pathetic poor people of all, the old ones whose lives are leaking away in a dark, forgotten room, surrounded by the pitiful relics of a lifetime of suffering? Could you stomach a trip to a county hospital, to an old people's home, to a Catholic hospital for unmarried mothers—not just a visit, a tour of inspection, but hours of heart-rending suffering perhaps, just sitting there and listening to the sick poor pour out the tragedy of their lives? Would you have the love and patience necessary to teach the catechism to a child not quite mentally deficient enough to be placed in an institution? No one who has never tried these works of mercy can know what bittersweet experiences they can be, how our very understandable natural loathing can be turned into a spiritual joy by the alchemy of God's grace.

Loving the poor is not something optional for a Christian; it is of the very essence of his faith, and it makes sense only in the light of that faith. It is easy to love lepers in Asia, when someone else changes their bandages; it is easy to love orphans in our own city, when devoted Sisters care for them day and night. But it is repulsive, it is awkward, it is sometimes embarrassing, it can make us uncomfortable to think about really and truly loving the poor in person.

When the followers of John came to Christ to ask if He were the Messiah, our Lord made the preaching of the Gospel to the poor the sure sign of His office as Saviour. Love of the poor has always remained the certain mark of His true followers, of His real lovers. As His beloved Apostle, St. John, remarks: "Yes, we must love God; He gave us His love first. If a man boasts of loving God, while he hates his own brother, he is a liar. He has seen his brother, and has no love for him; what love can he have for the God he has never seen? No, this is the divine command that has been given us; the man who loves God must be the one who loves his brother as well" (I John 4: 20-21).

Christ Himself has given us a very practical reason for this personal love of the poor. On the most momentous day of our lives, He will say to the elect: "I was hungry, and you gave me food, thirsty, and you gave me drink; I was a stranger, and you brought me home, naked, and you clothed me, sick, and you cared for me, a prisoner, and you came to see me. . . . Believe me, when you did it to one of the least of my brethren, you did it to Me." And others will hear, to their eternal sorrow, that the contrary of this is also true: ". . . when you refused it to one of the least of my brethren, you refused it to me" (Matthew 25: 35-46).

The Phenomenon
of Man

Francois Russo

S. J.

CONSIDERABLE ATTENTION has been given recently to a book translated from French into English and entitled *The Phenomenon of Man* (Harper). It is the most important of the works that came from the pen of a man who was both a member of a religious order and a well-known scientist. Born in France in 1881, in the Province of Auvergne, Pierre Teilhard de Chardin entered the Society of Jesus in 1899 after completing his secondary education at the Jesuit College of Mongré, near Lyons. He was ordained to the priesthood in 1911. From that time on he dedicated himself to the so-called earth sciences, and above all to paleontology. His scientific work made it necessary for him to spend long years in China, and to travel widely. He returned to Paris in 1946, and then in 1951 went to New York, where he died suddenly on Easter Sunday, April 10, 1955.

Fr. Teilhard was a member of the French Academy of Sciences. During his latter years in the United States, he was attached to the Wenner-Gren Foundation for Anthropological Research.

The author of *The Phenomenon of Man* was a scientist of international repute, to whom are owed several extremely important contributions in the field of human paleontology. Moreover, Fr. Teilhard was a man haunted by the apostolic needs of his time. All through his life he struggled to understand the human and religious meaning that lies behind the advance of the sciences and particularly of biology. Over and above his directly scientific works, he is to be credited with numerous writings of a general character that treat large philosophical and religious problems, especially in so far as they touch upon the sciences. The *Phenomenon of Man* is but the first volume of these works; four other volumes have already been published in France (Le Seuil, Paris). These writings of Fr. Teilhard often seem rather to resemble sketches, or the presentation of a piece of research as it might be proposed to intimate friends and not to the larger public, than the expression of fully elaborated thought. But *The Phenomenon of Man* is one work that Fr. Teilhard most explicitly wanted to see published. In its pages he brought together the essential and guiding ideas of a world-view which he kept progressively sharpening and reformulating all during his life, and whose basic insights date from 1916. This book, which was finished in 1947, was published only in 1955, a few months after his death.

One can distinguish in *The Phenomenon of Man* two levels of its author's considerations: on one hand, a *description* of the evolution of the world, where certain elements of hypothesis are already present; on the other, an attempt at an *explanation* of this evolutionary process.

TWO ASPECTS

For Fr. Teilhard the evolution of the world is viewed in four stages: pre-life (*la prévie*), life, thought, and hyper-life or a stage beyond life (*la survie*).

During the period of pre-life, matter passes from an undifferentiated state to that of organized forms which represent, first of all, the elements, and then bodies composed of a more and more complex structure. All this while, the universe in its totality is setting in motion a process of expansion which it will continue to pursue all through its history.

The appearance of life represents a passage through some sort of threshold. From this point on there begins a continuing development of living forms that mount up into more and more organized species—a process that ends in animal forms very close to that of man. Life has certain well-determined "manners," and its qualitative progression is clearly measured by means of what Fr. Teilhard calls a "parameter of cephalization." This means that the farther we advance in evolution, the more the complexity of the brain increases, at least for certain phyla. Among these phyla, there is one of "pure and direct cerebralization," which leads to man.

We find here, traced by the hand of a master, an admirable tableau of the story of life. These precise and stirring pages constitute, beyond all doubt, that part of Père Teilhard's work which is the most scientific in nature and also the least debatable.

After the appearance of life, the emergence of man constitutes a new and critical transformation. It is "the momentary pause of reflection." It is an extremely important moment in the history of life, and we shall perhaps never succeed in elucidating the phenomenology of its process with total clarity. The author writes: "At that point earth is reborn, or better, it finds its soul." This part of the book contains a masterly treatment of the paleontological problem of the origins of man—an exposé that requires only a few retouchings here and there in order to be brought up-to-date with discoveries which have taken place since it was written. These stirring analyses truly make us understand that "man is the ascending arrow of the great biological synthesis."

In a final stage, we confront the prolongation of evolution in the development of humanity. This development is presented essentially as a phenomenon of *convergence.* By this is meant a "coming together" of humanity—a process which in no way tends to form an impersonal all, but rather to effect a union which allows for differentiation and distinction within an ever more narrow solidarity and through a ceaseless interpenetration—the end-product of consciousness being constantly enlarged and augmented.

AN ULTIMATE CONVERGENCE

Thus, we see that the synthesis that Fr. Teilhard presents to us has evolution as its basic principle of explanation. Recognized at first in the realm of living forms, evolution is extended to the whole ensemble of the universe. Thus, there was already an evolutionary process at work before the appearance of life, and then, after the emergence of man, evolution goes on following its course from the very start in man's biological form. Finally, evolution is more and more evident in the course of the progress of humanity.

Each of these great stages of evolution, of course, has its own proper character, but the same fundamental dynamism runs through and sustains them all. Thus, what is to be has already been "fore-announced" by that which is and by that which has been. The evolution of matter somehow prefigures life. In fact, this is precisely why Fr. Teilhard calls it pre-life. To speak in general, "nothing could one day emerge as final on any of the divers thresholds—no matter how crucial these thresholds are in the successive leaps of evolution —which was not first of all obscurely primordial." Hence, we are in the presence here of a "cosmogenesis" whose "tendrils insist on reaching up and being prolonged in us. . . . Evolution is on its way into the realm of the psyche. . . . Thus, thought has part with evolution." Making his own the formula used by Julian Huxley, Fr. Teilhard dares to declare that "man discovers he is nothing other than evolution become self-conscious."

With respect to the convergence of humanity, this phenomenon appears as "a subtle shifting of the onward flow of evolution." Humanity, in its first movements of expansion over the earth, tended to branch off; now, however, it converges toward a point that constitutes the "superior pole" of all evolution—what Fr. Teilhard proposes that we call *Omega*. This final stage of evolution is of an "ultrapersonal" nature; at this point persons come together in unity and self-realization. (We have here a conception that is completely opposed to the totalitarianism of the Marxist when he discusses the "end" of humanity, a destiny wherein we discover in only a very feeble degree anything like care for the individual human person and his dignity.)

In order to clarify and give an account of this "up-flow" of life to achievement in *Omega,* Fr. Teilhard appeals to two pairs of notions: that of "complexity-consciousness" and that of tangential and radial energies.

Growth in the complexity of beings is accompanied—explicitly, at least, in the realm of animal life—by progress in psychic development. This fact leads the author to lay down as a general principle the notion that consciousness and complexity are but the "two faces"—one internal, the other external—of a single phenomenon that keeps showing itself all through the course of evolution. Hence, all things in a certain sense have a kind of "inwardness"; even inert matter has this character. The degree of complexity-consciousness constitutes the fundamental parameter which allows us to measure progress in evolution and the dignity of the beings that evolve. Thus, man, although quite lost in the immensity of space and time, appears as the summit of the cosmos, as its final achievement and its résumé, because he is the most conscious and the most organized of beings.

From the pair of notions that we have named complexity-consciousness, we pass on to the second pair, that of tangential energy and radial energy. Thus, the dynamism which, in certain areas of the universe, tends to go along certain privileged lines of development, ever at work to assure the growing complexity of being, cannot be understood except as springing from an energy of arrangement, called radial energy. We say "radial" energy but it is a dynamism which assures a progression of development. This energy comes to be associated with energy in its classical sense, the energy that Fr. Teilhard calls tangential. He calls it tangential because he conceives it to be only an element of the conservation of beings, and to be unable to assure the forward march of evolutionary progress.

NEED FOR SUCH A VIEW

It would be impossible to overemphasize how opportune is the effort at synthesis that is outlined in *The Phenomenon of Man*. New scientific data, especially in the realm of biology, have up till now remained quite unrelated. This makes it all the more necessary to bring these data together into a coherent and total picture. Such precisely is the task which so preoccupied Fr. Teilhard, and it is to his great credit that he was able to put himself in a frame of reference which—transcending the narrow scope of cosmologies that were completely exterior to man, and with which we have been too easily content up until now—is ample enough to permit the integration of man himself into cosmology. Such an enterprise is by no means a mere intellectual game or some sort of fancy speculation. It answers a pressing need of our era. Today, looking beyond the partial and disjointed world-views which have up till now been offered us, we seek a global insight. We want such a view to be founded on general principles, of course, but it must also take into account all the riches of scientific findings.

Fr. Teilhard was blessed with exceptional gifts as he set out to accomplish this purpose. He had great powers of analysis, wide culture, a forceful imagination, an aptitude for synthesis and, above all, that largeness of mind which scorns the shabby and the second-rate and puts no limit to its ambition to understand.

True, certain of Fr. Teilhard's descriptions and formulas have a certain poetic attraction about them, but it must be kept in mind that for him poetry constituted a genuine method of the phenomenological study of reality. I repeat that despite its appearances of poetic form the thought of Fr. Teilhard should not be ranged alongside the thought of authors of those numerous cosmogonies that are more or less literary or philosophical in nature, but which are also so careless in taking account of details of reality. Teilhard's formulations are at times daring, but the views he expresses in *The Phenomenon of Man* have their origin in the realm of fact. These views are deeply rooted in reality. His master ideas were born and matured in the womb of a real world with which the author's long career in research made him intimately familiar. Moreover, although these ideas may evoke criticism, they cannot be lightly pushed aside; for they embody a very remarkable attempt to answer the fundamental cosmological problems which preoccupy those gifted enough to possess at once a feeling for research and a desire to master difficult problems independently of immediate results.

Moreover, despite his highly personal style, we ought not be afraid to compare the work of Fr. Teilhard with those of a Descartes or a Leibniz. Like these men, Fr. Teilhard was haunted by the desire to grasp reality in a truly profound way, and to account for and unify that multiplicity of facts that has been brought into evidence by science. In his case as in theirs we find profundity wedded to true mastery of thought. He knows what he wants to say; he is not satisfied with words nor content with pseudo-explanations. What he affirms in his book is not the result of some totally conceptual deduction, but is intimately bound to an "experience" in reference to which he understands how to give an account of the real and intimate structure of things.

We are led quite naturally to ask whether views that are so ample and so rich really belong in any properly exclusive sense to the field of science. As he expresses them, are they not already filled with philosophy, and even with ideological considerations?

It is not easy to answer this question. Like all great creative minds, Teilhard was not slowed down by methodological discussions of any kind. Such exercises in the minutiae of scholarship seem never to have greatly interested him. Nevertheless, he was anxious to emphasize that his research was based exclusively on real phenomena, and that it was not dealing with either the principles of metaphysics or the data of revelation. Metaphysics and revelation certainly had a part to play in his thinking, but the views that we find expressed in *The Phenomenon of Man* are developed above all on the basis of the reality of phenomena that we can observe and understand with the help of the scientific method. In all truth, Fr. Teilhard could say that "in so far as man can distinguish in himself different levels of knowledge, it is not the believer, but rather the naturalist, who speaks in this book and asks to be understood."

Be that as it may, the views found in *The Phenomenon of Man* do not seem to be of the same type that one is accustomed to encounter in properly scientific treatises. Moreover, even if Fr. Teilhard should seem to us to have turned aside from science, this is not because he poses daring hypotheses for our consideration—every great scholar and savant does the same—but rather because his hypotheses introduce notions and considerations which lack that mark of objectivity and precision to which science is commonly accustomed. The "inwardness" of things, the radial energy of arrangement—concepts which for Teilhard are fundamental themes—are not truly scientific notions at all.

Must we therefore brush them aside as though they had no value? Not at all. Bear in mind that in the realm of physics the distinction between science and philosophy can be made without too much difficulty, but that it is not so easy to make the same distinction in the field of biology, in spite of the progress that has been made in methodology. Particular difficulties arise in the study of evolution, the field to which the aforesaid concepts have reference.

It is by no means proven that one can neatly distinguish the "scientific" and the "philosophical" in a study that sets out to understand life itself. If we attempt to imprison ourselves in too rigid or too scholarly a separation of these two orders of knowledge, we run the risk of impoverishing and stunting our investigation. Numerous treatises written in this narrow and rigid spirit give proof that such impoverishment is not only possible but real.

Some will object that Fr. Teilhard, by transcending positive science, is really engaged in philosophy. If so, then he should have concerned himself to a greater extent with principles and notions that have been tested. There can be no quarrel with this. But it must also be remembered that precisely here, in the field of cosmology, our classical views and concepts, valid as they may be fundamentally, today demand reappraisal. A work like that of Fr. Teilhard can be of great help in this regard. At first blush, of course, notions such as the "inwardness" of things and radial energy appear to be somewhat baffling, but he who reflects even a bit seriously on the world as made known to us by contemporary science will find them illuminating.

The author of the work in question was a philosopher in action rather than a professional philosopher. There can be no disputing the fact that Fr. Teilhard lacks the technical sureness of touch of a trained metaphysician. Yet his cosmological analyses are not for that reason of diminished importance. We may dare to criticize them or to revamp them, but if we are really anxious to enlarge the scope of cosmology in order to integrate into it all recent scientific knowledge, we must take his views into consideration. It is impossible to imagine how anyone could continue to teach cosmology without making generous allowance for the views of the author of *The Phenomenon of Man*.

CRITICISM OF TEILHARD

Thus, we see that the perspective or frame of reference in which the work of Fr. Teilhard is situated can be completely justified. Moreover, we may safely concede the riches and the profundity of the synthesis he proposes. Nevertheless, his thought calls for criticism on several points.

On the plane of positive cosmology, and quite independently of any philosophical or religious views to which it might seem to lead us, Fr. Teilhard's synthesis seems at fault in giving too great a place to evolution, and in presenting views as totally valid which in fact are still under discussion. Let us consider this point with particular respect to the realm of the physical world. Up to the present, while the thesis of the general evolution of the universe has by no means been set aside, it is equally true that it has not met unanimous acceptance in competent scientific circles. This general theory has as its most precise formulation the theory of the expanding universe, but today there are some who would oppose to the theory of the expanding universe a quite different theory—a theory of a pulsating universe, or a theory of irregular evolution; these, like the theory to which they are opposed, also rest on plausible foundations. Nevertheless, so far as the formation of the elements is concerned, the idea of the evolution of matter upward from an undifferentiated state toward more and more highly structured stages, which are represented by chemical elements of increasing weights, seems probable enough.

Moreover, the tight link which is asserted by Fr. Teilhard to exist between the world of pre-life and that of life in the general movement of evolution is not so solidly established as he affirms it to be. The "juncture" between the physical world and the world of life remains a problem which Fr. Teilhard has clarified less satisfactorily than he seems to think.

When he deals with questions related to the development of civilization, Teilhard appears to rely a little too exclusively on evolution. Evolution may be quite an essential aspect of human history, but it is difficult to go along with the seeming evaluation of Fr. Teilhard that evolution is the *only* principle by which to explain the dynamism of civilization. To insist too much on this one principle is to seem to fail to recognize realms like the history of art or the history of philosophy, which are likewise very important. Evolution, with its principle of linear growth, is not able fully to account for them. Moreover, in these fields we come upon patterns of evolution of a quite different type—cycles, regressions, etc.

When we regard it from the point of view of philosophy and religion, *The Phenomenon of Man* is again found to be other than completely satisfying. Let us

271

be very clear on this point. For the reasons outlined above, we ought not see in *The Phenomenon of Man* a metaphysical or theological work, and hence should not attempt to judge it as such. As is obvious, Fr. Teilhard has propounded certain views of man and his destiny which have a bearing on philosophical and religious problems. In fact, in a final chapter of his book, he has a treatise on the "Christian phenomenon." But here again he is dealing with considerations of *fact* and not with properly *doctrinal* affirmations.

In a word, Fr. Teilhard has in no way attempted in *The Phenomenon of Man* to give us the *total truth* regarding man. Such truth can come only from metaphysics and, especially, from revelation. Teilhard said this explicitly in his preface: "Let no one seek here a final explanation of things, a metaphysics." And again: "The book that I have written should not be read as one might read a work of metaphysics, and much less as one might peruse some sort of theological essay."

However, despite the care that the author took to write only within the framework of the phenomenal order, and to restrict what he has to say to that order, Fr. Teilhard—precisely because of his remarkable ability at synthesis—has presented us with a set of views on man and the world which to some little degree gives the impression of being *self-sufficient*. This, of course, is a problem that he himself recognized, for he said: "It is impossible to attempt a general interpretation of the universe without seeming to explain it from top to bottom."

The reader must not fail to note this problem about the work in question. One might wish that Teilhard's synthesis were *more open, more unfinished.* If it had been, the book would then be more useful in the work of building up a complete vision of man and the universe. This vision would have been one which, since it summoned up other sources than mere scientific experience, would have found a place for the very mystery of our freedom—for that mystery of evil which is not simply the mystery of the evil that we undergo (a problem which cosmology can discuss)—but also of that evil which is the product of our wills. This sort of evil is not very directly treated in *The Phenomenon of Man*, even though Fr. Teilhard was at pains to note that the fortunate evolution of the world that he envisaged depended on the free decision of man.

One should not try to find things in *The Phenomenon of Man* that are contrary to the faith. Even where Fr. Teilhard's views leap beyond the realm of strict positive evidence, they always allow complete scope for the teaching of the Church. It is impossible for us, here within the limits of this article, to examine this point in detail. Let us look at several essential observations.

The immanence and the spontaneity of evolution by no means rule out the transcendence of God. After all, evolution is only the phenomenal aspect of divine creation. Moreover, God's transcendence is demanded by the very exigencies of human action which, with its eternal striving for immortality, must constantly refer itself to a God who transcends the world. We have here one of the fundamental points of the thinking of Fr. Teilhard, and one that in other of his writings he calls the dialectical meaning of his thought.

Still other critics have felt obliged to note that in *The Phenomenon of Man* an excessive primacy is given to continuity in the development of beings. But this is to fail to recognize in Fr. Teilhard the notion of transformation, where continuity and discontinuity are indissolubly complementary to one another. Such critics also fail to recognize that the particular intervention of God, who creates the human soul, cannot be fully expressed on the phenomenal level, where we can find nothing more than a reflection of the mystery of creation.

Furthermore, so far as the mystery of original sin is concerned, is there any need to add that we would be guilty of a grave error of methodology if we reproached Fr. Teilhard for not having given this mystery an organic place in the cosmological synthesis he was making? In fact, it cannot be recognized in experience, because original sin is something which, in the last analysis, we know through revelation.

When examined attentively, the synthesis of Fr. Teilhard is seen to be less complete and less satisfactory than it might appear at first glance. Moreover, it is proper to read a book like this with a mind forewarned in regard to certain points of interpretation. But be all this as it may, Fr. Teilhard's synthesis is nonetheless a major contribution to our thinking about the world. Moreover, we must remember that for a world fascinated by the progress of science, a synthesis like that of Fr. Teilhard opens great windows to faith, and this in an age when such approaches are more than ever indispensable. One other notable achievement of this synthesis is that today, when the Marxists are attempting to monopolize the field of science, Fr. Teilhard demonstrates that science cannot find its fulfillment except in a spiritual dimension.

Let us therefore take up this book with the same simplicity of heart which caused its author to write: "I might well have deceived myself on a number of points. Let others, then, try to do better. All that I wanted to accomplish is to have made people feel the difficulty and the urgency of the problem, to comprehend its immense magnitude, and to perceive the form in which a solution must inevitably be found."

Should Men Hang?

Donald R. Campion

O N OCTOBER 21, 1959, Caryl Chessman won his seventh legal stay in an eleven-year battle to avoid California's gas chamber. The convict-author of the autobiographical best-seller *Cell 2245, Death Row* first heard the death sentence pronounced over his head in the Superior Court of Los Angeles on June 25, 1948. Now, two days before the U. S. Supreme Court intervened, Gov. Edmund G. Brown (despite his personal opposition to capital punishment) had turned down a plea for clemency submitted by Chessman's attorney. The execution had been scheduled for October 23.

Chessman's success in staying the law's avenging hand by complex legal maneuvers had long ago aroused international interest in his case. His book—a tract against the death penalty—won recruits to the abolition movement in California and around the globe. More than one prominent voice in other lands was raised on his behalf. *Osservatore Romano*, the Vatican City daily, recently labeled Chessman's "eleven years of awaiting the gas chamber" as an example of "immovable justice which has become supreme injustice."

Over the centuries the law has created a series of devices designed to protect the rights of any condemned person. The extreme uses to which Chessman and others have been allowed to push them serve to dramatize society's inner hesitancy about taking a life in payment for any crime. In a sense, then, the fate of the highly articulate prisoner in San Quentin has simply brought to the surface many already existing doubts about the wisdom of the death penalty. Should men continue to be executed?

Similar misgivings arose during the recent Truscott trial in Ontario. In the Canadian town of Goderich, on September 30, 1959, a jury found Steven Murray Truscott guilty of murdering a 12-year-old girl. Under Ontario law the death sentence is mandatory in such a case. What drew widespread attention to the trial was the age of the defendant—a boy of 14. In all likelihood, public opinion will never permit Truscott to be hanged. Indeed, many are now beginning to wonder whether a law which allows for the possibility of such a sentence is any longer socially desirable.

Dr. Benjamin Rush, pioneer psychiatrist, patriot and leading medical man of his day, fired the opening shot in the American campaign against capital punishment. Before a meeting of his fellow Philadelphians gathered in Ben Franklin's home in 1787, Rush read a paper entitled "An Enquiry Into the Effects of Public Punishment Upon Criminals and Upon Society." The substance, if not the words, of his case against hanging echoed as recently as a year ago in legislative discussions on the death penalty in California, Connecticut, Illinois, Indiana, Missouri, New Jersey, New York, Ohio and Tennessee.

A TREND TOWARD ABOLITION

Today, in the United States, 41 States and the District of Columbia still retain the gallows or its equivalent. When Gov. J. Caleb Boggs, on April 2, 1958, put his signature to a bill abolishing the death penalty in Delaware, he added that State to Michigan, Rhode Island, Wisconsin, Minnesota, North Dakota and Maine in the abolitionist ranks. Since that date, the admission

276

of Alaska and Hawaii to statehood raised their number to nine.

Most of the States, then, carry the death penalty on their books. But actual executions have become rarer each year. In 1958 the U. S. total was 48, the lowest on record since a national count was begun in 1930. Even more indicative of the trend are the annual averages for each of the last three decades. Executions averaged 167 a year from 1930 to 1939. During the years 1940-1949, the yearly average was 128. The figure was down to 74 for the nine-year period of 1950-1958. Thus, though the opponents of capital punishment have made little headway in fighting for its legal abolition, the death penalty seems destined to disappear at least by a process of increasing disuse.

Outside the United States, the picture varies. Four nations that reintroduced the death penalty for collaborators at the end of World War II quickly reverted to its abolition by law (Denmark, Norway, the Netherlands) or by custom (Belgium). Currently, most of the non-Communist countries of Europe, with the notable exceptions of England, France and Spain, do not execute criminal offenders. The death penalty has been dropped also in a majority of the Latin American republics. Closer to home, Mexico does not execute. But Canada, true to what promises to become peculiarly an Anglo-Saxon folkway, still clings to the noose.

Though England and Canada both retain the death penalty, it is not for want of abolitionist sentiment in these countries. Parliament in London has rung repeatedly with heated debates on abolition. Both in the 'thirties and again in 1950, Royal Commissions conducted extensive hearings on the subject. More recently, on this side of the Atlantic, the Canadian Parliament set up a Joint Committee on Capital and Corporal Punishment and Lotteries. The minutes of the committee's hearings constitute one of the best sources for up-to-date evidence and arguments for and against retaining the death sentence in a criminal code.

The story behind much of the drive to do away with capital punishment is one of gradual change in public sentiment throughout the Western world. In time this change made itself felt in our criminal law. Some 350 capital crimes existed in English law, for example, as late as 1780. These narrowed to about 220 by 1825. Today, murder remains the one crime for which an execution, in practice, will take place. Moreover, in addition to these modifications in the law, prosecutors insist that juries often mitigate the law's severity on their own in trials involving capital offenses. This accounts, it is said, for the difficulty encountered in getting a verdict of guilty where the death sentence would be mandatory.

Possibly the greatest change resulting from the shift in public opinion, however, has been in the way executions are handled. Today the authorities take great care to keep publicity to a minimum. In the not too distant past, on the contrary, the law appointed that a hanging or beheading be carried out in the most public manner possible. This often meant before a crowd of both sexes, young and old, gathered in a holiday mood and setting.

What accounts for the change in popular feeling and, in turn, in the law? To a great extent this reaction stemmed from a tide of humanitarian sentiment which swept Europe and the Americas in the 19th century. Church groups commonly proved to be the earliest and strongest supporters of the movement. Thus, many Quakers opposed capital punishment with the same intensity with which they struggled to free the slaves. Much of the present strength of the abolition movement, it is interesting to note, comes from the same sources. The following sample of resolutions taken by U. S. church bodies in the past year tells this story.

On October 17, 1958, the 59th triennial convention of the Protestant Episcopal Church went on record as strongly opposing capital punishment. Then, on January 2, 1959, the president and general secretary of the Massachusetts Council of Churches recommended that capital punishment be abolished immediately in that State.

Similar action was called for in Pennsylvania and New Jersey by the Philadelphia Yearly Meeting of Friends (representing some one hundred Monthly Meetings in the two States) in its session of April 1,

1959. Later that same month, on April 14, the 72nd annual assembly of the Texas Convention of Christian Churches (Disciples) denounced capital punishment as "cruel, inhuman and unjust." The assembly requested local churches to urge the Texas Legislature to abolish the electric chair.

Back once more in Pennsylvania, the Protestant Episcopal Diocese of Pennsylvania in its 175th annual convention (May 7) condemned capital punishment and asked that it be outlawed in the Commonwealth. Four days later, at Oak Lawn, Ill., the 116th annual meeting of the Congregational Christian Conference voted support of a proposal pending in the Illinois Legislature to suspend the death penalty for a six-year period by way of experiment. Outright abolition, however, was urged by the Colorado Congregational Conference on May 25—shortly after a similar move made by the Colorado Episcopal Diocese. Again in Illinois, at the end of June, the Methodist Rock River Conference summoned all Christians to take "deliberate and appropriate" action to end the death penalty. And in the East, the New York Yearly Meeting of the Religious Society of Friends, with members in New York, New Jersey, Connecticut and Vermont, on August 12 appealed to the Governors of those States to do away with capital sentences.

It will be noted that all of the above actions arose in Protestant or Quaker groups. Catholics and Jews in the United States seem to have had little to say on the subject in the past year. However, Rabbi Maurice N. Eisendrath, president of the Union of American Hebrew Congregations (an association representing one million Reform Jews in 565 synagogues), announced that the union would consider a resolution on capital punishment in its biennial assembly, at Miami Beach, Fla. in late November of 1959.

Despite the widespread support of abolition by church groups and other organizations, defenders of the death penalty still claim a solid measure of public support for it. Though philosophers, theologians, social scientists, the police and legal authorities have all had their say on the subject, the debate still goes on. Most current discussions, however, center around two basic issues. One is whether executions are necessary to satisfy justice; the other, whether such a penalty is necessary or desirable as a deterrent from serious crimes.

REASONS FAVORING CAPITAL PUNISHMENT

"A life for a life"—this remains the simplest version of the argument that justice demands death in some cases. Over the centuries, however, this rule of thumb has all but vanished from sight. It lies buried beneath a forest of distinctions on the morality of exacting such a price even for murder.

It may be of interest to note one corollary of the proposition that justice demands the death penalty. The claim is made that death should be meted out, at least for unusually heinous crimes, to satisfy in a legal manner the public's sense of outrage and its desire for vengeance. One wonders, however, whether the revolt against public executions in the old style does not point to a hopeful lessening of the cry for revenge.

Paradoxically, defenders of the death penalty sometimes also insist that an execution, in addition to being an economy measure for the State, is an act of kindness to the prisoner. The basis for this argument is the judgment that life imprisonment is a crueler fate than swift death on the gallows. Whether or not it costs less to hang a man by the neck than to keep him in prison for life would seem to depend on the price you attach to a great many intangibles. And as for weighing the relative humaneness of any mode of execution now in use, again your judgment will be influenced by deep-rooted factors in your own personality. In any event, the task of devising an objective method of making such estimates will not be easy.

Take, by way of example, the history of a recent experiment in Maryland. A few years ago that State substituted the gas chamber for the gallows. The change was widely hailed as a move to eliminate pain or torture from an execution. Yet, the late Fr. Joseph J. Ayd, S.J. (veteran sociologist at Baltimore's Loyola College and companion, over several decades, to all Maryland condemned men who walked the last mile to the gallows), could write soon after in the Baltimore *Sun*:

Had Arthur Koestler witnessed the recent gruesome gassing of a mentally underprivileged human (I.Q. 62) at the Maryland Penitentiary, he would have had added fuel for his remarkable book, *Reflections on Hanging*, and, maybe, some unkind words about Maryland's new gas chamber would have been brilliantly expressed.

IS IT A DETERRENT?

In the final analysis, however, the case for capital punishment today is based mainly on the claim that the retention of the death penalty affords society an effective protection by deterring potential evildoers. Advocates of capital punishment go on to insist that a comparison of crime rates in countries having and those not having the death penalty will support this claim. For example, this was the point of testimony by Walter H. Mulligan, president of the Chief Constables Association of Canada, before the Canadian joint committee on April 17, 1954. Speaking of policemen killed in the line of duty in those parts of the world where capital punishment has been abolished, he stated:

I submit that it will be found that the number is much higher than in those countries where the death penalty is still in effect, and this point is the main one in our submission that our Government should retain capital punishment as a form of security.

He then told the committee that his extensive contacts in police circles led him to believe that his view reflected the "general opinion among police officers on the North American continent."

In view of the forthright nature of Mr. Mulligan's statement, and because my own research on capital punishment convinced me that it was typical of the primary argument advanced everywhere in favor of retaining capital punishment, I attempted a minor test of its validity. The records on which the investigation was based came from the State police chiefs in 24

States (including the six in which the death penalty was abolished). They reported on all State police killed in these States during the years 1905 to 1954. From my analysis of these figures I concluded, in a report submitted to the Canadian joint committee in 1955, that the available data did not square with Constable Mulligan's claim.

In referring to this study—restricted as it is in scope—I do not pretend that it says the last word on the subject in itself. Its significance derives, rather, from the fact that it agrees with a series of other investigations of the anti-abolition claim. As Prof. Karl F. Schuessler of Indiana University wrote earlier in the November, 1952 issue of the *Annals* of the American Academy of Political and Social Science:

> Statistical findings and case studies converge to disprove the claim that the death penalty has any special deterrent value. The belief in the death penalty as a deterrent is repudiated by statistical studies, since they consistently demonstrate that differences in homicide rates are in no way correlated with differences in the use of the death penalty.

As this article is written, the Chessman and Truscott cases still hang fire. Bizarre elements in both these dramas will keep alive the discussion of questions raised in these pages. Moreover, on October 26, representatives of Sweden, Austria, Ceylon, Uruguay, Ecuador and Venezuela called on the United Nations to underwrite a study of capital punishment with a view to its universal abolition. This proposal, it is interesting to note, calls specifically for a study of the effect of abolition on the rate of criminality. Finally, it is most likely that in the coming year several State Legislatures will once again take up proposals to abandon the death penalty. What will be the outcome of these moves?

Certainly, the over-all trend is toward the abolition of capital punishment. Many factors lend support to this movement. Of fundamental importance is the influence of a more Christian or, at least, more humanitarian attitude toward the criminal. For a time this old-yet-new spirit seemed doomed to disappear in the bloodthirsty era of the 16th and 17th centuries. Today, to be sure, we may not be ready as yet to resume the

medieval practice of sending a murderer on pilgrimage to Jerusalem or Compostella in punishment for his crime and for his personal rehabilitation. Still, a wide sector of public opinion now inclines to the view that the execution of a prisoner is an unnecessary confession of defeat and an act of self-degradation on the part of modern society.

One final factor has, of late, won new adherents to the abolitionist cause. It is the growth of a critical attitude toward claims long made on behalf of the death penalty. Further research into the validity of these claims, particularly those concerning the alleged deterrent effect of this punishment, may well hasten the abandonment of the death penalty everywhere in civilized society. Then the gallows, the electric chair, the guillotine and the gas chamber can be relegated to our museums. There they will take their appointed places alongside the rack, the thumbscrew and other rightfully discarded instruments of earlier systems of justice.

God Knows Best

Pat Somers Cronin

EARLY TRINITY SUNDAY, some two months ahead of
schedule, I was wheeled into Mercy Hospital for
the birth of our seventh child. . . .

What is it about a Catholic hospital that makes it
seem that some peculiar protectiveness slips about you
even as you enter the doors? Perhaps any nurse anywhere would have greeted you as sympathetically, and
any orderly anywhere would have wheeled your chair
as gently. But would there have been anywhere, save
in a Catholic hospital, the statue of Christ at the Labor
Room door? And would there have been in His beloved
hands that prophetic scroll, "If you love Me, come
follow me"?

The moments preceeding birth, particularly premature birth, are emotion-packed for any woman. But
again, in a Catholic hospital, when all during labor you
have only to look at the crucifix and think over and
over through each pain, "If you love Me, come follow
Me," what is possible but complete resignation to the
divine Will?

However, life does mean hope and even a little boy
will fight for survival. "What is his name?" the doctor

asked, "Father is waiting to baptize him." "Eileen Marie," you said, having planned on another girl. "That won't do," the doctor smiled. Still groggy, you murmured, "Joseph Anthony," and only then could you relax. Father was waiting and little Tony joined the Church Militant, moments after his abrupt arrival into life.

Going back to your room, you questioned the attendant: "He is baptized?" "Yes, yes," you were assured, again gently, and I suppose gentleness is to be found in many, many secular hospitals too. At the nursery window you looked into the little incubator where Tony would spend only God knew how much time. But you and your weary husband were at peace; the matter was in God's hands now. What a blessing baptism is, surely a sacrament to inspire courage. Three A.M., Trinity Sunday: with all of Heaven rejoicing, little Tony had had quite a magnificent birthday!

In your room, still overcome by the actual fact of the baby's arrival, you faced up to his uncertain earthly future, discussing it in whispers with your husband. Two and one-half pounds, the doctor estimated; there had been no time for the usual accurate weight and height routine. But again, because you were a Catholic in a Catholic hospital, living at this dramatic moment under the roof with the Blessed Sacrament, you had only to turn to heaven and say to our Lord, "Dear God, it is in Your far-seeing Will; we have done our part, the rest is up to You." And because little Tony was named for your personal favorite, St. Anthony, who has aided you again and again, you turned to him, asking him to intercede for you, not for Tony's life, but for the manifestation of the divine Will.

During the long hours from three A.M., when sleep simply would not come, your mind dwelt on the phrase, "If you love Me, come follow Me." Surely, surely the baby would follow immediately; God had been most generous to give you such a direct sign.

But little Tony continued his valiant struggle, although Sister would never admit to more than a "pretty good, honey." "And," she added, "God sees so far ahead; sometimes He knows a soul may be lost unless He takes it right away." Where but at a Catholic hospital, you wondered gratefully, would the head nurse of the maternity department offer sage spiritual consolation as well as physical comfort?

The hours of Trinity Sunday dragged on, each adding to Tony's chances for survival. Over and over you said the rosary, content to rest and let God act. A few phone calls to your favorite convents and literally thousands of prayers were being said. What a wonderful thing, the Mystical Body of Christ!

Sunday evening your husband wheeled you down to see Tony, all pink and lovely, kicking gaily, even opening his tiny unseeing blue eyes. Toothpicks for arms and legs, you thought, but the little heart was beating and that little soul was ready. And here you were, in league with God, waiting, waiting for His word; how powerful God makes mothers and fathers; what a privilege to be parents!

Finally, after your nursery visit, you could succumb to that body-encompassing sleep that follows birth. The job is done; the body can rest. And when you awakened next morning, because this was a Catholic hospital, you had only to lie in bed, waiting for our Lord. This is something you will never accept as commonplace, that every single morning our Lord, preceded by a white-robed sister sounding a small tinkling bell, comes to any patient who wishes Him.

As you anticipated our Lord's arrival, you thought too of little Tony down the hall. He must have survived the night at least. Almost for him, you received our Lord, made your thanksgiving gratefully and then were amazed to hear the doctor's "Good-morning." The report was not good and something, surely another bit of divine generosity, propelled you from bed to take another peek at this littlest son. And what did this tiny bundle do? He curled his small fist and somehow managed a pint-sized wave. You smiled and tucked in your heart for all time that simple gesture.

Again in your room, you picked up the phone to prepare your husband for any news, but divine Providence and the hospital staff had raced ahead of you. Even as you held the phone in your hand, your dear strong husband walked in to give you the final news. In that short moment since your return from the nursery, little Tony, some twenty-eight hours old, had returned to our Lord.

Surely there are times of triumph for every mother and father, but what can ever equal this: to know with sublime certainty that a son is safely with our Lord, always and forever. Truly, He had spoken: "If you love Me, come follow Me."

Man is a toolmaker. Therefore his efforts to tame the refractory material world befit his rational nature: the accelerating pace of technology is a good thing, so long as man fits his mastery of things into a proper hierarchy of values. But many questions may be raised about the real value of our technological triumphs. They have not begun to solve the problem of giving all men real access to the goods necessary for human development. And there is a real danger that science may foster unhealthy pride in the heart of man and deaden in his heart the sense of sin. Does all this mean that there is some rationale behind that hostility to the works of science which sometimes exists among Catholics? Surely, in a world that belongs to God, there is some way of baptizing the science and technology that are changing its shape.

Men and Things

Christians
Confront
Technology

W. Norris Clarke

Gustave Weigel

Walter J. Ong

S.J.

I

BOTH THE NEED and the aptitude for technology are rooted deep in human nature. Man simply cannot live with security and dignity in this material environment of physically superior forces unless, by means of tools, he extends and intensifies the power of his own comparatively feeble body so that it can cope with nature. Thus we find that as far back as the presence of man is discernible in history it is accompanied by the use of tools. And the use of even the simplest tools is a rudimentary technology, differing only in degree from the technology of the great machines of today.

Nor is it merely a question of decent survival. If man is made as a living image of God, he must imitate in his own way the life of his Father in heaven. Now in relation to the material universe God is both its thinker and its maker—the supreme Artist. Hence man, His adopted son, must first strive to rethink the handiwork that his Father has thought up. (This is the fundamental justification for all pure science.) He must then strive to remake or transform creatively, by his own God-given powers, the world that his Father has made for him out of nothing and given him as his workshop. (This is the fundamental justification for all technology and art.)

The goal of all technology, then, is to make matter serve the human spirit as the most pliant instrument possible for authentic human growth. This involves both the gradual liberation of man from all inhumane, degrading, purely animal-like drudgery and subservience to matter, and also the positive transformation of matter to express man's own spiritual vision of the meaning and purpose of the universe.

Secondly, the unfolding of this basic aptitude is of its nature dynamic and progressive. Each successive achievement in technology builds upon what has gone before and opens up in turn new developments beyond it. As the range of possibilities constantly expands, the rate of development is able to advance more and more rapidly. This dynamic dialog of man with nature is inherent in the very presence of man as a rational animal in a material universe. To attempt to freeze this process, which by its very nature is developmental, at some supposed point of ideal equilibrium (determined by whom and on what evidence?) would be like trying to immobilize the growth of art or of human intelligence itself—indeed of any living thing, which dies when it can no longer put forth new fruits. The conclusion of all this is that progressive technology in some form or other is both natural and essential—hence basically good—for man if he is to fulfill his God-given destiny in the universe.

So much for the credit side of the account. On the debit side it must also be admitted that there are grave dangers inherent in the pursuit of technology, as in the use of all natural human aptitudes. These perils arise, it seems to me, from two main sources: first, lack of subordination to the higher spiritual good of man; second, lack of the proper rational control of the rate and timing of technological development.

The danger of the first is that what should be a mere

means, at the service of the spiritual growth of mankind, may become so all-absorbing that it will upset the proper hierarchy of values and reduce the spiritual intelligence of man to the role of a mere servant of technological progress pursued for its own sake. Technology would then become like an overdeveloped organ or the runaway growth of cancerous cells—a threat to the basic cultural and spiritual health of mankind.

The second main danger is that the tempo of technological development be allowed to follow unchecked its own inner dynamism, independently of its relation to the balanced over-all good of the people it is supposed to serve. Too rapid a tempo of change can produce an atmosphere of such constant flux and severe social dislocation that the people subjected to it will be in grave danger of becoming culturally rootless and deprived of all fixed landmarks as they are whirled hectically along by the racing current of "progress." Thus the ever increasing mobility made possible by the automobile (though not so much, strange to say, by the airplane) has so far proved to be a very mixed blessing, whose dissipating effects we have not yet learned to control.

Another form of the same danger is the so-called "enslavement of man to the machine." The harsh rhythms of the machine and its artificial environment will, it is said, dominate or destroy the healthy natural rhythms of the living body in harmony with nature as God made it. The example of the assembly line, with its impoverishment of creative ability and subjection of the workers to a monotonous, repetitive routine, is sufficient warning of where technology can lead.

All of these dangers are real and serious, in addition to the very special and obvious perils connected with the use of the immense power now at our disposal. I have no intention of trying to conjure them away by general optimistic affirmations of the "inevitable forward march of progress." The latter is a dangerous modern myth, a secularized distortion of Christian hope. Uncontrolled technology can certainly bring down disaster, perhaps irreparable, on our race. The only protection against it is a growth in man's spiritual and moral maturity proportionate to his growth in technical skill and power. Either we grow in both dimensions or we perish, like the overgrown monsters of our prehistoric past. But this is already a law in the development of every individual personality (for example, scientific geniuses with a child's knowledge of religion and morality). If individuals can solve it there is no reason why people generally cannot either. Actually, it seems to me that there is already a rapidly growing recognition on the part of both scientists and political leaders—who are also the ones most able to do something about it— of the urgent necessity of greater moral control over the exploitation of scientific and technological advances.

Furthermore, as technological development proceeds along its course among a people still endowed with basic biological, social and moral vitality—as I believe our people still is—certain laws of equilibrium and self-correction seem to be constantly and unobtrusively at work. Thus, losses in one area are compensated for by gains in another, or exaggeration in one direction generates its own counterreaction in the other direction. Thus the very mobility which seems, at least temporarily, to be weakening our roots in the family and the local community is at the same time strengthening our bonds with the rest of the world. The very increase in perfection of the means of communication at a distance, as in television, may eventually make it neither necessary nor desirable to move about so feverishly on a small scale as we now do. We may end up by visiting our friends and clients relaxedly on a two-way television circuit rather than by transporting ourselves physically to them along overcrowded highways or airways. Or by the mysterious providence of God it may happen that the insistent challenge of outer mobility may succeed more effectively than pulpit sermons in making us turn within and discover that it is possible to achieve a sense of permanence, self-identity and rootedness in more interior, supramaterial and universal values than we now believe capable of winning our allegiance.

What of the threatened enslavement of man to the machine? The danger is real. But I am convinced that it is limited by the very inner logic and laws of equilibrium of technology itself to certain transitory types of techniques and local or temporary abuses during periods of transition. The whole innate drive of technology is to substitute machines for man in all areas where monotonous, repetitive actions are the rule, and to leave man free for more intelligent creative or supervisory work. The supposed threat of a constantly increasing slavery to the machine, as some kind of inexorable drift inherent in the process of technology itself, seems to me to be largely a myth, without solid historical, psychological or sociological foundation. The true danger lies in the moral dispositions of those who use technology. The far greater peril is that men may become slaves to their fellow men rather than to their machines.

I believe, therefore, that if we have the courage to assume with full moral and intellectual maturity the responsibility of actively guiding and controlling the mighty power of technology that is now in our hands, far from being ruined by it, we shall be able rather to turn it into a profoundly beneficent instrument for the authentic growth of the human family. And no one has greater inner resources for rising to this challenge, nor more urgent motives for doing so, than the Christian.

W. NORRIS CLARKE

II

I HAVE BEEN asked to propose a counter-thesis to the essay of Father Clarke concerning a Christian judgment on technology. Fortunately I cannot make any substantial objection to the preceding article. For this I am grateful because I never like to disagree with the brilliant Father Clarke, and when the necessity arises it causes me pain. Hence most gladly I make my own the thoughts of the first essay in this trilogy. Perhaps, however, it will be possible to add some shadings to the reflections made by the preceding author.

The Prophet Ezechiel (28:26), speaking of the house

and family of Jacob, says: "Securely it shall dwell there, build houses, plant vineyards, fear no attack." St. Thomas, writing of what man can do without the help of grace (S.T., 1-2, 109, 2), says: "In the state of corrupt nature man can indeed act to achieve some particular good by the power of his own nature, as for example, the building of houses, the planting of vineyards and things of this kind." The employment of atomic power, which is today in the power of man, seems to be a far cry from the building of houses and the planting of vineyards. Yet it is more than pure whimsy to think that St. Thomas would include such a feat in his phrase, "and things of this kind." Technological progress derives from the cumulative knowledge of the human family. It is the fruit of the continuous struggle to possess the earth and to subdue it, which was the destiny divinely imposed on man according to the words in Genesis.

The malaise of moralists in the presence of the increased technological capacity of man has always struck me as unwarranted and irrelevant. Evolution seems to be the very basic pattern of the universe. Hence it seems only logical that technology among men should evolve into ever more complicated structures of power capable of ever wider efficiency. This evolution of technology should be welcomed, not lamented. The people who cry alarm because of the dehumanizing effects supposed to be inherent in the better tools and instruments that human intelligence has devised for our aid, rarely see that the high human activities they so praise were possible in past times only because vast masses of the human family were condemned by a humanly erected social system to be mere hewers of wood and carriers of water. The degree of humanism achieved by this numberless proletariat was certainly not high. In those days, in a vast sea of drab human misery, there were indeed little green isles of comfort and luxurious leisure where the few beneficiaries of the iniquitous system could discourse eloquently and elegantly on art, history, philosophy and the patterns of nature. To stand in rightful awe before the brilliant contributions of these few men and women, while overlooking the dull and tedious existence of the countless surrounding majority of their contemporaries, seems hardly humane.

Those who nostalgically praise those days of old usually do so because they wittingly or unwittingly share Plato's conception of mankind. In this vision there are a few individuals who are really men. They are the *aristoi*, the best, who in turn breed other *aristoi*. The rest by very nature must be treated as a good husbandman treats his horses and asses. He gives them what is necessary so that they can survive and be able to use their muscles to serve the master. Their own aspirations and desires are not consulted. They are expendable. Even their procreating capacities are exploited to assure the owner a continuance of an efficient physical force at his disposal.

In this cruel and un-Christian view of mankind, our human family is deterministically divided into two unequal groups: the "haves" and the "have-nots." By some kind of weird and unverified assumption, the real men are "haves" who beget real men who will be "haves," while the "have-nots" are subhuman and can only engender more subhuman "have-nots." Technological evolution endangers the privileged position of the hereditary *aristoi* because the lesser breed finally has an opportunity to enjoy leisure. Now they too will discourse about life and eternity. But since they are the great unwashed, it is asserted that they will vulgarize the arts and sciences. In this contemplation, the Platonic lover of aristocracy can only shudder.

For my part, I let him shudder—without any felt need to shudder with him. The Christian understanding of man, and indeed history itself, find no room for the postulate that human genius and human creativity come forth by some law of biological determinism. The genius is a glorious sport showing up in the most unexpected places. Improved technology gives the sport who happens to rise out of the masses the opportunity to develop his genius richly for the benefit of all. Improved technology gives leisure to all men. That very many will use it for creative ends is more than we can hope for. Yet it is true that some will do so and their contribution to culture and civilization will be a blessing.

Having made this basic recognition of the goodness of technology, we must now consider its ultimate value. Optimists, whether they be Christian or naturalist, usually look no further than the goods rooted in creation. They overlook, or at least do not take seriously, the dogma of original sin. They are always looking for man's better moment in the future. According to faith there will indeed be a golden eon at a point beyond history. However, before that point is reached, the ever-evolving human situation under the sickening influence of original sin will not change substantially.

Now technology is a phase of creation. But in this creation man himself will always be faced by his own sin and the consequences thereof. Selfishness, guilt, ignorance, anxiety and frustration will not be removed because of technological progress. The improvement of human know-how will not increase the amount of virtue in the world. The kingdom of God is not the fruit of the natural evolution of man. Only the catastrophic intervention of God, unmerited and undemanded by human efforts, will bring it about—after history ceases. In this evolving world, through the power of God and not through natural evolution, the Mystical Body of Christ gradually achieves its full stature. The growth of natural human potential is the setting in which the whole Christ matures. The setting does not enter causally into the process of maturation. Increased human efficacy furthers the designs of God's natural creation. However, the salvific will of God is distinct and only occasionally related to the creative drama. The heightening of man's creative power can readily also be the occasion of man's moral deterioration. It need not be so. Yet, whether it is or is not is a matter of indifference to the salvific designs of God. St. Paul says that where sin abounds, grace abounds more. It is not sin which produces grace. Grace is freely and independently given by a gracious God who uses the unfolding of nature as the framework for His saving bounty.

To put it briefly, the expansion of technological prowess, since it is a manifestation of God's creative will, is like all of God's creation—good. It should be hailed as such by all men. But it is *not salvific*. Of itself it neither hinders salvation nor does it hasten it. Salvation comes not from nature, no matter how effective it be. It comes from grace given on God's mysterious initiative. Before the kingdom of God arises, nature lies under the dominion of the Prince of this World. Salvation will not be of it. Only at the end will the order of creation and the order of salvation be identical. Although technology is a good thing, it is helpless to make man righteous. Man's hope can not be founded on increased human power, good though that be. Only faith and trust in the world to come can give substance to human hope. Gustave Weigel

THE OBSERVATIONS on technology by Fathers Clarke and Weigel seem to me eminently sound. Not knowing how to take exception to them, nor wanting to do so, and yet being constrained by a kind but persevering (that's why he has the job) editor to produce some sort of counterstatement, I can do nothing better than use their observations as points of departure, examining the implications of those observations in a more extended field.

The problem confronting the Catholic mind today is not the problem of tolerating the technological age, of living with it. This we do well enough. The problem is rather that of participating unselfishly in it, of contributing to it. Our present difficulties, philosophical, theological and other, vis-à-vis the age we live in seem to be in great part our inability to conceive of it positively and imaginatively.

We badly need a cosmology and a Christology sufficiently developed to enable us to lay hold of the technological age, and all it implies, with inspiration and vision. This means a cosmology and a Christology which will enable us to conceive of our entire evolutionary universe with a positive intellectual humility and enthusiasm. For our problem with the technological age is only one facet of a much larger problem—our problem with an evolving cosmos. Our technological age cannot be grasped as the reality which it is outside the framework of cosmic and intellectual and social evolution in which and as a result of which the technological age has come into being and achieved its own self-consciousness.

Our vision and enthusiasm should be without illusions, of course. As Father Weigel says so well, the expansion of technological prowess is not salvific. Men are not individually closer to God because of it. Yet, as he also says, this expansion is a good. There is in many quarters a growing awareness of this fact, but the Catholic consciousness as a whole, in the United States and elsewhere, still labors under a certain disposition not to welcome technological growth or the over-all movement of cosmic evolution as a good in its view of the over-all scheme of things. Evolution is not of course presented as an evil in most Catholics' world outlook. In fact, in this country at least, for the most part, it is not presented at all. A few articles and lectures are putting in their appearance now. But corporately we still react as though evolutionary processes were not there.

The unfolding of the basic aptitude of man to transform material reality, Father Clarke has well observed, "is of its nature dynamic and progressive." And Father Weigel adds the more general theorem: "Evolution seems to be the very basic pattern of the universe." No one can today adequately understand the material world, or those reaches of the spiritual world enmeshed in the material, such as human thought, without immersing himself in evolutionary studies. Courses in the details of evolution are a standard part of any biological training, but familiarity with the developmental pattern of God's universe is necessary as well for geology and astronomy and semantics and linguistics and an increasing number of other fields. Yet, strangely enough, in many quarters it is still thought possible to develop a Catholic world view with no serious attention to evolutionary fact or, at the maximum, with a permissive, tolerant gesture toward this great "basic pattern of the universe." How much of our corporate thinking about divine revelation gives any sustained attention at all to the possible meaning of the Incarnation for the real evolving cosmos as we know it, in which technology has now come to be?

One cannot fully understand a fact which one accepts reluctantly. When Marxist thought has stolen the march on Catholic thought, it has often done so by enthusiastically making its own a fact which Catholics have not had the courage or humility to warm up to. Father Weigel expresses a sympathetic interest in the massive and miserable proletariat of Plato's republic, the "have-nots" as contrasted with the "haves" who were Plato's *aristoi*. He does this in order to explain the forces at work in our technological age. A Marxist could urge, quite legitimately, that Marx had used this type of analysis and had felt the sympathy which it entails more than a hundred years ago: the "haves" and the "have-nots" form a perfect dialectical dyad for a dialectical penetration and understanding of the historical processes. Father Weigel is right in his analysis and in insisting that the lot of the proletariat ought to be changed, but

Marx was right first. He was right before some Catholics were, not because of his basic principles nor of his over-all aims, which were wrong, but because in this he was building upon a keen and enthusiastic awareness of the fact of change which some Catholics lacked. He seized imaginatively and creatively upon the emergence of a new technological order and upon the evolutionary nature of the universe and of human society, at a time when all too many Catholics were meeting the challenge of the age by talk of being satisfied with one's "state in life" (that is, with a static view of human society).

Certainly, we must not abandon what we already know and teach. But you are sure to lose if you are so cautious about keeping what you have that you feel no real enthusiasm for what is new and unknown.

The time is past when we can afford a merely permissive reaction to evolution or to such things as this technological age to which an evolving universe has brought us. We cannot even begin to understand technology or to make it our own and Christ's own if we regard it and other massive developments in a changing universe as incidental items, inconsequential or even unintelligible phenomena to which one need pay no great attention as human life creaks along in its supposedly unchangeable ruts. The age of technology is an era in the history of the universe, coming into being at a certain time just as dinosaurs and the first mammals and man himself did. Technology is a shape which material reality takes at a certain stage in its development, a stage at which it arrives when it has ripened over a period of some five or ten billion years for man's appearance and when human culture thereupon, over a period of probably some several hundred thousand years, has developed a store of experience such as we have at our command at present. The age we live in is a shape all things have today, different from—yet comparable to—other and earlier shapes.

What is the over-all Catholic educational effort doing to interpret with positive and creative vision this shape of things? What are we doing to interpret philosophically and theologically, imaginatively and inspiringly, a universe which everyone knows is in full evolutionary career? A retouched medieval cosmology is hopeless and inevitably false. If evolution is "the very basic pattern of the universe," it is not a thing to be discussed charily, handled gingerly, touched on incidentally. Although its details are even now not fully worked out, and probably never will be, cosmic evolution has been known to thinking men as a fact for generations. As early as *The Descent of Man* (1871), the sage and cautious Darwin notes that the principle of evolution is already "admitted by the majority of rising men" among natural scientists. This was almost a hundred years ago. The hour is getting late.

As long as change in the world was thought to be a simple cycle of life and death complicated only by the vagaries of human history stemming from unpredictable human decisions, one could enjoy a world view in which change was treated simply by contrast with non-change, as becoming is contrasted with being. Once we know, however, that created material being changes over vast eons in a directional pattern, in which more advanced forms of being appear only after less advanced forms, we cannot be so offhand. The study of the supposedly cyclic generation and corruption postulated by ancient philosophies no longer suffices. Knowing a vast number of details concerning the movement of matter through time and its greater and greater complexification, if only to understand ourselves better we need to puzzle out the *sequence* of changes which represent an activity proper to material being of which earlier man had been unaware. Protein molecules far postdate a world of simple inorganic molecules and atoms. Early geological deposits yield only simple forms of life, later deposits alone yield higher forms. And these become more and more advanced as time moves on. Moreover, species vary from place to place, as well as from age to age. The flora and fauna of the Western Hemisphere are quite different from those of the Eastern. And there is a long and complex sequence in human cultures, too.

301

Such facts were of course inaccessible to earlier "wisdom lovers" or philosophers, who lived before man had been able to accumulate all the vast store of observation and reflection on which we can draw today. But now that we know these facts, we cannot afford to disregard them in constructing our world view. Any wisdom, natural or supernatural, worthy of the name now has to deal with the fact of linear development in the history of material being and of human culture, in which the present grows out of a past different from itself and opens into a future different from both present and past. This is particularly true if we are to try to interpret the meaning of the technological age. For this age is most strikingly something which has not existed before and yet something into which the preceding history of human society and of human thought has led, as well as something pregnant with a future sure to be different from both present and past.

For the technological age is not only an epoch in the totality of cosmic evolution—all ages have been that—but it is also keenly conscious of the fact that it is an epoch in a total process. To interpret it to itself we must work out a world view which is thoroughly Christian and which also operates in close, imaginative, sympathetic, creative association with the facts of cosmic development, for this development is God's work and something humbly to be revered.

WALTER J. ONG

Sin, Sickness and Psychiatry

John R. Connery

S. J.

ARE SIN and mental sickness two faces of the same coin? If they are, psychiatry, presuming that it can cure the illness, can make saints of us all. Psychiatry, of course, makes no claim to produce sanctity. But there are psychiatrists who will say: "There are no sinners, there are just sick people." This is an extreme position, and more philosophical than psychiatric, but it illustrates the needless conflict that has in the past divided the theologian and the moralist from the psychiatrist.

The various aspects of this conflict are best illustrated in the different opinions advanced regarding the relationship between sin and mental sickness. Besides the opinion that would regard sin as sickness rather than an expression of the will of the sinner, there is a second opinion that, surprisingly, reverses the relationship. According to this opinion, sin, far from being the result, is really the cause of mental illness. A third opinion refuses to consider sin either as cause or effect of mental illness, but tends to regard it as a cure. Fortunately, these opinions, at least to the extent that they are objectionable to either theologian or psychiatrist, cannot today claim any large number of adherents. Nevertheless, it will perhaps be profitable to explore them, to understand more precisely just what is the relation between sin and mental disease.

THE PURPOSE OF CONFESSION

If sin were merely a symptom of mental disease, the psychiatric clinic could, and should, be substituted for the confessional. Sacramental absolution is not intended to be a cure for disease. The Church has a sacrament for the sick, but it is the sacrament of extreme unction, not the sacrament of penance.

It is quite true that the act of confessing one's sins, the acceptance of the priest and of his pastoral counsel can have some therapeutic value, but this is not the primary purpose for which the sacrament was instituted. The sacrament of penance is primarily a sacrament of forgiveness. Consequently, it presumes responsibility for sin and has no meaning outside of a context of responsibility. An opinion that reduces sin to sickness, then, is incompatible with the existence of a sacrament of forgiveness; it is unacceptable to those who hold the sacrament of penance to be an integral part of the Christian economy for fallen man.

There is, of course, a sense in which all of us are sick—we are all victims of original sin. But Catholic theology has never admitted that this sickness destroys human freedom. Responsibility for personal sin cannot be shifted entirely to the shoulders of Adam. Moreover, this sickness is not something that will yield to psychiatric treatment. Nothing short of a restoration of man to the state of original justice will remove it.

WEAKNESS OR MALICE?

Yet we must admit that we do not enjoy the freedom of Adam. Original sin has introduced a certain dissociation into our nature, a conflict between our instincts and appetites and right reason. We do not have the control that a perfectly integrated nature would have. Passions and emotions leading to sin arise spontaneously and often continue to make their demands beyond the intervention of the will. And when man does sin, it

304

is more often because he yields to these passions than because he deliberately arouses them. As theologians say, his sins are very frequently of weakness rather than of malice.

It is a strange paradox, too, that we do not begin to function freely until in a sense our freedom is already prejudiced. If the child could function freely from birth, he would be more his own master. But the child's early formation is directed by his parents. By the time he gets to the age where he can gradually take over personal responsibility for his conduct, he is no longer the same pliable person he was at birth. He has already been given a certain *formation*. It would indeed be incongruous if this early formation were incompatible with personal autonomy, but there can be no doubt that the child's life has already been given a distinctive moral direction which will not easily be changed. If the child has been properly formed, he will have certain moral assets to draw upon. Otherwise, he will begin his moral life with definite liabilities.

There are also other elements to be taken into consideration in estimating the extent of individual freedom. Even when a child begins to direct his own moral life, every action he performs influences his future. This is true of good actions, but it is true as well, and perhaps even more so, of sinful actions. No act can be isolated or erased from our past. It leaves its mark on our personalities and becomes a factor in our next decision. This will be particularly true if the act has become a habit. As has often been said, we *are* our past. If that past has taken a certain direction, it will become increasingly difficult to change it as time goes on. In common parlance, it will take greater will power.

This continuity with our past is admittedly a handicap where that past has been sinful, but it is also essential to moral progress. If one is to grow morally, he must be able to profit from past good conduct. Habitual good conduct in the past should endow him with a certain moral facility. Once such ease of operation is acquired in one moral area, the will can be released for conquest in other areas. This is the way moral progress is made. It is, if you will, the economy of moral development. It is not desirable, of course, to reduce moral conduct to a purely mechanical process. But it is not desirable, either, that good conduct should always be difficult. We do not necessarily measure the goodness of an act by the difficulty it involves. But a certain facility in performing moral acts is certainly consistent with liberty, especially if this facility is itself a testimony to constructive use of freedom in a person's past life.

At any rate, when the will goes into action, it can be confronted with an initial inclination toward good or evil. In fact, in the beginner the tendency toward evil may be more frequent. But whether this tendency is the result of original sin or early formation or previous habit, it will not necessarily be compelling in the sense that it will rule out human freedom. Even when it amounts to a pathological force, although there will be some impairment of will, freedom will not be ruled out completely. Sin, then, like good conduct, can be explained to some extent in terms of a person's past, but this does not prevent an actual commitment of the will in the present. To what extent there is actual commitment will depend on the circumstances not only of the person but also of the individual act.

GUILT FEELINGS

If it is an oversimplification to reduce sin to sickness, it is even more naive to consider sin a cure for mental illness. Fortunately, the reputable psychiatrist will not subscribe to any general theory of sin therapy. But it is not difficult to see how the temptation arises to resort to such therapy, particularly in the realm of sex. In his professional work the psychiatrist comes into contact with guilt feelings that not only disturb emotional balance but actually paralyze action. The curious aspect of these feelings is that they plague the innocent; the hardened sinner fails to experience them. It is easy for a psychiatrist whose theological or religious background is deficient to conclude that guilt feelings are the result of moral striving and that, consequently, the remedy consists in abandoning such striving.

The Church, of course, has always considered a

healthy sense of sin a moral asset, not a liability. The recognition of the self as a sinner is the beginning of conversion. It is quite true that this sense of sin grows as the Christian grows in sanctity. The Christian attitude, no matter how far along the road to perfection one may have traveled, always remains that of the publican rather than the pharisee, and the saints have always considered themselves the worst of sinners. One might be tempted to consider this a pious exaggeration; or worse, one might conclude from it to the pathological nature of guilt feelings. Either judgment would be a mistake.

The sense of sin is linked to the sense of God. As the creature comes into more intimate contact with infinite Sanctity and Goodness, it is quite natural that awareness of his own defects should be sharpened and deepened. Remoteness from God, on the contrary, removes the contrast necessary for the sinner to recognize his true condition. The only contrast available to him is that with other creatures, which is immeasurably less revealing. The sense of sin that the saints experience is neither insincere nor pathological. It is a genuine and healthy experience of the evil in themselves—however slight it may seem to others—against a background of infinite Sanctity.

There is certainly a sense of sin that is not religiously profitable, but a real handicap. It makes psychological cripples of its victims. This sense of guilt has nothing to do with religious truth but, rather, resists it stubbornly. For instance, it is not affected by sacramental absolution, and it turns a closed ear to the appeal of divine mercy. This is the sense of guilt which manifests itself in the scrupulous conscience; psychiatrists classify it as a form of obsessive neurosis. While the obsessive neurosis itself is no more common among Catholics than among others, the anxiety characteristic of it seems more often related to the sphere of morality among Catholics. The scrupulous conscience is a kind of "Catholic disease."

It is their contact with this type of guilt that has stimulated the attacks of some psychiatrists on the doctrine of sin. In a desperate attempt to alleviate these feelings they may even be tempted to have recourse to sin therapy. Yet most of those who take issue with the Catholic doctrine of sin and punishment are realistic enough to recognize that wrongdoing is not the cure for neurotic guilt feelings. But they would like to see the concept of sin disappear. In their opinion the world of obedience, sin and guilt is the world of the child, the world of the primitive, which the adult must outgrow and which adult society must leave behind. The adult, they feel, should be motivated by more positive and altruistic feelings.

The Catholic theologian certainly recognizes the importance of loyalty and love in the realm of motivation and he approves wholeheartedly of a morality founded upon charity. But it is difficult to see how a morality of love is possible without a morality of sin. How deep can that love be which does not recognize betrayal or experience remorse about it? One would rather expect that the deeper the love goes, the more profound the feelings of remorse will be. Guilt feelings are, indeed, the inverse expression of love. The loss of a sense of sin, therefore, far from being an indication of psychological maturity, must be traced to a loss of love, a loss of the sense of God. As such, the loss of a sense of sin must be considered a psychological handicap, tantamount to a loss of the sense of pain in the physical order. As long as sin is an objective reality, there must be a sense of sin. The whole concept of salvation and redemption in the Christian economy presumes this reality. It assuredly has no meaning without it.

There is, unquestionably, a great difference between a healthy sense of sin and a morbid one. The healthy sense of sin is linked to genuine fault; the morbid sense is unfounded. The origin of this morbidity is not always easy to detect, but one can point to certain factors in the early training of the child that can foster a scrupulous type of conscience. Overanxious parents, for instance, can easily pass their morbid fear of sin on to their children. Just by their association with them, the children can copy the anxious attitude of the parents toward sin. Similarly, overprotective parents, who attempt to lead their children's lives instead of teaching them personal responsibility, can deprive the children of the education they need in decision making. Since life will eventually demand such decision making, they will be overwhelmed with anxiety whenever they are faced with the task. Parents who are perfectionists, who constantly nag at children and make no allowance for the failings natural to children, can generate a kind of nagging conscience in the children themselves. Finally, parents who motivate their children primarily through fear and punishment, and, when it is necessary to bolster their own authority, introduce God to the children as a kind of superpoliceman, can easily cause the anxious conscience of the scrupulous person.

FRIENDSHIP WITH CHRIST

The child's first contacts with religion and moral duty should not be dominated by fear. It is clearly unfair to threaten with divine punishment a child who is as yet incapable of formal sin. The Christian must indeed have a sense of sin, but it should not be linked primarily with a fear for self and a dread of punishment; it should have that reference to love and to Christ that is basic to it. Sin consists primarily in breaking off a relationship of friendship and love with Christ. Similarly, recourse to the sacrament of penance and genuine penitence are not aimed primarily at personal security but at restoring this all-important friendship. Fear of punishment, which is at best emergency motivation, should not dominate the Christian's moral life. If the conflict between psychiatry and religion succeeds in correcting a negative approach of this kind to the Christian moral life, it will have been worth-while.

A third source of conflict between religion and psychiatry originates in the opinion that neurosis must be traced to sin. According to this opinion, it is because the patient has repressed his conscience, rather than because he has repressed his instinctive drives, that he develops a neurosis. Although this position is held by some first-rate psychologists and psychiatrists, it is vigorously opposed by equally competent representatives of these fields. From a religious viewpoint it does not have the objectionable features of the opinions already considered, but it is not necessarily true because it is religiously more agreeable. There are, indeed, good reasons for questioning it. First of all, there are many habitual sinners who to all appearances have average mental and emotional balance. Secondly, the scrupulous conscience, which usually must be classified as neurotic to some degree, does not ordinarily have its origin in past sin. For the most part, the scrupulous individual is as remote from sin as one can get.

THE CONFESSOR'S PROVINCE

But whatever may be said for the truth of the opinion that neurosis must be traced to sin, it would be a mistake to conclude from it that mental sickness is a simple moral problem. It is just as much a mistake to attempt to substitute the confessional for the psychiatric clinic as it is to substitute the psychiatric clinic for the confessional. Whatever may be the cause of the serious neurosis, it is not the province of the confessor to deal with it. The confessor will have to deal with the neurotic and psychotic penitent, but the disturbance itself is not his concern, any more than sin is the concern of the psychiatrist. Even if one were to grant that the neurosis or psychosis in a particular case originated in some moral failure, it has gone beyond the stage where it will yield to the ordinary moral solution. I suppose the best illustration of this fact will be found in the case of the alcoholic, although it is

310

by no means clear whether one is an alcoholic because he drinks to excess or drinks to excess because he is an alcoholic. At any rate, ordinary excessive drinking will yield to a moral solution. But the alcoholic seems to have gone beyond the point of moral return. Sacramental confession will not cure the alcoholic, any more than it will cure tuberculosis. As we have already pointed out in another connection, it is not a cure for disease. Mental disease is no more the province of the priest than physical disease.

A conflict between psychiatry and religion is just as needless as a conflict between medicine and religion. It is encouraging to see this conflict being resolved today in the recognition on both sides that each has its place and that neither can be reduced to the other. Religion will not eliminate the need for psychiatry, and psychiatry will not serve as a substitute for religion. The Christian needs the ministrations of the priest; he may also need the services of the psychiatrist. He must not expect either to do the work of the other.

The Vanishing Hero

Andrew M. Greeley

K ENNETH S. DAVIS ends his tragic biography of
Charles A. Lindbergh with an account of how
the motion picture, *The Spirit of St. Louis,* was
a box-office failure because few moviegoers under forty
either knew or cared about Lindbergh. In the closing
words of the book, Davis describes the famous *New
Yorker* cartoon in which a boy says to his father, as they
walk away from a theatre: "If everyone thought what
he did was so marvelous, how come he never got
famous?"

Davis sees this as the unhappy ending of a great
hero's romance with the American public. However,
there is more involved. Even those young Americans
who can grasp that flying the Atlantic alone in a 110-
mile-per-hour Ryan monoplane was an amazing feat find
it impossible to understand the tremendous ovation
which this accomplishment earned for the Lone Eagle.
That Lindbergh could have become one of the truly
important men in our land, offering counsel to the
powerful and the wealthy, and arguing in public with
the President, is beyond the belief of the present generation. As one young man put it to me, "So he flew

the Atlantic. So what?" It is not merely that flying the Atlantic has become a commonplace, but that heroism —or at least hero worship—has become a thing of the past. The Lindbergh phenomenon simply could not happen in 1959. The first man to the moon—in the unlikely supposition that he is an American—will never capture the public imagination as Lindbergh did in 1927.

One searches the national scene in vain for any trace of a hero. The attempt to build up Dr. Jonas Salk as a latter-day Edison had barely gotten off the ground when confusion over the safety of his vaccine and governmental bungling in its distribution destroyed his chances. Mickey Mantle (or, last year, Luis Aparicio) does not occupy in the imagination of the young anywhere near the place that Ruth or Gehrig or even Di Maggio did. College football stars, if we are to believe a recent article in *Harper's,* are no longer the toast of Big Ten campuses; the student body regards them as mere paid professionals. The "astronauts" are favored with complete coverage by *Life,* but few think they will beat some nameless Russian into orbit, and not many people really care. Tom Mix, Buck Jones, Gene Autry and Roy Rogers have been succeeded by the very nonheroic but indisputably "cool" Maverick Brothers. No longer do boys collect cards with pictures of home run kings or galloping halfbacks. Now, on the contrary, they save and trade pictures of ghouls, vampires, werewolves, two-headed monsters, dancing skeletons and assorted odd creatures from outer space—all furnished by the obliging manufacturers of bubble gum.

THE TIMES ARE SOPHISTICATED

Hardly anyone can remember the last time a leading character in a major novel was in any noticeable way an admirable person. The idols of campus radicals (such as they are) are no longer a Dewey or a Tugwell, but rather a Kerouac or a Corso or a Ginsberg. The typical labor leader in the public mind is not a crusading John L. Lewis or Phil Murray, but a smooth though tough negotiator like David McDonald. The efforts of several Catholic organizations to promote

313

prominent entertainers as model Catholics have ended disastrously. Even in the political world no leaders excite the admiration or the dislike caused by an F.D.R. —or even by an H.S.T. President Eisenhower was unquestionably a hero eight years ago, but it is dubious whether he remains one. A father figure or a "personality" perhaps, Dwight D. Eisenhower might well be called the last of the national heroes.

There are many reasons for the disappearance of the hero from the American environment. World War II was a disillusioning experience, and the disillusionment was compounded by the Korean debacle. We were sated with heroes during the war and found out later that many of the heroes had been created by publicity men for "morale purposes"—whatever that might mean. There was, of course, much bravery in both conflicts, but in mechanized, electronic wars bravery is often irrelevant and not infrequently useless. Most Americans, therefore, tend to feel that heroism is pointless and that a hero may be stupid or mad, or else that he is a chap who is running away from personal problems, or is incredibly naive. An alleged hero is greeted with scepticism and even distrust, but hardly ever with admiration.

Besides being disillusioned, we are also extremely sophisticated. A good number of us know enough about the techniques of publicity build-ups to be able to spot a smart public-relations man's handiwork a mile away. We are well aware that the world we live in is anything but an honest place, and we suspect that everyone who has done something outstanding or is alleged to be doing something outstanding has an "angle" somewhere that will emerge if we just wait around long enough. We know that big-time athletics is a business, not a sport—and if we happen not to know it, the antics of major-league baseball owners would certainly convince us. We know that major scientific discoveries are no longer made by isolated geniuses but rather by well-equipped teams working for big corporations or affluent foundations. We realize that the entertainment world is a land of what would charitably be called make-believe or, uncharitably, phoniness.

Hence, we at least pretend not to be surprised by the quiz-show scandals. (Despite the anguished moralizing of editorial writers, average citizens seemed remarkably unperturbed by the whole sorry spectacle. Most of them seemed to feel that if they were in the same circumstances as the hapless contestants, they would do the same thing themselves.)

We know that politics is a profession of eternal compromising where even the most shining knight must soon learn to "make deals" and ignore the many shady doings of his underlings. We know that "personalities" can be "merchandised" and "packaged" and that any connection between the public image of a "personality" and his real personality is entirely accidental. So we take our heroes with a grain of salt.

There seems to exist a kind of Gresham's law of publicity, according to which authentic greatness is corrupted by association with pseudo-greatness. Heroes are somehow tainted by association with "personalities." If the Lindbergh feat happened today instead of in the 1920's, he would appear on the Ed Sullivan show, have his picture on the cover of *Time*, be the subject of a serial biography in the *Saturday Evening Post*, star in a highly fictionalized movie account of his flight and trade wise cracks with Jack Paar. All of these "stunts" are harmless in themselves, but taken together they constitute the same type of treatment accorded to quiz-show winners, tennis stars, rising young "sick" comedians, the newest teen-age "singing" (the term is used loosely) sensation, beatnik poets and any other odd characters that temporarily awaken public interest in our blasé society.

THE RADIO AND TV DID IT

There may, of course, be a real distinction between celebrity and heroism, but such nuances are hard to catch in a mass-culture world. The nation is strongly tempted to lump all public figures into the same two general types of phenomena—the amusing and the diverting. If the chair next to Jack Paar is occupied one night by a medical missionary from Laos and the next night by a brash and clever starlet, there is little chance of the missionary's raising public respect for the starlet, but considerable danger that the starlet will subtly taint the public image of a real hero. (Obviously, I'm talking about Dr. Thomas Dooley; he seems to realize the chance that he is taking and is willing to run the risk. Perhaps there is no greater heroism than to endanger a reputation for genuine personal heroism in the service of something more important.)

The mass media are the great equalizers. They reduce everything to a homogenized common denominator. They have room for the bizarre and the peculiar, but no room for the truly different. "This is Your Life" and "Person to Person" carry this equalizing function to its logical absurdity. The extraordinary person is made to look ordinary. The hero, who is always just a little bit larger than human, is reduced to the commonplace, the banal, the trivial. And the public yawns and looks for someone else to stimulate its dulled sensitiveness. Heroism vanishes not in disgrace but in boredom.

Yet, there are other reasons for the vanishing hero than the equalizing influence of the mass media. For there are still heroes, even if we do not see them or try to convert them into something different from what they are. A year that has seen a Thomas Dooley and a Shirley O'Neill, the girl who tried to save a man from an attacking shark, can hardly be said to be a year without heroism. The human spirit is still capable of bravery against incredible odds. Man is still capable of breaking out of the ordinary run of everyday activities and doing the startling, the remarkable. There are still a few Americans who are willing and eager to dedicate their energies and even their lives to the service of their fellows. There is still a handful of young people searching for ways to make a significant contribution to human progress and happiness no matter what personal inconveniences, discomforts and even sacrifices are required. It is not heroism that has vanished but hero worship. If we Americans have allowed the mass media to taint heroism and even to destroy the notion of it in the market place of common ideas, the reason is not the absence of heroes but rather our fear of them.

SOMETHING GOOD HAS GONE

For the hero is a reproach to the rest of us. We seek eagerly for his feet of clay so as to find an excuse for our own laziness and indifference. In the late 1950's we Americans do not want heroes. Reaction to Dr. Dooley is a perfect example of our contemporary indifference to the hero. This "splendid American," in many ways so like Lindbergh, has stirred a completely different public reaction. As a young friend of mine observed: "If Dooley should die, a lot of people will weep, but there won't be very many who will want to take his place." In 1927 the public identified itself with Lindbergh. The young could see themselves doing the same thing when they got older. The old would have liked to see their children accomplish something like what the Lone Eagle had done. But precious few Americans want to go to Laos to heal the sick; in fact, practically no one would even give it a thought. Most parents would be gravely displeased if their offspring even suggested that such a vocation might be worthwhile. As a nation we admired Lindbergh and wanted to imitate him; today we are fascinated by Tom Dooley and cheerfully contribute money to his cause. And so the hero vanishes and is soon forgotten.

The vanishing of the hero is then part of the whole complex malaise which has settled upon our nation.

317

We want to be left alone so we can enjoy our Good
Life free from social responsibilities. We want to "play
it cool." Life is too complicated and involved, too confused and dangerous for us to depart from the comfortable routine we have carved out for ourselves from
the mess around us. The hero and the heroine refuse
to subscribe to our National Compromise with indifference. Hence, we have no room for them.

Such a state of affairs should be disturbing to a
religion which has based much of its traditional pedagogy on hero worship of Christ, the Blessed Mother
and the saints. In a world determined to "play it cool,"
one wonders how much relevance these models of the
Christian life still have. The ascetical dictum *"admiran-
dus sed non imitandus"* ("to be admired but not imi-
tated"), used at times of certain of the more spectacular
rigors of the saints, has at best only a limited area of
proper application; yet American Catholics are sorely
tempted to make it a guiding principle of their spiritual
life, and to place it side by side with that glittering
absolute of other-directed man—"Everybody is doing it."

The decline of public idealism between the age of
Lindbergh and the era of Dooley should be even more
troubling to Catholics. The healing of the sick in Southeast Asia is far more in line with the traditional Christian notion of heroism than the spanning of the Atlantic.
There still exists in our land some depth of interest in
scientific achievement, but the corporal works of mercy
occasion only passing fancy. It is not a question of our
trying to defend these principles of charity from direct
attack. That would be relatively easy. It is rather a
problem of maintaining them as vital parts of the life
of our Catholic people when all the world around us
acts as though heroic virtue were irrelevant.

When someone writes a pessimistic little piece like
this one, it is normally demanded of him that he provide
answers. A writer who attempts to describe a critical
problem is apparently thought to incur some sort of
obligation of coming up with a pat, easy answer. But
there are no easy answers. There never have been and
there never will be. If our nation is to survive we must
once again have popular heroes who will inspire us

to greatness through times of crises. The mass media must bear much of the blame for corrupting the image of heroism in the public eye. The media can be reformed, but only if the public wants this reform badly enough. The public will get authentic heroes again only when it feels the need for them. But there seems to be no way in which the public can be persuaded to face the reproach which heroism involves. Yet must not some way be found—and soon? For, as the atomic scientists keep warning us, it is two minutes to midnight.

Science and the
Catholic Tradition

Ernan McMullin

IT IS A STRIKING fact, and one often commented on, that
the underlying attitude of the average Catholic toward
the whole enterprise of theoretic science is usually assumed to be one of hostility. He is the inheritor of a
sad tradition of misunderstanding and misjudgment in
this matter, one which goes back more than three centuries to the period in which physical science, as we
know it today, was just beginning to take shape.

The Church's condemnation of Galileo marked—
though the Church's spokesmen could not realize it—
a moment of grave decision. Galileo had been eloquently (if not always convincingly) contending for
the freedom of the "new science" from theological
control. In his forthright *Letter to Castelli*, he argued
that

> the authority of the Sacred Scriptures has as its sole
> aim to convince men of those truths which are nec-
> essary for their salvation. . . . But that the same
> God who has endowed us with senses, reason and
> understanding should not wish us to use them and
> should desire to impart to us by another means
> knowledge which we have it in our power to ac-

quire by their use—this is a thing which I do not think I am bound to believe.

He was on the right track, as it turned out, but the theologians were not going to be easily convinced of this. Their supervisory competence in matters physical had too long gone uncontested for them to take kindly to a man who warned them bluntly that "professors of theology should not arrogate to themselves the authority to decide on controversies in professions they have neither studied nor practiced." Forgetting the caution of Augustine, who had written that "the Holy Spirit did not desire that men should learn things [from the Bible] that are useful to no one for salvation," and ignoring the lesson of Aquinas, whose successful efforts to establish the autonomy of philosophy had met with vehement opposition from the Augustinian theologians of his day, the theologians declared that the theory that the earth moved was formally heretical. This was equivalent to outlawing the upstart new science of the "mathematicians"; it was, in fact, a declaration of war.

It is easy to find excuses for the theologians. The die-hard Aristotelians whom Galileo had confounded were the ones who actually initiated the campaign to have his novel views declared heretical. As the denunciation to the Holy Office phrased it, the Galileans "were treading under foot the entire philosophy of Aristotle, which had been of such service to scholastic theology." Strong measures of repression were therefore demanded by the beleaguered philosophers, who were, as Galileo wryly put it, "unable to withstand assault on their own." In addition, the theologians themselves had been growing increasingly sensitive about questions involving the interpretation of Scripture; the Protestant challenge had made them much less receptive to developments in the concept of inspiration than their predecessors had been. The Church's reaction to the 17th-century crisis was thus very different from her reaction to the very similar crisis in the mid-13th century, when Aristotle's novel views in physics and psychology seemed to threaten the intellectual foundations of Christendom. That Galileo failed in his attempt to provide a way for the Church to assimilate the new learning where Aquinas had succeeded, is not so much an indication of a difference between the two men (though Galileo with his scorching polemic and soaring vanity stirred up a fierceness of personal opposition that the serene Aquinas never had to contend with) or between their aims, as it is an indication of the failure of nerve that followed the Counter Reformation, a failure which all but paralyzed intellectual initiative in the Church for two centuries.

A SUSPICIOUSNESS TOWARD SCIENCE

Physical science had not originated in the East nor in the Arab world, even though mathematics and technology were already relatively advanced in these areas, but rather in the Christian West, whose belief in the orderliness and "creatureliness" of the universe encouraged a constructive and theoretical approach to the problems of nature. In the early growth of this science, bishops like Grosseteste, Albert of Saxony and Oresme, as well as priests like Albertus Magnus, Bradwardine and Buridan had played a decisive part. In Galileo's own day, the contributions to science of priests like Copernicus and Mersenne were known to all; indeed, Galileo's strongest support came from priest-friends—Foscarini, the Carmelite provincial; Castelli, the Benedictine professor of philosophy; Ciampoli, secretary to Urban VIII; Dini, archbishop of Fermo. But within a generation all this had changed. Reactionism set in, and the intellectual forces of the Church gradually withdrew from the fields of secular learning which they had dominated for so long, back to the seemingly secure fortifications of a tried and true traditionalism. For the next two hundred years scarcely a single theologian, philosopher or scientist of the caliber of a Cajetan or a Copernicus was to appear behind those fortifications. Their places were taken by the preacher and the casuist. During the time when the "modern" mind was being molded by intellectual giants like Newton, Leibnitz and Kant, the Church was voiceless and intellectually almost impotent; she could take no part in directing the flood of new ideas. The age of Newman and Mercier and Lemaître was still a long way off.

But this unhappy story reveals only one of the causes of the latent hostility between scientists and Christian theologians that sometimes, even today, breaks out into open warfare. In England, the national church at first greeted the new science rapturously, seeing in it a wonderful manner of discovering (in Robert Boyle's phrase) "the footsteps and impressions and perfections of the Creator," of scrutinizing "the vast library of creation" (John Ray). But a nagging doubt soon arose. Did not the new physics lead to a mechanistic world-view which was incompatible with belief in the Christian God? And so the Anglican apologists began to find themselves on the defensive against allegations that they were promoting atheism (Bishop Bentley's reproach against Newton); they set about writing treatises like *The Darkness of Atheism Dispelled by the Light of Nature* (Charleston) and *The Wisdom of God Manifested in the Works of Creation* (Boyle). These works tried to provide a rational basis for a belief in God which would be acceptable to scientists. They searched for "such principles as might work with considering men for the belief in a deity" (Newton in a letter to Bentley). But their natural religion, with its emphasis on physical law and design, took little account of the supernatural side of the Christian message; instead of shoring up Christianity, natural religion soon began to displace it. As a recent writer puts it, "although their absorption in natural religion and the external manifestations of divine power did not dispute or deny any specific Christian doctrine, it did more to undermine Christianity than any conclusion of natural science ever did" (Westfall).

In the century that followed, Anglican theology was buried in the deist landslide. The Watchmaker God of the Newtonian world-machine (who had to intervene in the universe to keep planetary systems stable) became less and less believable as time wore on and scientific explanation was seen to be total in its own order. We do not *need* the hypothesis of God in physics, as Laplace explained patiently to Napoleon. Neither do we need it in biology, as Darwin's century was soon to discover. The diversity of species, the marvelous intricacy of organisms, the adaptation of living beings to their environment—all these and many other striking facts about the living world which had formerly been thought to be explicable only in terms of special divine "interventions," now appeared as natural corollaries of the all-embracing scientific concept of evolution. But the Anglican Church felt that the time had come to make a stand (American Protestant groups like the Baptists were later to come to the same decision), and so they joined battle with the "atheist" defenders of the new theory—Huxley, Haeckel, Tyndall and the rest. History repeated itself—except that the Anglicans lacked the canonical sword Galileo's opponents had been able to wield—and the results were just as disastrous as before.

And so, both ways were tried. The Catholic Church, after an auspicious start, lost confidence and treated the new science with suspicion as a potential competitor of theology. This led for a time to the eclipse of science within the Church and to a near rupture of the harmonious, but always precarious balance between faith and natural reason which had prevailed since the time of Aquinas. The Anglican churchmen welcomed the new science as a helpmate of theology; but it ultimately proved a Trojan horse to them. Here, then, is the background we must keep in mind when we talk of the "conflict" between science and Christianity. It will be seen that the tension is due to two main factors— the past efforts of theologians to regiment science and to extend their competence considerably beyond its proper limits, and the growing "Caesarism" of science, which seems to explain everything and to make supernatural modes of thought appear hopelessly old-fashioned. The "Catholic" attitude toward science has been strongly affected by these factors. The peculiar combination of bad conscience and inferiority complex they can give rise to is vividly illustrated, for example, by the statements about science and scientists that one sometimes finds in certain sections of the Catholic press.

CAN THE GAP BE BRIDGED?

There is a real problem to be faced here. Science has

unquestionably encouraged the spread of irreligion. Are we then to retreat from it, as some leading Protestant and Jewish thinkers seem to advocate? Are we to set science over against religion as an alien and hostile fact, or are we to incorporate it in our world-view as part of that total intelligibility which it is given to man alone to discover in God's universe? Does the advance of science pose a threat to the Christian's theological understanding of the universe?

To answer this last question, we must see something of what is meant by "explanation"—scientific, philosophical and theological. Each discipline proceeds in a different way to "explain" the same thing; each has, if you will, a different idea of what constitutes "explanation." For the scientist, the death of a dog will be "explained" in terms of a virus; for the philosopher, it will be "explained" in terms of matter and form; for the theologian, it will be "explained" as part of God's providence. Now the exponent of any one of these modes of explanation is quite liable to regard the other modes as being trivial or even spurious. For instance, the scientist may protest to the theologian: "Your statement that God is good is applicable to every contingency that can arise. Therefore, its truth cannot be tested and it explains nothing." Nor does it, in the scientific sense of the word, for science requires that an explanation be specific and thus, conceivably, falsifiable.

Of course, this objection will not be taken seriously by anyone who has first grasped the difference between these quite diverse ideals of "explanation" and has then satisfied himself of the legitimacy of each. Furthermore, an analysis of the methods of procedure followed in these disciplines shows that each of the orders of explanation is autonomous and—in principle, at least—complete in its own domain. This means, for example, that there cannot ordinarily be any question of science happening on "something it can never explain." Science is capable of explaining any repeatable physical phenomenon, according to its own sense of the word "explain."

These points are understood much better today than they used to be. It was once assumed that each kind

325

of being (a stone, a gnat, a star) was fashioned separately by God; this implied that the *only* explanation of why things are as they are is a theological one. The projection of a scientific framework back into the prehistory of our universe—in the theory of biological evolution, for example—indicates that the matter is much more complicated than this. We are beginning to see a continuous line of descent from the primitive nebula almost to man himself. Science has discovered the laws by which the stars evolved; we know why the earth is the sort of planet it is; we know a little, at least, of what brought about those genetic changes which produced more and more complicated animal nervous systems until finally one may have been sufficiently developed for God to infuse into it the breath of rationality, the human soul.

It is a majestic picture that science here presents to us, one after the heart of Augustine, who saw the whole plan of God's creation contained germinally in the original desolation. God is not "intervening" at every moment, as Platonic teleology and Aristotelian physics led medieval thinkers to assume. God is *transcendent;* He is no demiurge or watchmaker. His creation and conservation are one and the same, timeless and allwise. There are no last-moment additions to His plan: everything is allowed for in the original blueprint.

SCIENCE, TOO, IS GOD'S

Science now begins to emerge as an essential component in our understanding of God's plan. Man is still the pivotal point in the universe. The scientist realizes better than most of us that the rationality on which science depends can be found only in a single creature, and that this creature alone has the incredible power of encompassing the universe in the sweep of his mind, of becoming "potentially all things," in Aquinas's happy phrase. The whole history of the world has led up to this creature. The Aristotelian of Galileo's *Dialog* objected to the vast empty spaces between planets and stars in Copernicus's model of the universe as "vain and superfluous," because they did not serve man. Galileo's spokesman tartly replied that it is not for *us* to say what is vain. Nowadays we can answer this objection even more effectively. No longer is man's key role as the "crown of the universe" to be insured by the crude device of making his dwelling its physical center. We can understand that enormous spaces are necessary if somewhere, by the ordinary laws of physics, planetary systems are to appear. We can appreciate the fantastic time-scale that is required if on one of those planets an incredibly improbable and complex grouping of atoms is to occur, and if a new kind of matter which will have the power of adaptation and development is to appear. We can realize that a profusion of living creatures must try their luck in the struggle for existence if some day one of them is to be found a suitable abode for an immortal spirit. The advance of science does *not* therefore involve any weakening of the plausibility of theological ways of thinking, if it be properly understood. On the

contrary, it notably deepens our theological appreciation of the grandeur and nobility of God's plan for man and the universe.

It has often been said that Catholicism is lacking in a theology of the temporal order, that its otherworldliness and preoccupation with the absolute have made it dilatory in evolving a true humanism. That there is an element of truth in this allegation cannot be denied. Catholic thinkers, like Maritain, Thils, Dondeyne, Mouroux and Norris Clarke have been trying hard to remedy the fault. They have sought to validate proximate temporal ends for man. Among other things, they point out that advances in technology are liberating man more and more from his slavery to matter—to disease, hunger, climatic extremes, exhausting labor and so on. Man has tapped sources of untold energy. He is about to conquer the barriers of space. The range of his brain is being enormously extended by intricate electronic computers. He will soon be able to communicate almost instantaneously with any one of his fellows. His whole conception of work and of society is gradually being transformed. Three hundred years ago, science scarcely touched the daily life of man; the range of his mind and body, the energies at his disposition, even his means of communication were almost as physically limited as those of his primitive ancestors tens of thousands of years before. Today man's whole relation to the universe is changing at a pace that few have really grasped. Yet we are still only on the threshold of undreamed-of changes. Biology and psychology are at approximately the level of theoretical development that physics was in the time of Newton. What the next century will bring only God knows.

There are two points of view among Christians regarding this upheaval. One is that technology is a "bad thing," that it replaces God's image in creation by that of man, that it is a manifestation of the "original sin" of man's nature, a sign of his inordinate desire for knowledge and greed for power. This attitude (which is exemplified in the work of some few American Catholic writers, like Wilhelmsen and Carol Jackson) is partly Manichean, but is chiefly rooted in a "good-old-days" mentality which Catholicism somehow seems to foster among some of its adherents. The opposite view is that technology is man's way of obeying God's command to Adam to "dominate the earth;" it "transforms matter by imposing upon it traces, as it were, of rationality, of spirituality, even of humanity" (Thils). In remaking the universe in the image of man, science brings it nearer the image of Christ, too, thus helping it participate in its own way in the work of redemption (Dubarle, Teilhard de Chardin). It may even be (as D'Arcy, Malevez and others suggest) that in transforming the earth, science is preparing for that "glorified earth" on which the resurrection of the body is to take place and which will be entirely dominated by man.

Be this as it may, it is certain, at least, that the technological transformation of the world is in itself good. But it unquestionably poses man with the gravest challenge he has ever faced. The more man's capacities are magnified, the greater the dangers to which the weakness of his still human nature exposes him and his world. It is imperative, then, that man's spiritual growth match the increase of his physical potentialities. It is not merely that man needs new wisdom and new restraint as he gains command of nuclear and genetic forces. It it not just that the terrible new capacity he possesses for dominating his fellow man may turn his head and put an end to freedom on the earth. It is above all the fact of *knowledge,* the feeling of omnipotent reach, that can make the mind of man so swell with pride that it may set itself over against God.

In this growing crisis, the troubled scientist can find little solace in either of the great philosophical orientations which have, between them, dominated the intellectual arena for over three centuries. The tradition which stretches back from Nagel and Ayer through Mach and Hume to Locke and Hobbes, and which in its various manifestations has been labeled "empiricist," "phenomenalist" and "positivist," could never find room for the notion of a transcendent Creator. Within the limits of its own categories and starting-point, the most it could hope to achieve was either a rational affirmation of a limited God (the deism of the 18th century is an instructive example of where such an effort is bound to fail) or else an incompletely rational affirmation of a Creator. (The fideism of the later medieval nominalists or of many of the leading Protestant thinkers of today might here be quoted as examples.) On the other hand, the idealist tradition, represented in our own day by such great scientific figures as Einstein and Eddington, deifies the human mind, and therefore tends to accentuate rather than diminish the peril in which the scientist now finds himself. Existentialism may be regarded as an anguished attempt not so much to resolve as to underline this dilemma bequeathed to the modern world by Descartes. It recalls man to a sense of his own contingency, to wonder at the *fact* and not merely the modalities of his existence.

But this recall is not enough. If we refuse to move beyond the level of human frailty and fleetingness, the human condition becomes a horrid absurdity without a history or a meaning. It must be seen as demanding a total creative Cause as its existential ground. This requires acute metaphysical analysis of the kind in which Aristotle and Aquinas excelled and which contemporary thought is beginning to master again after many centuries of neglect. Here is where the realist metaphysical inheritance of the Christian can be of such immense service. Yet the very strength and complexity of this inheritance poses a great danger, too— the danger of treating the words of a master philosopher as things, of converting philosophy into history. Metaphysics more than any other part of philosophy requires an utter integrity, to which the memorizing of "theses" and the division of the history of philosophy into the "good guys" and the "bad guys," in the manner of a juvenile western, are altogether alien.

A KEY TO UNDERSTANDING NATURE

The passionate desire for understanding and comprehensiveness which distinguishes the true metaphysician can be seen in the best of contemporary Catholic thought—in the works of Maréchal, Maritain, Lonergan and de Raeymaeker. It is here (so it seems to me) that the scientist may find a way of relating man to nature and to his Creator. Man is seen as totally dependent upon God at every moment of his existence. Everything that he is or makes himself to be, the very fact that he is at all, all these find their ultimate ground in the Creator. Man accepts things as they are, tries to understand them and modify them. But the whole order of space and time, of man and materials, takes its being from One who stands alone, who conserves the world in being and does not merely modify it.

The scientific quest itself takes on its full significance only within this context of *creation*, of the universe as God's handiwork. This insight is probably the principal legacy that the Judeo-Christian tradition has bequeathed to philosophy, as Pieper and other historians of medieval philosophy have often stressed. Natural science is, then, in its own way a searching out of the intelligible imprint that the Creator has impressed upon His work. It is true that some have held that science tells us nothing of real structure; it is to be regarded, they say, simply as a convenient way of cataloguing phenomena. This was Bellarmine's contention against Galileo, and it echoed a distrust of the "mathematicians" which was common at that day among philosophers and theologians. It is the view of modern positivism, too—a view which, partly through the influence of Duhem, has tinged the whole of contemporary Catholic thinking on the nature of science. Though possessing a certain plausibility in the context of descriptive theories of motion, this view is utterly and demonstrably inadequate as an account of what science in general is doing. It makes the scientist either a collector of curiosities or a technologist.

Science, then, must be taken to disclose in some sense, however oblique, the hidden structures of the real. We can now begin to realize the true dignity of the scientist's vocation. It is he who is charged with interpreting the Book of Nature in which God reveals Himself no less surely—though much less clearly—than in the Bible. What the scientist finds is what God Himself has put there, the intelligible structures which are the proper objects of man's God-given intellect. Next to love of God and neighbor in the scale of values governing those spiritual activities which make us the "image of God" comes intellectual understanding. And foremost among the goals of that understanding is the scientific grasp of that created world to which God has fitted man's sensory powers. If we are to prepare for eternal life by the development, both natural and super-

331

natural, of our faculties of intellect and will, it would seem that scientific understanding is among the highest of natural activities, one that every Christian should hold in the most profound esteem.

The struggle which convulses the world today can, in a certain sense, be regarded as a conflict between two competing theologies of science. One theology assigns to science a messianic role in bringing about the millennium here on earth; secularists of the West and Communists of the East agree in making scientific progress the supreme norm for man. Christianity, however, sees its millennium elsewhere, and declares that prayerful union with God is more important to human destiny than is scientific research. The scientific exploration of the universe, as our late Holy Father so often emphasized, is good, but it attains its full significance only when it reverently respects God's overlordship. It must be carried out with humility; there must be a real ascesis of knowledge, of the kind that the Incarnation not only dramatizes and symbolizes, but also makes possible for the individual Christian. The Word of God freely limited Himself by assuming our condition, and even gave Himself over to suffering and death for the love of men. The scientist who looks upon nature and sees in it the imprint of this same Word cannot fail to realize that his commitment to truth must involve an equal commitment to love, and that the discovery of truth must lead man to humility, not to pride.

How Affluent
Are We?

Benjamin L. Masse

O UR COLLEGE hosts had done their homework; they
had planned exceedingly well. What more timely discussion topic could one have desired than
"Our Affluent Society"? Wasn't Professor Galbraith's
The Affluent Society on all the best-seller lists? Wasn't
it stirring economists to angry debate on half the campuses in the country? Wasn't it jolting complacent
businessmen and sending labor leaders into mental
tailspins?

Nor was the topic merely timely. It raised a host of
important questions, not only for economists and statesmen, but for theologians, philosophers, sociologists and
psychiatrists as well. What was the affluent society doing to the one and only absolute commitment man has
here below—the commitment to serve God and save his
immortal soul? What was it doing to the character of
individuals? What was its impact on family life and on
the community? Freed at last from the grinding struggle to overcome scarcity, were we falling victim to a
siren world of abundance? Were we, in short, going the
decadent way of the ancient Romans, masters of the
world but slaves to sense appetite?

What about all the economic problems our affluence was generating? Were we working too hard and too long? Were we building too many autos, refrigerators and television sets, and not enough roads and schools, parks and hospitals? Were individuals taking too much of the national product and the state too little? How could it take a bigger share without taxing us to death and coming to dominate our lives?

Surely, that was the sort of chow to feed the troops (the troops in this case being an invited group of businessmen, union leaders and public officials). Our academic hosts were right. If the social documents of the Popes are to have significance for our times, such are certainly some of the questions that must be posed and pondered.

But the play didn't run according to script. The discussion began well enough and Galbraith's blueprint for a happier future was being subjected to the sort of lively crossfire one expects whenever scholars and businessmen gather for dialog. Before the discussion reached the point, however, when it might be expected to continue under its own momentum, one of the professors gained the floor and proceeded to execute the maneuver known as the diversionary tactic. He announced that the Galbraith tome wasn't worth the paper it was expensively printed on. It was as phony as a three-dollar bill. It assumed that ours was an affluent society and then went gaily on from there. But was ours truly an affluent society? How many in the room, the speaker demanded, waving an eloquent finger in a sweeping semicircle, felt notably affluent?

That did it, of course. Our academic hosts remained perfect gentlemen. There was not the slightest sign of dismay over what was happening to the agenda they had so carefully planned. But from that point onward, the argument was not about the consequences of an affluent society; it raged over the bald fact of its existence.

Now from several points of view, this switch in the discussion might seem to have been a waste of time. Certainly, compared with other countries, American society is not merely affluent, but garishly so. What other country can pay its farmers not to produce? Or permit its industry to· practice a wasteful policy of planned obsolescence? What other country can finance a World War and at the same time raise the standard of living of its people? What other country can over a ten-year period lend or give to other countries more than $60 billion?

Nor is the United States well-to-do merely in reference to other lands. By any criterion of material wealth, it is simply and absolutely rich—period. It has vast natural resources. It has the greatest industrial machine known to man. Its citizens possess in abundance those goods and services which are recognized as evidences of wealth—telephones, automobiles, indoor plumbing, electric refrigerators, radio and television sets, motor boats, schools and hospitals. They spend a fortune annually on liquor, tobacco and cosmetics. In their search for pleasure and diversion they travel to the ends of the world. Never before has there been a society in which so many workers enjoy so much of what are commonly regarded as the perquisites of wealth. How can anyone seriously quarrel with Mr. Galbraith when he writes that "as an economic and social goal, inequality has been declining in urgency"; or when he notes that, subject to a few qualifications—including the major qualification that depressions be prevented—the age-old "preoccupation with economic security is largely in the past."

It is only when one ignores the forest and looks at the trees, so to speak, that doubts about the Galbraith thesis arise. It was the sudden descent from the global and national to the individual that detoured the conferees. Only those who did feel affluent—and they appeared to be a small minority—frowned when the professor suggested that all of us might take a long look at family-income distribution and then make our own estimate of the affluence of the U.S.A. He had taken such a look, he affirmed, and so far as he was concerned, his articulate colleague from Harvard had laid an academic egg.

But did Dr. Galbraith lay an egg, albeit a very lucrative one? Let us together have a look at the most recent estimates of national income distribution and make up our own minds about this business. (These estimates are the work of Mrs. Selma F. Goldsmith of the Office of Business Economics of the U. S. Department of Commerce, and appear in the April *Survey of Current Business.*)

In 1958, total pretax income of families and unattached individuals (consumer units) increased, despite the recession, by $6 billion over 1957. The total was $338 billion. However, since the number of consumer units also increased, from 53.5 to 54.3 million, average family income remained stationary at $6,220. The median income stood at $5,050, that is, half the country's consumer units had incomes above $5,050, half had incomes below that amount. The following table shows the distribution of income among consumer units:

Family Income	No. of Families (Millions)
Under $2,000	7.6
$2,000- $3,999	12.1
$4,000- $5,999	13.6
$6,000- $7,999	9.2
$8,000- $9,999	5.0
$10,000-$14,999	4.3
$15,000 and over	2.5

Over the status of the 7.6 million consumer units with an annual income of $2,000 or less, there won't be much argument. They scarcely consider themselves affluent, nor are they so regarded by popular estimate. In 1958, as in the preceding year, they represented 14 per cent of all consumer units. Since in large part these units are made up of farm families and unattached individuals, their economic status, while unenviable, is not quite so hopeless as the bald figures suggest.

Nor would families in the $2,000-$3,999 bracket look upon themselves as well-to-do, or be so described by others. If there are children in the household, these consumer units are barely able to get by. Even a single person earning $76 a week before taxes—the highest level in this bracket—is hardly in a position to indulge in riotous living. More than a fifth of all consumer units are in this category. Combining these two lowest brackets, we find that 36 per cent of U. S. consumer units might reasonably wonder what Dr. Galbraith is talking about.

It would take a Gallup Poll to find out whether the large number of consumer units in the next bracket—a fourth of all consumer units—consider themselves affluent, at least in the restricted sense of being reasonably well off. In this bracket, where incomes range from $4,000 to $5,999, are many of the nation's unionized and better paid workers. The bracket is also heavily populated by school teachers and government workers. At the risk of exposing the Editor-in-Chief to a flood of irate letters, I would guess that at least those in the upper half of this bracket, especially the unattached individuals and small families, have some feeling of being part of an affluent society. They can't send their children to college—unless the children work their way through—but they do enjoy many of the amenities of modern life. They can contribute to the week-end jam on our highways (in a second-hand car) and (with the aid of a long-term mortgage) swell the number of Americans who own their own home.

If Professor Galbraith's thesis makes any sense at all, all the remaining consumer units, those making $6,000 and over, must be deemed in some sense affluent. In this group are 21 million consumer units, or 39 per cent of all units. These are the families, notably the 6.8 million among them with incomes over $10,000, who set the affluent tone of American society. They are the ones for whom the big slick magazines are mainly published. They are the ones on whom Madison Avenue concentrates much of its frenetic energy. They are the darlings of Fifth Avenue and Detroit, and of all the centers of fashions and big-ticket consumer durables in the land. And, significantly for the Galbraith thesis, they are a growing percentage of all our family units. In terms of 1958 dollars, only 27 per cent of U. S. families had incomes of $6,000 or more in 1947. Last year, as we have seen, nearly two-fifths of our families had such incomes.

337

The late Hilaire Belloc, as I recall, used to argue that a dominant minority customarily establishes the character and sets the tone of a society. If that criterion has validity, the sizable minority with incomes of $6,000 and more—or even, perhaps, the smaller minority with incomes in the $8,000-plus class—stamps American society as signally affluent.

One reason some of Dr. Galbraith's critics are loath to accept this fact is the growing institution of the working wife. In 1940, less than 15 per cent of the wives of family heads were in the work-force. By 1958 the percentage had jumped to 28. Still more astonishing, the increase was as marked among the top two-fifths of our families—rated according to income—as it was among the other three-fifths. In fact, the closer one looks at the figures, the clearer it becomes that in many cases the dividing line between affluent and nonaffluent families is determined by the presence or absence of a working wife. In 1957, 41.2 per cent of the wives of working husbands in the top fifth of our families were in the paid labor force. In the next fifth, the percentage was 33.4. Those figures contrast sharply with the 16 per cent of working wives in the lowest fifth of our income classes, and with the 22.3 per cent in the next lowest fifth.

But, however great the sociological significance of this phenomenon, it doesn't change the economic fact of affluence—except in one respect. To the extent that many of our affluent families have sacrificed leisure for income, by sending the wife out to work, they are less affluent than the size of their billfolds suggests.

The conclusion would seem to be that Professor Galbraith was correct in positing an affluent society; and that, as a consequence, anyone who wishes to think realistically and creatively about our society must start from that fact. Among other things, the fact of affluence has enormous importance for our conduct of the Cold War. It means that if our leaders should decide that more strenuous efforts are needed to turn aside the Communist threat, they can safely demand much greater sacrifices than the American people are presently making. They can forget, in other words, the nonsense that the Kremlin, by keeping the Cold War going, is forcing us to spend ourselves into bankruptcy. That such a belief has gained some currency in the country, even in high councils, is itself, perhaps, another proof of our affluence. For too often one of the fruits of affluence is a certain softness of character which shrinks from sacrifice, and which, if indulged, spells the doom of men and nations. It was this softness which Sen. J. W. Fulbright had in mind when, rising in the Senate on July 8 and looking on the wreckage of the Foreign Relations Committee's mutual-security bill, he said bitterly that "we are determined to end up the richest, fattest, smuggest and most complacent people who ever failed to meet the test of survival." God grant the Senator is wrong.

Where Do We Go From Togetherness?

Katharine M. Byrne

T HE WORDS "Magazine of Togetherness" are no longer to be found on the cover of *McCall's*. What does the withdrawal of this familiar subtitle mean? Is this the end of another era? Is each man now to go his way alone, picking out his own underwear, pursuing a destiny apart from the other members of his bowling team? What happens to the American housewife of the ad writer's dream—the girl who, as Philip Roth has it, "couldn't buy a roll of ScotTissue unless her companion-helper-husband went along to help select the color"? And our children? Are they to sit around reading books or looking into space, or to gather in haphazard little groups composed entirely of other children? Will we abandon them to their unorganized devices?

These are serious questions to which precipitate answers will not suffice. But perhaps we should back up a bit. What is "Togetherness," anyway, and what could possibly be wrong with it? At first glance the word appears to describe an admirable ideal of shared familial experiences. It also suggests any number of pleasant pictures, often in four colors and on slick paper. The pictures usually include Mother, Father, Sister and Brother. Sometimes, with a nod to the national birth-boom, Brother and Sister are joined by Baby. If it is spring, Father may be planting a young tree just beyond the last flagstone of the patio. Brother holds the shovel, Sister carries the bag of fertilizer, and Mother stands by, decorous and deferential, with a tray of frosty lemonade. This scene offers only one of a number of heartwarming variations on the theme: parents and children engaged in mutually satisfying projects. Abroad, this companionable group might be seen eating off the tailgate of the station wagon. At home or away, they usually move as a unit.

If the mother does leave the house alone, it is to attend a PTA meeting, to act as a canister-bearer for a worthy childhood disease, to solicit money for new band uniforms or to set out the casseroles for the Cub Scout dinner. Father will venture beyond the range of the television set long enough to coach young ballplayers, to participate in a symposium on "Our Turbulent Teens," or to pressure local authorities for some significant community project, perhaps a new swimming pool for the children.

This is a world of children, and, as someone might viciously suggest, of adults who have never been anything but children first and parents afterward. It is an egalitarian world of family councils in which a four-year-old's vote is as good as his father's, and of schools where everyone sits in a circle and the teacher just happens to be bigger than the other members of the group.

FAREWELL TO PRIVACY

From the earliest days of the Togetherness movement, some there were who did not like that word. Hardly was the ink dry on the first "Togetherness" issue of *McCall's*, when an articulate opposition moved into print. It was, of course, among persons who had never purchased a copy of the magazine—and were now even less likely to do so—that the wheels of high-minded protest were set in motion. Joseph Wood Krutch, for one, writing in *The American Scholar*, announced that

341

at the first sight of the word "Togetherness" he felt a "little wave of nausea" come over him.

Thus, from the beginning, there were dissenting voices: those of persons who persisted in thinking of families as composed of individual members, each with a separate as well as a corporate destiny. These objectors saw in Togetherness a leveling process, an invitation to mediocrity, a cutting down to a least common denominator. And they set out to plead the case for apartness, separateness, or individuality; the right to spiritual and physical withdrawal, at least on a part-time basis.

Not that either condition is readily achieved in our time or in our places of residence. What are the possibilities for physical separation from those we love? Invasions of privacy are usually discussed as though they consisted only of wire-tapping, bugging, assailing of captive commuters by canned commercials, or the impudent questionings of a personnel department. But actually, parenthood, in our culture, is probably the greatest single invasion of the right to be let alone. What has the Fourth Amendment, guaranteeing the rights of the people to "be secure in their persons, houses, papers and effects," to say to the parents of a number of young children?

Physically, we are all in this together. New-house space is dearly purchased, if at all, and the old houses are running out. There is no place to hide. The French, in other times, built into their homes a *boudoir* (Fr., *bouder*: to pout), to which an adult female might retire in times of stress. Today's lady of the house will have to stand up and scream right in the middle of the living-dining-and-hobby area. Even "mommy's room" is likely to be shared by the ironing board, an electric train running around and under the bed, and enough Lincoln Logs to reconstruct Abe's birthplace.

Domestic privacy, the right to be alone now and then, used to be purchasable at low rates. Our mothers could summon to their aid the laundress, the nursemaid, the indigent and grateful relative. Even today, in other climes, the middle-class mother has the assistance of amahs, ayahs, scullions and nannies. It wasn't long ago

342

that the British family of *Mary Poppins* operated with
"Mrs. Brill to cook for them, and Ellen to lay the table,
and Robertson Ay to cut the lawn and clean the knives
and polish the shoes. And, of course, there was usually
a nanny to look after the children." In most of the
households we know the mother plays all these supporting roles herself, including that of Robertson Ay.

The world of hired help and adequate living space
is gone, but not without being missed. Even Mary
Drone, John Keats' wretched, unheroic heroine of *The
Crack in the Picture Window*, knew that the life of
community Togetherness in cracker-box identicality,
with endless talk of tots and toilet-training, was wrong,
but she didn't know what to do about it. Several of her
more literate sisters could have told her, and in no uncertain terms.

MESDAMES OF THE OPPOSITION

First among a recent group of Togetherness's detrac-
tors was Anne Lindbergh, happy to be tied by the
bonds of family love and necessity, but not willing to
be strangled by them. Her gentle protest, in *Gift from
the Sea*, is the classic plaint of a mother giving love and
time freely—but with a small reservation, asking to be
removed in time and space, occasionally, from the
exigencies of hems to be let down, items to be purchased, schedules to be met, and the endless tyranny
of telephones. Hers is a plea for the chance to replenish
the ever pouring pitcher, to preserve a small corner of
life untrammeled. Moreover, she is certain that, given
time out, she will return to the fray a better and more
understanding parent.

A more raucous voice on a shriller note is that of
Jean Kerr. In her anti-Togetherness tract, *Please Don't
Eat the Daisies*, Mrs. Kerr makes the basic assumption
that a parent is entitled to a considerable part of her
own life, even during the years of her children's early
childhood, a period of active and unavoidable Togetherness. Mrs. Lindbergh is gentle, tentative, inquiring; Mrs. Kerr's cry is loud and clear. It says, very
simply, "lemme-out-of-here." This girl wants to sleep
late and to write, and has been doing both with con-

343

siderable success. She loves each cereal-smeared little face, but not exclusively.

About housing, Jean Kerr could tell Mary Drone a few things. "I wanted," she writes, "a house that would have four bedrooms for the boys, all of them located some distance from the living room—say in the next county."

Of the period during which she and her husband were working on the musical, *Goldilocks,* she writes: "First we would locate the children and threaten them with violence and sudden death if they came near us. Then we'd take coffee and cigarettes and hide in the den." Lines like these must give us pause. As a writer who is a Catholic, what is Mrs. Kerr doing to our Mother Machree Fantasy? (This is the illusion which haunts one segment of Catholic writing—that unless the dear fingers are toilworn on a 24-hour-a-day basis, the mother doesn't really love her children.)

Another assault, this time two-pronged, was launched by a man and his wife named Smith. Elinor Goulding Smith is the author of books with such remarkable titles as *The Complete Book of Absolutely Perfect Housekeeping* and *The Complete Book of Absolutely Perfect Child Care.* (This last contains the Absolutely Perfect Chapter Title: "The Child, from One to Forty.") Mrs. Smith's answer to the "groupiness" of organized, adult-directed childhood is a prescription for developing an "ingoing" child. Her formula calls for no fuss, no muss, nor any procession of uniformed and mud-footed affiliates. "Just drop the child off at a library," she suggests, "or buy him another stamp catalog or a scrapbook for his bug collection, or a little formaldehyde, or a tub of tropical fish, or even a book, and he's safely and economically disposed of."

Now the literate females of the community may be accused of selfishness: turning their backs on their children because of the desire for a more ego-satisfying hour or two out of life. And, it must be admitted, they all are spiritual sisters of Joan, one of A. C. Spectorsky's *Exurbanites.* You remember Joan. She is the one who asks herself why, with her brains and good taste, she shouldn't start a small business, or write a book, or "put

344

up my onion soup with sherry that everybody always

raves about, and sell it by mail?" But not Mrs. Smith's husband, Paul Robert, who, in *"Where Did You Go?" "Out." "What Did You Do?" "Nothing."* sets up all his arguments for adult apartness from the *child's* point of view.

He is the one who comes right out and says that "parents are the natural enemies of children." And before you get excited about this premise, please note that it is just Mr. Smith's way of postulating a dual family-world, as opposed to the social monism of Togetherness. The title of his book is a reference to the mutually impenetrable curtain which hangs between a child's world and that of his parents. The book itself is a plea for the part-time freedom of growing children from the encroachments of interfering adults, with a special emphasis on the right of a child to breathe in and out without direction, and make his own way among his peers.

By last spring the pendulum was arcing wide with savage swipes. There was a Mercury ad featuring three crowded and uncomfortable males packed into the rear seat of a competitor's automobile, and captioned, "Are you suffering from too much Togetherness?" There were admonishing magazine articles and hortatory headlines. "Don't Be a Pal to Your Son!" cried the *Reader's Digest.* "What child wants a 40-year-old man for a friend?" sneered Al Capp in a New York *Times* interview.

Yes, it seemed only yesterday that the last father had been wrested from his beer can and television set, and pushed over to the third-base foul-line with his boy's team at bat. But now the order was being countermanded. He was being warned to get back into his

345

house-slippers, and to cultivate a stern look of authority; and advised coldly that a man in a chef's cap leaning over a hot barbecue pit does not present the proper "father image" to the young.

Someone even suggested an organization called "Fathers Anonymous," dedicated to the rehabilitation of reformed parents, erstwhile victims of the recent unpleasantness. If a member of the association should feel a cook-out or an all-family beach excursion coming on, he is advised to telephone another father, one who will speak firmly to him, strengthen his resolve, or even come over and hold his hand until the crisis passes.

Another straw in the wind came out of the Middle West when the leader of a Cub Scout Pack in Winnetka, a man described in newspaper accounts as a "former Cubmaster who is also an opinion research executive," announced that his youthful affiliates were being placed on inactive duty. This man, you must note, is not only a Cubmaster, but a poll-taker, sensitive to the wavering seismograph of buyer-reactions. And he has sent forth a ukase: "It's time that the kids started their own baseball games, or just went outside and kicked a can."

One can almost see the little IBM wheels turning madly in the ex-Cubmaster's eager, probing mind. (And in our world that "ex" pays highly: whose word is more impressive than that of an ex-narcotic, -Communist, or -drunkard?) This man is probably giving us the word from our alternate sponsor, with next week's prescription for family living. If the organized child is on the wane, let's start working on the Child Apart, the Pale, Skinny Kid with Glasses, reading a book, or the Lonely Scientist with his "600-power microscope with reversible plano-concave mirror with illuminator, 5-hole revolving diaphragm and zippered, simulated-leather carrying case." Or even, absolutely new and in time for the Christmas trade, a package of "non-toxic, non-allergenic and highly educational KANS FOR KIDS. Hours of Healthful, Solitary Fun. Just for Kicks."

If an epitaph to an era is now in order, let it be written by the small boy in a cartoon in this morning's

346

paper. He is standing in his backyard with a firm grip on his own football, and he is saying to the puzzled adult who is signaling for a pass: "I'd like to have you for a pal, Dad, but you're just not my type."

The John Birch Society

Robert A. Graham

L IKE THE influenza epidemic now predicted for next spring on the basis of known cycles, a new onset of such extreme "ultra" movements seems at hand and may well be already upon us. One writer claims there are today 2,000 right-wing organizations in the country, with a membership or following of eight million. No one knows how many persons are really active in these bodies, but it is already clear enough that they are in a position to make their influence felt. Is there reason to be alarmed about this revival of extremism?

In the opinion of many observers, the recrudescence of what is a chronic malady of American democracy will soon be cast off by healthy antibodies in the nation. Others, less complacent, point to perhaps lasting ill effects on the political system of this country. While most of the right-wing organizations now proliferating claim the highest patriotic purposes, the fact is that they weaken the fight against communism by indiscriminate charges against the most respected leaders of government and public opinion. The resulting loss of public confidence in our national leadership, it is feared, will seriously compromise the United States' ability to emerge from the current world crisis with its honor and its prestige intact.

Many of the new organizations now recruiting the extremists of the country in their ranks are small and insignificant both in numbers and in the quality of their leadership. This, however, cannot be said of the John Birch Society. This is no movement led by an obvious paranoid like the self-proclaimed Nazi, George Lincoln Rockwell, or by opportunists with a police record, such as the promoters of the Minute Men in Southern California. The JBS boasts of a national council comprising leading industrialists, military men and former government officials, as well as several well-known Catholic figures, one of whom is a priest. A fairly large number of Catholics seem to have been drawn to the society. Without accepting the estimate of 50 per cent of the total membership, we can believe society president Robert Welch's Catholic secretary, who told the editor of the Rochester *Courier-Journal* that there is "a high percentage of Catholics in the John Birch organization."

Yet for this organization of presumably responsible and conscientious men, Sen. Thomas J. Dodd (D., Conn.) has had words of sharpest criticism. Alluding to the JBS-propagated charges against such respected public leaders as President Eisenhower and the late John Foster Dulles, he spoke of an "affront to both decency and intelligence." This sort of charge, he said in a speech last March 31, "brings our leaders and our institutions into disrepute, it sows division, it makes it easier for the Communists and the 'ultraliberals' to equate opposition to communism with political lunacy." Senator Dodd's vigorous, practical anticommunism needs neither apology nor proof. This will not necessarily guarantee him against attack by the Birchites as a Communist.

What is this organization that called forth such a cry of protest from so respected and forceful an anti-Communist as Senator Dodd?

John Birch, after whom the society is named, was a young Georgia-born fundamentalist Baptist missionary in China when America entered the second World War. He become a captain in the Office of Strategic Services, and appears to have been instrumental in preparing the escape route of Gen. Jimmy Doolittle, who landed in China following the successful bombing of Tokyo. Killed by Red Chinese troops ten days after V-J Day, Birch is hailed as "the first victim of the Cold War."

On December 9, 1958, Robert Welch, a retired New England candy manufacturer, founded the John Birch Society at a meeting in Indianapolis. Its purpose: to cope with "the threat of the Communist conspiracy." Unless, he said, "we reverse forces which now seem inexorable in their movement, you have only a few more years before the country in which you live will become four separate provinces in a world-wide Communist dominion ruled by police-state methods from the Kremlin."

Growth of the new society was rapid, and it is now described by observers as "the base-organization of the extreme Right." It is so much to the right politically that it treats with disdain such conservatives as Sen. Barry Goldwater, former Vice President Richard M. Nixon and the late Sen. Robert Taft. According to the Attorney General of California, its membership consists primarily of "wealthy businessmen, retired army officers and little old ladies in tennis shoes." Nevertheless, it has aroused public attention and concern. It spearheads a campaign to impeach Supreme Court Chief Justice Earl Warren. Its material was used by Gen. Edwin A. Walker in his controversial right-wing activities in the U.S. armed forces in Germany.

The JBS is perhaps most known for its founder's sweeping charges against President Eisenhower, whom Mr. Welch has described as a conscious Red agent. Relying less on mass membership than on disciplined and organized (and perhaps often camouflaged) small groups scattered around the country, the John Birch Society seems capable of making its influence felt, if only by co-ordinating the efforts of other existing extremist groups that await direction.

Included among the estimated 60,000 members of

the society are, no doubt, a large number of ordinary citizens who seek to "do something" to combat communism. They are usually surprised and puzzled that an organization led by such a God-fearing man as Robert Welch, who patriotically aims to save the country from what they are convinced is imminent danger, should be subjected to denunciations and complaint. The attacks on the JBS they regard only as confirmation of the gravity of our national peril and proof of the extent of Red influence. These persons exhibit an amazing naïveté about the real issues at stake and what they are getting into.

Typical in this respect is the view expressed in a letter sent by a pious and apostolic Catholic woman and brought to this writer's attention. She wrote: "Critics of JBS all speak vaguely of extremism, questionable methods, fascism, etc., and they all sound as if they haven't even read the Blue Book. I read the Blue Book first two years ago, thought it made good sense and was impressed with Welch's spirituality. I read it again this spring when all the controversy arose and still feel the same way. I read his monthly bulletins fairly regularly. The only specific objection I have read about is Welch's contention that 'government is the enemy of the people' or something to that effect." For the writer of that letter, as for many others, the criticisms seem trivial compared to the great task undertaken by the society in fighting communism.

It is perhaps true that much of the criticism leveled against the John Birch Society at the beginning was based on instinctive fear of any right-wing organization and not on a detailed knowledge of the creation of Mr. Welch. After all, these movements are not new. They all tend to follow a common pattern, since they recruit from much the same reservoir of human temperament and political bias. They are usually anti-Semitic and anti-Negro. Many are also anti-Catholic. All are anti-Communist, but it usually turns out that they use the Communist issue as a cloak to cover such less admirable features as racism, bigotry and intolerance, both religious and social. Even the best of them invariably attract a host of dubious personalities all too ready to ride the crest of popular hysteria. The general public cannot easily forget the Ku Klux Klan or the Christian Nationalists of Gerald L. K. Smith.

The John Birch Society seems to have avoided the cruder manifestations of the extreme rightwingism of its predecessors. Accusations leveled against it on the score of anti-Semitism seem based on suspicion rather than on the record. While it opposes desegregation, it refrains from anti-Negro bias. Nevertheless, the JBS inevitably falls heir to the heavy legacy of distrust and revulsion that sad experience has left in the public's mind. The feeling is almost unavoidable that the old forces of bigotry are latent in the society, ready to burst forth at the right moment.

Critics of the society have found more concrete grounds for their attacks in the contents of the Blue Book already referred to. This is the "bible" of the society and consists of the talks Robert Welch delivered to the charter members in Indianapolis in 1958. The Blue Book is not just a collection of speeches; it is the acknowledged chief source of orientation on the principles, attitudes and program of the John Birch Society.

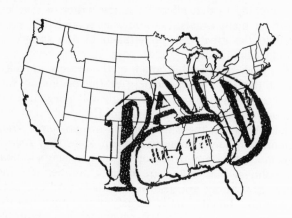

Many of the individual aphorisms in the rambling Welchian prose of the Blue Book are not particularly incendiary unless given an extreme and literal meaning. Mr. Welch believes, for instance, in "less government and more individual responsibility." A much-publicized slogan runs like this: "This is a republic, not a democracy. Let's keep it that way." Other statements are found which, though disturbing by their connotations, are capable of an innocuous interpretation, or are at least not as sinister as sometimes made out. For instance: "The greatest enemy of man is, and always has been, government." Democracy is defined by Mr. Welch as "the unbridled rule of demagogic men." It is "merely a descriptive phrase, a weapon of demagoguery and a perennial fraud." Taken in their ensemble, however, these and other statements of governmental philosophy reek strongly of distrust of the democratic principles upon whose validity the American system rests.

The authoritarian structure of the society is another object of criticism. In the Blue Book the founder leaves no doubt that it is he who will decide things. The society, he said, is to be "a monolithic body." It is not to be run on representative principles or on the principle of local autonomy: "The John Birch Society will operate under completely authoritative control at all levels." He declared also: "We can allow for honest differences of opinion. . . . But whenever differences of opinion become translated into lack of loyal support, we shall have short cuts for eliminating both without going through any congress of so-called democratic processes." Needless to say, these remarks confirm the picture of the society as an antidemocratic body.

There is no doubt that Mr. Welch is not only the founder but the main force of the society. He stresses repeatedly in the Blue Book the leadership principle, that recalls the grim Nazi precedent: "The men who join the John Birch Society . . . are going to be doing so primarily because they believe in me and what I am doing and are willing to accept my leadership anyway." His justification is the following pragmatic one:

"We simply are not going to be able to save our country from either the immediate threat of communism or the long-range threat of socialism by organizational leadership. Our only possible chance is dynamic personal leadership."

The methods proposed in the Blue Book provide another reason for criticism, by seeming to sanction the use of any means, fair or foul, in combating communism. "The front business," said Mr. Welch, "like a lot of techniques the Communists use, can be made to cut both ways." He advocates the pillorying of suspected Communists by techniques which he admits are "mean and dirty."

Such arguments against the John Birch Society, based on its antidemocratic principles, its authoritarian structure and its avowed readiness to use "short cuts" to achieve its ends, fail to impress, much less embarrass, the average Bircher. These features, they say, are necessary to prevent the society from degenerating into an ineffective debating society or from being infiltrated by Communist disrupters. Membership is voluntary,

and those who don't like the founder's ideas are perfectly free to take their leave. The accusations, in the Birchers' eyes, are mere caviling on secondary issues at the very moment when the nation faces mortal danger from communism.

The John Birch Society is certainly no model for a movement in the American democratic tradition. From this standpoint it deserves the castigation it has already received, and one must regret that its members treat so lightly these unpatriotic aspects of a supposedly patriotic organization. But the real danger of the society lies not in its organization and methods but in its impact upon the American national life at this moment. It is proving to be an instrument of division and a threat to the national morale. For, to justify its claim that the country is infiltrated by Communists, the John Birch Society has embarked on an unprecedented and arrogant campaign against almost all our leaders, Democrats or Republicans, liberals or conservatives. A man for whom President Eisenhower himself is a "dedicated, conscious agent of the Communist conspiracy," can only be said to use the Communist issue for his own purposes and to define "communism" in a sense all his own.

This now famous statement about President Eisenhower is dismissed by Birchites as antedating the foundation of the society and therefore as not being a JBS document. The statement was not repudiated, however, by its author. It still reflects, so far as the evidence shows, the frame of mind of Mr. Welch. The citation deserves quotation at greater length:

> While I too think that Milton Eisenhower is a Communist and has been for thirty years, this opinion is based largely on the general circumstances of his conduct. But my firm belief that Dwight Eisenhower is a dedicated, conscious agent of the Communist conspiracy is based on an accumulation of evidence so extensive and so palpable that it seems to put this conviction beyond any reasonable doubt.

This frightful distortion should suffice to damn the allegedly anti-Communist movement headed by Robert Welch.

Yet the society prospers. This is an uncomfortable fact that requires explanation. One element in the mushrooming of the John Birch Society is no doubt the widespread anxiety of the general public over the world situation, marked by what appears as a succession of defeats on the international scene. There is a strain in the body politic. To many, the history of the postwar years is, to quote one Birchite, a story of "defeatism, humiliation, incompetence, surrender and treason." The only explanation of the setbacks, for many a perplexed citizen, is Communist infiltration. A new "stab-in-the-back" legend is in the process of creation.

Robert Welch was formerly active in the National Association of Manufacturers and his views represent the extreme right wing of that right-wing group. His program expresses resistance to the trends of the past thirty years toward more government control in the economic life of the nation as well as the "welfare" phases of contemporary governmental policy. This is the "communism" he is fighting, not the communism of Marx or the Leninism of Moscow. Of late years, however, a new factor has entered upon the scene in the form of an upsurge of anti-Communist activity by fundamentalist Protestants.

It was not so long ago that Catholics were regarded as the most active foes of communism. This can no longer be said today. Dr. Fred C. Schwarz' Anti-Communist Christian Crusade is of predominantly Baptist inspiration. The National Educational Program of Dr. George Stuart Benson of Searcy, Ark., is another fundamentalist operation. It is no accident that the key centers of the John Birch Society are in the fundamentalist South and Southwest, and that Welch himself stems from this background. John Birch, be it recalled, was a fundamentalist.

To these Protestants, the charge of widespread Communist infiltration seems to make sense when they look at the National Council of the Churches of Christ in the United States. For years they have regarded with distrust the efforts of their NCCC brethren in the urbanized regions of the country to adapt Christianity to the social problems of modern times. This is "modernism," or "liberalism." It is socialism or communism, and they will have none of it.

Related to this tension within the Protestant body in this country was the uproar over the Air Force training manual last year. In that text, the author (who drew his material from one of the fundamentalist anti-Communist organizations) charged that the Communists had infiltrated the Protestant clergy. The National Council reacted with vigor to these charges and suc-

356

ceeded in having the manual withdrawn by the Defense Department.

The charge of Red infiltration of the Protestant clergy remains in the air, however, and Mr. Welch explicitly refers to it in his talks. As he himself reports, his remarks are usually matched by the query as to whether the Reds have also infiltrated the Catholic clergy as well. In a talk at Garden City, N.Y., October 9, 1961, Welch said that about one-half of one per cent of Catholic priests are "comsymps." When challenged on this statement by the Boston *Pilot*, Welch admitted that his figure was "simply pulled out of a hat, as a complete guess, and without any substantiation even being claimed." In the same letter, however, he revealed that by "comsymp" he means not merely a priest whose sympathies may happen to be turned toward "socialism," but, actually, a Communist who became a priest. So far does Robert Welch push his theory of Red infiltration.

Reference has already been made to the participation of Catholics in the John Birch Society. This is hardly the kind of Catholic-Protestant dialogue encouraged by the ecumenical movement. But it would be a serious mistake to contend that the Communist danger does not greatly worry Catholics. One Protestant writer, Dr. David M. Baxter, whose notes on the John Birch Society greatly aided this writer in the preparation of the present report, testifies that many Catholics, like others, were stampeded into the Welch camp by an hysterical fear of a Communist takeover. Dr. Baxter's own article on the society in the Catholic monthly magazine *Extension* brought this sample of confused thinking from a reader:

If America and Holy Mother Church are to survive in the face of our Catholic Action, our Catholic President and too much of our Catholic press, we sorely need the John Birch Society to keep us from destruction. As long as good people continue to give God their first allegiance, as Robert Welch does, there is hope that our Lady's Son will be appeased and we will enjoy an era of peace.

The writer of those lines is no doubt a very religious and sincere person. It evidently does not strike her as strange that Catholic Action (which is under the bishops' supervision) and President Kennedy (a practicing Catholic) and the Catholic press (also under episcopal supervision) should be a menace to our country and our Church and that only Robert Welch stands between us and disaster.

As A. A. Berle Jr. remarked recently at a dinner honoring Christopher Emmet, the key to the survival and influence of the U.S. Communist party is its success in focusing the issue not on itself but elsewhere. An attack on communism is automatically transformed by them into an assault on precious values of our society—civil liberties, social progress, democracy, even peace.

To date no remedy has been found to cope with this tactic of dodging and camouflage. The John Birch Society has made this problem more difficult than ever before. If allowed to proceed with its work of confusion and division, it will destroy the basis of a solid effective fight against communism carried on by such organs as the FBI. As it stands today, communism, which as an enemy of freedom and order should be the common foe of both liberals and conservatives, eludes (perhaps indefinitely, so far as our action is concerned) its final accounting. Indeed, applying Welch's own principle of "inversion," a perfect case can be made out for the thesis that Welch himself is a Communist, so much has he helped the Red cause in the United States.

After this lengthy analysis of the sad role of extreme rightwingers in the fight against communism, a word about the responsibility of the liberals is in order. These are not at all without blame for the situation that drives so many anti-Communists to extreme positions. The liberals seem to have adopted the old European slogan, "No enemies to the left." Not only have they predictably defended Communists in the name of civil liberties, but they have lacked both courage and consistency in carrying out their self-proclaimed devotion to freedom. There are few outspoken anti-Communist liberals. Outside of such persons as Berle and Emmet, and such

358

organizations as Freedom House, few have applied to the Communist totalitarian danger (internal or external) the same zeal they deployed for years against the Nazi totalitarianism and Nazi-like movements in this country. Until the liberals adopt a less ambiguous position in relation to communism, extremist groups like the John Birch Society will continue to win ready credence among average citizens for their scattergun accusations of infiltration and subversion.

On Turning Seventy

John LaFarge

F OR MOST PEOPLE the seventieth birthday comes in
silently, like Carl Sandburg's San Francisco fog.
The usual reaction to congratulations is: Why this
fuss *today*? Nothing new has happened. In fact, you
would hardly have noticed the event if you hadn't received retirement papers or read the passage in Psalm
89 (90) which defines the usual limits to human age.
That psalm, incidentally, was composed long before our
present days of regulated diet, vitamin tablets and other
aids to longevity.

This very unobtrusiveness of the 70th year, however,
inclines me to believe one should not wait until decrepi-
tude sets in before formulating some plan for life's last
lap. I don't believe that one should just trust to luck—
or the good Lord's merciful indulgence—so as to enjoy
various happy and pleasant latter-day moments. I don't
think it's enough to reread Cicero's *De Senectute* and
be persuaded that age is not such a bad thing after all.
Age, it is true, can be a time of harvest, of selection
and wisdom, with wonderful compensations all its own.
But for you, perhaps, it isn't quite so commendable.

Let it be clear to us that our Christian and Catholic faith is not content just to console us in old age, to shield us a bit from the rude blasts of the time-wind. Our faith can transform old age, just as it can transform each period of our life upon earth, and it is of supreme importance that we act in our faith's full consciousness: that we do not leave matters to mere hazard, but that we approach this period fortified with a definite purpose and program.

Old age, after all, is a natural phase of life. The burden of human weakness that we have inherited from our father Adam lies heavily upon it, both physically and morally. Yet it is endowed with a right, a nobility of its own. Since it is a humanly natural phase, one wants to make the best use of it. The latter years, in various ways, can repair the mistakes of youth or of the middle years. But who can repair old age when it has been wasted?

For this reason I propose a conscious and deliberate choice. People want something they can remember, something that will stick by them and serve as a rallying point when their minds become a little foggy. The words I propose will carry very different meanings to people in different states of life. They will mean one thing to a priest, another to a layman or woman. Yet I think they are applicable to all. Close to a dozen years of latter-day pondering have strengthened my conviction of their validity.

Old Age Is a Time of Prayer

I am not suggesting anything unusual, anything like the good old medieval idea when the conscience-stricken knight or the too-comfortably-cushioned prelate decided it was high time to retire to a monastery or hermitage and begin to "prepare for death." If, of course, you have drifted along to your 70th birthday without ever having made a spiritual retreat—or at least a really devout one—now, obviously, is the time to repair that particular lacuna. I am speaking of a deepening of value, rather than of any extension to our time schedule.

The latter years are a time when we simply allow ourselves to become more familiar with God and with His saints in heaven. We should let ourselves grow closer to that source of life, that ocean of love, toward which we are inexorably moving, just as the water-borne traveler on a great river begins to scent the first tang of the mighty sea to which the current is noise-lessly carrying him. It means talking much to God: to our Father in Heaven, to His Son, our Redeemer, to the Holy Spirit, who is our invisible and ever-working companion, and to Christ's Blessed Mother Mary.

We don't delude ourselves. Our minds may wander more readily in the later years. Troublesome memories of the past may obtrude, if we don't banish them at their first appearance. We may even forget prayers we used to know by heart.

But the main thing is that prayer become more and more a part of the texture of our lives. We dwell a little longer in meditating. We spend a little longer time in a visit to the Blessed Sacrament. We refer things to God more naturally and frequently. We do much praying for the Church, for the See of Peter, for all the body of faithful, for souls akin to us outside the visible Church, for so many great intentions. In our later years we become more conscious that we do not pray alone. The Church is praying with us and in us—the whole Mystical Body of Christ. With this, many things take on a new and fresh meaning, such as the prayers of the Mass and the Divine Office, the rosary and its mysteries. They are more specifically our prayers—especially if we have cherished since our youth some pious practice like the Angelus or Morning Offering or the *De Profundis.*

These latter years are a time for *listening,* listening for that Voice which could not make itself heard so well in the clamor of busier years. Now that voice begins to converse with us in the cool of the evening, speaking to us of what it all means and what we should really be thinking of.

We can become habitually thankful in our prayer, making the latter years a period of constant thanksgiving, in union with the divine Eucharistic thanksgiving each day in the holy Mass. We thank the Creator for these years, present and past. We think of all those who have not been privileged to enjoy them, those who died in infancy, in youth, in midstream. The *oblata* each morning are placed in our hands. Shall we not offer them consciously and joyously? Each day is a gift, ever more precious, mysteriously gathering up in itself all the value of all the days that have preceded.

Moreover, we pray silently and informally with all other *viatores*—fellow pilgrims, *sputniki,* as the Russians call them. For the curiously twisted thing about the Bolshevist jargon is its use of an honored and an-

cient term—the fellow-traveler on a sacred pilgrimage —to express the opposite of all that is holy: the Communist "fellow-traveler" here on earth, and the Soviet satellite, the "fellow-traveler" of the skies.

Let us pray for our fellow pilgrims here and in the world to come. In the latter years we live, or should live, in closer relationship with those who have already completed their term and are waiting to rejoin us in eternity.

Time, as it duly unfolds, becomes familiar with eternity. In our childhood we felt eternity's cool freshness, its bright simplicity. We return to it today, the time of the *Heimholung*, the ingathering into the Father's house. By the same token, it is the time of remaking one's life by reparation. Of that, a little later.

With every additional year the Church's traditional worship takes on new meaning. The Church is praying *in us and with us.* Our prayer becomes less purely private and is more absorbed into the great sacramental intercession of the Mystical Body of Christ.

Do I pray only for myself, or for my associates and friends, or for all mankind? It makes little difference. The Holy Spirit prays within me; it is His voice speaking through my own.

Largire lumen vespere
Quo vita nusquam decidat.

("Bestow upon us Thy light in the evening [of life], that our life may never languish."

—Hymn for None)

Is it my own personal life, or is it also the life of the whole creation that the Church prays for? It is either or both. It is the fulfillment of God's plan.

Old Age Is a Time of Charity

The second element in the program is that of charity, which is the new life into which we are reborn in baptism.

In the latter years you cannot, as St. Jerome says, practice anything like what you once could in the way of strenuous works for your neighbor. The area in which you can operate becomes gradually smaller. Your greatest hope is seeing that others carry on your works, perhaps much better than you could hope to do, for they can profit by your experience; perhaps less effectively, at least from your particular point of view. But with all this, the latter years offer countless opportunities for charity, many of which are appropriate to that very time. In those years you watch over your tongue, and see that it does not yield to the particular temptation for elders to listen to gossip and to disparage others. Old age is the time for *hidden* charity: a good word spoken here and there, a quiet service performed, visits to those in suffering, visits to others of the same age period whose predicament you can understand.

Most of us, unless we have had a particularly unhappy youth, remember how much we valued the kindness then shown us by older people, sometimes by the aged. The world of conversation with the young is a world each older person must construct for his or her particular self. There are infinite differences as to what each of us can contribute. Yet *give we can*, though apparently it may amount to no more than listening to what younger people say and providing for them the audience they naturally crave.

Even where age has taken the heaviest toll of physical strength and alertness, there is always something the older person can do to make life tolerable for those with whom he lives in daily contact. There are always ways and means to aid even those at a distance. It may be no more than a letter of congratulation or condolence or attendance at a wedding, a wake or a funeral; or greetings to newlyweds, or a word of encouragement to a struggling student, or a good word for the worker in some intellectual specialty who feels isolated and misunderstood. It may be the answering of questions out of our somewhat fading store of knowledge. Or the ordering of our affairs for our successor. Or the bit of counsel given to those who need it and whom we can really advise. Or encouragement to true creative effort—oh, this is a great *opus* for the aged! Or taking on the companionship of someone in the community or neighborhood whom one might, perhaps, instinctively avoid.

Nothing indeed can extinguish our capacity for love as long as the breath of life remains within us, and that love *is life*, its very breath and current. One of the deepest inspirations to one's life as a priest is to see those wonderful instances where a married couple have nourished a flame of true love that neither age nor custom can wither, that endures until the very end; indeed, beyond the grave itself. . . .

Love for the living and love for the dead. For our

faith teaches us that we can show our love for the faithful departed in a tangible manner. There are so many, so very many, in your later years, who are inscribed in your roll of remembrance. *Ipsis, Domine, et omnibus in Christo quiescentibus*: for those (whom I have named) and for all who rest in Christ. How much meaning those words gather!

Charity for those who are spiritually kin but separated from us by misunderstanding, by honest differences and, perhaps, by prejudice. Indeed, do we ourselves understand them as we ought? Certainly it is not mere chance that one has remained in close friendship with friends of one's youth throughout the vicissitudes of life, and that we can still forgather. Such things are God's working, the working of His Holy Spirit, in ways that we know not.

And there must be charity for the spiritually dead, for our enemies, if there are such; even for God's enemies, as long as they struggle in the uncertainties of this life. In my old age I can still, perhaps, represent for them the charity of Christ as I could not in younger and more active years. When age bears heavily upon them, they can more reasonably tolerate my own differences, more readily concur in those points of attraction or rejection wherein we coincide.

Old Age Is a Time for Courage

The two preceding items in our latter-years' program are more or less obvious. The third is less so and may seem to contradict our idea of age, belonging specially to youth. Yet it is, in a way, the most essential of all. This is the factor of courage.

Courage, of course, is what we elders demand and expect of the young. We tell them how brave we were in our own time, conveniently passing over various episodes of moral or physical cowardice. The middle-aged are to be guided by common sense, and the elders by the divine virtue of caution. Age is the time for prudence, for if's and maybe's, for looking before you step out, for seizing the railing when you step downstairs, for slipping a coat over your shoulders of a chilly evening, for going easy on cholesterol in your diet, for avoiding contentious argument; in other words, for sailing close to the wind and keeping your hand on the tiller.

Now there's plenty of good reasoning to be displayed for each and every one of these precautions. None the less, the latter phase of your life is not just a calamity to which you must somehow accommodate yourself. It is an adventure—your greatest adventure.

It is the time when you bet your final stake upon the great battle of life itself: when you place all your life, hopes and being in the hands of Him who gave His all for you; who hoped in you and for you, when you had forfeited any such grounds for His hope. And it's a precious privilege to enjoy this experience.

There are ample motives, then, for courage in our old

age: courage from a sense of destiny; from a sense, too, of the strength that can flow to others from your own example; for the multitude of mankind have no more respect for the cowardly aged than they have for the timid youth. The courage of old age is the courage of an exalted vision. Not the dreams of a visionary, but the glimpse of the reality and the foundations of things that is given by our faith, and the interpretation that our faith offers of the meaning of the universe—the sense of the truly sacred, of the genuinely and infinitely precious elements of our existence.

The fact that so little of life still remains is the added reason for being, as it were, prodigal of that little. Thus it was put by the patriarch Eleazar when, at the age of 90, he refused to listen to the kind advice of his cautious friends and went to torture and death, because, as he said in very blunt language, he'd "go to hell" before violating the holy law of God by eating the forbidden food.

The courage of old age is not an added decoration, a mantle of heroism in which we dress up and masquerade. The *material*, the occasion for courage, floats to our hand in the circumstances of old age itself.

The latter years are a time of diminution, no matter how you look upon them. They preface the total diminution which ends life itself. "Does the road wind upward all the way? Yes, to the very end" (Christina Rossetti). Our *habitual* courage consists in accepting this diminution, in living with it. The sense of achievement is rudely lessened. The circle of associates grows smaller. We find fewer capabilities for exciting adventures. We grow steadily smaller; after a while even our bodily stature may shrink. There is less we can say, less attention we can command, fewer opportunities to make our ideas and opinions known, greater perils of error and blunders, less control over our own functions, of mind or body, less ability to concentrate. We are becoming steadily—let us hope, gracefully—less.

Courage, then, consists in accepting this diminution just as it comes; not only accepting it, but welcoming it, going forth to meet it and embracing it with simple honesty, as the Christlike pastor of an old German parish in Ohio told me he and his parishioners would go forth and welcome the first Negro family to put in an appearance as residents.

It takes courage, therefore, to face, day by day, the manifold pinpricks of diminution. Indeed, one becomes accustomed to it, as a new rhythm of life—if in point of fact it *is* new, and is not a mere emphasis on diminutions that wafted their chilly breath upon you long ago in less propitious moments. It can steal over you in so many ways, as when you clear out your desk drawers or files and wonder how you happened to accumulate so much junk, and why you have such reluctance in disposing of it. You stroll in the library and realize finally (what common sense should have taught you long ago) how many areas of knowledge must remain forever unexplored, how many intellectual or imaginative byways you can hardly ever hope to investigate. You are grateful for honors or congratulations if any such have come your way; but now they point only to the past. They no longer presage any particular surprises still to come.

As I said, there is a courage of diminution, and it has its worthy place in the program of old age. It precludes certain conventional types of adventure. Yet the approach of the latter years is a vast liberation, not an imprisonment. It is the time now to speak frankly, since you no longer have anything to lose or anything earthly to gain. You may not speak at length, and your voice is croaky, but you can express the outcome of a life's experience—modestly, of course, but also confidently.

The natural difficulties of communicating with one's neighbor should not drive us in upon ourselves. On the contrary, it is the time for going forth and meeting people, for talking, a bit confusedly, perhaps, but in the depth of human warmth, with those whom you alone can reach. For the older one grows in the service of God, the more accessible one becomes for the young, the troubled, the doubting, the despairing and perplexed. Your advice, your warning, your prophecy, may be lost nearly a hundred times. But that hundredth time, like the slim notches of a Yale-lock key, may mean for another human heart the unlocking of life itself.

Old age is traditionally the time for exceptions and exemptions. Some of these, of course, must be. You need a bit more sleep, a bit more rest, less worry and responsibility. But may it also not be the time for a somewhat greater exactness, greater fidelity, in matters that do lie within its scope? In such a way, one can take a revenge, as it were, on the tyranny of time. You can make a little more room for eternity just when time has tightened its grasp.

Most of all, we remember that old age has a special work to do. With the merely natural apparatus that time offers us, we cannot turn back the hands of the clock nor erase by one iota what the Moving Finger may write. But with the help of the Eternal we *can* turn the clock back: we can rewrite our lives, and even rewrite the lives of others. Old age is pre-eminently the time of reparation. Into that great work of reparation enter all three factors that I have just mentioned: prayer, love and courage.

I have never been able to determine just where thanksgiving ceases and reparation begins. The two great actions are inextricably blended in the great prayer of the Church's sacrifice. We give thanks by offering, on our part, the sacrifice of atonement. We introduce the sacrifice of atonement by a solemn preface of thanksgiving. We give thanks at the end, after the great offering has been made, by partaking of the Victim's Body and Blood in reparation for the world's burden of sin and alienation.

This is the great *opus* of old age. This is its wonderful work, its glorious Amen; the response to the divine "Amen, I say to you. . . ." That Amen can never be in any way diminished as long as we keep it in our hearts and minds. In these years we are always busy with the great work of reparation: each day offering ourselves and offering the divine Victim—sacramentally or just spiritually—as an atonement for all the sins of the world. The facets of reparation are innumerable, yet they all blend into one great harmonious whole: the offering that is consummated with the offering of life itself. In our days of relative strength, while the light does still shine (*lucerna Dei antequam exstingueretur*), we can offer that final sacrifice, accept its manner and mode and circumstances wholly and entirely from the hands of the Creator, pray that it may be meet and just, fitting and salutary.

———"The Old"———

"WHEN THERE IS QUESTION of blood-relationship, three ancient traditions—the merely human, the Judaic and the Christian—agree that children are obliged to render concrete assistance to their needy parents. We must note that in one sharp controversy with his faithful enemies our Saviour explicitly and heartily condemned the failure to discharge this duty. . . . An impersonal government, paternal as it may wish to be or seem, cannot altogether assume the filial obligations that exist in the highly personal family."

Vincent P. McCorry, S.J., on the November intention of the Apostleship of Prayer.

There is a close link between classroom and commonwealth. It is in our schools that men are trained to take part in that civilized dialogue which leads to the rational consensus so vital to a healthy democracy. But what is happening in our schools today, particularly in our institutions of higher learning? The campuses are in political ferment, to be sure, but is that necessarily a healthy sign? Are our philosophers dutifully guiding youth's search for truth? And by the way, what is the responsibility of government toward all schools in our democracy? Should the state, for instance, assume the basic costs of education? Can it do so, without demanding a dangerous control of the whole process, to the ultimate harm of truth and human liberty?

School and Society

Only Higher Education, Mr. President?

Charles M. Whelan

PRESIDENT JOHN F. KENNEDY's education message to Congress contained several surprises, but none more disappointing than the statement on parochial schools:

> In accordance with the clear prohibition of the Constitution, no elementary or secondary school funds are allocated for constructing church schools or paying church school teachers' salaries; and thus non-public school children are rightfully not counted in determining the funds each state will receive for its public schools.

With one sentence Mr. Kennedy disposes of a problem which has vexed the best constitutional lawyers in the nation. Who's being dogmatic now?

In fairness to the President, we could hardly have expected an elaborate constitutional argument to the Congress. But in fairness to the people we could and did expect a silence respectful of the complexity of the problem and the traditional modes of constitutional adjudication. As an American, Mr. Kennedy is entitled both to hold and express his personal opinions. As a candidate, he was compelled to detail his position on Church and

State. But as President of the United States, speaking to the Congress of the United States, he should avoid unnecessary pronouncements on delicate constitutional issues.

Mr. Kennedy's warrant for the "clear prohibition" of the Constitution is undoubtedly the Church-State theory elaborated by the Supreme Court in the *Everson, Mc-Collum,* and *Zorach* cases. In the first of these cases, decided in 1947, the court affirmed that neither a State nor the Federal Government

> can pass laws which aid one religion, aid all religions, or prefer one religion over another. . . . No tax in any amount, large or small, can be levied to support any religious activities or institutions, whatever they may be called, or whatever form they may adopt to teach or practice religion.

One year later the court reaffirmed this position in *Mc-Collum* and held religious instruction on public school premises during public school hours unconstitutional. In 1952 the court sustained a released-time program off public school premises in the *Zorach* case, but did not explicitly temper the language of *Everson* and *McCollum.*

In view of these statements from the nation's highest tribunal, Mr. Kennedy has a prima facie case. He also enjoys the unquestioned support of distinguished constitutional lawyers like Leo Pfeffer, counsel for the American Jewish Congress and author of the best one-volume work on Church and State in America. The President can count on the active political support of such eminent and powerful organizations as the National Educational Association and the National Council of Churches. He cannot fairly be blamed for having incurred the endorsement of POAU and similar extreme groups.

What complaint, then, have the advocates of church schools, save that Mr. Kennedy has given the coup de grâce to a cause already lost? What refuge have they, short of saying the Supreme Court was wrong and thus conceding the President's proposition?

The answer is short and decisive. Mr. Kennedy's statement was erroneous, inopportune and unnecessary.

It is no disparagement to say that neither the President nor his Attorney General enjoy the reputation of great constitutional lawyers. If Mr. Kennedy were speaking simply as a private citizen, his opinion would not be recorded in the law journals of the land. The fact that he is President lends only political, not persuasive, force to his assertion.

A short survey of the professional legal journals would demonstrate to any inquirer that there is no clarity of expert legal opinion on the constitutionality of Federal aid to education through limited grants to church schools. It is the fashion of opponents of such aid to pretend that there is no question what the Supreme Court would do with such a program, and that the only people who think there is a serious argument for the constitutionality of such aid are Roman Catholics. The publications of such eminent non-Catholic legal authorities as Mark DeWolfe Howe and Wilbur Katz are simply ignored.

A GREAT amount of confusion could be saved if all parties to the controversy would agree to this statement of the question: May the Federal Government bear part of the cost of educating all of the nation's children in literacy, science and general human culture, regardless of the benefits which result from the program to religion or religious groups? Everyone is talking at present as though it were the name on the Federal check which determined the issue of constitutionality: if it is P.S. 101, it is constitutional; but if it is St. Mary's, it is a betrayal of the American way of life. I submit that it is an incontrovertible principle of American constitutional law that it is the purpose, and not the payee, that determines the check's constitutionality.

The only constitutional issue in Federal aid to education is whether the First Amendment means that Congress may not advance the level of national education by any method which even indirectly results in benefit to religious bodies. There is no decision of the Supreme Court on this precise point. All that the *McCollum* case decided was that government may not use its revenues and its coercive force to co-operate with the teaching of religion in public schools. *Everson* sustained the use of tax funds to provide transportation to church schools, and *Zorach* relied explicitly on the right of government to accommodate its programs to the religious interests of the citizens it serves.

Moreover, there are two significant facts in our constitutional history which militate for the legitimacy of Federal aid to education, regardless of the religious consequences. First, the Blaine Amendment was not adopted. In spirit and in letter, it would have forbidden every form of Federal aid to education which would result in direct or indirect benefit to church schools. This amendment repeatedly failed of enough votes in Congress to be proposed to the States for ratification. The failure of its adoption by the nation is the precise reason why it was adopted in New York and many other States.

The second fact supporting Federal use of church schools to advance general education is that the *Cochran* case of 1930 was not overruled in *Everson, McCollum* or *Zorach*. As is well known, *Cochran* sustained the constitutionality of state-supplied textbooks to church-school children. Opponents of Federal aid airily dismiss this case with the comment that the First Amendment issue was never argued. This is true only in form. The whole point and substance of the objection overruled by the Court was that the educational program could not be public because it resulted in benefit to a religious, and therefore necessarily private, group. The side effects of the program, the Court held, did not nullify its public character.

Cochran involved the due process clause of the Fourteenth Amendment; so did *Everson, McCollum* and *Zorach*. What puzzles the experts is the coexistence of these four cases with one another and with our total constitutional history. It is a brave prophet, indeed, who confidently predicts what the Supreme Court will decide.

In the clarity of his constitutional vision, however, Mr. Kennedy has succeeded in adding to the confusion. On what principle of law will he justify the enormous chasm in his program between higher and lower education? An admirable scholarship program, buttressed with supplementary grants to the institutions chosen, apparently raises no First Amendment problems; but once you descend to the high school or elementary level, there is no possibility of aid through church schools. Is it because lower education is compulsory that aid would be unconstitutional? Surely that argument cuts both ways; religious freedom becomes a joke when government itself makes the price too high. Is it because direct and unrestricted grants for construction or teachers' salaries are the only conceivable means of aid to grammar and high schools? What about scholarships, tuition payments, tax credits or deductions, with supplementary grants to the institutions of parental choice? "Education must remain a matter of state and local control," says Mr. Kennedy, "and higher education a matter of individual choice." Only higher education, Mr. President?

The Administration, however, has double reason for gratitude to its leader. Not only has Mr. Kennedy illumined the experts; he has saved his advisers the trouble of further thought. The speed with which he has done so should give them particular consolation and great hope. Less than two months after assuming his grave responsibilities, he has settled for them the position they must publicly take on an intricate constitutional problem. That is, they will take it or risk their jobs. With the necessity of uniformity in the Administration, I have no quarrel; but why should uniformity have been imposed, when it was not necessary to say anything at all?

No one would have been surprised if Mr. Kennedy had simply submitted his proposals to Congress without defining the unconstitutionality of a proposal he was not submitting. The basic models of the President's program are the Thompson and McNamara bills of last year; each passed its own House with scarcely a whisper of Church-State debate. For all practical purposes, the question of aid to education through limited co-operation with church schools was simply hushed up and ignored. Senator Morse was the one exception, and he made a speech in favor of its constitutionality.

The President has solid political reasons for refusing to champion aid through church schools. I affirm the propriety and the wisdom of his standing on those reasons. More importantly, I concede that, wholly inde-

377

pendently of Mr. Kennedy's position, there are sound arguments against the desirability of Federal aid through church schools. The dangers of excessive Federal control, of disproportionate complexity in administration, of imbalance between the public and church-school systems, and particularly of the use of such funds for segregated schools, are not mere chimeras. These arguments I understand and respect, even though I do not think they outweigh the contrary arguments in favor of the desirability of Federal aid once such aid is given to public schools. But what I cannot understand is why a President who had such excellent political justification for the omission of private schools from his program has chosen the deeper and swampier ground of constitutional law on which to take a stand.

The reason he gave Congress, of course, was to explain why non-public school children would not be counted in determining the funds each State would receive for its public schools. An equally good and perhaps more candid reason would be that he had decided in the national interest not to help them. Or was it that Mr. Kennedy did not dare to say that? Did he recognize that the discrimination would be too manifest unless hidden in constitutional clarity?

The Philosopher's Responsibility

James Collins

W<small>E COULD DEAL</small> very abruptly with the theme of the Catholic philosopher's responsibility in our world by saying that he has the same responsibility as anyone else in the guild—simply to do a good job at philosophizing. Nothing more need be said after that, provided we really understand what it takes to do the job. There are some disagreements about what it does take, however. It may be useful, therefore, to spell out some of the philosopher's responsibilities.

We have, for example, a share in the responsibility for long-range preparation of college students who show an interest in becoming philosophers. It seems to me we could improve our counseling of such students when we talk to them about the study of modern languages and the choice of a major subject.

TRAINING THE PHILOSOPHER

In order to avoid wasting valuable time at the graduate level, and to insure a real use of language resources in later life, the undergraduate who plans to work in philosophy should master both French and German.

For students of the sciences, translation of new research is systematically planned; the main objective is simply to make information available. Philosophical reading, however, demands something more than the transfer of information; the reader must eventually make a close study of sources. Norman Kemp Smith has provided fine renditions of Descartes and Kant, but the student who wants to become an effective philosopher must be able to consult the original French and German—and Latin—of Descartes and Kant. He cannot be fully confident about the bases of modern thought without attending to the pattern and nuance of Descartes and Kant, which elude even a well-turned translation.

More is at stake here than background erudition. Language deficiencies often limit the course of studies and thus hamper the comparative work which Catholic thinkers should be doing in the contemporary field. Often, a student will embrace some current trend in British or American analytic philosophy simply because he lacks the linguistic skill to explore any other regions. And then he goes along with the trend of many analytic philosophers to become rapidly impoverished in thought content, because they fail to consult other ways of thinking which are not reducible to questions about English usage or formal systems. A counterpart case is furnished by the student who knows French well but is vague about German; he then spends his graduate program in assimilating only the French approach to such philosophies as phenomenology and existentialism. His understanding of the roots of these movements is likely to remain forever slightly out of focus; he cannot make the thorough evaluation of them for which we are looking.

Another domestic responsibility we have is to counsel prospective philosophers about the proper value of non-philosophical studies. I would prefer to see these students do their major undergraduate work in something other than philosophy and develop a lifelong habit of cultivating other fields of interest. There is nothing so barren as a mind which has tried to specialize too early and too exclusively in philosophy, especially in the School philosophies, which introduce one into an autonomous world of terms and syllogistic rules.

The fact is that it takes time and experience to ripen the philosophical temper of mind, and to date there is no way available for artificially stepping up the process of maturation. Hence, while the undergraduate and graduate student is learning the rudiments of philosophy, he should also be feeding his mind with large doses of literature and the sciences, history and the arts. In doing so, he will discover his own way of overcoming the isolation that initially separates the Catholic philosophical mind from contemporary modes of inquiry. Sometimes it is suggested that desperate measures must be taken to remove the isolation. Some, for example, recommend sloughing off the entire philosophical tradition in philosophy and simply combining one's Catholic faith with some currently important tendency in philosophy. I am convinced that this procedure results in more of a net loss than a gain, particularly when the individual is asked to compare the merits of the philosophy of his choice with other alternatives. What we should do is, rather, to try the indirect route of deepening our hold on both the philosophical tradition and the liberal heritage in the sciences and humanities, to the point where we begin to feel confident about bringing them to bear upon some present issues. This is a very steep demand to make of the maturing philosopher, but the road to philosophical competence is an unusually steep one in any case.

There is one definite advantage in cultivating interplay between one's philosophy and the other cultural components. It gives the Catholic philosopher sufficient familiarity with problems in other fields to enable him to speak with wisdom about them.

The complaint is often heard today from jurists, directors of foundations and other administrators that they consult the philosophers in their midst for guidance on major human issues—but do so in vain. The analytic philosophers, who are in the majority, are quite adept at describing the logic of courses of action already taken and at pointing out flaws in all plans for future action. But they regard even their work in the moral area as a meta-ethics, which usually means a theoretical analysis that does not result in any definite practical recommendation or norms of choice.

On the other hand, the Catholic philosopher is apt to be embarrassingly rich in general recommendations which he does not know how to make concretely applicable to the particular shape of the problem confronting the practical man. Here, the individual thinker has to rely upon his own fund of experience drawn from his personal studies in the relevant natural and humane sciences.

THE PHILOSOPHER'S ROLE TODAY

An example of my point is furnished by a session of this year's meeting of the Western Division of the American Philosophical Association, which was devoted to the theme of the public interest. This theme was suggested by the urgent need to set up some working standards for determining when there is a genuine conflict between the private connections of a public officer and his official responsibilities. As the assembled philosophers probed into this matter, it became increasingly clear that much more than a procedural issue was at stake. It was important to settle the rules of adjudication, but there was, at bottom, a good deal of murkiness about the meaning of the public interest and about the grounds for upholding and promoting it, even at cost of sacrificing a political administrator's private advantage. To clarify the difficulties, analyses were given from many different philosophical standpoints. The official printed report mentioned St. Thomas and Yves Simon, but it was noticeable that no Catholic thinker had been invited to give an independent development in the light of present legal and political circumstances.

The pertinent point here is that some independent rethinking of the "conflict of interests" issue is required, and it must be done with resources drawn both from political philosophy and from acquaintance with relevant materials in political history and present-day economic situations. The theme of the common good may be more productive in this inquiry than the general topic of natural law. There is no easy equivalence between the common good and the public interest, any more than there is between moral good in general and moral value. But there is a definite relevance of the doctrine about the common good to what underlies our present talk about the public interest and the obligation to uphold it. One of the Catholic philosopher's prime tasks is to search out the points of insertion and make his findings available in public conference and readable prose.

We are beginning to realize that in our pluralist world more is required than agreement on some practical courses of action. We see a need for dialog concerning widely divergent general interpretations of human existence and the roots of obligation. I think, however, that the time is overdue for Catholic philosophers to perform their critical function in respect to the theme of dialog itself. There is a danger that dialog may be praised out of all proportion, and hence a danger that we may demand more of it than we can reasonably expect it to yield.

THE NATURE OF DIALOG

Recent probes into the role of religion in American society show the need not only of carrying on a persistent dialog, but also of clarifying the nature of dialog. Suppose that we want to understand and develop our human nature to the fullest. Can we do so if we consider only the individual man in isolation or as related solely to the world of impersonal things? A negative answer is required because isolated man merely talks to himself, and man, the shaper of things, does not profit by independent criticism. For full use of his capacities and for full understanding of what they are, the individual man has to enter into the society of persons. Only then can a man open himself to another (as well as to himself) on a person-with-person basis. This interpersonal relation constitutes the situation of the dialog, which is the mainspring for humanizing our social bonds.

For over a century now, philosophers have been examining this dialogal relation among men. From the time of Feuerbach and Kierkegaard down to Buber and Marcel, a remarkably broad zone of agreement has been developing among otherwise quite divergent thinkers. They refer to man's attitude toward nonpersonal things as an I-and-it relation, and they observe that this nondialogal relation is a powerful but onesided realization, since it leaves out the challenge of a free response from another person. The human individual is made for something more than dominion over things; he looks for a sharing in the goods of interpersonal life. This is possible only in the form of an I-and-Thou bond among persons engaged in dialog, whether the other person be a fellow man or God. Dialogal analysis is the philosophical study of the traits that unfold when a man reaches out to other persons and seeks to produce conditions of mutual understanding, critical integrity and, perhaps, love. The dialog itself is the interlacing of several mutual interpersonal efforts.

One of the lasting achievements of our century is to uncover the values of interpersonal communication, both among men and between man and God. But I would like to see the basic findings of existentialism and psychiatry about the unique reality of the I-Thou relation and dialogal intercourse kept distinct from the mass of loose variations and overextensions of these insights. At least two critical limitations should be respected. First, although a dialogal relationship establishes the conditions most favorable for studying questions about the human person and the acts of freedom, it does not automatically generate the evidence which will lead to sound conclusions about them or to firm agreement among the participants in the dialogal situation. Second, there is a wide range of significant philosophical issues, especially those concerning scientific methods and the domain of nature, which must be investigated by nondialogal means. Philosophy itself reaches farther than analysis of the dialogal situation, some of whose implications can be followed through only with the aid of other philosophical approaches.

A CASE IN POINT

In last year's televised study of Western ideals which was sponsored by the Rockefeller Foundation, two of the participants, Arnold Toynbee and Reinhold Niebuhr, described the West's commitment to respect for personal integrity, moral courage and the constant search after justice in society. The discussion became highly charged, however, when an observation was quietly introduced by the third participant, the only professional philosopher in the group, Prof. Charles Frankel of Columbia University.

While approving of the dialogally congenial traits of the Western mind that Toynbee and Niebuhr described, Professor Frankel said that he missed any mention of another outstanding trait—the search for truth and the readiness to accept objective evidence, regardless of where it leads. Frankel then pressed home the point that one of the triumphs of the Western mind is its investigation of the structures rationally attainable in nature. He left the impression that Greek and Judeo-Christian humanisms contained some strong convictions, but that it was left for the Enlightenment and the scientific method to sift these convictions, identify the sound ones and eliminate any views conflicting with a scientifically grounded humanism.

We may readily sympathize with the judgment, expressed in Crane Brinton's recent *History of Western Morals* (Harcourt, Brace; 1959), that Frankel takes too simplistic a view of the relation between the scientific mind and rational structures, as well as between the Enlightenment and Christianity. There is much more constructural activity, and hence more need for decision and a basis of intelligibility, on the part of the scientist than Frankel admits. There is also a much broader basis of intellectual content and independent, self-critical activity on the part of the Christian mind than he allows.

The main criticism which suggests itself to me, however, tells against all the participants in the discussion: it is unfortunate that anyone should be permitted to pit the values of dialogal existence against the truths about nature as embodied in a scientific ordering. The Catholic philosopher's acceptance of God as the creative source of both personal and nonpersonal realms of being, as well as his acceptance of the value of all our sources of experience, requires him to overcome this dichotomy.

The Catholic philosopher is clearly obliged to keep open the meaning of philosophy, so that it can include the method of object-analysis as well as that of dialogal analysis, the world of nature as well as the society of personal centers. He may well specialize in one of these modes of philosophizing and be thorough in working out its interpretation of human experience. But he should not succumb to the tendency to absolutize only one of these approaches and to reduce the other to a subordinate function.

The Catholic philosopher's respect for nature as well as man fits him for healing the split which has made intellectual strangers out of the existentialists and the naturalists, the phenomenologists and the analysts. His critical integrity will prevent him from following the momentary fashion of pretending that these two groups are saying the same thing in different ways. The problem of bringing unity and order into our philosophical world is much too genuine and complex to tolerate such an illusion for very long. But the Catholic philosopher can work deliberately and steadily to bring these two approaches within range for a mutual study of evidence that will benefit philosophy as a whole. This search for wholeness in the midst of a jagged world of natural events and interpersonal relations is the beacon of his professional labors.

Throughout this article I have referred to "the Catholic philosopher," without specifying any of the schools to which the individual thinker may belong. My reason for this usage is that at least a few things can be said in common about the present responsibilities of Catholic philosophers, before getting into further points of method and doctrine which separate them. Once in a while, these common tasks should hold our attention.

Give Me That Old College Tory!

John R. Strack

JOURNALS OF OPINION have been raising the dust lately
with a rash of articles denouncing conservatism
among college undergraduates. The phenomenon is
something of a menace, they suggest; the conservative
is out of place on a college campus. It is proper for
a young man to be wild, rebellious, anarchistic. If one
isn't a socialist at twenty, one's future is in doubt, and
so on.

Nowhere in all this, however, has any college conservative taken pen in hand to announce that his is
a noble and just cause, "one that is in the right because
it has stood the test of time, and sound because it is
rooted in our heritage."

A defense of what seems to be a much-maligned
movement is in order; and what better man to do the
job than a leading campus conservative himself? Hop-
ing to gain an insight into the nature of collegiate
conservatism, the writer, in a college way himself,
recently visited just such a conservative. Now, once
and for all, it is possible to quiet the fears of those who

eye with trepidation the future of the nation and its youth.

The audience was held in the headquarters of the Campus Watchbird & Safeguard Society, a group which aims to insure conformity between administration policy and student activity. The president of the club, a sophomore majoring in economics, motioned the writer into his office and waved him to a seat as he finished signing some papers. Shorter than most and rather stocky, he was wearing a carefully tailored and severely styled brown suit. From his vest he slipped out a cigar, offered it in a gesture of welcome and said in a tone of hearty camaraderie: "What can I do for you?"

When he was told that an explanation of the collegiate conservative's position was sought, he beamed, sat back in his leather chair, folded his hands across his stomach and said: "Well, now, I'm always glad to pass on to the students what little I've acquired in my time here. For it seems to me that the great hope of the future is the youth of the nation, and I shall consider worth-while whatever effort I can contribute to the encouragement of that youth. So, ask me your questions, and I will do my very best to provide you with the answers."

Q. Well, briefly, what is collegiate conservatism?

A. Collegiate conservatism, my friend, is not as some have said, the wave of the past; nor is it, as others have suggested, belief in the proposition, "What is, is right." Rather, it is a way of facing up squarely to the future of the problems of the past, a way of courageously confronting tomorrow's threat with yesterday's deterrent.

To the college man it means what Beatrice meant to Dante, what the essence means to the existence, or, in other words, what tracks mean to a train, only more respectable, of course.

Q. What sort of student do you think becomes a conservative?

A. One of my young freshman friends asked me that same question not too long ago, and I told him that if it isn't born in you, you'll never be a college Tory. One must have an almost inborn reverence for the venerable.

A serious turn of mind is not a handicap, nor is an impatience with ephemera; and an ability to dress tastefully doesn't hurt, either. The college conservative is a man who has learned early that if you go out walking on a dark night and watch the ground to avoid tripping, you won't see the stars, but you'll never trip, either. In sum, he doesn't go for this so-called "adventures-of-ideas" nonsense. He prefers to take his excitement in small, measured doses.

Q. How, then, do you answer the charges of faculty people that the conservatism of the college man is an almost unnatural thing, that college people pick up the conservative banner, not because they stand for the same things great conservatives of the past stood for, but rather because they want to escape the risks involved in a normal life, preferring instead the almost bloodless security of a perfectly controlled environment?

A. Well, let me repeat what I said at the dinner of the freshman Eternal Verities Club last month. The collegiate conservative does not answer the charges of his attackers; that is not his business. Instead, he looks to the erroneous motives of his assailants, to see what lies in their make-up that causes them to yelp like dogs at even the most established institutions.

We have been on campus almost a year now and know quite well what it means to face opposition. I think the best way to deal with opponents is to put them in their place, early. Now, who opposes us? Well, for one, the left-wingers and latter-day Bohemians do. Should this trouble us? No, everybody sees them for what they are. What we are concerned about is the effect they can have on the innocent, for too many people are being led astray by the "liberals." We must handle the problem the way a patient father would treat an unruly son, showing him his error and chastising him when he seems in danger of worsening, but leaving the door open for him to return home when his brief infatuation with unreality has run its course.

Q. Still, the arguments seem to carry weight with some people?

A. Correct, my friend! The innocent *are* being duped and I feel it is my obligation to answer some of these wild charges—just for the record.

First of all, we respect the way things are. Right now it is winter; we like that. We like also the organization of the campus, the wonderful balance of power between the Registrar's office and the Public Relations Department. The campus is divided so well that one or the other of these can influence every sphere of school activity from the surveillance of the department chairmen to the operation of the cafeteria. Nothing can get out of hand.

We see things this way: in every generation, it is given to a few men to offset the influence of the so-called "progressives" who would do violence to what we hold sacred. Now this does not mean that we are intolerant, that we select only those ideas and recognize only those institutions which support our own. Nothing could be farther from the truth.

Conservatives are simply not capable of discriminating between views that are different from and those that are opposed to their own. In philosophy, for instance, we try to see the whole history of thought from Saint Thomas to Hegel as a *unity* and we *accept* the Hobbeses and the Kants along with the Burkes and Berkeleys. In religion we do tend to have an affinity for negative theology, and we do have a team of crackerjack natural lawyers, but we don't begrudge anyone else the right to hold legitimate differences of opinion with us—all they have to do is ask us.

Q. Ask you?

A. Yes, ask us. As I was telling my history professor the other day, that crew-cut, white-haired chap who claims to be a liberal—he's not really, you know; beneath that plaid sports coat beats the heart of a tired old man whose spirit cries out from the depths to be delivered from his current persuasion—anyway, as I was telling him, ours is a student view that tells time in terms of centuries. Events of today, like this new drive to double the size of the university in a "Great Leap Forward," must be seen against the background of the more realistic, original and age-old aims of the founders of the school. Remember, as our national director, Maxim Waterbug, a man in whom we place our deepest faith, has said: "Enthusiasm repressed is preferable to foolishness expressed."

In this regard, we do not oppose change for itself; rather, we oppose it because it tends to disturb the way things are. Now we *want* to live with the future; we *accept* it as a fact of life, the same way we accept such things as the "curve" marking system and the inevitability of warfare.

But what we want from the future is a guarantee of the same order that prevailed in the past. If not, then we will impose order on it! If a teacher gives two A's a semester, we want some assurance that he will continue to do so. If he doesn't, we want to know why!

Man's great discovery in the universe is order. We see the stars wheeling about in their close-knit formations and imitate them when we put up our fences and build our sewers. The triumph of man the maker is written in the remotest regions of the earth. From the Hill of Arizona to the teeming cities of Spain we see signs of the orderly pressure man has exerted on nature. The more order the better, say we. That's the way we like it.

Now if you want to see an example of the dynamic application of order to a situation, take my own case. I'm a sophomore now, and will graduate in 1963. After that I'll take an M.A. in Business Administration at Harvard. I'll spend two and a half years with IBM and leave for a higher salary in the insurance game. I will take my vacations in the mountains and will choose a wife whose tastes in such matters will be compatible with my own.

Q. *But where in the world would you ever expect to find such a wife?*

A. No problem there, my friend. Why Mount St. Marycliffe College, for instance, teems with girls whose training makes them perfect matches for young men who see things our way. I'll have no trouble finding a mate; together we will raise three children, two boys and a girl—in that order—and will have our home paid for by the time I am 36. I will retire at 58 and in my 60th year will complete work on my autobiography: *Looking Backward—the Story of My Life,* I'll call it. I will revise it just before I die to include my last seven years. I anticipate being outlived by my widow by six and one-half years, but just in case, will leave enough to support her comfortably for eight years.

I will bring my children up as rugged individualists, and will train them to look to their own resources in everything. I expect them to be paying half their way by their 15th year. With luck, I think nothing will go wrong.

I hope to worship my God, love my family, protect my home, respect my neighbors and uphold the law in such a manner that my friends as well as my enemies will remember me as a staunch and upright supporter of the Establishment. I have submitted this plan to National Headquarters for review. I am proud to say that our Regional Headquarters has already given it an "Honourable Mention."

Q. *What do the conservatives plan to do on campus this year?*

A. Well, first we hope to play a larger part in influencing student opinion to favor what we support. For one thing, we support the idea of noninterference in local matters, like this sit-in fuss over the so-called abuse of social minorities. We feel that the business of students is studying and minding their own business. We want to demonstrate that we do have a positive program; we are *for* maintaining the present size of the school; we will oppose the "Great Leap Forward." Incidentally, we may construct a bird sanctuary to keep our eagles in, and we hope especially to distribute copies of *The*

Mercurial American: How to be Conservatively Conscientious, our best-selling bible, you know. This is the story of how a rich Massachusetts family is carrying the traditions of old Salem into the modern publishing and political worlds.

• •

With that, conservatism's exponent pulled out his pocket watch, saw that it was late and said: "You'll have to excuse me now, I must get over to the cafeteria. After that, I've got a rally to organize. This week our group is protesting this Peace Corps nonsense. Nobody's come out against it yet, and I'm afraid the thing may catch on. Nice talking to you."

Thus dismissed, the writer strolled off, eyes glistening, pleased to know the college Tories could still yet defend themselves well.

The Left Side
of Paradise

William F. Gavin

A S EXECUTIVE CHAIRMAN of the Take Umbrage Committee of Young Americans' Hysterical Organization of Stevensonites (YAHOOS), I would like to take
umbrage at the obviously slanted article, "Give Me That
Old College Tory" (AM. 4/8). John Strack is undoubtedly a tool of the Interests and I have no doubt that the
AMA, NAM and DAR were pleased no end by the
space devoted to the neo-neo-Fascists and anti-freedom-
of-riot groups which are infesting our otherwise dedicated outposts of the New Frontier.

I have long suspected that Fordham College was
harboring people who enjoy wearing "carefully tailored
and severely styled brown suits." Mr. Strack's enthusiasm for such anti-working-class mufti is his own business, but I'll bet my autographed picture of Arthur Mil-
ler that my own shredded T-shirt and humble khakis
(suitable for sit-ins, cook-outs and, depending on the
weather, small riots) are as worthy in the eyes of the
emerging nations as his brown (I'll bet his shirts are
the same color!) uniforms. Once the youth of America
takes to wearing suits, can fascism be far behind?

Mr. Strack seems to laugh off the fact that conservatism (so called) is sweeping the college campus. We of the YAHOOS do not take such a bright view of reactionary movements. Only last week we held a meeting, followed by a rally, to decide what course of action should be taken against the conformists in our midst. After passing our usual resolution denouncing Trujillo, States' Rights, William F. Buckley, brown suits, IBM, bloodless security, Trujillo, Franco, the American Legion, Catholic War Veterans, Trujillo, and, finally, Trujillo, we decided that no positive action was needed at this time. But now the picture has changed. If AMERICA is seen to be a tool of the Fat Cats, we and our brother organization, Socialists Against Private Spending (SAPS) must act; you can readily see that Mr. Strack and his tailfin-loving friends are in for it.

I have chosen to reply to Mr. Strack's fawning interview with the president of the Campus Watchbird and Safeguard Society, by publishing my own interview with Alger T. Wunwurld, a junior majoring in Non-Conformity and a founder of YAHOOS. Mr. Wunwurld was gracious enough to devote a few minutes out

of his busy schedule (he pickets the pickets who are picketing the Russian Embassy on weekends, and devotes all of his spare time to writing letters of protest to the New York *Times*. Recently he broke his own record by writing a letter of protest against his own letter of protest, protesting the lack of protest on our campus!) to state his considered views on the state of campus liberalism today. Taller than most and rather thin (he recently went on a hunger strike protesting the lack of hunger strikes on our campus), Mr. Wunwurld gave his answers while walking a picket line protesting the—oh, the hell with it.

Q. *Mr. Wunwurld, what is collegiate liberalism?*

A. Liberalism is many things. It is being for, instead of against, things.

Q. *For? For what?*

A. It doesn't matter, so long as you're for something. Take me, for instance, I'm for Stanley Kramer movies, the World Federation, Freedom to Riot, Murray Kempton, Dorothy Day, Linus Pauling, Social Security, Job Security, Old-Age Security, Folk-Singing, Mort Sahl and SANE.

Q. *But doesn't your insistence on security leave you open to the same charge offered against campus conservatism? Do you not also prefer "the almost bloodless security of a perfectly controlled environment?" It would seem that your desire for more security would make you more of a conformist than your adversaries.*

A. This isn't true. I'm surprised you do not realize the difference between the conformist pattern of the young conservative and the dissenting voice of young Liberals. Only a few days ago, I said to a history professor: "I'm against McCarthyism, provincialism, clericalism and sin, in that order." "We need more men like you," he said. You can see that I'm not afraid to speak out against what I feel is wrong in the world.

Q. *Yes, but isn't it true that most history professors claim to be against the same things and that your dissent is, in reality, merely a playback of what they give to you?*

A. Not at all! This professor, for instance, was against McCarthyism, clericalism, provincialism and sin, in that order. You can see the difference. Plenty of room for honest disagreement between faculty and students.

397

Q. Yes. Tell me, Mr. Wunwurld, what do young Liberals feel are the greatest problems facing America today?

A. Conformity, for one thing. We *all* agree that conformity is bad.

Q. Conformity? What kind of conformity?

A. Never mind, what kind of conformity . . . just conformity. We go in big for "adventures of ideas."

Q. What does that mean?

A. Oh, you know . . . adventures . . . and ideas. We're all for freedom of thought, freedom of riot, that sort of thing. Adventure. . . . Ideas. . . .

Q. You mentioned "freedom of riot." Just what do you mean by this?

A. We feel it's every American's birthright to riot for what he believes in. Rioting is the backbone of our nation. Where would we be without the freedom to riot, guaranteed to us by our forefathers? We believe it is the right of every freedom-loving person to disrupt the United Nations and attack guards with chains and razors, although we do wish they would wait until Adlai is finished speaking. After all, isn't the United Nations for all people? There are some in this country who would deprive students of this fundamental right. A good riot is proof of nonconformity and that's what we're *for*. It's "adventures of ideas" in action. The reactionary press and the Big Boys in Washington have used smear tactics against those patriots who rioted against the HUAC in San Francisco. Is this the way to impress the emerging nations?

Q. Mr. Wunwurld, it has been suggested that collegiate liberalism is an "unnatural thing," and that young Liberals, who demand more Federal aid for *everything, are in reality trying "to escape the risks involved in a normal life." Is this true?*

A. Quite untrue. If properly applied, Federal aid to education can increase the risks involved in a normal life. Think of the healthy risks the parents of children attending private-parochial schools will have to take if aid is given only to public schools. On the other hand, if we do breach that historic wall separating Church and State, imagine the ingenious methods which will have to be devised by those who agree with the *New Republic's* claim that the state should "draw people to its system of schools and away from centrifugal systems." You can readily see that Federal aid can involve enough risks for any 100-per-cent, anti-centrifugal American.

Q. *It has been rumored that contemporary collegiate liberalism has become dogmatic and is, in effect, illiberal. Is this true?*

A. I'm glad you asked me that. There seems to be a general misunderstanding of the views of YAHOOS, despite our efforts at free exchange of ideas. I suspect this misunderstanding is the deliberate and malicious work of the reactionary press and Madison Avenue. Let me clear up a few of the most confused ideas.

First, it is *not* true that we believe that social salvation is impossible outside the editorial page of the New York *Post*. We embrace all roads to understanding and progress. Only last week we sent out a task force to deliver copies of the *Nation* to underdeveloped areas that are infested with the blight of conservatism. Many YAHOOS swear by James Reston and Walter Lippmann, despite the fact that the writings of these gentlemen are found in what might be called areas of reactionary fall-out. Of course, it is true that we believe that all those who seek the one true road will read the New York *Post*.

Another distortion and, I feel, a truly shocking example of the power of the McCarthyites, is the vicious myth that YAHOOS apply a double standard in the realm of political morality. William F. Buckley, that unregenerate tool of the Interests and the Pentagon, in his *Up From Liberalism*, devoted an entire chapter to the Paul Hughes case. Buckley pretended to believe that the hiring of a con man by Joseph L. Rauh of the ADA to spy on Senator McCarthy was an example of gross hypocrisy, since Rauh had previously denounced the hiring of confidential informants in no uncertain terms. You can see for yourself that Buckley misses the point. Proof of this is the fact that I have never heard any YAHOOS or a single progressive professor question the motives of Joseph Rauh in this case, while it is a matter of record that McCarthyism is denounced regularly by students and faculty. If this so-called double standard was applied by YAHOOS, why wasn't the Hughes case discussed in Richard Rovere's scholarly, unbiased account of the McCarthy days, *Senator Joe McCarthy*? You can see that logically speaking, the YAHOOS position—a position distorted and twisted by perverse and medieval minds—is the only logical one. Do I make myself clear?

Q. *Quite. What do YAHOOS plan to do on campus this year?*

A. We are planning many things, despite the fact that "planning" is a dirty word in certain circles. We plan to have a music festival in which we hope Pete Seeger will sing and play, to be followed by a march on the United Nations building, where we will protest the fact that Pete Seeger is being denied the martyr's right to be in jail, where he was ordered when he was previously denied the right to refuse to deny that he had ever had been a Communist, a denial of which would have been ample proof that the right to deny is being forcibly denied patriotic citizens of this country.

Q. *Mr. Wunwurld, may I be the first to congratulate you on your old-fashioned spirit of protest?*

A. Thank you. Coming from one of the biggest YAHOOS and SAPS on campus, that is a compliment!

As MR. WUNWURLD strode off into the night, I was jostled by an oaf carrying a placard. This placard read "Hungary . . . Tibet . . . Poland . . . China. . . ." I'm still wondering exactly what that sign was supposed to mean. After all, what is there to protest about in these countries? I cannot remember ever seeing YAHOOS carrying a sign like that.

♦

And Mary Sang

Snow on the gray crest of Mount Hermon wakes
My Son is a river in the waiting landscape
Out of my desert valley He has made a lake

My Son is the sea I am set to drift on
Everywhere I look He is the horizon
From and to Him I move Who is all directions

My Son is rain in Silo and I the first flower
I reach to Him and all my roots are sure
He is the storm and the early spring shower

My Son is a white alb of water falling
In the cup of my hands I have held Him flowing
Beneath the ferns and rock He is a small spring

My Son is a well deep in the unseen flesh
He is the water rising and the surface at rest
My children drink of Him and be refreshed

JAMES F. COTTER

401

What is "America"?

What is "America"?

Thurston N. Davis

THE QUEST for self-identity, for self-definition, is on occasions a useful and salutary undertaking for us all. Not only persons, but institutions also, can profitably ask themselves who or what they are and how they came to get that way. For a journal like AMERICA, a fiftieth birthday is as good a time as any to face the mirror of candid self-scrutiny and ask what we have been trying to be and do for half a century.

However, as Hippocrates once said, though art is long, life is short. There are so few left who can tell us, step by step for fifty years, how AMERICA happened to choose each of the paths it took at every forking of the roads. The last member of the first editorial staff, Fr. James J. Daly, died in 1954. The two survivors of our relatively early days are Fr. Gerald C. Treacy and Fr. J. Harding Fisher. Our sole hope for anything resembling full self-identification rests, therefore, with these two distinguished veterans—and, of course, with Fr. John LaFarge, now rounding out his 33rd intensely active year on the staff of this Review.

AMERICA's North Star in this voyage of self-discovery must be the original "editorial announcement" of April

17, 1909. In it our founder and first Editor, John J. Wynne, who was likewise the father of *The Catholic Encyclopedia,* spelled out the objectives and the modus operandi of the Review he was launching.

AMERICA was created "to meet the needs of the time." One such need was for "a review and conscientious criticism of the life and literature of the day." Other needs were for

> . . . a discussion of actual questions and a study of vital problems from the Christian standpoint, a record of religious progress, a defense of sound doctrine, an authoritative statement of the position of the Church in the thought and activity of modern life, a removal of traditional prejudice, a refutation of erroneous news, and a correction of misstatements about beliefs and practices which millions hold dearer than life.

To accomplish these ends, Father Wynne saw that a weekly journal would be required. The topics that demanded discussion were "too numerous, too frequent, and too urgent," he said, to be handled by a monthly magazine. He saw this need as "imperative." Father Wynne noted that the weekly diocesan press of those times did not attempt to chronicle events of secular interest or to discuss contemporary issues in the light of Christian principles. Many of them were "excellent in their way," he said, but they were "limited in the range of subjects and circumscribed in territory." The United States needed a national journal something like *The Tablet* of London.

What was Father Wynne's program for AMERICA?
The new Review, he wrote, was to discuss

> . . . questions of the day affecting religion,
> morality, science and literature; give informa-
> tion and suggest principles that may help to
> the solution of the vital problems constantly
> thrust upon our people. These discussions will
> not be speculative nor academic, but practical
> and actual, with the invariable purpose of meet-
> ing some immediate need of truth, of creating
> interest in some social work or movement, of
> developing sound sentiment, and of exercising
> proper influence on public opinion.

Naturally, in its efforts to follow the course charted
by its founder, AMERICA has tacked this way and that
with the passing years, depending on who was at the
wheel and who happened to be his first and second
mates. After all, these plans and provisions of Father
Wynne had to be translated into the weekly reality of
ink-on-paper by the men who year after year wrote and
edited AMERICA's pages. Father Wynne made a brave
and distinguished start, but his editorship (1909-1910)
was not lengthy enough to give us grounds for judging
how fully he would have succeeded in realizing the
objectives he had plotted for AMERICA. His successor,
the scholarly historian, preacher and former Jesuit provincial Thomas J. Campbell, Editor-in-Chief from 1910
to 1914, put no new or peculiarly personal stamp on the
Review. But in the quiet years just before World War
I, Father Campbell did far more than keep the fran-
chise. The international coverage of those years was remarkably good, and Father Campbell's editorials were
models of vigor and clarity.

In 1914 an extremely forceful personality came on
the scene as AMERICA's third Editor. Richard Henry
Tierney soon impressed the young Review with a
polemic spirit, a readiness for controversy and a deep
concern for the international responsibility of American
Catholics. Father Tierney left the relatively quiet life
of a seminary professor to become Editor. As his biographer notes, "he threw himself into the turmoil of a

journalistic career with a bounding energy and enthusiasm. . . . He had full scope to show whatever individuality and originality and power and personality he possessed"—and he had these qualities in abundance. He soon became, in his biographer's words, "the journalistic spokesman of the Catholic Church in the United States."

Through the years of the first World War and after, the vigor and energy of Father Tierney's rather imperial temperament dominated the pages of AMERICA and made themselves felt in the larger world outside. Some of the flavor of that period—Father Tierney arguing with President Woodrow Wilson and two Secretaries of State in defense of Mexican Catholics, his attack (he was a total abstainer) on the Prohibition Amendment, his drive for funds for the relief of Europe's starving millions after the war—is caught in the pages of his biography, *Richard Henry Tierney,* by Francis X. Talbot (America Press, 1930).

When Father Tierney's health broke beyond repair in 1925, Wilfrid Parsons succeeded him. There were changes of emphasis under the new Editor, but no lessening of liveliness and controversy. Father Parsons was always in the thick of things. During his time AMERICA stayed shoulder-deep in the continuing controversy over the persecution of Catholics in Mexico. The fateful events of the Al Smith campaign, the rise of fascism in Europe, the Great Depression, the disputes over Fr. Charles Coughlin and the beginnings of the New Deal are only some of the big strands that run through the fabric of Father Parsons' years as Editor.

What was AMERICA under Father Parsons? A penetrating answer can be found in an article published by *Social Order* in March, 1958 to commemorate Wilfrid Parsons' 71st birthday. Myles Connolly wrote from Hollywood to say:

> The AMERICA office, as presided over by Father Parsons, was a combination of employment office, embassy, information center, marriage bureau, Travelers' Aid Society and Number 10 Downing Street.

It was Father Parsons who chose and remodeled our present editorial residence, Campion House on West 108th Street in New York City. His good taste and practicality mark every corner of it, from the great crucifix over the main altar in our chapel to the fittings of the editorial board room. Father Parsons left the editorship in 1936, but his heart was always at Campion House and his pen ever at AMERICA's service. On the eve of his death in October, 1958, his arthritic fingers were still tapping out the lines of his weekly column, Washington Front—as sprightly and informed a bit of political reporting as could be found in the American press. At our fiftieth anniversary we salute a great priest-editor and a dear departed friend.

AMERICA got a new look under the next Editor, Francis X. Talbot. Father Talbot succeeded Father Parsons just as Francisco Franco was coming to power in Spain. An historian, a man of letters, a facile and wide-ranging mind, Father Talbot immediately impressed a new and distinctive stamp on the Review he edited. For one thing, AMERICA was given a fresh format. "Farewell to Old Style," said AMERICA on June 27, 1936. "From now on titles will be big and bold, . . . and every page will satisfy the esthetic sense." Heavy black rules and sans-serif type predominated, and the magazine took on that strong, emphatic look which many thought excessively stark and harsh. If so, the new, rather "nazoid" face of AMERICA certainly belied the mild, poetic and gracious Editor of those times.

During all these years, Paul L. Blakely, a Kentuckian and a vigorous States'-righter, wore out at least a gross of typewriter ribbons composing the editorials for AMERICA's pages. Father Blakely, associate editor of AMERICA for 29 years, was one of the most prolific journalists of his time. Through the entire middle period of AMERICA's life, the magazine was all but identified with the name of Paul Blakely—and with John Wiltbye, his pen name. Mention of Father Blakely recalls two other great names of our middle years, William I. Lonergan and Joseph C. Husslein. The work of Father Husslein, who was a member of the AMERICA staff from 1911 to 1927, is discussed in some detail elsewhere (p. 139) in this issue.

In 1944 the Second World War was drawing to a climax and a close. International issues were the order of the day; a new world was struggling to be born; the menacing shadow of Red imperialism was beginning to grow and grow over Eastern Europe and Asia. It was right, therefore, that one who had been among the very first to sound the warning against international communism, who was so widely acquainted with world affairs, so gifted a linguist and so well travelled, should direct the policies of AMERICA during these crucial years of reconstruction. He was John LaFarge.

Father LaFarge has little in common with warmongers or polemicists, and these were the days of the great world quest for peace. During this time, then, John La-Farge, the wise irenicist, made a most vital contribution. But his objective—and the objective of AMERICA—was always peace with justice. Therefore, when justice demanded it, the Editor of AMERICA spoke out unequivocally—against the shoddy in art, against the backsliders in social justice, against the hatemongers—in a word, against the blind who happened to be leading the blind of those particular years. Father LaFarge farsightedly opposed the policy of unconditional surrender for Germany at a time when such a stand was most unpopular. He had pioneered in the field of interracial justice, and of course these preoccupations were mirrored in AMERICA during his years as Editor. Probably no other single white American has worked so long and so arduously in the cause of the Negro here and everywhere. A long spell of ill health—today fortunately belied by his seventy-nine ripe years—forced his retirement from the editorship in 1948.

Robert Hartnett succeeded Father LaFarge. Large in body, mind and sympathies, Father Hartnett had been a superb teacher. His former pupils, remembering provocative classes in political science at the University of Detroit, were saddened to learn that the university was losing him. He brought to his editorial work the refinements of a scholar. None but those closely associated with him as colleagues will ever know how meticulously he worked, how many hours he carved out of extremely busy days for reading and research, how faithful he was in scholarly correspondence, how exacting in demands on his collaborators—but primarily on himself.

To habits of scholarship Father Hartnett wedded the forceful, analytical and honest mind of a born debater. Perhaps the height of his debating career was the occasion when, before a large student audience at Yale, he took on Paul Blanshard. This was an era of great debates. The years during which this manly and priestly Jesuit presided over the policies of AMERICA were years when tension and controversy welled over in the United States. The infant United Nations made its first teetering steps on the world stage; Unesco was already under severe fire; China went Communist; the Korean War flared up and fizzled in a fire of frustrations; General MacArthur was relieved of his command; the Truman doctrine was formulated; Nato slowly gained ground in Europe; U. S. economic and technical aid programs were debated in the light of isolationist or internationalist preoccupations. Concern over Red espionage and the infiltration of Communists, later brought to a head in the notorious Rosenberg case, had set the stage for Sen. Joseph R. McCarthy. AMERICA under Father Hartnett turned to each of these problems as it arose, and the AMERICA record of those years, so obviously marked with the genius of its editor, is there for all to read. During the final months of his editorship in 1955, Father Hartnett set in motion detailed plans for a new format for AMERICA. The present dress of the Review dates from Oct. 1, 1955.

The foregoing account is necessarily most incomplete. For one thing, it discusses Editors-in-Chief as though they alone were responsible for AMERICA. Doubtless, each of these men gave a distinctive cachet to the Review, but their work could never have been done without the constant assistance of many lay collaborators and, above all, of teams of dedicated Jesuit associates. These fellow priests, both associate editors and business and circulation directors, have for fifty years given AMERICA unique strength in depth and unusual organizational stability. Elsewhere in this volume we list all their names. But it should be noted here that during the last fifteen or twenty years AMERICA could not have been published without able colleagues like the late Francis P. LeBuffe, Joseph A. Lennon, Cornelius E. Lynch, Joseph P. Carroll, Edward F. Clark, Joseph C. Mulhern, James P. Shea, Stephen J. Meany, the late Daniel M. O'Connell, Paul A. Reed, Joseph F. Mac-Farlane and Patrick H. Collins—men who labored in the office now directed by Clayton F. Nenno, who became treasurer of the America Press in 1958.

Associate and contributing editors who have given long and distinguished service to AMERICA during the last two decades are John A. Toomey, the late Gerard B. Donnelly, Edward A. Conway, Allen P. Farrell, the late Albert I. Whelan, Vincent P. McCorry and two long-time members of our present staff, Robert A. Graham and Vincent S. Kearney. For shorter terms during the same period AMERICA benefited from the presence on its editorial staff of Gordon George, William J. Gibbons, J. Gerard Mears, W. Eugene Shiels, Edward J. Duff and the late John P. Delaney. Still more briefly on our masthead during these years were the names of

FATHER WYNNE   FATHER CAMPBELL

William A. Donaghy, John Courtney Murray, J. Edward Coffey, Philip S. Land, Louis E. Sullivan, Richard E. Twohy, John J. Scanlon, Richard V. Lawlor, Daniel Fogarty, Thomas J. M. Burke, Joseph Small and Francis J. Tierney.

Charles Keenan, Managing Editor for many of his sixteen years on the staff, deserves special mention, be-

410

cause during these years—to paraphrase Parkman—not a line was turned or an apt parenthesis entered but Keenan led the way. A native Irishman, a man slight in bodily frame, Father Keenan loomed large in AMERICA's world as an editor's editor. Two other distinguished contemporary veterans of the present staff, Harold C. Gardiner and Benjamin L. Masse, assuredly deserve space in this issue for the articles in which they discuss AMERICA's contributions to the fields of literary criticism and Christian social thought. Finally, how can we ever express our gratitude to all the others—clergy and laity, here and abroad—who have given the fruit of their talents to our Review?

W HAT IS AMERICA? It is not merely the approximately 70,000 pages bound into the hundred volumes that now, the product of fifty years, span fifteen feet three inches on library shelves. Depending on how one appraises it, AMERICA is something more or less than the sum of those pages. It is what each of its editors and contributors, and all of us together, have made it. By our individual and collective failure or success we must measure the net gain or loss of fifty years.

Frankly, we are not ashamed. Of course, we could have done better. Even by the standards of an essay-writing age, there were probably too many general essays in our early volumes. In expressing its opinions, AMERICA has never laid claim to infallibility, nor does it do so now. However, there were moments when we spoke with too strident, too intransigent, too dogmatic a voice. There were other occasions when that voice sounded too cloistered, too timorous, too studied. But if at times mistakes were made in emphasis or attitude or expression, they were at least the mistakes of honesty. This same honesty compels us to say that the overwhelming part of our work has expressed exactly what we wanted to say as we wanted to say it.

AMERICA set out to be and still is an "opinion" magazine—a journal of Christian opinion. A journal of opinion is not a family magazine. It does not attempt to amuse, entertain, instruct or edify, though it may happen to do all these things at one time or another in the performance of its specific function. An opinion-journal exists to express self-consistent opinions, proposals and criticism and to foster discussion of them by competent minds. (An AMERICA department, State of the Question, is intended to create a forum for discussions of this nature.)

There is no better definition of a journal of opinion than the one formulated several years ago by Father Hartnett:

> It is a magazine which has a definite, coherent outlook in terms of which its editors and contributors analyze and reach judgments about current events and trends, especially in the social, economic, political, literary and (in some cases) religious fields. It addresses itself to a general readership, to those persons who, regardless of occupation or station in life, are interested in analyses terminating in judgments, based on a coherent outlook, about current events and trends in the fields mentioned.

A magazine of this nature, if it adheres to its principles, will not appeal to everyone; its circulation will remain relatively limited; it will never be a "popular" journal. In fact, if it is conscientiously performing its function of expressing ideas and opinions, it is likely at times to be exceedingly unpopular, at least in certain quarters.

Among the 310 publications that currently are members of the Catholic Press Association of the United States, strictly speaking only AMERICA and *Commonweal* can be described as weekly journals of opinion, though *Ave Maria* is now moving into this category. Outside the field of the Catholic press, the *New Republic, Christian Century, New Leader,* the *Nation,* the *Reporter,* and most recently the *National Review*—each with its own political or ideological point of view —likewise fit the definition. Of course, opinion journalism is not necessarily restricted to the field of the weeklies and biweeklies. The monthly *Atlantic* and *Harper's* in the secular field might be called opinion journals. Among Catholic publications there are the

Catholic World, published since 1865 by the Paulist Fathers, the *Voice of St. Jude* and the monthly of the Passionist Fathers, the *Sign*—all of which have made significant contributions to opinion journalism.

But has not the day of the opinion journal passed? Looking back thirty, forty or fifty years, it is possible to understand the role once played by these journals. A generation or so ago, the sociology of communication was vastly simpler. So were the dynamics of opinion-making. But there have been so many changes in the intervening years. In those earlier times public opinion was a much more limited thing than it is today. Opinion-makers then aimed their shafts at an elite, for it used to be sufficient to reach the leaders of society.

Today, however, the opinion-maker must reach everyone, for everyone weighs the same as everyone else in the egalitarian scales of the Gallup poll. Digest magazines bring capsulated opinion to everyone's bedside.

FATHER TIERNEY

FATHER PARSONS

Radios beam Fulton Lewis Jr. to our dinner tables. Three big national television networks project the images of opinion-molders like Edward R. Murrow into our living rooms.

But there were no Arthur Godfreys, Edward Murrows, TV networks or big book clubs when AMERICA was founded in 1909. People then would have stared in wild surmise at the phrase "communications media." There was advertising, of course, but no Madison

Avenue. The opinion-molding of the movie industry had not yet begun. In 1909, Henry Luce, an eleven-year-old boy at Hotchkiss School, had not so much as dreamed of his *Time-Life-Fortune* empire. There were lobbies in the Washington of 1909, but not the smoothly tooled, opinion-making lobbies of today. The Rockefeller brothers, either mere infants or still to be born, were not issuing—as they did in 1958—important opinion-making statements on education and the national security. Universities were for the most part just liberal arts colleges, not a great formative bloc of influence in the democratic process. The Federal Government of those days might well have wanted to influence public opinion, but it hadn't one-tenth of its present panoply of agencies and instrumentalities for doing so.

In this mid-century quest to establish once again the identity and definition of AMERICA, we do not discount these contemporary realities. It is quite true that today opinion-making has become the objective of all the above as well as of a score of organizations like the Fund for the Republic, but this development does not impair the usefulness of or diminish the necessity for the journal of opinion. There is no conflict between the opinion journal and, tor example, the Fund for the Republic. The Fund operates on a high level in the field of mass adult education, and it approaches this legitimate and necessary work in a creative manner. But the area of the Fund's influence is distinct from that of the opinion magazine, and its occasional telecasts, releases and brochures, though powerful in the world of opinion, lack the constantly repeated impact of the weekly journal read at leisure by the thoughtful few.

In fact, the small-circulation journal of opinion has a more vital role to play than ever before. The relatively simple days of 1909 are gone. There are so many new problems, so many emerging issues, all of them intertwined one with the other in the most complicated ways. There is a plethora of opinion about each phase of every single problem. All these new questions, arising from the rapidly changing configuration of our times

414

and our society, demand analysis and discussion.

Vast and knotty international problems are cropping up from week to week and year to year. Again, U. S. society confronts in 1959 a problem which it was only commencing to recognize in 1909, that of religious pluralism. Today, all sorts of questions relating to intergroup tensions and to methods of trustworthy and fruitful communication between and among the diverse segments of our society have given public discussion of opinion a fresh framework of reference. Think, moreover, of the speed with which science and technology have developed in the last half-century. They raise hundreds of questions of the greatest urgency.

If they were here today, what would Fr. John Wynne and his first board of editors think of the long roster of topics—all of them pressing, perplexing and complex—that supply the grist for today's opinion journalism? They make quite a litany: space control and intercontinental ballistic missiles; hydrogen bomb tests and manned satellites to the moon; automation and the problem of the new leisure; a tangle of questions relating to urban life, suburbia, working mothers, slum clearance, city planning and juvenile delinquency; the mental-health menace, psychiatry, applied depth psychology and the new-fangled arts of persuasion. There is the new problem of how to control our vast abundance of foodstuffs; and all the related questions of an affluent society. There are new questions of public health and plans for voluntary health insurance. What about the "censorship" problem? What is beating the "beat" generation? Is the very meaning of "nature" changing? How are we to think of the bulging population of the world? With what alternatives can we confront the rising wave of neo-Malthusianism?

Father Wynne and his first AMERICA staff would have a difficult time picking and choosing today among these and a thousand other questions. Africa is in danger of slipping into the Red camp. Southeast Asia shudders under the shadow of the Red Chinese commune plan. How long can we count on the solid support of Latin America in the battle of the free world against tyranny? What are all these new freedoms—to read, to travel, to criticize, to know? To what extent is John Dewey's instrumentalism responsible for the alleged failure of education in the United States? Was the legal positivism of Justice Oliver Wendell Holmes a cause or a mere symptom of the declining health of American law? Father Wynne and his companions could take at least some measure of comfort from these last two questions. They would recognize the name of the younger Holmes. And in 1899—ten years before AMERICA—John Dewey had published *The School and Society*. But I suspect that most of these questions—along with conceptions like mass culture, baby sitting and supermarkets—would be as unintelligible to Father Wynne as the titles of a double-feature recently playing at our neighborhood theater: "The Blob" and "I Married a Monster from Outer Space."

FATHER TALBOT

FATHER LaFARGE

THIS IS ALL very well, say the devil's advocates at this point. We concede that you Jesuits of 1959 deal with a vastly greater proliferation of topics than did your predecessors. But is anybody reading you?

AMERICA goes directly to approximately 50,000 persons or libraries each week, and its circulation continues to grow. Moreover, we have good reason to believe that our readers are a most communicative lot, and so the magazine regularly gets passed along to a much larger group. Last year, when a friend gave us a check and asked that AMERICA be placed in 40 university or college libraries, we were hard put to find that many that didn't already have it. Early this year the chaplain at Leavenworth Penitentiary wrote: "The men here pounce on AMERICA as supplemental reading for their college courses. It is in constant circulation and demand." AMERICA is frequently consulted in the Congressional Library. The British Museum requested and got a complimentary subscription. AMERICA is clipped for dossiers used at State Department briefings. Moscow's *Literaturnaya Gazeta* is one of our subscribers. *Time* (May 28, 1956) backed into a compliment by saying that AMERICA "comes up to any secular standards." It is a special source of encouragement to us that so many editors, Catholic and non-Catholic, read AMERICA regularly. Many of them have been kind enough to tell us that, even in realms where they decide to differ from us on points of policy, they look to our Review for balanced Catholic opinion.

Newsweek and *Time* have cited AMERICA, we believe, more frequently of late than any other periodical of its type. AMERICA's editorials are frequently guest editorials not only in the Catholic press but also in the U. S. secular press and in the overseas edition of the New York *Herald-Tribune*. Our articles are sometimes "lifted" by foreign journals—often without a credit line. AMERICA is one of two Catholic periodicals on the tables of the reading rooms of the Harvard and Yale Clubs of New York City. The librarian at the National Press Club in Washington, we hear, recently posted a notice calling back missing copies of AMERICA needed for binding. Of course, AMERICA is indexed in *Readers' Guide to Periodical Literature* and in the *Catholic Periodical Index*.

Let us further clarify AMERICA's identity. It is a Catholic journal. At the top of our masthead, under the word AMERICA, we print "National Catholic Weekly Review." Again in the masthead, just above the names of the full-time and corresponding editors, we publish this legend each week: "Edited and published by the following Jesuit Fathers of the United States and Canada." This serves further to identify AMERICA as a

417

Catholic review published by Jesuit priests of North America. The reader who gives this legend a moment's consideration will immediately understand that the good ship AMERICA is not sailing under the flag of the Society of Jesus as such. Our Review is not the official publication, or an official publication, of the Jesuit order. AMERICA is no more and no less than it claims to be in this published self-identification. That is, it is a Catholic weekly review, the supervision of whose editorial content has been turned over to an Editor and a limited number of associate editors appointed to this work of weekly journalism by the provincial su-

FATHER HARTNETT   **FATHER DAVIS**

periors of the eleven provinces of the United States and Canada. (The French-Canadian Jesuits publish their own review, *Relations*.)

Allow me to repeat that AMERICA does not exist to publicize "the Jesuit line"—there is no such thing—on the temporal issues of our day. Individual Jesuits are free to, and often do, disagree with us; their letters, disputing some point of editorial policy, frequently appear in our Correspondence. Likewise, as is perfectly obvious, AMERICA does not pretend to be an "official" voice of the Church in any sense whatever. Despite the constant plaint of certain bigots that Catholic opinion is a frozen iceberg of conformity, any moderately informed person knows that apart from the defined dogmas of the Church and the principles of the natural moral law, Catholic opinion, especially on temporal issues, is variegated to the degree that one might almost say that its disarray is the most notable thing about it. All this is elementary, but is needs to be stated from time to time, and our fiftieth birthday is a good occasion on which to repeat it.

WHAT PRINCIPLES and policies actually define and characterize AMERICA? Obviously, AMERICA strives to be contemporary, to write and rewrite up to its deadline about strictly current events and contemporary trends. Its editors labor to stay "on top of the news"— ahead of it, if possible. But these are not distinctive traits. Any news magazine accomplishes this weekly feat and gives more extensive coverage than AMERICA.

AMERICA is specified by its concern for moral questions. This concern lies at the heart of what we may call the corporate personality of a journal like ours. Our preoccupation is with the moral hits or misses, the spiritual triumphs or failures of man in all the varied enterprises of the modern world. Almost every human event—from the closing of Little Rock Central High School to a sputnik racing into orbit—has certain definite moral and religious overtones. Our ears strain to catch these notes, from whatever source they come.

No one should look in AMERICA's pages for comment by neutral observers. We are not neutrals. We are deeply committed. Obviously, as Jesuit priest-journalists, we are committed to our holy faith. Secondly, we are committed to the moral law of God, as this law is promulgated through the universal forum of human conscience. We are committed, on a wide and varied field of subjects, to the principles enunciated by the Popes, the Vicars of Christ, and in the annual statements of the American hierarchy.

We conceive it to be a large part of our task to point out how, in concrete and specific cases, the universal teaching of the sovereign pontiffs and of the bishops on social, economic, scientific and cultural topics can be applied and implemented. It is not enough for us to compose disquisitions on the naked principles of justice or on rights and obligations in the abstract. Our effort is to find out how, and according to what prudential judgments, these universal norms may be translated into laws, institutions and attitudes.

There are universally valid principles on racial justice. But how do fair-minded people go about changing attitudes regarding the desegregation of Virginia's high schools? What can American Catholics do toward helping Negroes into the ranks of white-collar employment? Anyone with a mere nodding acquaintance with the social encyclicals of recent Popes acknowledges the right of workingmen to form unions of their own choosing. But what of right-to-work laws? What remedies are there for the recent hardening of attitudes between labor and management? Is it true that congressional investigations of labor racketeering have gone so far that they are now harming the cause of labor itself? We address ourselves to problems such as these. No one will quarrel with the principle that college students should read deeply and widely under proper guidance. AMERICA does not devote space to this obvious major premise. We are in business to discuss whether a book like James Joyce's *Ulysses* is proper fare for a student in a Catholic college seminar, and under what conditions.

In these and a hundred other editorial concerns, AMERICA's attitude is and should be characterized by the widest and most universal of interests. Nothing, absolutely nothing, that concerns the good of the human person on any level of life should ever be outside our purview. The inspiring meditation on the Incarnation of Jesus Christ, found in the second week of the *Spiritual Exercises* of St. Ignatius, founder of the Society of Jesus, sets our editorial policy in this important respect. I wish there were space to quote pertinent passages from this meditation, but those interested may consult it for themselves. Let it be noted that it is in a meditation on the *Incarnation* that St. Ignatius gives us this amazing picture of universal human diversity, struggle and suffering.

It is no exaggeration to say, therefore, that every single line of type in AMERICA bears, or should bear, in some manner at least, on the meaning and consequences for daily life of the Incarnation of the Son of God. Catholicism draws its philosophy of life from the central reality of the Incarnation, from the fact that the Word became flesh and dwelt among us. The never-ending work of the Church is to elaborate, on every level of life and for every clime and time, the conclusions to be drawn from this shattering event. In that phase of the Church's deathless mission AMERICA has, we feel, a small but not insignificant part to play in the world of contemporary American life.

AMERICA is independent. As is obvious, of course, we acknowledge complete and unqualified dependence on the dogmas of our revealed religion and on the dictates of the moral law. But in the entire field of human affairs, wherever there is an area for prudential judgment, we gratefully recognize the immense freedom that we enjoy as editors. Our cordial relations with subscribers, advertisers, benefactors and that esteemed and valued group known as the AMERICA Associates are such as in no way to infringe on our editorial freedom. We ourselves act as censors of what we publish. There is absolutely no shadowy specter of "publishers" hanging over our shoulders, reading our galleys or inserting changes in our page proofs. Our considerable independence is made possible, of course, by the trust that our ecclesiastical superiors have been good enough to repose in our prudence. Without this leeway it would be almost impossible to publish AMERICA.

We are not beholden to any political party or any special interest. We take stands on public issues, but we do not endorse political candidates nor involve ourselves in partisan politics. We have never done so, and we have no intention of changing this policy. I think it is fair and true to say that not for one moment have we ever consciously deviated from the principle laid down in 1909 by John Wynne: "AMERICA will aim at becoming a representative exponent of Catholic thought and activity without bias or plea for special persons or parties" (AM. 4/17/09). Perhaps, on second thought, we have harbored one bias—a bias for the poor. But that would have been all right with Father

421

Wynne, since the poor are not "special persons" and they usually have no "special parties" to speak for them.

One final pillar of policy. AMERICA shuns an editorial attitude that is nagging, negative or contentious. We fail in this at times, to be sure, but our overarching concern is to write positively and constructively. We are fully aware of the terrible evils of the world. The twist in man's nature, product of original sin, is a cosmic tragedy to which we do not shut our eyes. We tend to look editorially, however, for what is promising and hopeful. We make no secret of the value we set on Christian optimism and on the habit of hope.

We are encouraged to pursue this policy by a statement that appears at the very beginning of the *Spiritual Exercises* of St. Ignatius Loyola, in a brief note that is called the Presupposition to the Exercises. In it St. Ignatius says: "Let it be presupposed that every good Christian is to be more ready to save [put a good construction on] his neighbor's proposition than to condemn it. If he cannot save it, let him inquire how his neighbor means it; and if he means it badly, let him correct him with charity." If in the future AMERICA should ever habitually set its course athwart the spirit of this Ignatian principle, it will in my opinion have ceased to justify its existence.

THE IDEAL of the Jesuit is not pure contemplation. His vocation is rather that of the contemplative in action. This double polarity of Jesuit life, certainly of the life of a Jesuit journalist, is symbolized for AMERICA's editors by the location of the house they live in. Campion House on West 108th Street in New York lies halfway between Upper Broadway and Riverside Drive. When we leave our residence to take a walk, we must choose between two courses. One is a contemplative stroll along the tree-lined, Old-World paths of Riverside Drive, with the Hudson River flowing quietly by at our side. The other is a brisk walk up or down the teeming and shabby sidewalks of mid-Manhattan's Broadway—a multilingual, interracial neighborhood to which all the nations of the earth seem to have sent delegates.

Like contemplation and action, these two city streets go unswervingly along, meeting only in the mind of the one who must wed them in a synthesis of the two things they represent. Perhaps at times in our fifty years we have walked too frequently on one rather than the other. But for the most part I believe we have mixed in just proportions the hustling immediacy of Broadway with the reflective quiet of the Drive. In the year 2009, when AMERICA celebrates its centenary, we can only guess where its editors will be residing. But wherever they are, you can take it for granted that two such paths as I have described will still meet at a crossroads in their editorial sanctum.

Editorial

Our New Editorial Table

A MASTERPIECE WAS UNVEILED in our editorial office during the last week of March. It was delivered to our door with no fanfare and considerable incongruity when a rather battered truck jockeyed for space on our traffic-lined street and three husky men in old work clothes hopped out, swung open the doors and gently maneuvered the masterpiece into the editorial sanctum. The three "workmen" were two young Jesuit seminarians from the house of philosophy at Shrub Oak, N. Y., and a Jesuit lay brother.

When the object of their maneuvering was stripped of its protective case and paper wrappings, a truly magnificent table gleamed out in the editorial board room. It is 12 feet long and of trapezoid shape. Under the satin sheen of the finish, the oaken grain has been matched in a lovely design; the angle-joints are so silky-smooth to the touch that they seem no more than penciled lines. Every ounce of its 400 beautifully designed and executed pounds bespeaks the craftsman whose loving care and pride in his work has produced this masterpiece of the cabinetmaker's art. And who was the artist-craftsman? He was the Jesuit lay brother.

Several days after we had rejoiced in our new table,

we read an address given at the sixth annual convention of the National Science Association at Denver. Dr. Howard E. Wilson, dean of education at the University of California at Los Angeles, delivered a severe indictment of one aspect of American culture and education. The problems that science teachers face, he charged, are problems that are deeply rooted in a "tradition of sloppy craftsmanship" on all levels of American education and work. This blight, he stated, extends from the garage mechanic who does a slipshod job of repairing a car to the would-be English teacher who does not bother about proper punctuation and good grammar. Yet our times demand precision as never before.

The successful career is, of course, a legitimate goal, but there is a deeper motivation to inspire worker or scholar to forswear "sloppy craftsmanship." It is the motive of proper pride in one's work. The unsung [What? After *this* tribute?] Jesuit lay brother to whom we are indebted labored for 175 long hours over his masterpiece. He was not struggling toward a successful career. But he was driven to achieve the perfection of his craftsmanship, because he knew the dignity of his work. He knew it because he realized that any legitimate product of the human hand and brain *is* human—and therefore Godlike. He knew, too, that any such human work has been sanctified by the Son of God—was He not known as the "son of the carpenter"?

The burden of inculcating such an esteem for the job at hand lies heavily on our whole educational establishment. But it lies primarily on the home. It is within those walls that children must first learn, not merely that "what's worth doing is worth doing well," but worth doing perfectly for their own sake as human persons, for the sake of the work and for the glory of God.

We shall sit around this lovely table twice every week, discussing and hammering out editorials and comments and the entire policy of this Review. We can only hope and literally pray that our work, in content and style, will reflect—week in and week out—the hatred of "sloppy craftsmanship" that shines out of every shimmering grain of our new board-room table.

Morals in the Market Place

M ANY A CORPORATION EXECUTIVE probably rubbed his
eyes in disbelief when he opened the September
issue of *Fortune* and started reading Louis Finkelstein's
"The Businessman's Moral Failure." Disdaining a soft
approach to his audience, Rabbi Finkelstein, who is
chancellor of Manhattan's Jewish Theological Seminary,
starts his homily with this stern, uncompromising para-
graph:

> If American businessmen are right in the way
> most of them now live, then all the wise men of
> the ages, all the prophets and the saints were fools.
> If the saints were not fools, the businessmen must
> be.

Dr. Finkelstein then proceeds to document his indictment with a litany of vivid detail. Not only do businessmen, he says, have a false view of their role in society—a view which emphasizes their place on the economic ladder rather than a concern for the civilization
which they dominate. They tend in many lamentable
ways to transgress in their daily actions the ethical laws
that apply to their calling. The author instances crooked

427

tax returns, bribery of purchasing agents, suborning of legislators and law-enforcement officials, use of wire-taps to learn the secrets of competitors, violations of building codes, spreading of false information by insiders in order to make a killing in the stock market, false advertising and a number of other malodorous practices. "It is impossible to conduct business in the U. S. today," a fast-rising young executive confided to Rabbi Finkelstein, "without breaking the law." Even if this is an exaggeration, the author comments, there is a great deal of skulduggery in the marketplace. The disturbing truth is, he says, that the U. S. businessman

> is preoccupied chiefly with gain, coasting on the spiritual momentum of the past, divorced from our sources of inspiration. He is a leading citizen of a largely hedonistic nation propelled by meaningless drives toward materialistic and frequently meaningless goals.

Only those who do not know Rabbi Finkelstein will imagine that his indictment springs from hostility to businessmen, or to our system of capitalistic enterprise. On the contrary, he has been led to criticize the American businessman because of his high regard for him and his role in our society. "The fate of the world," he asserts, "hangs on his decisions." Or again: "Today's crisis demands the businessman's leadership in the area of human behavior," for the world needs "ethical leadership from those it respects as supremely practical."

Nor is the Jewish leader's message merely negative. His program for placing ethics on the corporation agenda may differ in detail and emphasis from the Holy Father's teaching on the duties of businessmen, but it is in basic accord with it. Like Pope Pius XII, Rabbi Finkelstein is warring on the maxim "business is business." He is calling for the supremacy of ethics in business, as in all other phases of life. He would save our business civilization from moral decay by having businessmen concentrate, not only on profits, but also, and even more, on saving their immortal souls. The heartening thing is that the editors of a plush businessman's magazine like *Fortune* apparently agree with him.

Puerto Rican Pastoral

THE CATHOLICS of the mainland United States were quite unprepared to read in their morning papers that several Catholic bishops living under the American flag had, late in October, jointly forbidden their people to vote for a certain political party. Whatever the record may show elsewhere, such a prohibition is unprecedented in American Catholic history.

Up to the present, our American democratic system has unfailingly given the Church wide latitude and ample opportunity to voice its convictions on moral issues, to preach the Gospel and to take the means necessary to defend its liberty and well-being. Down through the years, as a result, the weight of Catholic leadership, like that of the Protestants, has been able to influence for good the course of national life. But a sharp line has invariably been drawn this side of the voting booth.

Thus, it has always seemed unnecessary, improper, even something of a profanation, for the authority of the Church to be extended, through the pulpit, to the point of a formal prohibition against voting for one particular party, or for an individual candidate. The record of the Catholic Church and of her priests has been without blemish in this respect.

For generations it has seemed evident to American Catholics that only the gravest peril to civil order, or an imminent threat to the Church's very existence, joined to a complete (and highly unlikely) breakdown of the democratic process itself, could be conceived as justifying the use of such an extreme measure.

Consequently, the U.S. Catholic remains profoundly confused and bewildered—not to say embarrassed—by the action of the bishops of Puerto Rico. In a joint pastoral read in all their churches on October 23, they forbade Catholics to vote, in that Commonwealth's November 8 elections, for the Popular Democratic Party headed by Gov. Luís Muñoz Marín.

Catholics on the mainland, together with most of their fellow Americans, are in a state of considerable ignorance concerning the true character of the PDP and the peculiar circumstances on the Island which led to the bishops' exceptional step. Perhaps, too, they do not understand the Latin temperament of the Puerto Rican political leaders who, while American citizens, rule the Commonwealth under their own constitution and who are heirs, not of the Anglo-Saxon traditions of New England, but of the culture and traditions of New Spain.

It may also be that, contrary to widespread belief, the pastoral did not impose a formal obligation in conscience, but was simply a way of articulating a long-standing grievance of the Church against the Puerto Rican powers-that-be. Any fair-minded observer in the States must also concede that Church leaders are in a better position to judge the moral issues involved than are outsiders who do not bear before God the responsibility of shepherds of souls in Puerto Rico.

Here on the mainland, few Catholics—and even fewer Protestants—are aware of the long struggle of the Church's leaders with Governor Muñoz and his party. That these grievances are important, and that they touch moral and religious issues, seems evident. In a land overwhelmingly Catholic, the governmental party has consistently advanced public policies offensive to the moral sense of Catholics and alien to the traditions of the Puerto Ricans. Passages in the party's own program, as published in the public press, have been interpreted as an open repudiation of this tradition and as an insult to the Church.

No Catholic should presume to pass definitive judgment on actions taken by responsible Church leaders in distant regions under circumstances difficult to evaluate. Obviously, however, American Catholics can and must decide whether such a course can be regarded as a model of what is proper for their own country. What is involved here is nothing less than the conception that we American Catholics entertain about the function of ecclesiastical authority within the American democratic system. Is the attempt to use Church authority to determine, by formal prohibition, how a man votes, an action that is necessary or desirable in this country?

It happens that in October U.S. Catholics found themselves with two examples to study and to choose between. During that very month, the French hierarchy issued a grave declaration on the moral problems posed by the continuing conflict between the Government of France and the Algerian nationalists. In France, the hierarchy's statement was met with wide attention and respect on the part of those to whom it was addressed. No Frenchman—not even a secularist or Freemason—challenged the right of moral leaders to offer guidance to their coreligionists at a time of widespread public confusion and anxiety.

In Puerto Rico, on the contrary, the bishops' letter stirred up a storm of controversy even in the churches in which it was read. Public officials denounced it as "incredible medieval interference in a political campaign." The difference in the reactions may stem, not from any divergence of viewpoint over the respective hierarchies' right to speak about public issues of moral import, but from a difference in the manner in which this vital mission was exercised.

The French document limits itself to setting forth guide lines by which French Catholics can form thei: consciences, and on the basis of which they can perform their civic duty with peace of mind. The Puerto Rican pastoral adds the suggestion of coercive action by ecclesiastical spokesmen. It does so, moreover, in that very area of civic life, the voting booth, which a democratic state necessarily surrounds with a maximum of privacy and independence. In this atmosphere the individual citizen is presumed to be able to come to a free decision—a choice enlightened, it may be, by the guidance of those he trusts and reveres, but a choice responsibly made by himself.

Catholics in the United States cannot but wonder about the nature of a situation which would persuade Church leaders to embark on a course of action so open to misinterpretation, not to say futility. It must indeed be a grave situation, for, in a healthy democracy, such a step as that taken by the Puerto Rican bishops can only be viewed as a profound disruption of normal political processes.

Under any circumstances now conceivable to the American Catholic citizen, there is no substitute for reliance on the established procedures by which the moral forces in a democracy are free to defend and promote the sound development of the common good and to secure, at the same time, the liberty and well-being of religion.

Standing outside the Puerto Rican discussions as they do, U.S. Catholics must regret the turn of events which now threatens to embitter that island Commonwealth with the fruits of prolonged civic dissension. Surely, too, they must regret the circumstances which have, in a sense, put the Church's prestige at stake in the coming Puerto Rican elections. More directly of concern to them, however, as it must be to all their fellow Americans, is the understanding of how this incident may be made to affect and influence events closer to home.

At this point and in this hour, history offers enlightenment and reassurance. It clearly affirms that American Catholics stand at one with their fellow citizens in loyal allegiance to those principles of conscientious citizenship which undergird our nation's attempt to preserve the structure of a free and democratic society. Indeed, the very difficulty that American Catholics feel in comprehending the pattern of events in Puerto

Rico testifies to their unquestioning conviction—incul-
cated, by the way, in the parochial schools now flourishing in this free country—that human dignity and the
freedom of the Church have been and will remain best
guaranteed by the wholehearted and unswerving support all Americans pledge to the democratic rules that
lie at the core of our most cherished civic institutions.

◆

OUR LADY OF TAOS

Mary, narrow, lean as a bow,
Spreads her thin hands
From her hand-span waist
Gowned in green gauze
The brown hands of Indian
Women have wound, round-
Haloed in white wax roses,
Closed eyelids veiling black
Moon-down eyes, the ark
Of her womb a room
Beneath the tented pale-
Wrapped breast, the night-colored
Hair: the fair linened altar
At her feet, the neat, caped,
Plaited, tender leather lady,
Moon-shod monstrance mother,
Mounts her crescent as a
New moon rides the mountain's
Rim; old image of older mother,
Mother of oldest meaning—
All things are younger than she
Save her undying Son.

NANCY-LOU PATTERSON

433

Looming Moral Thunderheads

THE renowned classical scholar, Prof. Werner Jaeger, calls education by its Greek name, *paideia*. In its profoundest meaning *paideia* is the work of handing on the cultural heritage of our race from one age to the next. If so, then all of us—for in this school everyone is a teacher—must be concerned over the present general misunderstanding of what is meant by the natural moral law, and over the particular difficulty we encounter in bringing its true import home to a rapidly growing number of our physical and social scientists.

Today one is inclined to write the phrase "natural law" within quotation marks. For people by and large (many Catholics included) no longer know its significance. Speaking historically, this blackout of the natural moral law is a relatively recent development. For two centuries and more the tradition of the natural law flourished in our oldest American universities. One has only to examine the evidence in the archives of Harvard and Yale—the big folio sheets on which, each spring for decade after decade, there was imprinted that almost unvarying list of ethical "theses to be defended" by senior-year students in their oral examinations. All the way from the 1630's to the 1850's and later, this scholastic tradition of ethical learning persisted without substantial deviation at Harvard, Yale and elsewhere. Then, about a century ago, simultaneously with the transforming process by which our older colleges passed from religious to secular control, the living tradition of the natural law was broken. Today few American secular educators even know that it once existed.

One who does honor the tradition, and who conceivably regrets its passing from the academic scene, wrote a letter that was published in the New York *Times* on December 14. John Herman Randall Jr., Woodbridge Professor of Philosophy at Columbia University, stated:

> In view of the justifiably great public interest in the recent statement of the Catholic bishops [that of November 25, 1959, relative to the promotion of artificial birth control], I should like to suggest that the level of discussion would be raised if it were focused on the central issue, the meaning of "the natural law" in Catholic thinking. This idea has so completely disappeared from non-Catholic thought about moral questions that I am afraid very few non-Catholics understand its meaning. . . . It would be immensely helpful in bringing together all sensitive men of good will if an informed Catholic teacher would try to explain to all of us just what Catholic thinkers mean by "the natural law" of morality.

We wrote to Professor Randall that same day, inviting him to take part with us, not in a debate, but in a common attempt to elucidate the question of the natural law itself and the problems raised by a widespread public failure to recognize its principles and appreciate the relevance of its applications. His gracious reply, indicating that he was at least tentatively willing to join us in such an exploration, has encouraged AMERICA to project plans for it in a coming issue.

Obviously, it is the birth-control question that has provoked this fresh and welcome interest in the natural law, with which, of course, the morality of artificial birth control is intimately connected. A number of Protestant leaders, some of them prominent in their advocacy of birth control as a solution to the so-called "population explosion," are entering the discussion of the natural law through the birth-control door. Many of them are concerned to explain to themselves and their followers how it is that official Protestant doctrine in this field has shifted so radically during the last two generations.

The scrupulously fair-minded dean of Union Theological Seminary in New York, John C. Bennett, recently noted that Protestant systems of ethics "have their day and lose force" and that "neither Luther nor Calvin can be said to be a guide on specific moral issues." As Dean Bennett remarked, in 1908 the Anglican Bishops were unequivocally opposed to contraception; opposed it again, though less vigorously, in 1920; gave permission for its "conscientious use" in 1930; and appeared as its advocates in 1958.

Commenting on Dean Bennett's statement, Robert Hoyt, editor of the Kansas City-St. Joseph *Reporter,* wrote with tact and insight in his December 25 issue:

The absence of principles and laws in Protestant morality makes one wonder about the future. For example, at present there are influential secularist thinkers making the same arguments about homosexuality that their forebears were making earlier in the century about birth control. They are ridiculing the Christian teaching on sexual perversion as another example of the power of inherited inhibitions. . . . May we expect that Protestant leaders of thought, subjected to the pressure of this new ethical fashion, will gradually find it possible to regard acts of homosexuality as morally neutral? What limits are there in the methods of Protestant theology to prevent such an adaptation? For that matter, what action of any kind—no matter how shockingly evil or perverse it may appear to the Protestant conscience today—can be definitely and permanently outlawed as un-Christian, unnatural, inhuman?

On Fighting Communism

IF THE READER will turn to the "State of the Question" in this issue, he will see that, as we anticipated, the reprinting of Gerard E. Sherry's editorial on negative anticommunism provoked a lively response. By way of adding to the discussion, we should like to sketch in broad strokes the only kind of anticommunism which seems to us to be at the same time informed and Catholic.

At the risk of offending sophisticated readers, we begin by making the fundamental point that communism is both a movement of social protest and a conspiracy aimed at world conquest. As a form of social protest, it appeals to the victims of capitalist oppression and colonial exploitation, promising them a better and happier life in a society devoted to equality and justice. As a conspiracy, communism poses a double threat to the non-Communist world—the threat of direct, or military, aggression, and the threat of subversion, or indirect aggression.

It is scarcely necessary to argue that an intelligent and effective anti-Communist program must be well-rounded and all-embracing. It must be directed not only at blunting the appeal of communism as a social protest, but also at exposing and checking its conspiratorial drive for power. Such was the program sketched in 1937 by Pope Pius XI in *Divini Redemptoris.* Referring to the anti-Communist role of the Catholic press, the Pope wrote that "its foremost duty is to foster in various attractive ways an ever better understanding of social doctrine." In addition to this "foremost duty," the press should also, he explained, "supply accurate and complete information on the activity of the enemy and the means of resistance. . . ."

On the anti-Communist program thus outlined, there ought to be general agreement among Catholics. Some of our coreligionists, however, seem surprised—when it is called to their attention—at the priority the Pope gives to propagating the Church's social teaching. Clearly such Catholics are not well acquainted either with the social implications of their faith or with the state of affairs in the world today. They don't understand that even should Khrushchev call for baptism tomorrow, Catholics would still be obliged to strive zealously for social justice. They don't appreciate, either, the appeal of communism in underdeveloped countries, whose leaders are impressed both by the industrial progress of the Soviet Union and its official policy of racial equality. Such Catholics seem blind to the pressing necessity of demonstrating to the world, by our solicitude for justice here at home, the superiority of our way of life to the Communist way.

Whence it follows that a Catholic segregationist, for instance, no matter how loudly he may discourse against communism, is scarcely an anti-Communist at all. Like the Catholic who opposes foreign aid, he is, rather, an unwitting ally of the Kremlin. And the same is true of reactionary business men, of crooked labor leaders and of dishonest politicians.

But waging an anti-Communist war on the social front, though indispensable, is not enough. To the subversive activities of the Communist Fifth Column, it is only a partial answer; and to the Red Army, with its missiles and bombs, it is no answer at all.

In dealing with communism as a conspiracy, two questions are of capital importance. One has to do with methods; the other with emphasis.

With regard to methods, anti-Communists differ on the importance to be attached to democratic procedures in combating the Communist plot. Some would cut constitutional corners to wage a more effective fight. Others insist on giving Communists the full benefit of all the rights and immunities they are sworn to destroy. Unless communism is fought with clean democratic hands, say the constitutionalists, we risk being infected by the very totalitarian poison we abhor. That this danger is not negligible appears today from the persistent effort in some quarters to turn "liberal" into a smear word and to stigmatize as "socialistic" all proposals for social reform. The blurring of ideological lines is not the least of the temptations which earnest anti-Communists must stoutly resist.

There remains the question of emphasis. In some areas of the world the threat of indirect Communist aggression is obviously greater than the danger of direct aggression. This is true of a country like Indonesia, as it is true of the Middle East and Africa generally. The opposite, however, is true of the United States, since over the past decade it has become agonizingly clear that far and away the bigger threat to our security is Soviet power as symbolized in the Red Army. That doesn't mean that our domestic Communists, no matter how discredited they are right now, can be safely ignored. On the contrary, they must be watched and exposed and checked at every point (and, of course, our security agencies must be ever alert to Soviet espionage). But it would be a fatal error, we believe, so to concentrate on the Soviet Fifth Column in our midst as to miss the greater threat from abroad.

That is the reason this Review has consistently supported big appropriations for defense and mutual security. That is why we have frowned on proposals for tax relief. That is why we have approved all sorts of foreign commitments—from the Truman Doctrine on

Greece and Turkey, through the Marshall Plan, to Nato and Seato. We have thought—and still think—that the only hope of stopping further Communist expansion by force—and the only hope for peace in the short run—is to maintain a clear margin of military superiority over the Soviet Union.

We have been disturbed, consequently, by the preoccupation of some Catholics with our domestic Communists. Too often, we note, this preoccupation is accompanied by coolness toward Nato, by hostility toward foreign aid, by complaints about taxes, by opposition to desegregation, even by defeatist fears of Communist infiltration of Catholic schools and other Catholic organizations. In short, we are led sadly to suspect that some of the anticommunism in Catholic circles is no more than a form of escapism from the anxieties and frustrations of a harsh and turbulent world.

We are fighting for our lives against a shrewd and implacable foe. We cannot afford to make mistakes. If with our knowledge of communism we combine a realistic appraisal of existing situations; if, in addition, we never lose sight of the lessons of justice and charity read to us by all the recent Popes, we should be able, with God's help, to fight successfully, and with much greater unity, for values we hold dearer than life itself.

Woman and the Common Good

IN MOST pagan societies womankind has an inferior status. She is the first of the male's chattels and a social cipher. It is the Gospel that ultimately powers the trend to give woman the suffrage, free her from civic disabilities and allow her to enter careers where she may use her talents for the upbuilding of the common good.

Despite female emancipation, the male still harbors the illusion that woman is the "lesser man." He fosters a stereotype of the female which emphasizes her lower intelligence, emotional instability and general ineptitude to engage in activity that transcends home economics. Obviously it is to the advantage of the lordly male to perpetuate this stereotype and to encourage its submissive acceptance among women. In this way the male employs tradition and prejudice to prevent the distaff element from encroaching on such typically male preserves as architecture and engineering, government and politics. One of the great pities of the modern world is that women so generally subscribe to the stereotype created for them by the dominant male, and thereby hinder their own achievement of status as well as hamper their power to contribute significantly to the betterment of the whole human family.

Somebody ought to inform June's girl graduates that the masculine posture of superiority finds cold comfort in the Church's attitude toward woman's place in society today, even though the Church deplores the philosophy of individualism that atomizes society and tends to eject woman from the home and make her a mere economic competitor of the male. Woman needs no Magna Charta of her rights and duties in the modern world: all the elements of her status and vocation were repeatedly emphasized in the many addresses of Pope Pius XII. Perhaps it will be good to summarize some of the basic positions of the papacy right here.

1. Male and female enjoy an absolute equality in personal dignity and value. Man and woman both enjoy a common temporal destiny, one toward which all history moves, and which was indicated in the command that Adam and Eve received together: "Increase and multiply, and fill the earth and subdue it and rule over it. . . ." Scripture does not say that men shall do the ruling while women do the multiplying.

2. Because of this shared goal, there is no field of human activity which must remain closed to woman; her horizons reach out to the regions of politics, labor, the arts, sports. Granted that the primary function and sublimest mission of woman is motherhood, still her personal perfection can be attained in other ways. Not all women are called to motherhood, neither is it possible for all to find their maximum personal development in the atmosphere of the home. "Woman's place is in the home" is a neat generality that reflects the ideal pattern of a perfect human society. It is not a precept of natural or divine law, least of all in an era of social upheaval that tends to debase woman, destroy the family and endanger the common good of all the world.

3. Despite the fact that woman's supreme throne is the home, modern conditions specifically demand female participation in public life, both social and political. It is the right and the duty of woman to take an active part in the movements of the day. The fate of

human relations is at stake everywhere. The mission of woman is urgent, to cooperate with men for the total good of country and society generally.

The paramount principle of social and political action is always the achievement of the common good, not the preservation of historically male prerogatives. So far, unfortunately, the male of the race has not distinguished himself in securing the welfare of humanity. It is not impossible that history may yet see women assuming a dominant role in the direction and control of community activity, and with the Church's blessing, too. Today, of course, this is still a "man's world." It will be a long while before the male crawls into the doghouse and growls: "Move over, Rover."

◆

IDYLL

Peace flowed along the River Tyne,
As Bede, the boy, sang in his stall,
Peace brought by angels drawing near
To serve the hours canonical.

Culling from out the Fathers' mead
The flowers of truth, the quiety Bede
Himself became a meadow rare:
The flock of Christ had pasture there.

Then lest his children learn a lie,
He taught them still, Death standing by,
Closing in peace and God's pure praise.
The lovely idyll of his days.

SISTER M. PAULINUS, I.H.M.

443

The Still, Small Voice

MORALITY MAY SEEM to be expiring, but it is not yet dead. Proof of its vitality lies in the fact that the word "conscience" is being heard again in the land.

For most of us, conscience probably means the still, small voice of the inward judge who levies praise or blame on our past actions. Conscience in this sense is a source of peace or remorse—a soft pillow or a gnawing worm.

But in the strict sense, conscience is not an assessor of dead choices but an imperative guide. It is nothing else than the final judgment I make on the moral quality of an action I am here and now on the point of performing. In the more crucial moments of the last stages of deliberation, it gives out with the "must" or "must not" that are the characteristic notes of inescapable duty. Conscience in this sense is the most personal and private experience in the world, and yet it puts on us the absolute necessity of obeying, for the moral judgment of conscience is nothing else, ultimately, than the will of God as known to us here and now.

We must remember that the judgment called conscience is not an irrational impulse that wells up from the Id, nor a censorious delivery of some mysterious Superego. The judgment of conscience is a work of human reason, and in fact it can be expressed as the conclusion of a syllogism. This, in truth, is precisely what links conscience to the realm of morality: the major of the syllogism is a general moral precept and its minor applies the precept to the contemplated choice of the will. In this sense conscience is not really private at all. The majors that preside over our choices are drawn from the authority of parents or the state or the Church, or even from our knowledge of natural law or divine revelation. But in every case, if they possess any genuine binding power over the human will, that power must be derived from God, who alone has the final right to put shackles upon the liberty of the human will.

Forming the judgment of conscience is not always easy. We are subject to error and lie under the influence of passion. Sometimes, too, we find that our moral judgments are complicated by conflicting loyalties. St. Thomas More faced such a decision when he had to choose between obeying Henry VIII and what he conceived to be the more pressing claims of God. Many are starting to ask now what a Catholic President would do, if he faced a choice between "national interests" and "Church doctrine."

When such perplexities arise, every man is ultimately bound to do the will of God as he sees it. If he acts with complete sincerity, he commits no moral fault, even though his choice is objectively in error.

That sincerity before God is not enough for those who pose a religious test for Catholic candidates. For them, conscience is dandy, so long as it is not a Catholic conscience. In this case they remain distrustful and suspicious, like Aaron in *Titus Andronicus:*

". . . for I know thou art religious,
And hast a thing within thee called conscience,
With twenty popish tricks and ceremonies,
Which I have seen thee careful to observe. . . ."

Southerners as Americans

AMERICANS coming back from Europe always express the feeling that while abroad they "discovered" America. In much the same way, the first earthlings to return from another planet will likely have a lot to tell us, not so much about possible non-earthlings as about ourselves. A stay away from home is always a revelation.

Many a Southerner, too, has found that living in another part of the country has helped him find out what it means to be a Southerner. As an instance of this, nine respected Southern scholars—born, reared, largely trained in the South, but now doing research or teaching in the North—have just published a provocative, hard-hitting analysis called *The Southerner as American* (University of North Carolina Press, $5).

Mere latitude apart, what is the South, and what is a Southerner, anyway? The most important fact about the Southerner is that he is an American. But an American with a difference. He is pictured as different in accent, though even that is a varying and vanishing trait. The main difference lies in his history, true or fanciful; he is a man burdened with that history. After the Civil War, many Southerners, having tasted that un-American thing, defeat, escaped into a warm dream, a sentimental myth, the tragic Lost Cause. Today a new, revisionist school of Southern historians has for some years been demythologizing the fictitious South.

This stock-taking by the revisionists has already yielded meaningful results. It is now clear that the Old South was not really old, nor was it uniformly idyllic: the ante-bellum mansions of Natchez, Mobile and Charleston were few and far between, and three-fourths of all white Southerners owned no slaves. Slavery was not the paternalistic or neutral thing it was once held to be; indeed the great majority of slaves did not remain loyal. Nor was the corruption of Reconstruction entirely the fault of one race or region; it continued unabated even under restored white supremacy. Jim-Crowism, in the form we have known, is a recent, not a venerable social myth and usage. And research has quite exploded the concept of a monolithic South, together with the notion that the Civil War happened because there were "two civilizations"; the war came very largely because of that "peculiar institution"—the fact that the South possessed slavery and slavery was found profitable in the South.

The tragedy of Southern history—and vestiges of this regrettably remain—has lain in the inner conflict of true, self-reliant, freedom-loving Americans doing violence to their best selves by depriving fellow human beings of much of their humanity. The Southerner has been deeply Christian, and it has taken soul-wrenching casuistry to reconcile Christian charity and justice with the "peculiar institution." Many a Southerner—and Northerner—has thought it, but few have been so blunt as the politician who proclaimed: "I believe more in the purity of the Anglo-Saxon race than I do in the principles of democracy."

Out of this inner paradox of the South, and partly because of it, has come a sort of victory of pen over sword—not in cold historiography, but in the literary word. From Poe to Faulkner and Flannery O'Connor, the Southern writer shows a more-than-American tragic grandeur. Even the lowly of Yoknapatawpha County, Faulkner's Bunrens and McCaslins, have dignity and

447

stature. Here is an awareness of the local, the regional, the highly individual. Southern characters, in and out of books, have time to be neighborly and personal. Surely these are precious human values in a largely homogenized, undifferentiated America.

The new upsurge of racism and race-baiting demagoguery seems only a noisy death gasp. There is a New South intent on being its true self, fully American, Christian, authentically human. It may take some time for this South to win out.

◆

PURE DESERT

The more one runs in the spiritual
life the less tired one gets.—PADRE PIO

This is pure Gobi desert, you declare.
I see, past sandstorms (of exaggeration)
And rage of flesh at ghostly motivation,
Pink health invade your prayer.

Pure desert, you complain, though now you walk
Who once had shuffled through the arid miles.
Sighting a day of flight, I shelve my smiles
And share your pilgrim talk.

All true ascesis as a desert lies,
Hot wind, hot sand, no water and no way.
The ego agonizes through each day.
Freedom is when it dies.

I coax you onward: soon first breeze of bliss,
Soon sun that scorches cooled to sun that warms.
Your youth will dance when shady lanes lock arms
With each green oasis.

JESSICA POWERS

448

Patient, Doctor, Human Life

A BISHOP of the Church of England recently made headlines by telling British medical men that they have no moral obligation to keep elderly persons alive by "extraordinary means."

We have no quarrel with Doctor Mortimer, who is Bishop of Exeter: most of his quoted remarks could have been drawn from Catholic manuals of morality. But if the press thought his comments newsworthy, then it is time to emphasize the most basic principles that bind both patient and physician in the preservation of human life.

We all recognize that man has a positive duty to protect life when it is threatened by injury, disease or the debilities of advanced age. For although life is not a supreme good, to be maintained at all costs, it is certainly the fundamental natural good that makes possible the achievement of every other valuable goal. The root question, then, is this: what is the minimal required standard of responsible stewardship for man when his life, which is God's exclusive property, is threatened by any of the many ills that assail our mortal frame?

Catholic moralists agree that we are bound to take *ordinary* means to preserve life, but that *extraordinary* means, generally speaking, are not obligatory. The crux of the problem lies in the meaning and application of these two terms.

Probably most moralists would agree that ordinary means are those which lie at hand and are in common use among doctors and surgeons. In the average well-organized community of today, therefore, it would seem reasonable to regard intravenous feeding, blood transfusions or injections of insulin as ordinary means of preserving life. We might say the same thing of using the oxygen tent or of a growing number of routine operations and amputations, even major ones.

Extraordinary means are usually regarded as those which entail great hardship, suffering or expense beyond that which men would prudently consider proper for a serious undertaking, according to the state of the individual in question. That too may be called extraordinary which offers no solid hope of success or utility. Examples of such extraordinary procedures would be the continuation of a costly treatment after a patient has fallen into a terminal coma, as well as some of the more drastic operations on the heart and brain. No one would doubt that Fred Snite, who spent more than 18 years in an iron lung, at a probable cost of a million dollars, took an extraordinary and nonobligatory means of keeping himself alive.

We simply do not have any neat formula for applying these sound norms of convenience and utility. Hence, in particular cases, it is often difficult to impose a clear duty of employing a specific means of preserving life. Fortunately, when life is at stake, the human instinct is to seek help over and above the hazy minimum that morality rigorously demands.

The medical man's duties are stricter than those of his patient. He must not only do the minimum to which the patient is bound, but also do whatever the patient reasonably requests as well as what professional standards require. It is by close adherence to a certain moral rigorism that medical men maintain the reputation for setting a high value on life. It is by never yielding to defeatism that yesterday's extraordinary means of preserving life become today's commonplace, and thus contribute immeasurably to the enrichment of humanity and the nobility of medical art.

The Day

Which the Lord Has Made

IN A SERIES of dramatic flashbacks on Good Friday, the Church unrolls her memories of the suffering and death of Jesus. The recollections are bitter indeed.

On Holy Saturday, the Church is mute. Here is the one day in the year that has no service of its own. The altar of sacrifice is denuded and the tabernacle stands empty. The Church tarries numbly at the tomb and wills to know the void that is in her life when Christ is gone.

But neither Friday's grief nor the Sabbath loneliness is marked by despair. The grief is softened by sudden thrills of hope, the sense of abandonment is lightened by throbs of expectation, up to the moment when the Church, as if unable to repress her remembrance of the hour when death was swallowed up in victory, anticipates the rapture of Easter in the vibrant gladness of its Vigil.

Now indeed her joy is great, as the flood of triumphant happiness transforms the ugliness of yesterday's defeat. The whistle of the lash and the thud of the hammer are blotted out by the merry clangor of bells and the thunder of the Alleluia. The purple flecks of Christ's blood redden gloriously in the light of the paschal candle. The poignancy of Good Friday's Reproaches yields to the almost extravagant fervor of the Exsultet. In a kind of inspired daring, the Church presumes to rationalize the abysmal blunder of Adam, the ultimate folly of his prevarication in Eden: "How truly necessary was that sin of Adam, which was blotted out by the death of Christ! How fortunate was that sin which occasioned for us such a redeemer!"

Is the Church justified in these unrestrained outbursts of joy? We can answer that question by posing another. What is the central fact in the long narrative of human hopes and fears? What is the axis of revolution about which the world of history turns? It is not the emergence of language, nor the discovery of fire, nor the invention of the wheel. It is the event that took place between the darkness and the dawn of the day "which the Lord has made." "On this day, God, you overcame death through your only-begotten Son, and unlocked for us the gate to everlasting life."

To the eyes of faith, human history could never again be a story of damning sin and crushing guilt, of wrenching grief and farewells forever, after that moment when the portals of hell were shaken and the grave gaped and the One who bore our iniquities burst His cerements in lightnings of glory. For with the same thrust of omnipotence that exalted the name of Jesus above every name that is in heaven or on earth, grace began to rush like a torrent over the wastelands of mankind's sorrow and despair. The earth began to flower with the hope that men could live in newness of life, a "holy and sanctified people." Even more, the resurrection of the Prince of Life was an earnest of their own regeneration from the burnt ruins of the world. History is not closed by the mordant kiss of the worm. It opens on the day when this corruptible body puts on incorruption, and mortality robes itself in everlastingness.

"I am risen, and am still with you, alleluia." We must not forget that Christ is our hope, the author of our faith and the cause of our joy, even in these sad days when the "sky grows darker yet, and the sea rises higher."

A Great Inaugural

IN EDITORIALIZING on President Kennedy's Inaugural Address, one is tempted to string together a dozen sparkling quotations and let it go at that. For the materials from which this relatively brief address was fashioned are the heady stuff that history is made of. As Lincoln assuaged the spiritual anguish of a war-sundered nation in his Second Inaugural, as in his First Inaugural Franklin Roosevelt stirred to new hope and enterprise a generation mired in the despondency of economic depression, so did John F. Kennedy rally an apprehensive people to face with confident energy the seemingly insoluble problems of our times.

To some readers this comparison with deathless documents of the past may seem farfetched. After all, nothing the President said on January 20, as a bitter cold wind swept over snow-covered Capitol Hill, has not been said before. The contemporary challenge to freedom is plain for everybody to see. The rise of Castro in Cuba has dramatized the Communist threat to the Western Hemisphere. The anarchy in the Congo, which the Soviet Union and its stooges are recklessly exploiting, has raised the specter of newly independent nations trading 19th-century colonialism for 20th-century slavery. The civil war in Laos provides only the most recent reminder that our unity with "those old allies whose cultural and spiritual origins we share" is less firm than it ought to be. And as background for all this, we have been living for more than a decade now with the awful and frustrating knowledge that while "man holds in his mortal hands the power to abolish all forms of human poverty," he also holds in the same fragile vessels the ability to destroy all human life.

What was there, then, about this Inaugural which in the opinion of some raised it far above pedestrian levels and destined it, perhaps, to a high place in history?

It was written in excellent modern style—lean, terse, evocative. It was rich in literary, biblical and historical overtones. To old friends and ambitious foes, to our neighbors in the hemisphere and the masses of people in underdeveloped lands everywhere, it said with precision, and with feeling deep but disciplined, exactly what should have been said. And the address was studded with quotable gems: "Let us never negotiate out of fear. But let us never fear to negotiate"; "For only when our arms are sufficient beyond doubt can we be certain beyond doubt that they will never be employed"; "If a free society cannot help the many who are poor, it cannot save the few who are rich"; "And so, my fellow Americans: ask not what your country can do for you—ask what you can do for your country."

But it was none of these merits that touched the Inaugural with greatness. What gave it distinction is suggested perhaps by a line from one of our American poets. "Each crisis," wrote John Greenleaf Whittier, "brings its word and deed." Early in the address, one sensed that President Kennedy was bringing the word that answered the need of our troubled age. Harking back to our revolutionary past, he sounded his keynote:

Let the word go forth from this time and place, to friend and foe alike, that the torch has been passed to a new generation of Americans—born in this century, tempered by war, disciplined by a cold and bitter peace, proud of our ancient heritage —and unwilling to witness or permit the slow un-

doing of those human rights to which this nation
has always been committed, and to which we are
committed today.
And what did that torch signify? It signaled that this
generation is called, as other generations were called
before it, to testify to its loyalty to the American dream:

Now the trumpet summons us again—not as a
call to bear arms, though arms we need—not as a
call to battle, though embattled we are—but a call
to bear the burden of a long twilight struggle, year
in and year out, "rejoicing in hope, patient in tribu-
lation"—a struggle against the common enemies of
man: tyranny, poverty, disease and war itself.

Is this challenge one to deplore, to be fearful of, to
shrink from?

In the long history of the world, only a few generations have been granted the role of defending
freedom in its hour of maximum danger. I do not
shrink from this responsibility. I welcome it. I do
not believe that any of us would exchange places
with any other people or any other generation. The
energy, the faith and the devotion which we bring
to this endeavor will light our country and all who
serve it—and the glow from that fire can truly light
the world.

Surely, that was the word today's crisis called for—a
word that scorned cynicism and routed despair, that
soared above sterile caution and the diffidence that sires
defeat, that found challenge exhilarating, a word that
echoed the ringing words Shakespeare put into the
mouth of King Henry V on the eve of Agincourt:

From this day to the ending of the world,
But we in it shall be rememberéd . . . .
And gentlemen in England now a-bed
Shall think themselves accurs'd they were not here,
And hold their manhoods cheap whiles any speaks
That fought with us upon Saint Crispin's Day.

So it was that the word spoken by the President—a
man who for all his youth has endured pain and lived
with death—wedding American idealism and American
power, summoned free men to a grand crusade.

From the word born of the crisis to the deed it de-

455

mands the gap is wide and treacherous. This, too, the President knows. Counting "a good conscience our only sure reward," he concluded, "let us go forth to lead the land we love, asking His blessing and His help, but knowing that here on earth God's work must truly be our own."

So it must be. Without God's help the deed will not be done. With it, we cannot fail.

Catholics and Others

JUST A WEEK AGO everyone who could manage it hustled off to a TV set to see the show: the historic and gripping solemnities that surrounded the Inaugural of the dynamic young man now formally empowered to speak for 180 million Americans. From Florida to Alaska, from Maine clear out to Hawaii, from Capitol Hill all the way down to 1600 Pennsylvania Avenue, from the shining top hat on his head to the last burst of band music outside the White House—it was a red, white and blue day! On such a day there are no political parties in America—there are only Americans. And all together we prayed that the new President would be equal to the gigantic tasks ahead.

Almost all our Presidents have had, each of them, a distinctive style, a special stamp—something they gave us to remember them by. In a thousand ways President Kennedy will impress his name and face and decisions on his time and on the conciousness of children yet unborn. But what will be the singular Kennedy cachet?

Washington is the man who crossed the Delaware and fathered his country; Jefferson is a wigged Virginian squire from Monticello; Lincoln freed the slaves and spoke briefly and tersely at Gettysburg; Teddy

Roosevelt charged up San Juan Hill; Coolidge was a silent man and chose not to run in 1928; a second Roosevelt smiled, smoked cigarettes in a long holder, talked admirably over the radio and put through the New Deal. The popular imagination is limited; it cuts a man down to a few sharply defined lines of truth or caricature, drawn with the brush of sentiment or pride or partisan pique.

How will Mr. Kennedy be remembered? For those of us who grew to adulthood with him here in the United States, who in 1928 were around to observe and now remain to remember what happened, who watched fascinated last fall as history proved that 1928 would not repeat itself, the answer is obvious. He will be remembered as a Catholic and as the first of his Catholic kind to be elected to the Presidency. (Strange, isn't it, that so few people could confidently tell you the precise religious affiliations of any former President, including Mr. Eisenhower.)

On November 8, 1960, with the election of John F. Kennedy, the full first-class citizenship of U.S. Catholics was at long last ratified. How do these now fully enfranchised Catholics regard their coreligionist in the White House? They respect him as their President, and they can't deny—whether they voted for him or not—a certain natural pride that he happens to be a Catholic. But there is no gloating in the Catholic attitude. Catholics look for no special preferments or special favors, and they will get none. They would be disappointed in the President if he ran things any other way. But they do want justice, particularly with respect to their schools, and they want the President and the Congress and the country at large to think hard about giving it to them.

With Mr. Kennedy in the White House, things are bound to be different for American Catholics. We shall all have fresh confidence, new courage, fewer resentments, and an easier feeling about shouldering our share of the common day-to-day work of America. Look for this in hundreds of ways—and we sincerely hope that you will not look in vain. With it now clearly established that our country does not accord prior rights

458

to Anglo-Saxon Protestants, you can expect to find Catholics turning up in all sorts of places where, formerly, nursing real or partially imagined resentments, they never quite felt at home: on all the citizens' committees that heretofore they frequently seemed to shun —committes to clear slums, organize municipal orchestras, build new wings on public libraries, raise money for the Red Cross, and all the rest. We shall be surprised if, from now on, Catholics don't take a more active and constructive interest in the public schools—to which they choose not to send their children.

In a word, it isn't hard to think that with a Catholic President in Washington, we Catholics might even call a halt to our old game of mutually excommunicating each other as "liberals" or "conservatives," and form a new citizens' front called COAU—Catholics and Other Americans United. It's time we did.

Values in the Space Race

WHY CONQUER SPACE? Practical minds often brush off the mastery of this forbidding environment as if it were no more than cosmic boondoggling or a game of "follow the leader" in which we or the Russians will be the first to encounter slimy little green men on Martian meadows.

From the short-range viewpoint, the current race into the unknown is politically and psychologically imperative. From the long-range point of view, man's triumph over gravity, no less than the invention of the wheel or of writing, puts humanity on the threshold of a new era of history that will enlarge our horizons immeasurably.

● In our own century, the development of the airplane profoundly influenced the strategy of warfare. The only assumption compatible with our security is that the future of military power is inextricably linked to the art which is the junction point of today's most advanced technology. That art is rocketry. Russia got there "fustest with the mostest," and her presumptive lead creates a threat of control which must not be disregarded. Control of space holds a completely unexplored potential for control of the globe. To cite just one possibility: the nation which puts in orbit one deliverable megaton bomb, as Sen. Stuart Symington has observed, "literally holds the sword of Damocles over its adversaries."

As long, therefore, as we live in a world without law, we must achieve that slender measure of safety which comes from wedding military science to the exploration of an environment which may provide war with its most dangerous dimension. We must either control space or be able to counter control by another power; in any event, we must master its difficulties.

● United States technological prestige has been appreciably dimmed by Russian successes in space. The USSR is not only enjoying its new role as the paladin of science; it is determined to play it boldly for every propaganda value that may accrue. The Soviets have literally hitched their wagon to the stars. After all, is there a better place to display one's prowess than the open skies?

Prestige is defined as the power to command esteem. It is a prime psychological value rooted in brilliance of achievement. France and Red China are seeking prestige diligently: so are Russia and the United States. Why? Because prestige is the basis of world leadership.

In today's world, justifiably or not, space feats have become the primary symbol of world leadership and a criterion of ideological superiority. Russia uses every conquest of space as a compelling argument for the Communist way of life. Since the United States aspires to remain the leader of the free world and a strong locus of values for the uncommitted nations, the implications are clear. If we are in the race for space, we must not lag on the laps; technological prestige tends to create political power, just as scientific competence tends to produce military supremacy.

We dare not neglect psychology, therefore, any more than we dare neglect physics. The world is no longer content to bow to affluence or be captivated by grants-in-aid or noble slogans. But it is powerfully drawn by a technology that springs from a way of life which promises to end want, injustice and inequality every-

461

where.

● Of course, the basic and enduring justification for the thrust into space lies in its ability to increase scientific knowledge and contribute to the welfare of mankind. As Wernher von Braun said on April 28: "This is a period of dynamic evolution which is pushing outward the horizons of human kowledge with explosive force." The impulse toward that evolution comes from nothing more mysterious than human curiosity. But the desire to know is a tendency of our nature as radical as the instincts of self-preservation and procreation. In God's design, it is what makes possible the material and spiritual advancement of the human species. Space may or may not be the last frontier, but it is certainly an endless frontier, whose margins fade forever as we move. Despite its formidable challenges, history counsels no other attitude toward it than optimistic expectation.

Let's Stamp Out Summitry·

D IPLOMACY is the theory and practice of international
negotiations. Its traditional formalities are the
etiquette of nations. Its institutionalized processes are
designed to preserve civilized communication between
sovereign powers, even when the most delicate issues
are at stake.

Centuries of experience have taught the West that
diplomacy is most effective when it is exercised by
specialists in foreign affairs. Its pursuit demands the
skill of the artist, the single-mindedness of the career
man and—increasingly today—the intimate knowledge
of details and their interrelations that characterizes the
practical scientist. Effective diplomacy is not the province of the amateur, however powerful, prestigious or
presumptuous he may be. This is especially true in the
era when the portfolios of the Big Powers are loaded
with plutonium and the heavy fears of all mankind
brood over the conference tables.

SHEER SHOWMANSHIP

Yet the ascendancy of the high-level amateur over
the professionally competent is the pattern of Big Power
diplomacy that has become ever more dominant from

463

the "horse-trading" days of Teheran and Yalta to the obscene "heavyweight match" that was scheduled for May 16 in Paris.

What judgment should the ordinary citizen pass on these jet-assisted take-offs whereby Mr. Eisenhower seeks to give Chancellor Adeuauer periodic assurance that we will not scuttle Berlin, or Charles de Gaulle hopes to attain a little bit more status with Prime Minister Macmillan? What are we to think of the swashbuckling summitry whereby Nikita Khrushchev strives to slug out international problems of the most vital nature in a fantastic brand of "diplomacy" of his own contriving, while accredited foreign ministers watch the water buckets in the corner of the prize ring?

What we have seen of personal summitry so far is hardly encouraging. It diverts the time and energy of the highest officials of government into channels of futility. It produces neither fruitful agreements among allies nor genuine relaxation of tension anywhere. It is a hasty process whereby the weightiest matters receive cursory discussion and immature decision. In the words of Sir Ivone Kirkpatrick, who was once United Kingdom High Commissioner for Germany: "So far as I am aware, no summit meeting has had any result except to create in the minds of all the participants a sense of weary and angry frustration."

Some of the perils of summitry, particularly as they affect the President of the United States, were explored in the April issue of *Foreign Affairs* by Dean Rusk, former Deputy Under Secretary of State. The basic obstacle to effective diplomatic communication on the Presidential level is that it is difficult or impossible for the President to give proper preparation to the business of international negotiation without serious neglect of his political and constitutional duties at home. Thus the constant climbing of summits adds intolerable burdens to the discharge of an office that many already consider an impossible task. According to Mr. Rusk, "the process needs time, patience and precision, three resources which are not found in abundance at the highest political level." Moreover, the raw confrontation of heads of government involves added tensions because every summit, in a sense, is a court of last appeal, where the costs of miscalculation are multiplied by the seriousness of the issues and the power of the men who take part.

If inadequate preparation, limitations of time and accidents of personality make personal summitry a hazardous gamble even in tête-à-têtes among leaders who are allies, the psychological barriers to meaningful diplomatic dialogue are infinitely higher in the staged summit. These affairs tend to be as stylized as a ballet, as elaborate as a Hollywood colossal and as public as life in a goldfish bowl. The expanded conference table is flanked by cameramen, messengers and translators. The principals are backed up by battalions of experts with their position papers and a mania for writing *ad hoc* memos. The press hovers in the wings, anxious to score beats and put calculated leaks on the wire. Under such circumstances a summit is not a meeting of minds but an exchange of propaganda-slanted speeches. There is no genuine dialogue on issues, no reasoned harmonizing of differences, but only an artificial debate. Is this the way to pursue effective communication between nations? It makes as much sense as if Rome and the separated churches of the East were to stage a council of reunion in the piazza in front of St. Peter's.

PSYCHOLOGICAL WARFARE

The gravest risks of personal summitry are inevitably associated with confrontations of East and West, whether they take place in the intimacy of Camp David or in the Elysée Palace. For here, because of the very nature of Soviet political strategy, true communication becomes fundamentally impossible. Soviet diplomacy is not intended to be a form of communication, but a tool of political and psychological warfare. As Dean Acheson pointed out just a year ago, its aim is not rational debate but propaganda. Hence its lifeblood is publicity. The conference table is turned into a grandstand. The forms of negotiation are prostituted to project images of power that are meant to deceive, divide and overawe. And in this clash of the megaphones, the odds favor the Soviet Union. The free world lies open to the sound and fury, but the Iron Curtain rises too high to permit an effective counteroffensive.

The supreme example of the perils of personal summitry was just given to us in Paris. In what was patently the Biggest Show on Earth, the Russian lion-tamer took the abashed American cat by the scruff of its neck, just to teach it a lesson—in Soviet diplomacy. Such obscene buffoonery, disgraceful at any time in international relations, is intolerable in what may be the twilight of oncoming nuclear darkness. Its utter irony was that it made impossible, at least temporarily, civilized negotiation between the United States and Russia: the rupture of rational dialogue was done in the very name of the art whose core is communication. No further argument is needed to bring in question the whole trend to summitry that we see today.

The policy of personal summitry needs immediate reappraisal in the light of the recent debacle in Paris. At best, it is comparatively ineffective. At worst, it envenoms international relations. If such a reappraisal restores to honor the old-fashioned diplomacy with its high style and painstaking attention to detail, the world will be the gainer. Let's return the portfolios to the foreign ministers, when we are dealing with our friends. As for the assumption that, in dealing with the Soviet Union, it does no good to talk with anyone but the boss, that depends on how firmly we resist his yen for summitry. He will give Gromyko a fat portfolio when he really wants to negotiate.

A last note of warning. Khrushchev, the incurable optimist, is ready to let bygones be bygones. He is already looking forward to a new summit. He is currently giving us a time of grace in which to regret our iniquities, nurse our fears and elect a President "who can negotiate." Whoever that President may be, let him remember the indignity his office met in Paris. Let him remember too that he already lies under an ultimatum; he has been served notice that he must capitulate on Berlin or suffer the consequences of his obdurate refusal to "negotiate" in the interests of peace.

Second Thought

Second Thought

The Threshold Moment

IT HAS BEEN five years since Msgr. John Tracy Ellis of the Catholic University of America delivered his paper on the condition of American Catholic intellectual life. The substantial and spontaneously affirmative response of American Catholics to Monsignor Ellis's indictment indicated that many were not complacent about the quality of Catholic education or about its product.

Indeed, most of those who would have disputed his thesis held their fire prudently for a year or two. And when they did speak out, it was not to directly dispute the thesis, because at its critical points it was indisputable. Rather the lament was over "Catholic breast-beating." Apparently public *mea culpas* were more scandalous than the conditions that occasioned them. Likewise, the critics did not challenge the validity of Monsignor Ellis's evidence. They questioned his methodology. Thus, although Monsignor Ellis had devoted only two paragraphs of his 200-paragraph paper to *Who's Who in America* and the lack of Catholic representation therein, one journalistic critic launched what was an ostensibly massive attack by questioning the relevance of that single piece of evidence.

I mention these negative tactics, not to refute them at this late date, but primarily to emphasize how sporadic and ineffectual they were and how pathetic they were by comparison with the realistic and rueful acknowledgment of our intellectual disabilities by the many hundreds of Catholics—teachers, school administrators and concerned nonacademic people—in whom Monsignor Ellis's paper had struck a sensitive nerve. Almost as one, the realists agreed that some remedial action was indicated.

All of which, however, brings me to my central question. It is this: "What has been done to remedy the situation Monsignor Ellis described in 1955?"

If Monsignor Ellis had been only half-accurate in his evaluation of American Catholic intellectual life, obviously it would take more than five years to correct the deficiencies he had found and which he had so painstakingly, charitably and candidly listed. Impatient as I tend to be in these circumstances, I am prepared to concede that a five-year reform program would have been an impossibly foreshortened crash program. But I am wondering what has been done in terms of reform and whether or not the future is promising.

I am wondering for three reasons:

1. Monsignor Ellis's indictment was a gravely serious one.

2. Initial response, particularly on the Catholic college and university campus, was one of reform enthusiasm.

3. Talks I have had in the last four or five months with lay, clerical and religious intellectuals, while they have not left me uneasy about the future, have not reassured me either.

Perhaps we ought to reread Monsignor Ellis's paper to recall just how serious were the defects he had discovered in his scrutiny of the intellectual life of American Catholics.

He spoke then of the "paucity of scholars of distinction" in Catholic higher education; of the "perpetuation of mediocrity"; of the "senseless duplication of effort and the wasteful proliferation that have robbed Catholic graduate schools of the hope of superior achievement"; of the failure of American Catholics to recognize "scholarly accomplishments" in fellow Catholics and to "lend them their support"; of the "vocationalism and anti-intellectualism" present in the schools; of the "pervading spirit of separatism" in both American Catholics at large and the intellectuals; of the "failure" of American Catholics "to have measured up to their responsibilities to the incomparable tradition of Catholic learning"; and of our "failure to produce national leaders and to exercise commanding influence in intellectual circles."

The first response on the Catholic college and university campuses was indeed gratifying. Monsignor Ellis's paper became not only the principal topic of discussion among professors over coffee; it was an object of formal departmental and interdepartmental study and analysis in our schools. Significantly, the few denials of its realism and accuracy did not come from the schools.

I suspect we will never know with anything like scientific accuracy which educational reforms and corrections can be traced to Monsignor Ellis's study. I don't think that kind of information is particularly important. What is important is whether there have been reforms; whether that first, instinctive, enthusiastic affirmation that greeted Monsignor Ellis's statement has spent itself fruitlessly and has now dwindled with no discernible effect or promise.

The kind of evidence that would be reassuring here is not limited to the easily recognizable action, such as the elimination of wasteful duplication of efforts; conspicuous recognition and reward by the Catholic community of scholarship; palpable attempts to discourage Catholic separatism; insistence on newer, more rigorous academic requirements.

Talking with Catholic intellectuals can yield evidence of a less obvious, but perhaps just as important, kind. Has there been a shift in the attitude, a change in the atmosphere, so far as the academic and nonacademic Catholic community is concerned? Is there not only remedial desire and pressure, but also the freedom to translate that desire and direct that pressure into action? There seems to be no clear-cut answer to these latter questions. We seem to be on a threshold at the moment. We can go forward, but we can also go back. Our schools, I think, hold the key to that larger question that goes beyond the schools, the question of whether the future of the Church in America will be shaped and determined in its essential features by the forces of reaction, separatism and the siege mentality, or by the forces of progressiveness, openness and intellectual respectability and influence.   DONALD MCDONALD

◆

In Our Town

In our town the Lion's Club remembers
Christmas with a crèche of strong black timbers—
larger this year with tiny bulbs that flick
like city lights. And right there by the track
where the New York Central makes it tremor
four times a day. So nice to see a glimmer
of something new on the long gray ride home.
Everyone's heard of it and they come
from up the line to see the crib, and smile
that we thought of it. They say it's all
we're known for, only borough in the valley
that has no tree, or bright red lights strung willy
nilly across Main Street.
                    But we only nod
and share a secret by the small straw bed.

                              MARY ANN MAC NEIL

Washington Front

Washington Front

PROGRESS IN RACE RELATIONS

TWENTY YEARS AGO the Swedish scholar Gunnar Myrdal argued that the Negro in America was caught in a vicious circle. The Negro, he said, was the victim of prejudice, which made it difficult for him to secure adequate income, housing, education or even the right to vote. However, a break in any part of the circle would modify all of the factors arrayed against him. Such a change could create an entirely new arrangement of forces—this time favorable to the Negro. If, in other words, the Negro's opportunities for education or voting increased, then each of the other factors would also take a turn for the better. These changes would make it easier for Negroes and whites to work together. Prejudice would be reduced, thus making it still easier for Negroes to get jobs, education, housing and the right to vote. Whether the first crack in the circle resulted from improved conditions of life for Negroes or from the lessening of prejudice made no difference. The effect in any case would be cumulative.

The Myrdal analysis looks remarkably good in retrospect. In 1940, in spite of some degree of equality in unemployment relief and pressure from the Supreme Court to force equality before the law, no one could contemplate the Negro's position in society with much optimism. The war brought fair employment practices. Negroes moved to the industrial centers of the North, increasing their political power. White primaries were outlawed. The dire -predictions of the fearful failed to materialize. Prejudice was reduced.

Under the Truman Administration the armed forces were largely integrated. The place of the Negro in many of the industrial unions was made secure. In 1948 the two major parties stated their support of political, social and economic equality. The support of the parties for civil rights was in part the product of their desire for votes from the increasing Negro electorate.

The developments of the 1940's made it easier for the Supreme Court to outlaw segregated schools in 1954. During the six years following the court's decision 12 per cent of the schools of the border and Southern States were desegregated. The number of Negro voters in the South has continued to climb—aided by the work of the Attorney General's office and the Commission on Civil Rights. Congress passed two civil-rights laws. To-day only 16 Senators can be counted on to vote against civil rights.

There seems to be a kind of geometric rate of change in the status of the Negro. More was accomplished in the 1950's than in the preceding five decades, but the break in the circle in the 1940's was essential for this development. Aided by the cumulative effect of the work of the last two decades, the Kennedy Administration should be able to make really great strides toward racial equality. HOWARD PENNIMAN

Comment

Comment

Inaugural Prayers

A religious people are delighted that their government, in its Presidential Inaugurations, formally acknowledges the place of God in the business of the state.

But we deferentially observe that the four prayers offered at the Capitol on Jan. 20 were too wordy for an already cold and gusty day. God was addressed bilingually, several times reminded of the calendar and pluralistically praised, thanked and besought. Secularists must have felt that organized religion was seizing a golden opportunity to turn a civil event into a specific act of worship. A continuance of this trend could wind up by making obnoxious the whole concept of recognizing the Almighty from the public platform.

Public prayer is difficult for men, even when they profess one faith in a common sanctuary. When the occasion is civil and the petitioners are of many faiths, due regard must be shown for all circumstances. Perforce, the theme of the prayer must reflect some comm denominator of commitment. For that, the pious should not be sermo ized, neither should the indifferent wearied, nor even the atheist needles provoked.

Ideally, public prayer on civil occ sions should sound only the essent notes of praise and repentance, thanl giving and petition. It should do so w directness, simplicity and a quick ame It will lose nothing if its sense a sentiment echo the familiar themes the Judeo-Christian tradition.

In January, 1965, esteemed clerg men will do well to limit Inaugu prayers to one or two minutes at mo The norm of public prayer is not fu ness of utterance but sincere engag ment of the people's heart.

Here is a model. The occasion w public, the need desperate, but t message brief: "Lord, remember when thou comest into thy kingdon God listened, and that's what counts.

476

p Mehitabel!

Are we missing out on the finer—
ad furrier—things. of life? With Inter-
ational Cat Week starting on Nov. 6,
n't it time to improve our cat I.Q.
bit?

Do you realize that there is no Cat
xplosion, despite tabby's addiction to
asual motherhood? The cat population
as been stable since the Great De-
ression. America boasts only 21 mil-
on cats. Any judgment to the contrary
s based on wanton extrapolation from
he cat density of a few jungle areas
a urban centers.

Do you know that 50 per cent of our
ats have to scrounge for fodder on Skat
tow? And that only four per cent live
n Park-Avenue-type pads? Are you
ware that even pampered pets have to
orm milklines at the icebox or do
ockroach patrol in the pantry?

Do you know that a well-fed feline
aas an overkill potential of 13 rats per
aight, and that the mouse potential de-
ies calculation?

The Golden Age of cats came in
.ncient Egypt; those were the days
when a cat had a better chance of being mummified than a statesman. Since
then the cat has suffered a colossal loss
of puss: although Castro touched most
bases in his UN oratorathon, the Maximum Leader forgot to press a resolution against catocide.

Another point. The family with a cat
is a family without delinquents. Cats
build character. How can kiddies go
wrong, if all their time is taken up in
feeding, grooming and scratching the
Velvet Menace?

Cats have a program: what this country needs is a good five-cent fish head
with catnip dressing. Beyond that, all
the cat asks is freedom to roam and
tighter dog-walking ordinances. The independent cat scorns the dog as a fawning satellite who will bootlick his master
for a synthetic bone.

Beware the cat. It's just waiting for
some Karl Manx to rise and mew:
"Mousers of the world, unite. You have
nothing to lose but your bells and
bows."

;even Against Space

On April 9, with a happy flourish,
he Space Administration czar un-
nasked the seven heroes who will be-
ome our first bona fide "space rats."
A composite sketch of Captain Icarus
hows that he is a military test pilot of
34 and packs 164 lbs. of splendidly co-
ordinated grit into a moderate frame.
He totes an egghead I.Q. and has a
strong yen to become a rocket jockey.
Moreover, he is highly motivated (his
wife is keen on lobbing him into orbit:

477

any connection?) and, sure enough, he is a believing *Protestant.*

Ay, there's the rub! No good for Administration spokesmen to say "That's just the way the rocket tumbles." We predict:

1. Some bilious editorial apologete will darkly ask: "How does it happen that from the volunteers among our 80,000 military pilots, not one Catholic filtered through the Space Curtain?"

2. Some communion breakfast orator will harangue the Knights: "Instead of asking where are our Catholic Salks and Einsteins, let us ask where are our Catholic astronauts? Columbus et al. were of our faith. Are the *Niñas, Pintas* and *Santa Marías* of the cosmic seas to be piloted solely by heretic helmsmen?"

3. A Catholic educator will demand a look-see at the 566 "Who am I?" ques-

tions used in screening the fledgli spacemen. Were those questions slant to put a Catholic profile in a poor ligh

4. Inevitably some aspiring politi will stir our bile to a boil by observir that a space team without a Catholic like an All-American team without Notre Dame player: serves us right the Commies beat us to the moon!

But in all seriousness, our prayers with these brave men in their arduo training and their perilous flight. frightens most of us, even in quiet re erie, to think of the day when the fi of the seven thunders into the blu spins about the earth dizzily, and the endures the fiery buffeting of re-entr We hope indeed that our first Magella of the empyrean may have God for h co-pilot.

Wesley Rides the Rockets?

Zealous John Wesley, mounted on a horse, rode 250,000 miles in evangelizing England and Ireland to Methodism. His form of the Gospel, transferred to America, was well adapted to lay preaching and frontier life.

Is Methodism getting ready for space? Are astronauts, doubling as preachers, going to ride the rocket circuit to the frontiers of Alpha Centauri?

Celebrating the 175th anniversary of U. S. Methodism, Washington Bishop G. Bromley Oxnam recently asked if the seminaries were preparing mission-

aries to share our riches with th cosmos.

Hmmm. . . . We hope *all* the sec will move slowly before men begin t contaminate the planets with the scar dal of disunity, or transfer the confus ing ecumenical dialogue to the stars, c show the universe a Word whose pearl luster is muddied by private interpreta tion.

Christ gave no command to evangel ize the Outsiders; His Gospel is fo earthmen. Are we to preach repentanc to those who perhaps never sinned, o baptize the unredeemed? Would ishop Oxnam demand faith of those /ho never got a revelation, or whip up ogmatic squabbles among those who ever doubted, or encourage sectarian agmentation among those who perhance were never divided? The nought is gruesome.

What's more, those stellar jaunts will e centuries long. Pity the devoted ilot-preacher. The tree of U. S. Methdism, during the last 175 years, produced 22 branches. What will the faith-

ful astronaut come home to, after preaching near Epsilon Eridani? One awful thought—he may make his earthfall only to find there is no such thing as Methodism; since he went out on circuit, the ecumenical problem has been solved, and all the earthbound Methodists have "come home to Mother," the Mother Church, that is! Could be!

Let Bishop Oxnam take thought. Cosmic Christianity is more than a challenge. It's a caution.

Queen of Spacemen

In the catalog of saints there are patrons galore. Brewers and weavers ave them; so do wet nurses, plasterers nd gravediggers. Travelers call on St. Christopher and aviators invoke the Little Flower. But so far as we know, here is no official patron of astronauts. Ve have protectors against hernia, nakes and earthquakes. But we have no intercessor against the perils of last-off, orbiting or re-entry, no guarian of voyagers through the "deserts f vast eternity" that lie beneath the noon, the sun and the distant stars.

The rocket launchers may adopt St. Barbara as their own. The communications engineers in the blockhouses already have St. Gabriel for their advocate. But neither of these, nor even the

many patrons of mariners will suffice for the pioneers who navigate in the bowels of space ships. These men need a patron who is powerful on earth and in the heavens, too.

One of our readers suggests that in selecting such an advocate no better choice could be made than Mary Assumed into Heaven. After death our Lady was in a very physical sense borne through outer space, and surely she may be called queen of the starry deeps as well as Queen of Heaven.

We like the suggestion that Mary be chosen patron of the astronauts who will soon be probing the solar system. Certainly there is nothing to hinder devout spacemen from seeking confirmation of the choice by the Holy See.

Dormididactics

You never heard that word before? No wonder; we just invented it. We're giving a name to the latest of the black arts—the art of teaching students while they are asleep.

Yes, there are psychologists who think we are wasting one-third of our lives by wandering aimlessly in the land of Nod. Why dream, when precious sack-time can be used to absorb a packaged course in sociology or history? What this country needs is an efficient mechanical tutor to drill us in facts and figures while we are knitting up the "ravell'd sleave of care."

We dread to think of successful assaults on the citadel of sleep. If the experimenters are lucky, the next generation will not be troubled by teacher or classroom shortages. Live teaching will be supplanted by nocturnal imbibition of knowledge at the hands of a patient, fully transistorized pedagogue. We can even do away with the schools; surely the taxpayer will welcome the day when a bedside squawk-box wi' give us all the benefits of a university. As for students, why should they spen' four years in college? We can see th' day when they hibernate for thre' months with a mechanical educator an' emerge with a bachelor's degree.

Somehow, though, it doesn't seem right to invade the realm of Morpheu' with packaged pedagogy, nor to mak' liars of poets who used to call slee' by such pretty names as the balm o' woe, sore labor's bath or the prisoner' release. As for Macbeth, now he ca' rest in peace. 'Twas not Macbeth di' murder sleep; 'twas the experimenta' psychologists.

The pay-off, from *Tiny Tim's Gar den of Verses*:
"Now I lay me down at ease,
To learn in sleep my ABC's;
If I should die in bed alone,
Please, Lord, switch off
  my Dormiphone."

To Bind in Conscience

Political discussion often uses the expression "Catholics are bound in conscience" as though it were an indication of some specifically Romanist syndrome. Let us scotch this error once and for all. Let us see what it means to bind in conscience.

Any dictionary gives us a clue. Literally, to bind is to tie or fasten tightly; and thus we bind sheaves, books, madmen and prisoners. The root idea in binding is to impose some form of constraint or immobility.

But for centuries our language has sanctioned figurative usage of the word "bind." We speak of binding ourselves by oath or contract. In the strictest sense, we speak of being bound by law, conceived as an externally imposed guide of choice and action. All these metaphorical uses connote some limitation on our freedom of movement. They imply a constraint that operates not by brute force but by moral influence.

Doesn't our experience of the "still small voice" of conscience bear this out? It is conscience that makes us aware of obligations. It is conscience that prods us to do our duty. It is conscience that makes us chafe under the yoke of law.

It is conscience that issues categorical imperatives, those unique forms of necessity which do not physically compel, yet which cannot be resisted without guilt, remorse and the awareness that we have deviated from rectitude.

To bind in conscience, then, is simply to put one under the moral necessity of pursuing a determinate course of action. To be thus bound, of course, is not a uniquely Catholic experience; it is the common lot of all men who are in bondage to Duty, the "Stern Daughter of the Voice of God."

⚜

Anyone for Steno?

If you can believe the "Help Wanted" columns, a girl doesn't just go out and get herself a job these days; she is lured into employment by promises of Sutton Place glamor, easygoing bosses, slow dictation and the "opty" to meet what abbreviated ad lingo calls "impt. ppl." Here are some samples from a single page of the Oct. 16 N. Y. *Times:*

• SECY. Unique exciting posit for brite gal who cannot stand routine. Aver skls ok. No pressure no tests.

• SECY. "Sutton Place." If you can't afford the rental live vicariously & at least work in this posh atmos. Lovely office lovely view lovely people who say 'thank you.'"

• SECY. This is the opty you've been waiting for! Wk with nicest boss in NY. Meet NY's top echelon! Non pressure, inform atmos.

• SECY. This furniture showroom is fab! What a lovely place to start your career! Loads of pub contact! Non pressure! Lt steno ok.

• SECY-RECEPT "Plush." Meet and greet, take a few letters, be pleasant & cheerful & a fine job in a fine firm is yrs! Coffee on the house.

• SECY. Plus bonus. Easygoing boss who's not around much & all benefits. Be yr own boss.

• SECY–JRS. Your opty to enter the stimulating, fascinating, exciting Busn. World. These are positions for brite gals in highly attractive offices staffed by young men on their way up to exec and sales mgmt.

What, no wedding rings on the house?

⚜

Science

SCIENCE

The Tunguska Mystery

It isn't every day that I can wrap up astronomy, flying saucers and Soviet science in one package. But I have the chance now, thanks to a weird event that took place in the upper valley of the Podkamennaya Tunguska, in Central Siberia, on June 30, 1908.

It was a cloudless morning. Precisely at seven o'clock a fiery object, blazing like the sun, swept into the earth's atmosphere from the south and exploded with a cataclysmic crash in the marshy scrub forest of the Siberian wilderness. What followed was awe-inspiring.

For a hundred miles around the big blast, water gushed from the ground or was swept in sheets from the lakes and rivers. The earth shook and concentric ridges formed on its surface. At 250 miles a black mushroom cloud was seen boiling up into the stratosphere. In selected directions, it appears, fences were toppled at a distance of 250 miles. Horses and men were bowled over at Kansk, 450 miles from the blast. The sound of the blast was heard 600 miles away and at the same distance (in Irkutsk) disturbances in the earth's magnetic field were recorded.

Other effects were noted on an even wider scale. The Tunguska object produced air waves that circled the globe twice. The seismic shock of the crash was registered in Washington, D.C. The atomized debris of the explosion, rising some sixty miles into the air, created luminescent clouds which gave much of Asia and Europe a series of "white nights."

It took many years for scientists to bring together the few facts I have cited. The Tunguska phenomenon happened in one of the most remote and uninhabited areas on earth. It was not until 1921 that a Russian expert on meteors began to gather eyewitness accounts of the catastrophe. Even he was not able to penetrate the actual site of the blast until 1927. The first aerial survey of the region took place almost thirty years after the original event. In fact, it was not until 1958 that the USSR sent a large and well-fitted expedition into the bleak tundra area.

What was the nature of the object that hurtled from the sky back in 1908? The conventional scientific explanation is that a stone or nickel-iron meteorite, moving at many miles a second and weighing possibly a million tons, intercepted the earth in its flight and hit the scrub forest with a terrific jolt of blast and fire. We are all aware, of course, that the earth sweeps up many meteors in its orbit and that some of them are quite hefty.

The meteoritic theory immediately runs into grave difficulties. Searching has uncovered no meteor fragment anywhere in the impact area or beyond it. No trace of a crater has ever been found at the site of the explosion. Are we to believe that a large and solid mass was so completely vaporized by heat that it left no trace of itself?

Another puzzle: at the very center of the Tunguska explosion a forest of about 700-800 square miles was entirely destroyed, with the charred trees stretching radially outward along the ground for from 20 to 40 miles. Yet in the middle of this devastated area, in a circle about one mile across, the detonation left the trees erect, but with their crowns and branches shorn. How could a meteor have produced such an effect?

A second, but rather beatnik, explanation of the Tunguska affair has been popular in semi-scientific organs of the Soviet press for the last fifteen years. Its originator was science writer A. N. Kazantsev, who argues that the explosion was caused by the disintegration of a spaceship that unwisely entered our atmosphere. Conceivably, the alien vehicle was made of "anti-matter," and quite inevitably vanished in a burst of sheer energy when it invaded the environment of the earth. Kazantsev's theory enjoyed new popularity in 1959, after inspired amateurs investigated the Tunguska territory and reported unusual radioactivity at the site of the explosion.

This curious report brought about a new official expedition to the explosion site in 1960, under the leadership of Dr. V. G. Fesenkov. This study did not confirm the reports on radioactivity, but did result in a third theory about the Tunguska object.

Dr. Fesenkov thinks that what struck the earth in 1908 was a small comet, several miles in diameter and weighing perhaps a million tons. Since comets are presumably composed of dust and frozen gases (they are often called "flying gravel pits"), such a theory could explain why the explosion left no crater and why the object disappeared without a trace. It simply bored into the atmosphere at 25 miles per second and vaporized when its kinetic energy turned into heat as a result of friction. Dr. Fesenkov feels that his cometary theory is supported by the fact that the object approached the earth from a direction opposite to that of the earth's motion around the sun, whereas meteorites always orbit the sun in the same sense as the earth.

We must conclude, I believe, that the Tunguska mystery still clamors for a satisfactory explanation. There is no doubt Soviet scientists will continue to give the matter considerable attention.

Celestial visitors like the Tunguska object were once quite common, when the solar system was young. But objects of a comparable magnitude probably do not strike the earth now more than once in a hundred thousand years. Thank heaven! If the Tunguska object had arrived just four hours and 17 minutes earlier, it would have landed on St. Petersburg (now Leningrad). The results of such a calamity may be left to the imagination.

L. C. McHugh

Melting the Snowman

Last September the conqueror of Mount Everest, Sir Edmund Hillary, set out from Katmandu on a search for the Abominable Snowman. Four months later, in the London *Sunday Times*, he said: "In spite of our efforts, the *yeti* still remains a very real part of the mythology and tradition of the Himalayan peoples and it is undoubtedly in the field of mythology that it rightly belongs."

For many centuries, all along the rugged flanks of the vast Himalayan range, there have been popular legends of a hairy wild man that dwells in the timberline forests and inaccessible icy caves of the world's loftiest mountains. Reports of these strange creatures began to reach the West at the turn of this century. By 1953, I would say, the Snowman had achieved a status like that of the Flying Saucers: there was lots of "evidence" for its existence, if you didn't ask too much concreteness and took an optimistic view of the value of human testimony. Its mewing or yelping cry was heard by various mountain people. It was fleetingly sighted in Tibet and in the northern parts of Burma, Sikkim and Nepal. Respectable explorers—British, American and even Russian—saw and photographed its tracks amid the eternal snows. Some even examined specimens of its scalp, which is sometimes preserved as a relic in Tibetan monasteries. There were even reports that mummified *yeti* were to be seen in some of these remote lamaseries.

Admittedly, none of this evidence took the scientific world by storm, although it did arouse considerable speculation. Any reader who wants to bone up on the lore of the. Snowman can consult pp. 127-183 of *On the Track of Unknown Animals,* by Bernard Heuvelmans (surely one of the most fascinating books ever seen in print). There one will find all the reasons why, if the *yeti* really exists, it is so hard to track down, describe with exactness or even classify as to type. I mention this last point because it is important to realize that legend provides for several kinds of Snowmen. The broad classifications run thus:

1. *Nyalmo,* a real giant that can attain a height of 16 feet. This is the most elusive of all Snowmen, found only above an altitude of 16,000 feet. *Nyalmo* may be only a fiction derived from the native Tibetan principle that "the higher you go, the bigger the *yeti.*"

2. *Rimi,* probably identified with the Sherpan *chuteh* and the Tibetan *metoh-kangmi* or "filthy man of the snow." This hairy ginger-and-black monster, sometimes eight feet tall, has long arms, bowed legs and a somewhat human face. Like all Snowmen, it has a high conical skull. It is normally vegetarian and tends to travel in groups at the 13,000-foot level.

3. *Yeti,* the garden variety of the species, also known as *yeh-teh, mi-teh* or *rackshi bompo.* The *yeti* proper flourishes on the flanks of Everest. It is never larger than a small man. In most respects it looks like a small edition of the *chuteh;* however, it is usually reddish in color and relishes human flesh.

4. Hillary, finally, allows for the *thelma,* a *yeti* no more than two feet high which (being the smallest) fittingly lives down in the jungle. It has human features and likes to pile sticks and stones in little mounds.

While *nyalmo* and *thelma* are almost

surely fictional, descriptions of the *chuteh* and common *yeti* are so widespread, persistent, detailed and supported by various kinds of indirect evidence that some respectable investigators feel there must be some anthropoid reality behind the *yeti* story. Heuvelmans, in the book I mentioned above (published by Hill & Wang, 1959), believes that the evidence for the Snowman is no worse than that which has admitted many a fossil or living species to the halls of paleontology or zoology.

Accordingly, Heuvelmans thinks that a giant anthropoid biped really dwells in the Himalaya. It is a primate, omnivorous, with a flat face and a conical skull; it reaches a height of from five to eight feet, depending on age, sex or geographical range. He gives it the name of *Dinanthropoides nivalis*, "the terrible anthropoid of the snows."

No doubt Sir Edmund views this nomenclature wryly. The *yeti* tracks he found turned out to be those of foxes and wild dogs, distorted by the heat of the sun. His *chuteh* skins, when examined, proved to be the pelts of the very rare Tibetan blue bear. The scalps which were shown to him as relics of the *yeti* were given special study; the scientific conclusion was that they were not scalps at all, but were molded from the skin of a rare member of the goat family.

Sir Edmund, of course, would be the first to admit that his fruitless search and explaining away of purported evidence do not actually disprove the existence of the rumored Snowman. It is very difficult to prove that something which might possibly exist, does not exist in point of fact. It may be assumed that the search for the elusive *yeti*, like the effort to establish the reality of Flying Saucers, will continue to engage the energies of those who have the resources and opportunity for such bizarre forms of research.

Here's a final fillip to disturb the unbelievers. Since 1934 the Dutch paleontologist von Koenigswald has discovered several molars, almost human in character, amid the fossil curiosities of Hong Kong and Cantonese apothecary shops. The peculiarity of these teeth is that they have five or six times the bulk of human molars. Whatever wore them, back in Pleistocene times, was probably 11 to 13 feet high. In any event, there is growing evidence that a huge ape called *Gigantopithecus*, inhabited Kwangsi Province in South China, half a million years ago. How would you go about proving that this big primate had no cousins that still survive in the relatively unknown stretches of the mighty Himalayan mountains?

L. C. McHugh

Hummingbirds

Crawford H. Greenewalt is not only president of E. I. du Pont de Nemours & Company at a staggering $600,000 per year; he is also a distinguished amateur ornithologist.

Since 1953 Mr. Greenewalt has lugged 250 pounds of photographic gear more than 100,000 miles in a dedicated effort to make a portrait gallery of hummingbirds in "living color." Sixty-seven plates of 57 species, together with new material on the iridescent coloration and flight techniques of what the naturalist Audubon called a "glittering fragment of the rainbow," form the substance of Greenewalt's 250-page book, *Hummingbirds,* which was issued by Doubleday & Co. during November.

I have not seen Mr. Greenewalt's book, already hailed as a "classic of natural history," because its list price is $22.50. But happily, the "poor man's Greenewalt" can be found on pages 658-679 of the November issue of the *National Geographic.* There you will see not only a summary of Mr. Greenewalt's studies on hummingbirds, but also 23 magnificent color reproductions of his work, some of them photographed at speeds of one 30-millionth of a second.

British and Continental lyric poets, who often pay tribute to the thrush, the skylark, etc., have generally ignored the glittering glory of the hummingbirds. Why? The answer is simple. They were not familiar with these flying sapphires, topazes and amethysts. Hummingbirds are the boast of the Western Hemisphere; they range the mountain and the plain, the forest and the desert, from Alaska to Tierra del Fuego. They are found nowhere else.

This does not mean that hummingbirds are rare. It is true that only one species (the ruby-throat) is found east of the Mississippi, and even in our West there are no more than eleven breeding species. But over their entire range, the suborder of the Trochilidae counts at least 319 species: hummingbirds will be found wherever and whenever flowers bloom in the Western world. If hummingbirds seem rare to us, that is because they are not much given to

migration, and most of the species inhabit a band that is five degrees wide on either side of the Equator. The center of the world, from the viewpoint of a hummingbird, lies in Ecuador, which is home for half the known species.

Everybody knows that hummingbirds are tiny. One Cuban species of *zumzum* is only 2¼ inches long. The giant of hummingbirds is the Andean *Patagona gigas;* its 8½ inches sound impressive until you see how much of it goes into tail and bill, and learn that the whole bird weighs less than an ounce. Our American ruby-throat, in fighting form, weighs in at 150 to the pound. Smallest of the known hummingbirds is the South American *Calliphlox amethystina,* which can balance a dime on the scales but is a lot more colorful.

No description of hummingbirds can overlook the fact that these living gems have an extraordinary power plant that enables them to expand energy faster than any other warm-blooded animal. To hover in the air like a helicopter, a hummingbird must burn up fuel, per unit of weight, ten times faster than a man running nine miles per hour. Even when it sinks into torpor (a state like hibernation) at dusk of a day on which it has not fed well, a hummingbird uses up its reserve energy at the rate of a man taking his morning walk.

♦

Such prodigious living explains why hummingbirds eat 50 to 60 meals a day and take most of their food on board in the form of sugar (nectar from flowers), which is high in food value and quickly convertible into energy. To absorb enough calories to live the normal life of a hummingbird, a 170-pound man would have to eat 370 pounds of boiled potatoes every day. To hover like a hummingbird, a man would have to perspire at the rate of 100 pounds of water per hour, just to keep his skin temperature below the boiling point of water. That's really living it up!

Some of the most remarkable facts about hummingbirds involve their flight techniques. Some species can beat their wings 80 times a second. All of them have wings that develop power on the upbeat as well as the downbeat. Most remarkable of all, hummingbirds have a "reverse gear" that enables them to fly backward almost as well as they can fly forward.

But not even the hummingbirds have everything! Their legs are so poorly developed that they cannot walk about at all. Worst of all, their spectral beauty is not matched by their vocal performance. Hummingbirds are not songbirds. Mr. Greenewalt found only one species whose operatic capabilities would excite the envy of even the lowly English sparrow.

Lack of a musical repertory does not lead to neurotic withdrawal in a hummingbird. The little bird is both bold and curious, disdainful of man's presence and extraordinarily pugnacious. It can afford to manifest these traits because it is faster than a rapier in the face of danger.

Too bad more poets cannot observe the flashing gems whose Indian names signify such things as "tresses of the daystar," and whose scientific nomenclature translates into expressions like "fiery topaz" and "golden torch." But our own priest-poet of the South, John Banister Tabb, who perhaps knew only the ruby-throat, paid it this lovely tribute:

A flash of harmless lightning,
    A mist of rainbow dyes,
The burnished sunbeams brightening,
From flower to flower he flies.

L. C. McHUGH

The Hurricane

The hurricane is a meteorological monster spawned in tropical seas. Our very name for these rampaging atmospheric vortices probably comes from an old Carib word that meant "evil spirit" or "storm god." But for the scientist, the Atlantic hurricane is identical with the Asiatic typhoon and the Australian willy-willy. The only difference is that the homegrown variety gets its start in the Gulf of Mexico, the Caribbean Sea, or more often in the southern stretches of the North Atlantic.

Everybody knows that the Weather Bureau nowadays christens every newly born Atlantic hurricane with a girl's name. The reason for this is neither humor nor sentiment, but the need for a short, easily pronounced identification tag in emergency situations. When Ione was zooming in on Washington, D. C., back in 1955, the local weather number was dialed 395,000 times in a single day.

Names like Donna and Ethel also point up the fact that every hurricane

ıs an individuality of its own. When
ıe talk of these storms in a general
ıay, we have to use broad averages to
ıver their characteristics.

Hence, in general, we can say that
ıe hurricane season runs from May to
ıctober; outside these six months, hur-
ıanes are rare. As for frequency, At-
ıntic hurricanes have averaged about
ıght per year since 1890. Their span
ˈ life runs around nine days, although
ı duration of five weeks is not unknown.
ıven the size of hurricanes varies con-
ıderably, but usually a fully developed
ıorm stretches over a diameter of about
ı0 miles.

◆

Only a hardy meteorologist would
ıssert that he knows for sure how a hur-
ıcane is born, and perhaps we are
ıolish to outline the most popular cur-
ınt theory in a few sentences. But it
ıould go like this: Somewhere on the
ıcean, a low-pressure mass of hot, moist
ıır, squeezed by opposing trade winds,
ıarts rising up a heat chimney in a
ıiral movement. As the air rises, it
ıols. As it cools, the water vapor con-
ıenses and heat is given off. The heat
ıırther warms the rotating air, which
ıecomes even lighter and rises more
ıwiftly. Meanwhile, more hot, moist air
ıwirls in at the bottom of the chimney—
ıs much as a million tons a second.
ıhus moisture and heat feed the grow-
ıg monster at an increasing pace; in a
ıw days it has turned into a symmetri-
ıal storm of wind, cloud and rain—a
ıw-pressure heat engine that tends to
ıweep west and then veer north like a
ıteam roller out of control.

Fortunately, every hurricane has a
ıuicidal mania. Its northern motion de-
ırives it of new heat. If it rolls over
ınd, there is no water to feed it. Both

factors cause the hurricane to dissipate
its energy budget in a few days.

The most unique part of a hurricane
is its eye, a central area about 14 miles
in diameter where the wind is no more
than a breeze and the sun shines fitfully
through filmy clouds. Seen from the
eye, the inner edge of the hurricane
looks like a curtain of cloud that may
rise seven miles high. This circular surface represents the region where the
centrifugal force of the spiraling winds
just balances the pressure that tends to
force the air inward toward the center
of the storm.

The chief destructive forces that are
associated with the hurricane are tides,
floods and winds.

Historically, the most dangerous spot
to tarry in during a hurricane is a
coastal area. As the hurricane moves
toward the land, it drives a mighty
surge before it, one that acts like a tidal
wave. The Galveston hurricane of 1900
killed 6,000 people; most of them
drowned in a tidal surge.

On land, a like danger to life lies
in flooding. A big hurricane can deposit
from three to six inches of rain over a
million square miles. In limited areas,
the total rainfall commonly reaches 20
or 30 inches. It was flooding that caused
most of the deaths and damage done
by Diane in 1955.

As for property damage, most of it
is due to wind. Most hurricanes attain
wind velocities of at least 100 miles per
hour sometime during their life. Back
in 1955, Janet touched 175 miles an
hour at Chetumal, Mexico, before the
anemometer disintegrated. Engineers
who studied the effects of a big wind
that swept the Florida Keys in 1935
estimated that its gusts must have
reached 200-225 miles per hour.

489

Obviously, every hurricane is a titan of energy, even though its mechanical efficiency is abysmally low. An average hurricane expends heat energy at the rate of 16 trillion kilowatt-hours per day; that's 8,000 times the total electrical energy generated each day in the United States. The energy budget of a respectable hurricane is equivalent to 500,000 atom bombs every 24 hours.

Such a fantastic quantity of energy shows how hard it will be to kill a hurricane, unless we can find some weakness in these giants that will enable us to trigger off a self-destructive cha reaction while they are still at sea. has even been suggested that the w. to nip a hurricane in the bud is to p off an atom bomb in its eye while it still a baby. The trouble with that su gestion is that we don't know enoug about hurricanes to estimate the effec The bomb might dissipate the baby strength. On the other hand, it mig only rouse the baby's fury and make squall more lustily.

L. C. McHug

Vanishing Wildlife

At one time the passenger pigeon nested in North America in larger numbers than any other vertebrate land animal on record. The 19th-century naturalist Audubon once observed a single flock of these birds that contained more than one *billion* individuals. But the pigeon was a tasty morsel and reckless slaughter made it disappear from the countryside by 1906. The last known specimen died in captivity in 1914.

Only last-minute conservation efforts saved the American bison from a like extinction. This huge beast once roamed over most of the United States and Canada. As many as 60 million buffaloes provided the Indians with food, clothing, shelter and fuel. Neither strength nor numbers saved the buffalo herds from wanton destruction. In 1889 there were only 541 bison left in the United States and even fewer in Canada.

What befell the passenger pigeon and the bison is part of the pattern of extermination that often follows ma wherever he hunts or fishes, clears th forest or plows the plain.

It is possible that Stone Age ma played a part in wiping out the wool mammoth and the giant sloth. It is ve probable that the European lion an the North African elephant did n wholly disappear until Roman time Altogether, it is estimated that 106 sp cies of mammals (not to mention birds have become extinct since the time Christ. Wildlife conservationists thin that as many as 600 animal species a in peril of extermination at the prese time.

What is most distressing about th world's vanishing wildlife is that th rate of extinction is rising. About on species a year is disappearing from th earth right now. Man's careless wast ot one of the earth's most precious an irreplaceable resources runs on apac in field and forest, in lake and river an sea—whenever the God-appointed stew

d of lower nature invades the bio-
•here and exploits it for his utility and
ofit.

Although nature was unusually lavish
  endowing the United States with
sources, her prodigality was more
an matched by the human tendency to
quander them. It was not until 1908
at we realized our timber was not
exhaustible. It took the dust-bowl days
  impress us with the necessity of con-
rving the soil. Even today we are
ossly ignorant of the extent to which
uch of our wildlife is being depleted.
There are perhaps 50 species of ani-
al life that are seriously threatened
  the United States today. The Cali-
rnia condor, our largest soaring bird,
umbers no more than 60 individuals.
ver the vast stretch between Alaska
d Florida, there are probably no more
an 1,500 bald eagles. It is doubtful
at there are 800 grizzly bears in the
tire country. Coyotes and bighorn
eep are growing rare. The flamingo,
e snowy egret and the great white
eron are vanishing.

Sometimes, of course, conservation
ethods help a species to stage a come-
back. The trumpeter swan was thought
to be extinct in 1900. They now number
700. Strong public interest is an even
more potent savior of wildlife. The
whooping crane was reduced to 14
specimens in 1938, but numbers 38 today, thanks to the unusual publicity
that attends its every migration.

The ethics of man's religious and
social life is well developed. It is hardly
a century since man began to realize
his natural duties as the husbandman
of the earth's resources. It is only today
that he is developing a rudimentary
conscience to guide him in his attitudes toward earth's flora and fauna.
We are just beginning to see that good
stewardship may imply more than wise
economic use of our abundant riches.
The good life of man on earth embraces
elements of beauty and companionship
with nature, too.

A population explosion may someday
blow most of our wildlife into outer
space. But does anyone want to hasten
the day when there will be no violets
by mossy stones and no lark to sing
at heaven's gate as "Phoebus 'gins
arise"?

L. C. McHugh

Poems

The Human Condition

En route through space
And ice Siberia-bound
The bus stops now and then
Time out prisoners
Bethlehem town Last
Time to look around
Be back in fifteen minutes
All of you
And I mean
Fifteen minutes

Move along murderer
Move along jade
Fifteen minutes of sheep
Cattle stable hay
Not much here to take away
Where is endless sleepless
Night in day out of time
Out of space
Past all frozen sun

Lift him up Cain
Let every eye see
You kiss his frail fingers
He will not shrink away

Give him your apple Eve
It belongs to him
Drink the wine his mother
Pours to the ruddy brim
Drink   For on your journey
The sun itself grows dim

All aboard now
Time shouts again
All aboard flesh souls sin God
With you amen

SISTER MARY AQUIN, B.V.M.

FALCON

On the other side of our hill
spring comes sooner;
the frost is gone by noon there
and winter with clenched teeth singing
and April chill—
on the other side of our heart.

Warm on the smooth rocks our faces
search high in the light,
homesick and pale for the sight
of a bird on the shouldering sky
where the huge air races—
on the other side of our heart.

The valley is silent and still
and the grasstops unstirred
where the ants work, but one arrogant bird
has found where the air is and mastered it
over our hill—
on the other side of our heart.

Downwinging the stream he floats,
tight wing sliding
perfect and black there, riding
his wind; and the grace of his flight
stops breath in our throats—
on the other side of our heart.

Children wild and white, debating
ironeyed of love,
we follow a taut wing above—
small heart in a towering pride—
while we sit waiting—
on the other side of our hill.

ROBERT B. BROCK

"O" Antiphons

"O" Antiphons vocal again on tongue
enjoin us: take to the attic rung
and from the cedar trunk bring out
hillside, a stable, and devout
ceramics—shepherds and kings
in apprehensive poses;
open the cardboard cases where
upon the kapok whiteness, stare
Mary and St. Joseph; and shed
cocoons of cotton from a carven head
of the cradled Child.
               On strings
our youngest one disposes
tissue wings upon a tree
and squeals a challenge: "You'll see
the Infant smile if you bend low
enough."
        So eagerly we go
the depths of creeping things.
Here faith discloses
no paltriness about our wooden crèche
wherein, upon the straw, we have
the Child, whose curve of lip
transcends the clay of flesh.

SISTER MARY HONORA, O.S.F.